M000288382

Cities and Homelessness

Cities and Homelessness

Essays and Case Studies on Practices, Innovations and Challenges

Edited by
Joaquin Jay Gonzalez III *and*
Mickey P. McGee

McFarland & Company, Inc., Publishers
Jefferson, North Carolina

ALSO OF INTEREST AND FROM MCFARLAND

Senior Care and Services: Essays and Case Studies on Practices, Innovations and Challenges, edited by Joaquin Jay Gonzalez III, Roger L. Kemp and Willie Lee Brit (2020) • *Veteran Care and Services: Essays and Case Studies on Practices, Innovations and Challenges*, edited by Joaquin Jay Gonzalez III, Mickey P. McGee and Roger L. Kemp (2020) • *Cities and Homelessness: Essays and Case Studies on Practices, Innovations and Challenges*, edited by Joaquin Jay Gonzalez III and Mickey P. McGee (2020) • *Legal Marijuana: Perspectives on Public Benefits, Risks and Policy Approaches*, edited by Joaquin Jay Gonzalez III and Mickey P. McGee (2019) • *Cybersecurity: Current Writings on Threats and Protection*, edited by Joaquin Jay Gonzalez III and Roger L. Kemp (2019) • *Eminent Domain and Economic Growth: Perspectives on Benefits, Harms and New Trends*, edited by Joaquin Jay Gonzalez III, Roger L. Kemp and Jonathan Rosenthal (2018) • *Small Town Economic Development: Reports on Growth Strategies in Practice*, edited by Joaquin Jay Gonzalez III, Roger L. Kemp and Jonathan Rosenthal (2017) • *Privatization in Practice: Reports on Trends, Cases and Debates in Public Service by Business and Nonprofits*, edited by Joaquin Jay Gonzalez III and Roger L. Kemp (2016) • *Immigration and America's Cities: A Handbook on Evolving Services*, edited by Joaquin Jay Gonzalez III and Roger L. Kemp (2016) • *Corruption and American Cities: Essays and Case Studies in Ethical Accountability*, edited by Joaquin Jay Gonzalez III and Roger L. Kemp (2016)

LIBRARY OF CONGRESS CATALOGUING-IN-PUBLICATION DATA

Names: Gonzalez, Joaquin Jay, III, editor. | McGee, Mickey P., 1949– editor.
Title: Cities and homelessness : essays and case studies on practices, innovations and challenges / edited by Joaquin Jay Gonzalez III and Mickey P. McGee.
Description: Jefferson, North Carolina : McFarland & Company, Inc., 2021 | Includes bibliographical references and index.
Identifiers: LCCN 2021011551 | ISBN 9781476673103 (paperback : acid free paper) ∞
ISBN 9781476640556 (ebook)
Subjects: LCSH: Homelessness—United States. | BISAC: SOCIAL SCIENCE / Poverty & Homelessness | POLITICAL SCIENCE / Public Policy / City Planning & Urban Development
Classification: LCC HV4505 .C58 2021 | DDC 362.5/920973—dc23
LC record available at https://lccn.loc.gov/2021011551

BRITISH LIBRARY CATALOGUING DATA ARE AVAILABLE

ISBN (print) 978-1-4766-7310-3
ISBN (ebook) 978-1-4766-4055-6

© 2021 Joaquin Jay Gonzalez III and Mickey P. McGee. All rights reserved

No part of this book may be reproduced or transmitted in any form or by any means, electronic or mechanical, including photocopying or recording, or by any information storage and retrieval system, without permission in writing from the publisher.

Front cover image © 2021 Shutterstock

Printed in the United States of America

*McFarland & Company, Inc., Publishers
Box 611, Jefferson, North Carolina 28640
www.mcfarlandpub.com*

Jay and Mick dedicate this book to everyone working together
to end homelessness in the United States
and around the world.

Acknowledgments

We are grateful for the support of the Mayor George Christopher Professorship at Golden Gate University as well as GGU's Pi Alpha Alpha Chapter and ICMA Student Chapter. We appreciate the encouragement from President David Fike and our wonderful colleagues and students at the Edward S. Ageno School of Business, the Department of Public Administration, and the Executive MPA Program.

Our heartfelt "Thank you!" goes to the contributors listed in the back of the book and the individuals, organizations, and publishers below for granting permission to reprint the material in this volume and the research assistance. They all expressed support for practical research and information sharing that benefits our citizens, communities, and cities.

AARP Public Policy Institute
Administration for Community Living
American Society for Public Administration
Deborah Bailey
William Bare
Willie L. Britt
California Department of Housing and Community Development
Samantha Carr
Damon Conklin
Denver Homeless Out Loud
eRepublic
DaVina Flemings
Rachel L. Fontenot
Karen Garrett
Golden Gate University Library
Coral H. Gonzalez
Governing
Paul Harney
Michelle Hong-Gonzalez
Jim Hynes
International City/County Management Association
Kaiser Health News
Alexandra Logsdon
Amanda L. McGimpsey
Rachel D. McGuffin
Deidre L. McLay
Ginger Miller

National Coalition for the Homeless
James P. Nicholls
Joshua Odetunde
PA Times
PM Magazine
Sukhdeep Purewal
Alan R. Roper
Claire Moeller Rygg
Ruth Astle Samas
San Francisco Department of Homelessness and Supportive Housing
Kurt Schake
Benedict Serafica
Michael Silliman
Substance Abuse and Mental Health Services Administration
theconversation.com
Town of Bedford, Massachusetts
University of San Francisco Library
U.S. Department of Housing and Urban Development
U.S. Department of Labor
U.S. Interagency Council on Homelessness
Virginia Commonwealth University's Center for Public Policy
White House
Kayla M. Williams
Johanna L. Wong
Jason Yergler

Table of Contents

Part III. Services, Innovations and Challenges

A. Affordability and Inclusion

B. Health

Appendices

Preface

Homelessness in America's cities is like the Lernean Hydra from the Greek legends, a gigantic water snake-like monster with nine heads, one of which was immortal. Cutting off one or two of the different heads of the homelessness monster does not kill it. Problems today for the homeless are similar to those from past years. The homeless population continue to be poor, they have no or tenuous ties to their family and friends, they suffer from debilitating conditions caused by physical and/or mental health challenges, alcohol and/or substance abuse and they don't have or don't want a home in which to live. Today, compared to the period between the 1950s to the 1970s, more homeless persons are sleeping on our city streets versus residing in flop houses, shelters or Single-room occupancy hotels (SROs). Rates of homelessness reflect trends in the country's economy, social inequities, inclusion as well as factors in the individual's health or lifestyle.

In most cities, homelessness is the result of multiple factors leading to poverty and loss of material security and include:

- Substance abuse;
- Lack of affordable healthcare;
- Mental illness;
- Physical disability;
- Loss of job opportunities or benefits;
- Lack of and decline in available public assistance programs;
- Increasing proportion of women, children and minorities among the poor;
- Increase in home foreclosures;
- Lack of affordable housing; and
- Natural, climate change, and man-made disasters.

Substance abuse is often a cause of homelessness. Addictive disorders disrupt relationships with family and friends and often cause people to lose their jobs. For people who are struggling to pay their bills, the onset or exacerbation of an addiction may cause them to lose their housing. Substance abuse was the single largest cause of homelessness for single adults as reported by 68 percent of cities in U.S. Conference of Mayors' survey.

A lack of affordable healthcare also is a concern. Overwhelming medical costs is one of the most common reasons for bankruptcy and poverty. Serious health problems or disabilities can also lead to homelessness. Contrary to popular belief, many homeless people with severe mental illnesses are willing to accept treatment and services. From 20 percent to 25 percent of the homeless population in the United States suffers from some form of severe mental illness. In comparison, only 6 percent of Americans are severely mentally ill. Mental illness was the third largest cause of homelessness for single adults as mentioned by 48 percent of cities in the U.S. Conference of Mayors' survey.

A decline in funding for cash assistance programs has resulted in an increase in homelessness and poverty, especially among individuals with disabilities and families headed by females. A public policy exacerbated the decline in affordable housing for the poor as the federal government withdrew its role in subsidizing low income housing alternatives. Until the 1980s, the federal government was the primary source of low-income housing subsidies. Federal support has been substantially reduced since then.

Traditional social and economic inequities by race and gender reinforced by the increasing proportion of women, children and minorities among the poor also contribute to their increasing number among the homeless population. The homeless are less likely to have regular or strong connections with family, friends or other social networks. Their lack of social capital and inclusion increases their vulnerability to disabilities and deprivations, or both.

Changes in the American workforce, nature of work, an economic recession and a pandemic have resulted in the loss of employment opportunities, especially among low-wage workers. More individuals and families are living in poverty and at risk of losing their housing. A direct relationship exists between the reduced availability of low-cost housing and the increased number of homeless persons. The extremely low rate of replacement or construction of low-income housing has not kept up with the increase in the homeless population. The articles provided in this book reveal that the major reasons for the growing homeless population is the lack of affordable housing, especially for those who are poor or at risk due to physical and/or mental limitations, substance abuse or family violence. We are witnessing today how the social, economic and political environments and a diminished stock of low-income housing are making it very difficult for people, especially low-income people, to afford a safe place to live. An increase in home foreclosures is resulting in a loss of housing among homeowners and an increase in evictions among renters. The lack of affordable housing as Federal support for low-income housing has decreased in recent years, a trend that is particularly hard on renters. Meanwhile, "rental costs continue to rise, placing low-income individuals and families in the difficult position of trying to pay higher housing costs on lower wages" (https://sunrisehouse.com/addiction-demographics/homeless-population/).

Women and people of color are also particularly vulnerable groups. "Homeless women are a large and diverse group, constituting one fifth of the U.S. homeless adult population" (https://pubmed.ncbi.nlm.nih.gov/8724230/). Although most homeless women do not have major mental illness, homeless women exhibit disproportionately high rates of major mental disorders and other mental problems. Rates of mental disorders are highest among whites and women without children, and important variations by subgroups of homeless women of color reinforce the need for disaggregated analysis. Homeless women are also vulnerable to unwanted pregnancies, adverse birth outcomes and sexual and physical assaults. Among low income women, being pregnant may put them at a higher risk of homelessness.

Children and youth are an increasingly visible and vulnerable part of the homeless population. "One of the subpopulations is youth who are under the age of 25 and living on their own (without parents or children). This group is 7 percent of the total homeless population. In recent years, coordinated efforts at all levels of government have also targeted veterans (7 percent of the total homeless population) and chronically home-less people (18 percent). This last group consists of people with disabilities who have been homeless for an extended period of time or repeatedly" (endhomelessness.org). Homeless children are much more likely to experience physical, mental, emotional, edu-cational, developmental, and behavioral problems and are less likely to have obtained health care services. Very young children are likely to be accompanied by their mothers. There is an increasing number of runaways/throwaways or homeless youth living on their own with little or no contact with their family or friends.

Our book provides a comprehensive review of 69 articles and two appendices to help guide the reader through each one of the homeless issues addressed above and is organized into four parts: Introduction; Cities vis-à-vis the States and the Feds; Services, Innovations and Challenges; and The Future; plus the appendices.

Part I, the Introduction, provides six articles addressing the general scope and nature of the problems of homelessness. Each of the articles examines one or more of the differ-ent heads of homelessness. Central to the discussion within this section include an over-view of the *Martin v. Boise* ruling from the Ninth Circuit Court of Appeals in September 2019 and the effect on how communities treat homeless people as well accounts on what cities, large and small, are doing to provide temporary encampments and long-term solu-tions to homelessness. Insights are offered on whether local laws, bans and restrictions directed at the homeless are making matters more punitive than helpful. Essays reveal the strong opposing positions which exist, the high cost in public treasuries to reduce the number of homeless, several myths surrounding homelessness, sheltering and medi-cal care programs for the homeless, and the changing narrative spoken today because we are all witnesses to the simultaneously occurring decay of cities matched by the agoniz-ing hardships experienced by the homeless and homeless families living in tent cities or parking lot encampments.

Part II contains three separate sections categorized as cities, states and the fed-eral government. The thirteen essays in Section A, "Cities," contain program and policy reviews and recommendations for action concerning modern approaches to homeless-ness in San Diego, California; providing permanent supportive housing for homeless in Sacramento, California; exploring homeless work programs in Santa Rosa, California; a scathing opinion editorial concerning President Trump's September 13, 2019, "attack" on the homeless; a community partnership proposal for the homeless in Sutter County, Cal-ifornia (note: an interesting story awaits you about the Sacramento River Bottom Home-less); strengthening homelessness public-private partnerships in the City of Seattle and King County, Washington; a care not cash program for the homeless in San Francisco; and the City and County of San Francisco's strategy for tackling homelessness in their community.

Jason Yergler, a young Washington State resident and Golden Gate University exec-utive master of public administration graduate, starts his essay in this section with the following words, "The issues surrounding and contributing to homelessness in the United States are numerous, highly nuanced, and stem from a variety of causes. The mul-tifaceted problem where homelessness exists affects everyone in the communities. Due to that omnipresent level of impact, it is not surprising that massive sums of resources are allocated to combating the causes of homelessness and supporting individuals cur-rently homeless or at-risk of homelessness." This and other articles within the "Cities" section describe the importance for public administrators and social service agencies to re-examine and redefine the partnerships and proactive collaborative approaches needed to resolve this complex problem of homelessness. Cities struggle to pay for resolving the homeless population problem. This section provides recommendations on ways to provide the homeless with housing and funding medical and mental health care, work and skill training and alcohol and drug rehabilitation/counseling programs.

Lack of housing is claimed to be one of the primary reasons for an increasing homeless population, especially in the State of California. Three of the four essays in Section B, "States," describe the State of California the housing crisis with attention focused on the causes of the extreme housing shortage, the resulting increase in housing prices, the construction workforce gap, barriers to creating new housing construction. local government responses to state severe housing shortages and requirement for public and private investment to solve critical housing challenges. Key housing challenges in the State of California regarding housing affordability are described followed with recommended options for addressing those challenges. California's Housing First Policy is reviewed in this section and provides detailed information on the Housing First approach to serving people experiencing homelessness: "Under the Housing First approach, anyone experiencing homelessness should be connected to a permanent home as quickly as possible, and programs should remove barriers to accessing the housing, like requirements for sobriety or absence of criminal history." The fourth and final essay in this section focuses on Rhode Island and how it became the first state to pass a homeless bill of rights. The bill prohibits discrimination based on housing status. The article chronicles the leadership of the Rhode Island Homeless Advocacy Project homelessness and the partnership with the state legislature, the Rhode Island Coalition for the Homeless (RICH), the state chapter of the American Civil Liberties Union (ACLU), the Interfaith Coalition to Reduce Poverty, and other community organizations to pass the legislation.

The four essays in section C, "Federal," reveal detailed reports from the Housing and Urban Development, the Department of Labor, the Interagency on Homelessness and the White House. The "HUD Reports on Homelessness Unchanged in the U.S. in 2018" indicate that homelessness in the U.S. remained largely unchanged from 2017 to 2018 with "552,830 persons experienced homelessness on a single night in 2018, an increase of 0.3 percent since last year…. Thirty-one (31) states and the District of Columbia reported decreases in homelessness between 2017 and 2018 while 19 states reported increases in the number of persons experiencing homelessness." Notwithstanding efforts to find solutions to ending homelessness, state and local partners struggled against strong obstacles such as lack of housing and rising rents. The HUD report provides interesting key findings to include a 13.2 percent decrease in homelessness since 2010 and a decline in the number of families with children experiencing homelessness declined since 2017, 2.7 percent and since 2010 29 percent. The report provides detailed information on family homeless; veteran homelessness; chronic homelessness; and HUD programs to ending homelessness.

The U.S. Department of Labor's report on "Ending Chronic Homelessness through Employment and Housing Projects" details the department's cooperative agreements with partner agencies like HUD to enable persons who are chronically homeless to achieve employment and self-sufficiency, thereby preventing unnecessary institutional placements.

The U.S. Interagency Council on Homelessness report, "Home, Together: The Federal Strategic Plan to Prevent and End Homelessness," describes the leadership role and responsibilities of the U.S. Interagency Council on Homelessness as it leads national efforts to prevent and end homelessness. The strategic plan in the report outlines import-ant objectives, performance measures and population-specific goals to include end homelessness among veterans; end chronic homelessness among people with disabilities; end homelessness among families with children; end homelessness among unaccompa-nied youth and end homelessness among all other individuals.

The final report in this section provides "The White House Housing Development Toolkit: Executive Summary." The Tool Kit Executive Summary describes the some of the barriers "including zoning, other land use regulations, and lengthy development approval processes … (which) has reduced the ability of many housing markets to respond to growing demand." This toolkit highlights actions that states and local jurisdictions have taken to promote healthy, responsive, affordable, high-opportunity housing markets.

Part III, "Services, Innovations and Challenges," describes services, innovation and challenges within seven separate homelessness problem areas: affordability and inclu-sion, health, substance abuse, veterans, seniors, women and domestic abuse, and youth. Affordable housing remains a major reason for the increasing homeless population. The "Affordability and Inclusion" section, contains six articles on affordable housing and pro-vides a compilation of affordable housing key findings, development, perceptions and barriers, citizen engagement and inclusionary housing policy. For example, the Interna-tional City/County Management Association's essay highlights key findings from their research on housing affordability impacting local governments in the United States and an essay from the Town of Bedford, Massachusetts, describes the successes achieved in their program to increase their inventory of affordable housing development over the past 14 years.

Essays from the Center for Public Policy at VCU's Wilder School, the California Department of Housing and Community Development, Michael Silliman and Deborah Bailey write that housing affordability is, not surprisingly, a very serious problem in the United States. They offer topics such as weak financial management, low education and income level impacts, and racial differences as having significant impact on meeting cur-rent and future housing needs. Silliman highlights the enormous scale of the problem in various cities and suggests that one of the tools cities can use to respond in the face of this affordable housing crisis is to collect open sourced data and mapping and offers examples of how volunteers use civic mapping to find and track current affordable housing. Baily writes that "Inclusionary housing is a concept and public policy decision whose time has come for America's cities and counties" and ends her essay saying that "inclusionary housing does not lead to our greatest fears of urban decline. Instead, it points us to our greatest hopes—communities that work for citizens from all walks of life."

The second section, "Health," contains six articles starting with Sacramento Coun-ty's work to reduce the number of mentally ill homeless, how funding to house the men-tally ill homeless is a financial gain and not a drain, how hospitals are experiencing a sudden increase in the number of homeless patients, on finding homeless patients a place to heal, the record number of homeless dying on the streets of Los Angeles, and the resurgence of "medieval diseases" created by homeless living in unsanitary condi-tions. Articles in this section focus on the severely mentally ill people who are suffering from chronic homelessness and how city, county and regional governments are work-ing to care for and provide services while trying to reduce the homeless rate of its men-tally ill citizens. Research undergirds these essays which provide interesting findings and conclusions regarding the positive correlation between programs that focus directly on solving housing, treatment, and rehabilitation as well as other resource issues among the mentally ill persons and programs which are proactive in reducing system and funding fragmentation as being the most successful in lowering the amount of mentally ill homeless that are on the streets. Organizations such as Sacramento Steps Forward and Pathways and programs such as Assertive Community Treatment are highlighted as having have led to success in reducing the number of mentally ill homeless by funding community-based plans.

An argument that "Cutting funds to house the homeless would cost us more money than it would save" is followed by an essay describing the massive increase of homeless patient visits (about a third of the mentally ill homeless) to California hospitals in 2017—with the public paying the bill. Healing a mentally ill homeless person is not only expensive but the process is problematic. Going back out to the street to heal is not an optimum remedy for immediate or follow-up medical treatment. An essay on finding homeless patients a place to heal is presented in this section and describes how it is attempted in Santa Clara County, California, with only 15 beds and a population of 7,394 homeless people. It's complicated. Still, the homeless are dying on the streets. Anna Gorman's and Harriet Blair Rowan's essay describes probable causes for the record number of homeless dying on the street of Los Angeles each year and the percentage of deaths are increasing year after year. The homeless, not just in Los Angeles, are dying on sidewalks, alleyways, parking lots, riverbeds, freeway on- and off-ramps. Living on the streets is somewhat of a death sentence for many suffering from chronic health problems, diseases and often exposure to severe weather conditions. Some are dying of medieval diseases such as typhus diarrheal disease shigellosis, *Bartonella quintana,* which spreads through body lice and causes trench fever and other diseases caused by living in unsanitary conditions. An article in this section describes the ways our homeless are dying of quickly spreading diseases caused by living in overcrowded conditions, contaminated with human feces, weakened immune systems and limited access to health care.

The two essays in the "Substance Abuse" section are "Addicted to Homelessness" by Johanna L. Wong and Willie L. Britt and "Homelessness Programs and Resources" from the Substance Abuse and Mental Health Services Administration. Substance use disorder and homelessness appear to be correlated. Findings from these studies find that majority of unsheltered homeless have at least one disability and cite their disability as a drug or alcohol problem. The results of the case study analysis indicate that despite entering and exiting treatment, individuals with substance use disorder experienced high rates of recidivism and relapse. The Substance Abuse and Mental Health Services Administration (SAMHSA) is the agency within the U.S. Department of Health and Human Services that leads public health efforts to advance the behavioral health of the nation. Their report provides many interesting findings regarding the connection between chronic homelessness and serious mental illness. Risk factors such as mental and substance use disorders, trauma and violence, domestic violence, justice-system involvement, sudden serious illness, divorce, death of a partner, and disabilities can exacerbate homeless personal vulnerabilities. The report concludes that housing and shelter programs can help address the root causes of homelessness, permanent supportive housing offers safe and stable housing environments to help people manage mental and substance use disorders and interventions to prevent homelessness are more cost effective than addressing issues after someone is already homeless.

Nine essays are included in the "Veterans" section. Helping to solve the homelessness problem is not easy. Hard work is needed to address specific challenges for individual homeless veterans while searching the horizon for sources of help and especially financial support. Homelessness is a solvable problem. The report from the U.S. Department of Veterans Affairs highlight many of the successes achieved by national, state and local leaders are saying about these successes and include statements like, "We've re-tooled programs and systems to be more coordinated and overall more effective at finding our most vulnerable Veterans, triaging their needs, and then navigating them to the most appropriate housing resources and supportive services" and "Today, we say with certainty that Miami-Dade is treating its Veterans with the respect they deserve."

The essays that follow cover specific programs and work which have led to government and non-profit veteran organization successful homeless treatments and support in local communities such as the Monterey County Veteran Transition Center, the Sacramento Steps Forward Program, Sacramento County, California, and the VA Greater Los Angeles Healthcare System, West Los Angeles Medical Center. JoNel Aleccia provides a poignant essay where veterans in several states including California, Oregon, Colorado and Vermont do not have the "right to die option of euthanasia." Patricia Kime describes an uplifting essay concerning the nursing home care veterans receive from caregivers willing to share their homes. The program is called Medical Foster Home Program where aging veterans are providing long-term nursing home care in private homes. In the next essay, Rachel D. McGuffin reviews and examines the potential benefits, problems and funding of tiny homes, some as small as 250 square feet, to house the chronically homeless population, especially for veterans.

The "Seniors" section includes seven essays on seniors/aging population and homelessness. The homeless population is changing and is getting older and sicker. Kushel compares adult homeless population demographics from the early 1990s to 2018 to inform "policymakers and the general public that the homeless are aging faster than the general population in the U.S. and that this shift in the demographics has major implications for how municipalities and health care providers deal with homeless populations."

In their essay, Shannon Guzman, Janet Viveiros and Emily Salomon offer several housing policy challenges and solutions to support aging with options for Americans to include for example:

Challenge: The population of older adults is rapidly rising and expected to reach 20 percent of the U.S. population by 2030. Many communities are lagging behind in supporting policies and programs that will address the needs, including housing, of older adults.

Solution: Local jurisdictions can use programs such as the AARP Network of Age-Friendly Communities or similar initiatives to address the housing and other needs of all residents regardless of age.

The essay "The Need for Safe and Healthy Homes in Order to Age in Place" by Rachel L. Fontenot and Willie L. Britt focuses on the impact that home repair and safety modifications has on making it possible for the elderly homeowners to age safely in their homes. A San Francisco based non-profit organizations serving elderly homeowners was the setting for this case study. Claire Moeller Rygg and Willie L. Britt's essay on "Accessibility Solutions for Colton Hall" centered on the adequacy of handicap access to public historical sites and how lack of access limits the opportunity for persons with a disability to simply visit, never mind enjoying, which is often taken for granted by those who are not physically impaired (mobility, vision or hearing). Key observations are made regarding the ADA of 1990 and the balances required to manage issues of accessibility for historic buildings while preserving their structural integrity. Colton Hall, City of Monterey, California, was the setting for this essay.

Joshua Odetunde, in his essay on "Engaging Nonprofit Sector Institutions for Housing Seniors," reminds readers that "promoting social change, public policy administrators particularly need to engage with nonprofit sector institutions in community real estate management for mutual benefits in local housing markets across the United States" and that "Effective engagement of nonprofit sector institutions is indispensable to ensure social justice in community development and urban planning for seniors." The International City/County Management Association essay on "Township Taps Former Mayor for Age-Friendly Initiative" describe how Teaneck, New Jersey, has formed task forces from its elderly population to make Teaneck an age-friendly and livable community. The former mayor of the town is identified as the motivational catalyst for Helping the Age-Friendly Initiative come to fruition. The process for identifying older adult top concerns and what kinds of task forces were formed are described and explained. The final essay in this section is from the Administration for Community Living (ACL) and focuses on Advancing Independence, Integration, and Inclusion Throughout Life. The ACL funds services provided by networks of community-based organizations with investments in research, education, and innovation. It is the ACL's belief that "older adults and people of all ages with disabilities should be able to live where they choose, with the people they choose, and with the ability to participate fully in their communities." The essay describes their vision, mission and strategic plan to help older adults remain in their communities and "preserve a critical connection to meaningful memories, people, places, and things. These connections with the familiar can be particularly important for older adults."

The four essays in the "Women and Domestic Violence" section include a case study on the City of Pacific Grove's program to provide safe parking for homeless women; a general discussion on women veterans and homeless women; minorities; and finding shelter in a housing shortage environment for survivors of domestic violence. "Safe Parking Program for Homeless Women in Pacific Grove, California" by Deidre L. McLay and Mickey P. McGee started as a research case study "to determine the effectiveness of the One Starfish Safe Parking Program in Pacific Grove, California, a non-profit organization serving adult women who live in vehicles." Program participants, program staff, parking lot provider, city police and government officials were interviewed. Performance outcomes were also measured to evaluate the effectiveness of the program. The conclusion, lessons learned and final thoughts reveal whether the program was effective.

In "Veteran, Minority, Woman and Homeless" Ginger Miller provides a first-person account of her journey from a happy childhood, honorable service in the military, her husband's PTSD and then their descent into the world of homelessness. She tells a story of how pride and patriotism along with lots of work helped pull her family through this terrible nightmare and made her remark "an incredible comeback and I am grateful to God!" Alexandra Logsdon and Kayla M. Williams next describe the growing population of homeless women veterans explain the some of the characteristics associated with homeless women veterans to include factors related to sexual assaults, unemployment, disabilities, degraded physical and mental health conditions, household alcohol abuse and exposure to domestic violence and emotional abuse. Rebecca DeSantis, in "Finding Shelter: Addressing Housing Challenges for Survivors of Domestic Violence," reflects on an issue communities must face when tackling domestic violence—housing for survivors. She points out that domestic violence is the leading cause of homelessness for women and children and that more than half of domestic violence victims who need housing services do not receive them. She outlines some important steps that local governments can take to address housing challenges for survivors of domestic violence and decrease survivors' vulnerability.

The three essays on "Youth" begin with Jon Ruiz's "Helping Homeless Youth" followed by Ryan Jensen's and Katelyn Hansen's "Navigating Student Housing Challenges" and Stacey Havlik's "The Hidden Homelessness Among America's High School Students." Ruiz describes Eugene, Oregon's homelessness challenge and reports that "Oregon is one of three states with the highest rate of homeless youth in the country." The article centers on how the city united to form a youth-informed community movement, 15th Night, to end youth homelessness by helping unaccompanied students stay engaged in school, safely housed, and off the street. The Collective Impact model framework and initiative and the five principles of the 15th Night program are described in detail.

In "Navigating Student Housing Challenges" by Ryan Jensen and Katelyn Hansen, housing challenges created by large student populations intruding into traditional single-family neighborhoods. They center their essay on a 2017 Strategic Housing Plan which analyzed university and local housing issues in order devise cohesive housing strategies.

"The Hidden Homelessness Among America's High School Students" by Stacey Havlik focuses on 13 to 17-year-old students experiencing homelessness, which is estimated to be about 700,000 young people nationwide. School counselors are a critical resource for students experiencing homelessness to not only help them stay in school and work towards going to college but to also help homeless students' basic needs.

Part IV, "The Future," has five essays covering suggestions on how shelter design can help people recover from homelessness and how improving resident services can be achieved by using blockchain technology. Our libraries today provide a sanctuary for people who are homeless or mentally ill. An essay explores whether or not libraries have become the front lines for the crisis of homelessness in the U.S. The Honorable Judge Ruth Astle Samas suggests that criminalization of homelessness is not the answer and housing the homeless in jails is not good public policy. She reviews the Homeless and Caring Court and describes the significance of the 2018 U.S. Court of Appeals, Ninth Circuit decision, *Martin v. City of Boise* 902 F. 3rd 1031 and how the ruling is impacting cities in their efforts to end homelessness. The final essay is on how tents and reusable containers vans may be the most effective and low-cost transition shelters, especially for disaster victims and the homeless.

The appendices feature a comprehensive glossary of definitions, terms and abbreviations and acronyms significant in the understanding of homelessness, and an FAQ compiled by Denver Homeless Out Loud.

PART I

Introduction

1. A Potential Turning Point in How Cities Treat the Homeless*

Mattie Quinn

A federal ruling from the Ninth Circuit Court of Appeals in September 2018 is already having an effect on how communities treat homeless people.

Martin v. Boise has been making its way through the courts since 2009. At issue is whether Boise, Idaho's ban against sleeping on the streets—a so-called anti-camping ordinance that exists in many places across the country—violates homeless people's Eighth Amendment rights, which protect against cruel and unusual punishment.

The victory: "As long as there is no option of sleeping indoors, the government cannot criminalize indigent, homeless people for sleeping outdoors on public property on the false premise they had a choice in the matter," wrote Ninth Circuit Judge Marsha Berzon.

The defeat: The court ruled that shelters can turn people away if they don't comply with religious rules or if they have reached capacity.

Boise is appealing the ruling and plans to continue as usual in the meantime. "As far as we're concerned, the ordinance stands until we hear differently from a final court," Mike Journee, a spokesman for the city, told the *Idaho Statesman*.

Still, homeless rights advocates are cautiously optimistic the case could catalyze cities to finally figure out long-term solutions for chronic homelessness.

"We want communities to see this as an opportunity, not a limitation. Criminalization of homeless, any way you look at it, is never a positive step," says Eric Tars, senior attorney for the National Law Center on Homelessness and Poverty. "From a fiscal standpoint, it costs communities more to cycle these people through law enforcement than actually providing shelter or giving them resources."

Research shows that the criminalization of homelessness is expensive and often ineffective. According to a 2018 study by the University of Denver, six Colorado cities spent $5 million enforcing anti-homeless ordinances over a five-year period. "Reducing or eliminating anti-homeless ordinances would achieve governmental goals of reducing ineffective spending," the study found. Similarly, San Francisco spends around $20 million a year enforcing its anti-homeless ordinances.

Meanwhile, a 2015 report found that Massachusetts saved taxpayers $9,339 for every homeless person that it helped house instead of penalized.

The September ruling has already spurred several cities to act.

---

*Originally published as Mattie Quinn, "A Potential Turning Point in How Cities Treat the Homeless," *Governing*, November 28, 2018. Reprinted with permission of the publisher.

Modesto, Calif., dedicated a park for homeless people to camp. But the city stresses that this is a temporary solution while it works toward increasing the number of available beds in shelters and that it will continue to enforce its anti-camping ordinance in other areas. Olympia, Wash., called off a sweep of a homeless encampment. San Francisco and Portland, Ore., officials said they will stop prosecuting homeless people violating city sleeping ordinances. And Los Angeles officials said they are working on new guidance regarding encampments.

As cities look for long-term solutions to homelessness, Tars says they should avoid taking the easy route of passing more laws against homelessness and instead invest in "upstream" programs, which cost more in the beginning but can end up saving communities more money down the line and in other areas like health care. Upstream solutions include opening up vacant lots to people living out of their cars and using bond money to create more affordable housing.

But, Tars says, these investments can be a tough sell.

"You get this push from the business community that we need to do something, and we couldn't agree more," he says. "Where we differ, however, is that businesses and others will say to do the quick and easy thing. Whereas when you have more thoughtful approaches, you have to acknowledge those costs up front."

How Philadelphia Is Helping the Homeless

Philadelphia isn't impacted by *Martin v. Boise*, but Tars says cities that are should look to its efforts to combat homelessness as a model, particularly the Hub of Hope.

One of the city's train stations was a de facto place for homeless people to sleep. With the population it wants to help already there, the city converted it into a permanent walk-in resource center where homeless people can shower, do laundry, and receive health, housing and legal aid. The space offers dinner on the weekends and in December will expand evening meals to four times a week. They cannot, however, sleep there anymore.

The Hub of Hope sees about 250 people per day, and they saw 80,000 people in 2017, according to David Hollomon, chief of staff for Philadelphia's Department of Homeless Services. Law enforcement likes it, says Hollomon, because it gives them a place to redirect homeless people.

Meanwhile, Philadelphia has created enough low-barrier housing—where the only requirement to get a bed is to not be under the influence and to not incite violence—to clear three out of four of its homeless encampments, redirecting 50 people to some form of shelter and helping 67 get a photo ID (which is required to receive some government aid). While this doesn't account for everyone in those encampments, Holloman says not everyone chooses to go to a shelter.

"Everyone in the city has been clear that we're not criminalizing homelessness. We didn't ever want to be perceived as doing that," Holloman says.

Tars worries, however, that no matter what cities do, they won't make a significant dent in homelessness until they address the lack of affordable housing throughout the country.

"[The ruling] gives us a really important tool, but the danger is we're not solving the overall affordable housing crisis," he says. "More families are paying a higher share of their income on housing, so my fear is that unsheltered homelessness is just going to continue to grow."

2. Why Turning Homelessness into a Crime Is Cruel and Costly*

Joseph W. Mead *and* Sara Rankin

Increasingly, local laws punish Americans who are homeless.

By severely restricting or even barring the ability to engage in necessary, life-sustaining activities in public, like sitting, standing, sleeping or asking for help, even when there's no reasonable alternative, these laws are essentially persecuting homeless men, women and children.

As law professors who study how laws can make homelessness better or worse, we encourage cities, suburbs and towns to avoid punishing people who live in public and have nowhere else to go. One big reason: These "anti-vagrancy laws" are counterproductive because they make it harder to escape homelessness.

Many Paths to Not Having a Home, and More Laws

Why do at least half a million Americans experience homelessness at any time?

Researchers find that most people who become homeless have nowhere to live after being evicted, losing their jobs or fleeing an abusive partner.

Many emergency homeless shelters are perpetually full. Even those with beds to spare may enforce rules that exclude families, LGBTQ youth and people with pets.

And when homeless people can stay in shelters, often they may only spend the night there. That means they have to go somewhere else during the daytime.

As the number of people facing homelessness increases, local residents are demanding that their elected officials do something about the homeless people they encounter in their daily lives. The leaders of cities, towns and suburbs are often responsive.

But more often than not, municipalities don't address the underlying problems that cause homelessness by, say, providing sufficient permanent housing, affordable housing or shelters with minimal barriers to entry. Instead, criminalizing homelessness is growing more popular.

Over the last decade, city-wide bans on camping in public have increased by 69

*Originally published as Joseph W. Mead and Sara Rankin, "Why Turning Homelessness into a Crime Is Cruel and Costly," *The Conversation*, https://theconversation.com/why-turning-homelessness-into-a-crime-is-cruel-and-costly-97290 (June 20, 2018). Reprinted with permission of the publisher.

percent while city-wide panhandling bans rose by 43 percent, according to the National Law Center on Homelessness and Poverty.

Advocates such as the American Civil Liberties Union frequently challenge these laws in court. Judges often strike down such laws on the grounds that they violate constitutionally protected rights, such as the freedom of speech or due process.

Still, more and more communities keep trying to outlaw homelessness.

Criminalizing Homelessness Is Ineffective

Not only do we and other legal experts find these laws to be unconstitutional, we see ample evidence that they waste tax dollars.

Cities are aggressively deploying law enforcement to target people simply for the crime of existing while having nowhere to live. In 2016 alone, Los Angeles police arrested 14,000 people experiencing homelessness for everyday activities such as sitting on sidewalks.

San Francisco is spending some $20 million per year to enforce laws against loitering, panhandling and other common conduct against people experiencing homelessness.

Jails and prisons make extremely expensive and ineffective homeless shelters. Non-punitive alternatives, such as permanent supportive housing and mental health or substance abuse treatment, cost less and work better, according to research one of us is doing at the Homeless Rights Advocacy Project at Seattle University Law School and many other sources.

But the greatest cost of these laws is borne by already vulnerable people who are ticketed, arrested and jailed because they are experiencing homelessness.

Fines and court fees quickly add up to hundreds or thousands of dollars. A Sacramento man, for example, found himself facing $100,000 in fines for convictions for panhandling and sleeping outside. These costs are impossible to pay, since the "crimes" were committed by dint of being unable to afford keeping a roof over his head in the first place.

And since having a criminal record makes getting jobs and housing much harder, these laws are perpetuating homelessness.

3. How Local Governments Can Build an Effective Homelessness System*

Cynthia Nagendra

On a single night in January 2015, 564,708 people were considered homeless in America. That's more than half a million people without a roof over their heads. And this, along with rising rents, continues to be a growing challenge in the nation, especially for local governments.

We know that housing is the solution to homelessness. So how can local government leaders help residents quickly exit homelessness and stay housed? There are many interventions that work to effectively resolve homelessness but the key doesn't lie only with programs. The key to ending homelessness is establishing a systemic response in your community—a system that is transparent, inclusive, goal-oriented, and fundamentally accountable for getting people into housing so that all instances of homelessness in your community are rare, brief, and nonrecurring.

Below, we break down the key pillars of an effective homelessness system. We'll cover:

- How local government leaders can leverage evidence-based interventions that are proven to have the best outcomes.
- How to bring together the various systems in your community that are best positioned to support this effort.
- How leaders can use data to ensure that the resources they allocate are responding to the needs of people experiencing homelessness.

Pillar 1: Leveraging Evidence, Measuring Outcomes

An effective system must be focused on outcomes:

- Are you reducing the total number of homeless individuals and families?
- Are you reducing the length of time that someone experiences homelessness?
- Are you reducing returns to homelessness?

*Cynthia Nagendra, "How Local Governments Can Build an Effective Homelessness System," *PM Magazine*, https://icma.org/blog-posts/how-local-governments-can-build-effective-homelessness-system (November 17, 2017). Originally published in the November 2017 issue of *Public Management (PM)* magazine and copyrighted by ICMA, the International City/County Management Association (icma.org); reprinted with permission.

Tip for Leaders: Local governments need to keep an eye on these numbers. If your system isn't addressing these three benchmarks, it's time to reorient your approach. That includes looking at the outcomes of existing programs and deciding how to allocate resources to the most effective interventions. Rapid Re-Housing is one example of an intervention that has been proven to be effective in meeting all three primary outcomes for most people experiencing homelessness.

Pillar 2: Building a Coordinated Coalition

It's only natural that local governments will often try to "match" a problem or an issue with a specific department. However, people who are experiencing homelessness will touch various systems. The homeless response system should be coordinating strategies and resources with each of them, potentially including child welfare, health and human services, education, criminal justice, and others, to achieve better outcomes.

Tip for Leaders: Local leaders need to be *conveners*. They need to help identify those sectors of the community that are impacted by homelessness, as well as the "usual suspects" (social services, nonprofits, philanthropy, etc.), to align as many cumulative resources as possible, and utilize them in a strategic and coordinated way instead of putting them into siloes or separate programs.

Pillar 3: Investing Wisely

Knowing where to invest your resources can be an overwhelming responsibility. Which programs are right for your community? Are they sustainable? Can you use data to support them? Will the broader community support your efforts?

Tip for Leaders: Evaluate existing resources and how they are being used. Are they supporting interventions and activities that make measurable progress toward system outcomes to end homelessness? Align local spending with evidence-based interventions and established federal priorities and strategies for ending homelessness. This approach brings the potential to leverage a combination of local and federal funds and helps ensure that you are investing in proven, evidence-based solutions.

To learn more about how to prevent and end homelessness in your community, visit the National Alliance to End Homelessness at endhomelessness.org.

4. Busting Three Common Myths About Homelessness*

Paul Toro

As a young psychologist in the 1980s who had researched treatment of the mentally ill, I was concerned by many reports suggesting that the growing number of homeless people may be due to deinstitutionalization.

Over the past 30 years, my research group and I have conducted a wide range of studies on homelessness. In our work, we've found that Americans hold a number of myths about this population. Some of these myths have some basis in fact, while others have little or no validity.

Myth 1

The homeless and "poor will always be with us." This statement about the poor, attributed to Jesus in Matthew 26:11, can be taken out of context to suggest that people need not be concerned with caring for the poor and homeless. According to such an interpretation, assistance to the poor is a waste of time. Most Biblical scholars disagree with such a pessimistic interpretation.

But will there really always be poor people? Rates of homelessness vary widely across nations. In our telephone surveys of random samples of citizens across 10 developed nations, the chance that a given citizen had experienced homelessness at some point in their lifetime varied between 2.2 and 8.6 percent.

It's not yet clear what explains this variation. Is it the quality of social and health services in different countries? Could different patterns of substance abuse or immigration explain it? In any event, at 6.1 percent, the U.S. has one of the highest rates among developed nations.

If nations vary so widely, that suggests national policy changes could reduce high rates of homelessness. In the past decade or so, the U.S. has dramatically ramped up resources devoted to eliminating homelessness among veterans. Thanks to these efforts, veteran homelessness went down 35 percent between 2009 and 2015, outpacing the 10 percent total reduction in homelessness.

---

*Originally published as Paul Toro, "Busting 3 Common Myths About Homelessness," *The Conversation*, https://theconversation.com/busting-3-common-myths-about-homelessness-93035 (July 5, 2018). Reprinted with permission of the publisher.

Provided with ongoing support services, the homeless mentally ill and other homeless persons can maintain themselves in permanent housing over long periods of time.

Other research suggests that homelessness can be prevented among vulnerable groups. For example, in a statewide evaluation, youth exiting foster care and detention facilities in Tennessee were randomly assigned to a special outpatient program or to a control group. Those in the program spent significantly less time homeless over the next year and also had other positive outcomes, like higher employment income.

Myth 2

Homelessness affects only very limited segments of American society. For sure, homelessness is more likely to affect those who are poor or otherwise disadvantaged in our society. But homelessness appears to touch the lives of a wide range of Americans, including some who average citizens would never have thought to be vulnerable.

Many people mistakenly believe that most of the homeless are mentally ill. Studies done by our group and others over the last 30 years have found that only one-quarter to one-third of homeless adults show a documented serious mental disorder, like schizophrenia, major depression or bipolar disorder.

Substance use disorders among homeless adults are much more common. Sixty to 75 percent of homeless people struggle with substance abuse at some point in their lifetime, versus 16 percent among the general population. Both serious mental and substance use disorders are less common among homeless mothers, their children and unaccompanied homeless youth.

Recently, studies have shown that college students suffer from high rates of homelessness and food insecurity. A recent survey of over 40,000 students across the U.S. found that 9 percent of university students and 12 percent of community college students had been homeless in the past year.

Over three decades, my team has interviewed thousands of homeless people. We have very rarely found anyone who we might consider to have "chosen" a homeless lifestyle. Yes, there are women, youth and others fleeing violent or otherwise very difficult life circumstances. Yes, there are some with severe mental or substance use disorders who have no other alternative to the streets or homeless shelters. If given the "choice" between a mental hospital, a jail or a homeless shelter in a dangerous area of town, some will, with good reason, take to the streets.

Myth 3

The public has developed "compassion fatigue" when it comes to homelessness. Starting in the late 1980s, researchers have conducted a series of public opinion surveys on homelessness in the U.S. and other developed nations. In the 1990s, some in the U.S. media started to suggest that the public was experiencing "compassion fatigue," the feeling that homelessness had become an intractable problem that no longer needed so much societal attention.

However, the evidence doesn't support this at all. For example, surveys continue to find that a majority of the public would pay more taxes to help the homeless.

Perhaps it's an issue of perception. My team analyzed the media's interest in homelessness over the past 40 years, focusing on four major U.S. newspapers: *The New York Times, The Washington Post, Chicago Tribune and Los Angeles Times.*

There was virtually no media interest in homelessness prior to 1980, when Ronald Reagan began his first term as president. Interest then took off, perhaps due to actual increases in the numbers experiencing homelessness. This curiosity peaked in 1987, the same year that the first major federal funding was passed, then declined as the media became interested in other topics.

Since 1995, media interest has been steady at a relatively low level. Given these findings, perhaps a more accurate conclusion is that the mass media have experienced "compassion fatigue."

5. Why There Are So Many Unsheltered Homeless People on the West Coast*

MARGOT KUSHEL

One-quarter of homeless people in the U.S. live in California, despite Californians making up only 12 percent of the population.

Not only is homelessness more common on the West Coast but it is also more visible, because a higher proportion of homeless people are unsheltered. In the U.S., 24 percent of homeless people sleep outside, in vehicles or somewhere else not meant for human habitation. But that varies greatly from place to place: In California, 68 percent of homeless people are unsheltered, compared to just 5 percent in New York.

Visitors to the West Coast may be shocked to find the tents that line cities from San Diego to Seattle. Like a modern-day *Grapes of Wrath,* the tents are a stark reminder of the suffering of the thousands living outside, homeless.

What's to blame for such high numbers of unsheltered homeless on the West Coast? The reason isn't drug use, mental health problems or weather. Rather, it is due to the extreme shortage of affordable housing.

Life Unsheltered

As a physician and researcher who provides medical care for people experiencing homelessness, I have seen firsthand how devastating homelessness is to health.

Being unsheltered is terrifying, humiliating and isolating. People living without shelter lack access to toileting facilities, sinks and showers. They have no way to store or prepare food and no protection from the elements. Hunger is common.

Sleeping in makeshift beds or on the ground, they get little sleep. They must contend with having their possessions stolen. They face frequent forced moves, which disrupt relationships and make it difficult for family, friends or service providers to find them.

People who are unsheltered are at high risk of physical and sexual abuse. If they struggle with substance use disorders, their use of drugs and alcohol occurs in public,

*Originally published as Margot Kushel, "Why There Are So Many Unsheltered Homeless People on the West Coast," *The Conversation,* https://theconversation.com/why-there-are-so-many-unsheltered-homeless-people-on-the-west-coast-96767 (June 14, 2018). Reprinted with permission of the publisher.

leaving them open to arrest. There are no places to refrigerate or store medicines, no place to receive mailed appointment reminders or a visit from a visiting nurse, no place to dress a wound or plug in medical equipment like oxygen. Without access to hygiene facilities, they are at high risk for communicable diseases like hepatitis A.

Unaffordable Housing

Some assume that homelessness is so common on the West Coast because people move here when they become homeless, but data do not support this. Most people experience homelessness close to where they lost their housing. My team's research in Oakland found that 81 percent of older adults who are homeless became homeless in the Bay Area. Only 10 percent had lost their housing outside of California.

Instead, the high rate of homelessness can be attributed to the lack of affordable housing in these regions. The West Coast suffers from rising costs of rental housing, stagnant incomes for low-wage workers and a decline in federal support for affordable housing. For example, California has gained 900,000 renter households since 2005, but lost $1.7 billion in state and federal funding for affordable housing.

Extremely low-income households—defined as those with income less than 30 percent of the area median income—are at the highest risk of homelessness. Nationally, there are only 35 units available for every 100 extremely low-income households.

In the West, these shortages are more severe: Nevada has 15 units available for every 100 extremely low-income households; California has 21.

In 2017, for the first time in 13 years, Los Angeles opened its wait list for housing choice vouchers. These vouchers allow households to pay 30 percent of their income in rent, with the rest paid by the government. There were 600,000 applicants for just 20,000 spots on the list, highlighting the enormous unmet need.

Who Pays for Homeless Services

Why are people on the West Coast so much more likely to be unsheltered than homeless people in other parts of the country? It reflects differing government priorities.

New York City, where there is a legal right to shelter, spends approximately $17,000 per homeless person per year on homeless services. Massachusetts spends approximately $14,000 per year. Los Angeles, by contrast, spends approximately $5,000.

With enormous numbers of people living outside, West Coast cities are scrambling for solutions. Some cities, like Seattle, have created sanctioned homeless encampments, bringing hygiene facilities and other services. However, the U.S. Interagency Council on Homeless cautions that this approach is costly and doesn't provide a solution to homelessness.

Other cities are following San Francisco's example and creating navigation centers, homeless shelters with added services. Unlike typical shelters, these centers allow people to come in groups, bring pets and belongings and stay all day.

Many areas have passed tax increases to fund new housing and services. These efforts show modest success but continue to struggle against the unfavorable housing conditions that lead people to become homeless in the first place.

So where can we go from here? There are solutions to homelessness, but, in my view, these will not succeed without solving the affordable housing crisis that is the underlying cause of homelessness.

For people who are chronically homeless and have disabling conditions, permanent supportive housing is highly effective. This type of subsidized housing offers supportive services, without the requirement that people be sober or engaged in medical care. Studies show that expanding permanent supportive housing has reduced the number of people experiencing homelessness in many parts of the country.

The success of permanent supportive housing has been overshadowed by increases in people becoming newly homeless due to the lack of affordable housing. In my view, preventing and ending homelessness will require a commitment to creating housing that is affordable to all.

6. How the Homeless Create Homes*

Susan Fraiman

The number of people facing housing insecurity, already on the rise, began to climb more steeply as a result of the Great Recession. This upward trend will likely be exacerbated if President Trump's proposed cuts to food stamps, Medicaid and housing subsidies are enacted, which will force even more to make a choice between food on the table and a roof above their heads.

To those who are safely housed, a homeless person is apt to inspire feelings ranging from fear and disgust to pity and guilt.

Such negative responses are rooted in longstanding myths about "hobos," "Bowery bums," and "bag ladies." Some may believe that homeless people are free spirits who simply prefer to live outside. More likely, they're viewed as misfits—dysfunctional, threatening, potentially criminal.

Above all, they are not like us.

In my book, *Extreme Domesticity: A View from the Margins*, I examine ethnographies, journalistic accounts and memoirs that have been written about homeless people and communities.

While the accounts describe individuals living in different decades, cities and circumstances, the homeless people portrayed all possess an impressive degree of agency and resourcefulness, even though they can't take the comforts of home for granted.

Homemakers once, they are homemakers still: however challenging, their efforts to satisfy basic domestic needs resemble those of people everywhere.

Changing the Narrative

The guy on a median, working the cars with his scrawled sign. The woman camped on a sidewalk with her bundles. The sleeping figure curled under a roof of cardboard.

These are only the most visible cases of homelessness. But many rotate among friends, stay in emergency shelters or live in their cars. Most are previously employed, and some still are.

The majority aren't consistently homeless. Instead, high rents, low wages and insufficient federal aid combine to produce recurrent bouts of homelessness—a cycle of

*Originally published as Susan Fraiman, "How the Homeless Create Homes," *The Conversation,* https://theconversation.com/how-the-homeless-create-homes-78581 (June 28, 2017). Reprinted with permission of the publisher.

25

instability. As Harvard sociologist Matthew Desmond noted in his recent book *Evicted,* millions of families are forced from their homes each year.

A large number are children. In 2016, youth under 25 accounted for 31 percent of the overall homeless population. In addition to LGBT teens and those aging out of foster care, a recent study identified a more surprising subgroup of unhoused kids: community college students. Many lack sufficient financial aid and are earning poverty wages. A full 13 percent leave class with nowhere to go.

Dealing with Daily Needs

We tend to equate the absence of secure shelter with the absence of a domestic life. Is it even possible to make a home without one?

But for people coping with homelessness, everyday domestic concerns become all the more urgent and all-consuming.

Is this a safe, dry place to sleep? Does my kid have cereal for breakfast? Where can I take a shower? When does the soup kitchen open? Where can I store my medication, papers and photos? How can I create some privacy and coziness in a public place?

The sources I survey in my book suggest that answers to these problems are as diverse as the people experiencing homelessness. In *Travels with Lizbeth*, writer Lars Eighner recalls his years spent sleeping in makeshift camps and eating out of dumpsters, accompanied by his beloved dog. At one point, he nests for weeks in a stand of bamboo, reading and writing by the light of an improvised oil lamp.

Jonathan Kozol, in the book *Rachel and Her Children*, tells the story of Annie, a woman who dreams of a sparkling house full of books and plants. In the meantime, she and her family of four make do with a room in the Martinique Hotel, a decaying building in midtown Manhattan serving as a homeless shelter. Braving squalid conditions, Annie cooks dinner on a hotplate and serves it on the bed, while still making sure the kids' homework is done.

Documented by anthropologist Jackson Underwood, the "bridge people" live under Los Angeles' freeways, camping together, divvying up labor, fighting with and caring for one another. Like any extended family, they share food, drink, cigarettes, clothing and cash. When Jerry and Suzi are sick, Mack brings them breakfast every morning: scrambled eggs, ravioli or grilled cheese.

No home is just given. Every home is the product of someone's daily labor and creativity. In this sense, the so-called homeless—under duress but carrying on with familiar routines of cooking, cleaning and caring—aren't so different from the rest of society.

Creating Something from Nothing

The 2000 documentary *Dark Days* introduces us to life in a shantytown located in a railway tunnel beneath the streets of Manhattan. It's no paradise, as the rats, garbage, arson and violent backstories make clear.

Yet against all odds, the men and women we meet in the film have managed to domesticate their underground wilderness. Hardworking and innovative, they cobble together the necessities and even a few small luxuries: a dartboard, toaster oven, dogs, cats and a gerbil named Peaches.

Along abandoned railroad tracks, residents live in rigged up wooden houses, furnished with items dragged in from the street. A man named Henry was able to tap into the power grid, so there's a ready supply of electricity for cooking, shaving and watching TV. Sanitation is poor, but sometimes there's running water from city pipes.

People fuss over meals concocted on hotplates. Noting the merits of buttermilk in cornbread, a woman named Dee explains, "We're homeless people, but if you know how to cook, cook right." Others are shown sweeping, brushing teeth, preparing for a day's work collecting cans or reselling found goods.

Supplies are stacked on tables and shelves. Someone has painted a Dali-esque mural on rough tunnel walls. The film itself is a creative act that emerged from the community: It was first proposed by one resident and executed by a crew of tunnel dwellers.

Mobilizing to Take Action

David Wagner's *Checkerboard Square: Culture and Resistance in a Homeless Community* is a 1993 study of street people in a midsized New England city. Like *Dark Days*, it shows that being homeless doesn't necessarily mean being isolated. Wagner challenges the view that homeless people are "socially disorganized, disaffiliated and disempowered," finding that many of the women and men he studied not only retain ties to mainstream society but also participate in well-defined subgroups, from what he calls the "Politicos" to the "Social Club."

The Politicos, for example, erected a tent city to protest policies detrimental to the poor and insecurely housed. Working alongside community organizers, interacting with journalists and city officials, these homeless activists succeeded in bettering conditions and gaining a voice for people living outside.

Wagner describes, too, how members of the Social Club gathered at the Friendly Center, an innovative community space for those with mental health issues. Staffed as well as frequented by the people it served, the Center challenged mainstream views of this population as broken and needing to be fixed. Most Social Club members were women who defied the stereotype of the hapless bag lady: they were eloquent advocates for alternative mental health care. They helped to lead the tent city and spoke out forcefully on behalf of homeless women and the mentally ill.

Being without reliable shelter is traumatic. But it's only dehumanizing if you're regarded as less than human. In fact, being homeless brings out the very things that make us human: our creation of domestic rituals, care for others, ingenuity in shaping our environment.

It may even inspire efforts to change the society that leaves some out in the cold.

PART II

Cities vis-à-vis the States and the Feds

• *A. Cities* •

7. Modern Approaches to Homelessness*

Amanda L. McGimpsey

In the modern era, public administrators must re-examine complex social problems like homelessness. The recent Hepatitis A outbreak in San Diego exemplifies a city being forced to redefine their approach to a decades-long social problem. The city must now explore issues of place, its relationship to community partnerships and vertical government structure.

In the 1980s, the City of San Diego made a large push to make Downtown San Diego a tourist destination. To this end, San Diego offered significant benefits for homeless services to move to the outlying East Village district of Downtown. The goal was to group homeless populations into specific areas to consolidate access to services, and to clean up the rest of Downtown. While this was in theory an innovative approach, unfortunately the relocation efforts for these services were largely promoted by the city government without consulting with the service organizations. This approach did not offer long range, sustainable funding.

In the 1990s, recognizing that the area needed additional support, the City Council developed a comprehensive plan to bring more funding into this area and setup more locations around the county that could address issues of homelessness in similar ways. However, while this plan had the best of intentions it was only partially implemented and funded. The East Village continued to be one of the few neighborhoods in San Diego with an accumulation of services but did not have the full support and funding from the city in order to make it a success.

By the time Petco Park was developed in the area in the 2000s, the East Village area served the largest homeless population in the county. As the area rapidly began gentrifying with the development of Petco Park, luxury condos and trendy restaurants, the homeless population continued to grow. Yet funding from the city and federal government continued to be prioritized for other types of services not offered in the East Village.

This leads us to 2016, when gentrified residential and business communities began demanding that the homeless population be moved from East Village. Mayor Faulkner was struggling with the public relations nightmare of having the fourth largest homeless population in the country and a growing chorus of angry residents and businesses. That

---

*Originally published as Amanda L. McGimpsey, "Modern Approaches to Homelessness," *PA Times*, https://patimes.org/modern-approaches-to-homelessness/ (February 14, 2019). Reprinted with permission of the publisher.

is when the Hepatitis A outbreak began spreading through the homeless population of East Village, killing 20 people and infecting over 500 others, including homeless individuals and community members.

Facing the political aftermath of the Hepatitis A outbreak, the city responded with more direct engagement such as regular street cleanings, more public restrooms and setting up temporary housing near East Village. But they also continued to rely on community partnerships. The key challenge that San Diego must solve is how it can ensure administrative accountability while networking with these services. In order to avoid repeating historic mistakes, San Diego will need to transform from a vertical approach to a more horizontal approach so it can build the capacity to manage these partnerships effectively.

San Diego should also reconsider how it organizes its approach to homelessness. In his *Notes on the Theory of Administration*, Luther Gulick outlines four distinctive forms of organization: By process, by clientele, by place, or by major purpose. He argues that to be truly effective, public administrators can not pick parts of each approach. They must instead choose only one approach. To do otherwise will lead to dilution and the organization will not work.

For the last 50 years, San Diego has been organizing by place. The homeless population was purposefully channeled into the East Village with the goal of being able to centralize services. However, this strategy has proved ineffective and the city should reconsider other forms of organizational approaches that may be more sustainable.

The East Village must also overcome issues of hyperpluralism, where groups or factions become so strong that the government is unable to function. San Diego must resist the temptation of repeating history. The city should not appease business owners and gentrified communities by moving the homeless population into another undeveloped area just like they did 40 years ago. This strategy does not work and San Diego's government must develop a more city-wide approach that involves listening to all stakeholders—most importantly, the homeless themselves.

To develop a horizontal form of management, San Diego officials must focus on being adaptable to new challenges, developing the capacity to manage effectively and consistently and show a willingness to redefine their role to better scale to the issues at hand. It is the administrator's job to maintain effectiveness by being highly adaptable in the modern era.

8. Permanent Supportive Housing for Homeless in Sacramento, California*

James P. Nicholls III *and* Rachel D. McGuffin

Permanent Supportive Housing Model

Over the past decade, diminishing financial resources across federal and local levels has led to a downward trend of funding available for public services. One of these services includes efforts to decrease the homeless population, especially in states with large homeless populations like California. These efforts have resulted in the recognition that housing is an important part of health care service delivery for persons who have experienced homelessness. Local, state, and federal stakeholders are working to find creative avenues to access the funding and support needed to address this problem.

U.S. policy continues to shift towards addressing long-term homelessness through permanent supportive housing rather than relying on shelters and transitional housing. In 2010, the U.S. government endorsed the Housing First approach to permanent supportive housing as the preferred solution for chronic homelessness (Graham, 2015). Whereas other programs require people to engage in psychiatric or substance use treatment and attain stability and sobriety before they can receive housing, Housing First offers permanent supportive housing without these prerequisites. This approach bundles financial support for housing with offers of psychiatric, medical, and social rehabilitative support.

Some Housing First programs use a "scattered site" model, providing subsidized rental support for a private-market apartment coupled with outreach from clinicians and social workers who regularly visit the tenant and assist as needed. Other programs use a "project-based" model, accommodating formerly homeless tenants in a building where comprehensive psychosocial services are available (Kertesz, et al., 2016). The definition of permanent supportive housing, regardless of model is as follows: A direct service that helps adults who are homeless or disabled identify and secure long-term, affordable housing. Individuals participating in permanent supportive housing generally have access to ongoing case management services that are designed to preserve tenancy and address their current needs (Rog, et al., 2014).

---

*Published with permission of the authors.

Sacramento, California: A Case Study

The City of Sacramento is no exception to the problem of housing the homeless and reducing its long-term promulgation. The Institute for Social Research from California State University Sacramento for Sacramento Steps Forward (a nonprofit local homeless advocacy group), the 2015 through 2017 Point-in-Time Count reported the homeless population in the Greater Sacramento area increased from 2,822 to 3,665 individuals, and the projected growth of homelessness is determined to be at a rate of thirty percent every two years.

In response to these rising numbers, nine mayors of the major cities in California, including Sacramento Mayor Darrell Steinberg, collectively approached Governor Jerry Brown with a proposal to set aside funds for affordable housing, including housing for the homeless. As a result of their efforts, in 2018 $1.5 billion became available for affordable housing throughout the State of California (Legislative's Analyst Office, 2019). The City and County seats of Sacramento passed a resolution in 2017 to convert Housing Choice Vouchers (rental subsidy anywhere in the U.S.) to Project Based Vouchers (project specific rental subsidy) to bridge the homeless population from the streets and hospitals to permanent supportive housing developments.

Assistance for the homeless population became so great in the City of Sacramento that four medical leaders in the area including Sutter Medical Center Sacramento, UC Davis Health System, Kaiser Permanente Sacramento Medical Center and Dignity Health, developed a referral system for sheltering the homeless. These large medical organizations paired with WellSpace Health (formerly the Effort) and other bodies like the Salvation Army for standardized shelter placements, case managements, and medical treatments.

Mercy Housing, which is one the U.S.'s largest affordable housing organizations and developers, in California has also partnered with health providers, such as WellSpace Health, to contribute to the permanent supportive housing and wrap around services. According to Mercy Housing California, WellSpace Health provides services in an on-site health clinic (a 5,000-square foot facility) in Sacramento on the ground floor of a downtown high-rise apartment and commercial-use building on Seventh (7th) and H Streets. This apartment community has provided permanent supportive housing and direct/on-site medical services to the 150 residents, whom have been homeless and likely received referrals from the temporary shelters, such as Salvation Army. As of 2019, Mercy Housing California (MHC), is the largest regional division of Mercy Housing, Inc., a nationwide organization. In California they have offices in Los Angeles, San Francisco, and Sacramento. MHC has developed and operates 134 affordable housing communities with more than 9,190 units serving lower-income seniors, families, and people who have experienced homelessness. In addition, MHC provides an on-site health clinic and supportive services for residents and those in the community (Mercy Housing California website, 2018).

Mercy Housing California has developed a model in Sacramento that includes permanent supportive housing with wrap around services that begins with a developer and ends with on-site services for the homeless population:

1. Developer that builds housing specifically for permanently housing homeless.

2. On-site management company that has experience working with this type of clientele.

3. On-site healthcare clinic that provides residents and non-residents with immediate care without an appointment rather than waiting for hours in an emergency room; patients can receive same-day care for the evaluation and treatment of illnesses and injuries that need prompt attention but are not life-threatening.

4. On-site resident service provider/case manager that promotes a sense of community by creating daily activities to bring the community together and provides individual case management services.

Benefits of Permanent Supportive Housing

The process of discharging patients from emergency care to the streets or to a temporary shelter has not provided a solution to house the chronically homeless. Some of these affected individuals may be down on hard times, veterans with PTSD (post traumatic stress disorder), have a substance abuse problem, have a medical/mental health issue that is not being treated or another reason as to why homelessness is their status of living.

Research has found participants in permanent supportive housing programs like Housing First remained stable and reported higher perceived choice as well as fewer visits to crisis (Larimer, et al., 2009). It is important to note that no differences were found in substance use or psychiatric symptoms. The researchers' concluded that the participants in the Housing First program were able to obtain and maintain independent housing without compromising psychiatric or substance abuse symptoms (Tsemberis, et al., 2004). Larimer and colleagues found that Housing First participants had significant improvements in the use of shorter-term housing and housing units to assist with sobriety. Additionally, they concluded that housing tenure was related to better personal improvement in the community (Larimer, et al., 2009).

A study, conducted in San Francisco, of 100 homeless individuals received immediate housing resulted in significant reductions in crisis service use when supportive housing placement was coordinated for the homeless population. The study revealed that supportive housing can accomplish a number of specific policy goals, in part, "namely ending homelessness by providing a stable residential setting and reducing emergency department and inpatient hospital use in populations with mental illness and substance use disorder who lived largely on the streets. As such, it demonstrated that public hospital savings can offset part of the costs of providing supportive housing to this population," (Martinez & Burt, p. 999, 2006). As Housing First becomes more widely available, assessment of residential stability, cost-effectiveness, levels of psychiatric symptoms, substance use, and community integration will continue to be important outcome measures.

Although this research supports that housing stability with supportive programs leads to reducing homelessness, the model itself cannot be successful without community integration and the available resources for provision of services. However, new Housing First programs should "expand their repertoire of services so that they can improve outcomes in the number of other domains (including health, wellness, self-management, employment, and social integration) and help homeless individuals identify and realize individual capabilities that are important to them" (Ellen & O'Flaherty, p. 53, 2010).

Barriers to Permanent Supportive Housing

Three main barriers to making permanent supportive housing a reality in Sacramento include garnering local support, access to funding, and finding willing housing developers to both build and operate the housing facilities. As Tighe states, "Public support for planning programs and initiatives are an important component of its success but opposition can be a powerful impediment. When siting unwanted land uses such as affordable housing, neighborhood opposition can be a particularly effective barrier. Understanding the factors that influence opposition is a necessary precursor to successful planning initiatives. Planners can manage public opposition and influence attitudes toward affordable housing" (Tighe, 2010).

The key stakeholders rely heavily on public funding and grants to develop permanent supportive housing. These resources come from taxpayers and investors, which are then distributed at federal, state and local levels to those applying for the funds. Some programs are competitive; therefore, not everyone that applies receives an award. However, there are programs such as non-competitive four percent low income housing tax credit programs and non-competitive tax-exempt mortgage revenue bonds that are awarded to all that apply. One 2019 case study conducted with fifteen key stakeholders in Sacramento, including members of local governments, non-profit building developers and non-profit health providers showed that each stakeholder in the varying categories all cited funding as the main barrier to project completion (Toro, 1999).

The last barrier details finding competent and willing housing developers. Experts working directly with the homeless rely heavily on low-income housing tax credits from the California Tax Credit Allocation Committee, and other local, federal and state funds to build all types of affordable housing, not only permanent supportive housing. This leads to a fierce competition of who gets what funds. To maintain an effective permanent supportive housing community, the development needs operating assistance, such as rental subsidies provided by the Housing Choice Voucher Program and the Veterans Affairs Supportive Housing Program. There is limited permanent supportive housing communities, the wait lists range from one-to-three years in Sacramento alone.

Recommendations

The six recommendations below to reduce the homeless population apply not only to Sacramento, but state and federal wide programs.

1. Currently, the California Tax Credit Allocation Committee's Regulations (Qualified Allocation Plan) adopted in December 2017, provides only thirty percent to special needs housing (e.g., permanent housing for homeless with supportive wraparound services). This provision must increase to 50 percent in order to deal with the rising population of homeless.

2. Internal Revenue Service needs to provide a tax credit to for-profit hospitals that will incentivize funding of the development and ongoing costs of medical and health facilities and services to the homeless population when partnering with a developer that serves at least 75% of the units in the development to the homeless population.

3. Local housing and commercial impact fees must include one-to-three percent tax rate of annually collected fees towards housing homeless programs.

4. State legislation must re-instate the Redevelopment Tax Increment Housing Program; however, the revised legislation will fund only permanent supportive housing with wrap around services that aligns with the recommended Special Needs Housing requirements (above) for housing homeless by the California Tax Credit Allocation Committee and must have at least 75% of the units in the development targeting the homeless population.

5. Increase the supply of temporary housing and extend the term of occupancy from the current thirty days to a two-year transitional housing program with life-skills to maintain a home and employment.

Conclusion

These recommendations need to be considered with high priority as the homeless population continues to grow. Local agencies struggle to pay for minimum services for the homeless, and it is becoming more apparent that agencies working at the local, state and federal level must find a way to work together to solve this dilemma. Building permanent supportive housing developments for homeless would reduce the number of homeless living on the streets and potentially those who suffer from premature death. Developers such as Mercy Housing California have been successful in developing permanent supportive housing developments across California; therefore, other developers, non-profit and for-profit, should be financially incentivized to build permanent supportive housing developments.

REFERENCES

California tax credit allocation committee (2017). California tax credit allocation committee regulations implementing the federal and state low income housing tax credit laws: California code of regulations title 4, division 17, chapter 1. Retrieved from http://www.treasurer.ca.gov/ctcac/programreg/2017/20171213/clean.pdf.

Considerations for the Governor's Housing Plan (2019). The California Legislature's Nonpartisan Fiscal and Policy Advisor. Retrieved from: https://lao.ca.gov/Publications/Report/3941.

Ellen, I.G., & O'Flaherty, B. (2010). *How to house the homeless.* New York: Russell Sage Foundation.

Graham, M. (2015). San Diego tries Housing First for homeless. Retrieved from: https://www.calhealthreport.org/2015/01/20/housing-first/.

Kertesz, S.G., Baggett, T.P., O'Connell, J.J., Buck, D.S. & Kushel, M.B. (2016): Permanent supportive housing for homeless people—reframing the debate. *The New England Journal of Medicine*, 375, 2,115–2,117. doi 10.1056/NEJMp1608326.

Larimer, M.E., Malone, D.K., Garner, M.D., Atkins, D.C., Burlingham, B., Lonczak, H.S., Tanzer, K., Ginzler, J., Clifasefi, S.L., Hobson, W.G., Marlatt, G.A. (2009): Health care and public service use and costs before and after provision of housing for chronically homeless persons with severe alcohol problems. *JAMA*, 301(13), 1,349–1,357. doi: 10.1001/jama.2009.414.

Martinez, T.E., & Burt, M.R. (2006): Impact of permanent supportive housing on the use of acute care health services by homeless adults. *Psychiatric Services*, 57(7), 992–999. doi: 10.1176/ps.2006.57.7.992.

Mercy Housing California (2018). Retrieved from: https://www.mercyhousing.org/california/.

Rog, D.J., Marshall, T., Dougherty, R.H., George, P., Daniels, A.S., Ghose, S.S., & Delphin-Rittmon, M.E. (2014): Permanent supportive housing: assessing the evidence. *Psychiatric Services*, 65(3), 287–294. Retrieved from https://doi.org/10.1176/appi.ps.201300261.

Tighe, J.R. (2010): Public opinion and affordable housing: a review of the literature. *Journal of Planning Literature*, 25(1), 3–17. doi: 10.1177/0885412210379974

Toro, P.A. & Warren, M.G. (1999): Homelessness in the United States: policy considerations. *Journal of Community Psychology*, 27(2), 1,520–6,629. doi: 10.1002/(SICI)1520-6629(199903)27:2<119::AID-JCOP2>3.0.CO;2-I.

Tsemberis, S., Gulcur, L., & Nakae, M. (2004): Housing First, consumer choice, and harm reduction for homeless individuals with a dual diagnosis. *American Journal of Public Health*.

9. Exploring Homeless Work Programs in Santa Rosa, California*

NICOLE TRUPIANO *and* WILLIE L. BRITT

There have been countless studies on the causes and remedies for America's homelessness. In 2016 there were 1,877 who found themselves homeless in the streets and in shelters in the City of Santa Rosa, California. This number has grown slightly from 2015, which is cause for concern for the city. This study reviewed how the potential success for reducing homelessness in Santa Rosa may center on a work program that "works" for multiple stakeholders to include citizens, elected officials, community-based organizations and the homeless populations.

Facing growing numbers of people without homes, many communities and agencies are faced with the task of deciding what services to offer the homeless. The 2016 annual Point-In-Time Homeless Count organized by the Sonoma County Community Development Commission reported that there were 2906 homeless individuals living in Sonoma County. This document clearly defined that "Connecting homeless individuals and families to these support services helps them create the bridge to mainstream support services and helps to prevent future housing instability." This leads us to the question, what programs will work best to accomplish this goal?

The growing number of homeless in Santa Rosa is a point of contention for residents who want to be empathetic and help people who are being economically and otherwise challenged, but also want to keep the streets clear of garbage and feel safe conducting their business downtown. It was quoted, "'if you were to look at the public perception of homelessness, it is that 20 percent who are there (on the streets) longer (than two weeks) that people see and are overwhelmed. That 20 percent frames most of the public perception of homelessness." The public is concerned and even overwhelmed at the amount of people on the street, as noted by the city's local paper, *The Press Democrat*. "In response to a resident who expressed concern about making homeless services so generous it draws people to the city," a councilman answered, "that is not what people should fear." These concerns that services are catering to the homeless rather than helping them reintegrate into society and to being productive members of society is something many residents express.

---

*Published with permission of the authors.

Background and History

Santa Rosa was discussing emergency programs to get the homeless off the streets and into temporary housing. Such efforts include safe camping, where those without permanent housing can camp on city property and have access to facilities and temporary shelter along with a safe place for their belongings, without fear of being moved along by police. "On October 11, 2016, the Santa Rosa City Council approved CHAP (Community Homeless Assistance Program) to allow property owners to use their properties or facilities for safe parking, safe camping, the placement and maintenance of portable toilets and access to existing bathroom facilities, provision of temporary overnight shelter, and storage for personal belongings.... The new program (CHAP) allowed for year-round operation and expanded activities such as safe camping under the Council's recent action declaring a local homeless emergency in Santa Rosa" (Homeless Services Webpage).

Other efforts include, "better coordination of services among key City departments, regional participation through the Sonoma County Continuum of Care, improving access to services through a Coordinated Entry system, sponsoring a street outreach team, and increasing the availability of shelter and housing options for the unsheltered" (Santa Rosa Homeless FAQs). The City Council formally declared a local homeless emergency in August of 2016. "This move should give the City additional flexibility to address the homeless crisis. Furthermore, the Council is hopeful that this action will rally community support for shared-based long-term solutions" (Santa Rosa Homeless FAQs webpage).

While looking at emergency provisions, Santa Rosa was also looking into long-term solutions such as building more affordable housing and partnering with Sonoma County and non-profit agencies to provide more support and outreach programs. One such program is the mobile bathroom trailer, which moves to different locations throughout the city to provide those in need with a clean place to use a restroom and shower. "Over the years 2015–2016, the City more than doubled its investment in homeless services with a budget in 2016 of approximately $1.7 million. The City reorganized in 2015 with the intension of focusing on affordable housing and homeless services through the newly formed Housing and Community Services Department. Additional support was allocated to the Homeless Services Program and several programs were introduced or expanded" (Santa Rosa Homeless FAQs). Of the additional services mentioned, a mobile bathroom-shower trailer was launched to help coax homeless into services, "Homeless Outreach Services Team (HOST) program is a multi-disciplinary street outreach team operated by Catholic Charities. The HOST trailer is an outreach tool for HOST's efforts to engage unsheltered homeless into services and would be staffed at all times by Catholic Charities during its operation" (Join the City, 2016). Santa Rosa was spending $1.7 million to help the 1,877 homeless on the streets, but that money was being spent on emergency provisions and short-term solutions.

Causes of Homelessness in Sonoma County

According to the 2016 Sonoma County Point-In-Time Homeless Census & Survey respondents indicated that the primary cause of homelessness is a lost job. The second biggest response from respondents, behind loss of a job was substance abuse,

"Twenty-one percent of respondents reported alcohol or drug use as the primary cause of their homelessness." An argument with family or friends that they were asked to leave increased from previous years, followed by eviction, with divorce/separation/breakup as the lowest percentage reason for homelessness. Other obstacles to obtaining permanent housing include the lack of affordable housing in Sonoma County, "67% of survey respondents indicated their inability to afford rent as the number one obstacle to them being able to obtain housing." Not enough income or lack of employment was a close second with 52 percent of respondents indicating those as obstacles, followed by lack of money for moving costs, no housing availability and bad credit.

Health was another category looked at in the point-in-time survey, in which 42 percent noted drug or alcohol abuse and 39 percent noted psychiatric or emotional conditions. Physical disability along with PTSD, traumatic brain injury, chronic health problems and AIDS/HIV were all categories in the survey.

Sonoma County boasts many programs for the homeless, including many shelters, safe camping and parking, a mobile bathroom/shower trailer, and countywide there are a number of job training services. These job-training programs assist people in finding stable jobs. They provide employment training and educational programs for youth or people over 55. These programs help with creating resumes and computer training, but there are no programs in Sonoma County, or more specifically Santa Rosa, that actually pay homeless to work.

Causes of homelessness are many, they are complex, and they are as individual as those persons experiencing poverty are. Affordable housing, lack of job skills, lack of education, and issues with substance abuse are among the most debated. While there are many studies championing the use of one method to help end homelessness, affordable housing or job skills coaching, it seems that the best approaches are multifaceted and individualized. Homelessness will not end by imploring singular methods, but instead aspects of each must be employed together to resolve the issue. Cost effectiveness will be achieved when methods refrain from competing but work together to reintegrate the currently homeless population into society and the workforce.

Survey Administration

Survey data was collected using an online survey questionnaire of ten questions. The survey was sent out to about thirty-one people or general email addresses with a request to forward the survey link to anyone else respondents knew who provided services to the homeless. Forty-one responses were received from various service providers and stakeholders in Santa Rosa. The hypothesis asked if homeless work programs were implemented in Santa Rosa, would the programs help reduce the number of homeless on the streets? Although not every participant answered the question, those who did, 66.67 percent (20 of 30) disclosed that their clients would be willing to work if offered a job. Many participants noted that their homeless clients would most likely need a flexible job that could allow them to continue treatment programs for drug/alcohol abuse, mental illness or would be able to accommodate some physical disabilities.

Respondents also noted that without stable housing, holding a job for long is difficult due to issues such as cleanliness or needing to spend time on basic survival. The fact that 66.67 percent of respondents indicated that their clients were willing to work shows that if a flexible work program was implemented, it would be a benefit to Santa Rosa and could help get homeless off the streets and on a path to reintegrating into society. If homeless can learn the skills they need to be productive in society, and they are given the opportunity to do so in a flexible environment that allows for them to continue necessary treatment, that could eventually help place them into a more permanent job placement.

The survey also asked in what capacity these stakeholders worked with the homeless. Some were mental or behavior health professionals, police officers, program managers, and volunteers who help feed or clothe the homeless. The diversity of respondents gives this research a variety of answers to help understand the plight of the homeless in Santa Rosa and to help understand if implementing a work program would help to move them off of the streets. The survey also asked where homeless clients were currently living. Some said in shelters or with friends, but most noted that their clients lived on the streets. This shows us that it would be important for a work program in Santa Rosa to partner with other city or county programs to help house those in the program so that they may have better chances at succeeding in getting off of the streets through a work program.

Homeless Services Commonly Used in Santa Rosa

Santa Rosa has many services for the homeless. The Redwood Gospel mission run by Catholic Charities is one of the biggest in Santa Rosa that feeds, shelters and offers the homeless church services. The Catholic Charities in addition provides additional supportive services and services for elderly and immigration. The Living Room is another service that provides a day center providing referrals to resources and access to telephones and computers, help with job searches, counseling, therapy and offer necessities like sleeping bags. The Living Room also provides a parenting program and necessities for mothers. There are more than 10 homeless shelters and faith-based organizations providing shelter and support to the homeless in Santa Rosa. Additionally, the City of Santa Rosa provides a mobile bathroom where homeless can shower and get a "clean start" as the program is called.

These programs provide emergency shelter and necessities to the homeless. Instead of only offering services to triage the problem, Santa Rosa needs to move towards solutions that can permanently reintegrate homeless back into society. A work flexible work program with wraparound services could be the key to getting Santa Rosa's homeless off the streets, and into occupations that will lead them to become productive members of society.

Conclusions and Recommendations

Facing growing numbers of people without homes, many communities and agencies are faced with the task of getting homeless off of their city streets. Santa Rosa declared a homeless emergency to leverage assets that may help get some homeless off the streets and into temporary emergency shelters, but these services do not solve the problem in the long term.

This study was performed to find out if homeless work programs were implemented in Santa Rosa, would they reduce the number of homeless on the streets? The study found that experts working directly with the homeless felt that a work program alone would not get homeless off the streets, but a work program along with counseling and affordable housing could help. Survey respondents also noted that the work programs would need to be accessible to people with various disabilities and/or medical conditions since this is the reason many of them could not hold a job in the first place.

This survey showed that lack of a job is not the leading factor for homelessness in Santa Rosa, so a job program alone cannot be the only solution. The solution must be multifaceted to accommodate the assortment of homeless individuals on the streets in Santa Rosa. Respondents were adamant that a major component of the solution needs to be affordable housing. Since affordable housing still needed to be improved in Santa Rosa, perhaps the notion of priority at certain shelters for work program participants would be sufficient until Santa Rosa is able to offer more affordable housing.

Life skills trainings were common themes of survey responses. Many answers echoed the need for not just job skills training, but also for basic life skills trainings such as conflict management, time management, interpersonal communication, basic budgeting or learning how to open a checking account. These are the skills that experts recommend will help the homeless in Santa Rosa. If this work program could not only offer stable housing through shelters, but also offer substance abuse treatment, basic life skills and job trainings courses, then these wrap around services would help get homeless off the streets and back into the job market and help reintegrate them back into society.

Four recommendations were as a result of this study:

- By June 2018, Santa Rosa should present a homeless work program with wraparound services pilot to the City Council for review.
- When Santa Rosa implements their work program in 2018, wraparound services should include drug/alcohol counseling, basic job skills training, financial management, and interpersonal communication trainings to name a few. Some of these services already exist throughout Sonoma County, so partnering with existing services will be key.
- Santa Rosa staff should work with current Santa Rosa Housing Department staff to give priority shelter to work program participants. Again, there are many existing shelters and the City should partner with some of these shelters to give the work program participants priority shelter.
- Santa Rosa should develop a plan to track program success in reducing the number of homeless on the streets in Santa Rosa. This plan should be reviewed by other agencies to compare criteria and be set in place before program operations begin.

10. Trump's Attack on the Homeless and Learning from Berkeley's Practices*

JIM HYNES

On September 13, 2019, President Trump announced that he would like to enact a policy to allow local law enforcement authorities to have the ability to "round up" homeless people and involuntarily relocate them to federal detention facilities. This harkens back to Nazism with the rounding up of the Jews and other "undesirables" or the mass encampments of Japanese Americans in the 1940s, arguably the greatest mistake in FDR's otherwise exemplary presidential leadership. This is a totally misdirected and counterproductive policy proposal that should not have even seen the light of day. Baffling, and even more troubling, is why there is nobody around Trump to counter his hateful, misguided, emotionally impulsive, counterproductive and uninformed positions?

Homelessness is an existential urban crisis of our country and we all experience it nearly every day. It's not so much about the issue of homelessness, a symptom of a larger urban crisis; as it is Trump's privileged view, "ugly and disgusting encampments" (God forbid on my golf courses) in which the vermin should be stamped out, and the fact that there are power hungry sycophants around him that will sacrifice their own moral, spiritual and religious tenets in the interest of power and treasure regardless of the impact on the underclass or even our shrinking middle class.

I spent almost my entire professional life fighting for the rights of the homeless yet at the same time using my position in executive management for the city of Berkeley to do the right thing to hold the homeless accountable and responsible for unacceptable behaviors. I needed to balance the basic human rights of the homeless with the concerns of taxpaying businesses and residents of the city. There is never an easy answer on such complex social problems, but Trump thinks that he has a simplistic meat cleaver solution—one that will only create more chaos, confusion and ambiguity by targeting a new boogie man, which is the marketplace of his choice. Nothing good can come from this.

Based on my formative years in the California Assembly in the 1980s working on mental health policy reform, the early part of my career in Berkeley focused on transforming the local mental health system to one that addressed the most seriously mentally disabled, and through several federal grants, it worked. The city's mental health department applied for and received two annual grants of $150,000 each year under the federal

*Published with permission of the author.

Substance Abuse and Mental Health Services Administration (SAMHSA) Community Action Grant program to adopt best practices into local mental health departments. The first year of funding was used for a stakeholder consensus building process centered around adoption of the documented best practice, Assertive Community Treatment. The second year of funding was used to implement Assertive Community Treatment (ACT) and to restructure the entire department to focus almost exclusively on the most serious and hardest to reach mentally disabled, in particular the homeless suffering from mental illness, usually with co-occurring substance abuse disorders.

As good as that was, the bigger problem was solving the growing housing afford-ability crisis, the increasing wage gap and abdication of homeless resource support from places other than the most progressive local Bay Area cities. Yes, the economy looks like it is doing well, but for whom? If the adage that the "rich get richer and the poor get poorer" is apt, the data clearly show that now is the time it fits best. Homelessness is a symptom of this, as is the struggle that the middle class and even upper middle-class have to pay the bills. Many of us are one paycheck away from homelessness, so try to be a bit compassionate to others. It could be you next. To paraphrase: "First they came for the socialists, then the trade unionists, then the Jews, and I did not speak out. But then they came for me and there was no one to speak for me." What next? The homeless?

Homelessness is not a singular issue or homogenous population. We have college students living in RVs next to elite campuses who cannot find affordable housing, young families with inner city service jobs having to commute long distances from the exurbs and living at or below the poverty line. For many, a verifiable urban dystopia of unlivabil-ity exists.

It is not just about mental health, and that is significant. Mental health gets wrapped up into much bigger problems about geographical and income disparities. We should not forget that when deinstitutionalization was proposed in the 1960s in California under then Governor Ronald Reagan, the concept was that the money used to cover the cost of state mental hospitals was to follow the former patients into the community and be used to create a "community based mental health" system with support services, jobs training and housing. But it never happened, instead it went to prisons, our new de facto mental health system.

It's history now, but we should also not forget that there was a progressive idea about the mentally disabled, taking us to an understanding that mental illness is an equal opportunity problem. We all have loved ones affected by this, whether it be depression, schizophrenia, manic depression, alcohol and drug dependence, suicide, etc., and our family members and friends should live amongst us in safe, supportive and affordable conditions. This is not just a family duty, it is a social right.

However, despite Trump's hateful rhetoric, there is hope. And that is knowing that local communities have exerted leadership and marshaled the resources to improve life for the homeless. One such community is Berkeley, California.

The city of Berkeley has been a leader on social and environmental issues in many ways. Berkeley blazed the trail in supporting everything from free speech, to animal rights and dog parks, to climate action planning, to mental health and homeless services. Berkeley has exercised a strong urban-based leadership position on the issues of the day. Berkeley prides itself on being innovative, forging a path of leadership on controver-sial, highly conflicted, contradictory and paradoxical contemporary issues. Leadership on mental health and homelessness issues has not been different.

Besieged with a growing homeless epidemic in 2008 with the economic downturn coupled with extant mental health and homeless problems, an outcry by both homeless activists over the human suffering and from the business community over the economic decline of the core commercial areas, the city had to act. With the support of both the business community and housing and mental health activists, the Berkeley City Council enacted the Public Commons for Everyone (PCEI) ordinance. The process of enactment and implementation of this ordinance represents a solid case study about how communities can muster the political forces within their respective communities to effect change locally. This recognition of the power of local government, and cognizant but not reliant on the role of state and federal "big government" demonstrates the power and importance of urban-based leadership solving local problems.

PCEI was developed as a compassion-based approach to homelessness. It was and has been funded by a 25 cent per hour increase on parking meters throughout the city, raising $1 million annually in revenue earmarked to the programs and services stipulated under PCEI, which includes not just mental health and social support services, the "carrots," but also programs and services to improve the aesthetic image of the city. These include:

1. More funding for social worker positions to support assertive outreach and engagement with the homeless community, and support individuals to stay housed once housed;

2. Funding to support 24/7-bathroom access for the homeless, and the general public;

3. A centralized real time database to provide information to outreach workers and police on shelter bed availability on any particular night. Lack of bed availability signaled to police not to enforce on lodging in public laws, whereas if beds were available on a particular night, and an individual refused to avail themselves to that resource, then police could legitimately enforce on such laws as lodging in public. Conversely, if no beds were available on a particular night, then lodging in public laws were not enforced. In retrospect, this policy approach was extremely valuable since it shielded the city from lawsuits on violations of the constitution for cruel and unusual punishment, as has been seen recently with the Boise, ID case in the Supreme Court;

4. Additional funding to help people get advocacy for SSI benefits, which is critically important to getting needy individuals in housing and getting support services to maintain them in housing;

5. Funding to the Public Works Dept. for "green machines" which are sidewalk cleaners that operate similarly to street sweepers but scaled to the size of urban sidewalks, as part of the city's "crime and grime" program

6. More public seating and replacing old dilapidated seating with new green ornamental wrought iron and attractive seating;

7. More trash receptacles, and replacement of old worn out receptacles to improve overall appearances and prevent littering; and

8. Funding for an "ambassadors" program staffed by previously homeless people to act as paid greeters and guides to Berkeley visitors, and to act as conduits to homeless support services and programs, in the two major urban nodes of Berkeley, downtown and Telegraph Avenue, adjacent to UC Berkeley

The net effect of these approaches is that the program housed and maintained in housing through social support services for over a year 74 percent of the hardest to serve in the Berkeley community, far above the national average for programs of similar design and stature.

On the "stick" side of the balance sheet, the following was included under PCEI:

 1. Established more stringent regulations on smoking in public places such that it is now prohibited to smoke in any commercial zone of the city;
 2. Reduced the warning requirement for sleeping in public from two warnings to one warning; and
 3. Eliminated the requirement that a complaint to the police department needs to be registered before police can enforce on lodging in public.

None of these revised laws made a significant difference in numbers of citations issued

Perhaps more significant than the content of PCEI, the stakeholder consensus building process was key to its passage, implementation and success. City staff created "arenas" for public discussion to work out disagreements and sticking points over an 18-month planning process. It included 20 separate meetings with various boards and commissions with sometimes three consecutive meetings with specific commissions. It also included multiple meetings with the business community, non-profit service provider agencies, the police union, various city departments, most notably the Fire Department charged with transporting the "frequent flyer" individuals from the streets to the emergency room (20 percent of the individuals represent 80 percent of the transports) and the Housing and Health Departments. Given the high profile and political nature of this initiative, the work was led by the city manager's office and included three city council meetings, formal and informal meetings with elected representatives, and also included several town hall meetings where all stakeholder groups were invited to air their differences, and negotiate and forge consensus, albeit at times shaky. It was a constant time-consuming process of negotiation and renegotiation, essential for authentic dialogue, engagement and democracy.

While the ultimate solutions to homelessness will require a massive investment in housing and mental health at the national and state level, impossible under the current administration, it behooves all communities around the country to heed the lessons of Berkeley and other communities that have addressed these thorny problems locally. These communities should attempt to adopt similar programs, perhaps not literally since other communities' needs vary greatly, but certainly with a focus on the hardest to serve homeless individuals. At the same time, communities need to take stock of their unique political dynamics in relation to the stakeholder consensus building processes required to effect meaningful change in service to the most destitute amongst us, the homeless.

And despite the lack of political and moral leadership on housing and mental health at the national and state level, there is additional hope at the local level, certainly in Berkeley, where the local city government and the University of California (UC) are collaborating as a matter of mutual self-interest to resolve the decades old problem of the homeless population at People's Park and affordable housing for students. They are undertaking a bold plan to repurpose People's Park.

People's Park was the site where student activists aligned with free speech and civil rights principles stood up against the National Guard ordered there by then–Governor Ronald Reagan, resulting in death and injuries similar to Kent State. The idea of People's

Park was noble, however, the last fifty years have been ignoble. People's Park has become a constant source of concern about mental illness. The homeless population has created a drain on community, business, UC and city of Berkeley resources. To some, People's Park is considered hallowed ground, akin to an historic free speech battleground. To others, the Park is a problem site which can and must be repurposed.

A potential solution might be to use the land to build student housing, housing for the homeless, and a memorial to the ugly events that occurred there in the 1960s. The community consensus building process around People's Park is under way, seeking compromise between the divergent perspectives, and there is an upbeat prognosis that a comprehensive redevelopment plan for change will emerge. With the city's support, the UC Berkeley campus is working with a local affordable housing developer to build and manage a facility with 75 to 125 units of permanent supportive housing for formerly homeless individuals, a campus-built and managed facility with 700 to 1000 beds for students, and a smaller portion of open space that will include a memorial to the historic role of People's Park.

Local communities have a twofold challenge. First, by fighting for affordable housing, and the homeless and mentally disabled at the state and national levels, and second, in lieu of leadership at the state and national levels, that they take matters into their own hands and resolve these problems locally

Both challenges are surmountable. It can be done but it takes moral courage, time, patience and leadership. To paraphrase John F. Kennedy from his September 12, 1962, moon speech: "We do these things not because they are easy, but because they are hard."

11. Community Partnership for the Homeless in Sutter County, California*

SUKHDEEP PUREWAL

There is a homelessness and housing crisis in California. The number of homeless individuals and families is staggeringly high and there are more homeless people living on the streets today than ever before. There has been a major increase in homelessness since the 2008 recession. More than 8.7 million people lost their jobs in America during the 2008 recession (Center on Budget and Policy Priorities, 2019) and some of them ended up homeless. This economic recession along with mental illness, alcohol/drug addiction, domestic violence, affordable housing and the shortage of housing are major contributors for the increase in the homelessness population.

The total homeless population in the United States is approximately 540,000. According to the HUD, as of September 2018 there was a population of approximately 134,000 homeless population in California. That figure represents more than a 14 percent increase from 2016. Some of the general causes of homelessness include lack of affordable housing, not enough jobs, growing drug or alcohol abuse and physical and mental illness. As the population of California has grown to over 40 million, the population of homeless have also grown and is at 25 percent of the total U.S. homeless population.

California is the second most expensive state to live in the United States. The high cost of housing along combined with the lack of affordable health care, mental illnesses and addiction to drugs and alcohol have caused a sharp rise in the homelessness population. An *American Psychological Association Journal* article titled "Recovery in Homelessness," states that "recovery is the process through which one learns to overcome, manage, or live with the negative consequences of physical illness, mental illness, alcohol or drug misuse, or trauma. Homeless individuals endure many, or all, of these experiences."

The River Bottom Homeless Problem

During a Sutter County Board of Supervisor's meeting in February 2019, a homeless lady addressed the living conditions of her homeless community living at the Sacramento River Bottoms. She stated clearly that they do not want government help. She said the food

---

*Published with permission of the author.

that is provided and services that are brought to them are fine, but they do not want to move or want any government interference in the way they live their lives. She appeared to have been using drugs when she spoke. She stated her age as 40 but looked much older. She admitted that drugs and alcohol had aged her body. She did not have a tooth in her mouth and she looked as if she had not showered in years. She stated she was a representative for the homeless community and she was speaking for the majority of people living in the River Bottoms. "There is a better way to spend tax dollars than bothering us," she said. She stated the belief that they had right to live at the River Bottoms as their own personal property and that government should not and could not interfere with their "homes."

The board was convinced that something needed to be done about the homelessness situation at the River Bottoms. The board gave direction to staff to find a location for a homeless shelter. This lady was angry at the board's decision. She returned to the podium to voice her objection but acted recklessly and was escorted away by security personnel.

The topics she spoke about caught my attention and I started to wonder about the substance abuse problem in the River Bottoms. I was determined to investigate further and find the scope of the problem of the homeless population living at the Sacramento River Bottoms area. The day after the meeting, I visited and was shocked to see how bad the River Bottoms had become. I discovered hundreds of needle syringes along with other drug paraphernalia, pipes and garbage along the levee. I had seen pictures and heard community members talk about the problem at the River Bottoms several times. I discovered that the problem was worse than I had imagined.

As I approached the highest peak of the levee that overlooks the river, I saw trash everywhere. I pulled out my binoculars to take a closer look. I saw tents, RV's, boats, wood frame homes and even cars. The River Bottoms had been transformed into a community of temporary homes for the homeless. These were talented individuals who could frame buildings and weld. They had created semi-livable houses; some houses even had garages. The residents also found ways to get cars and recreation vehicles through the sandy beach to their makeshift riverfront properties.

After visiting and speaking with many members of the River Bottoms homeless population, I became convinced that many did not want any help. The consensus opinion was that they much preferred that the county would leave them alone. I reported back to the county administrator what I had discovered; he did not believe me at first. After further discussions, he decided he wanted to take a closer look for himself. Once he witnessed the living conditions of the River Bottoms homeless population, he was also convinced that something needed to be done quickly.

In the 2018–2019 budget, the State of California allocated over $500 million to local jurisdictions to provide housing for the homeless. More funding and other resources are in the pipeline for solving the crisis. Sutter County has records and relationship with most of the homeless living in the river bottoms. Expanding on these relationships and finding out the motivating factors to help someone move up the Sutter County chain is key to ending their time at the river bottoms.

Recommendation

Based on the use of these local funding opportunities provided by the state and the dire health and safety conditions for those homeless living at the River Bottoms and elsewhere in Sutter County, community leaders should begin the process for developing a two phase solution to help solve the homelessness problem in Sutter County.

The Office of the County Administrator should collaborate with business and non-profit agency leaders to develop and coordinate the building of a 40-unit housing area. This housing area location must be approved by the County Board of Supervisors. For residency in housing area, homeless individuals must have demonstrated adherence to tent city rules, take their prescribed medicine on time, do not abuse alcohol or drugs and follow tent residency rules. The county will work with non-profit support agencies to provide food for tent residents. The Behavior Health Center Medical should assess and evaluate what and how much social services support can be provided. County departments of security, safety, fire, education and job training/résumé building services and support should also be evaluated to determine what and how much resources can be provided for this homeless problem solution.

Phase 1

The Office of the County Administrator should collaborate with business and non-profit agencies to identify, develop and establish a tent city at a site large enough for the homeless population in the County and provide tents and flooring and support for food and water, security, medical, health and social services to include substance abuse counseling daily and waste management. The goal for residents is to become a productive member of society. The goal for Tent City administrators is to help, support and provide basic services for homeless population residents of Tent City to become productive members of society.

This "Tent City" shall be designed to provide housing for Sutter County homeless who decide not to participate in the step-up program to live in a designated area. This option allows for the jurisdictions to have control, while the homeless can have the comfort of all their materials and pets in one location. Some communities in California like Yuba County and the City of Modesto have experimented using a tent city to help solve their homeless population problem. While it is still too early to determine the effectiveness of this solution, it seems worthy enough of a project to specifically address the River Bottom homeless population.

After six months living in the tent city, staff will review and counsel each homeless person. The review will provide staff with the necessary answers to determine relocation out of the tent city to another more permanent living location. Once staff have evaluated each person and determined eligibility, they will send them to the other location and start the step-up program. Once the tent city Phase 1 is completed, the remaining homeless will be lifted from the river bottoms to the tent city. Once there, the homeless can be provided with services that are necessary for them to survive as well as find the help they need.

Phase 2

Phase 2 (Step Up Program) provides the eligible homeless population access to approximately 40 tiny homes. This tiny home community will provide all the necessary amenities that are needed for daily living, including showers and AC installed in each unit. At this location, the county will focus on their weaknesses and continue any medical help they need. Each day they will ready and county will provide classes for them to get them ready to be a functional member of society. The Step-Up Program provides a safe and healthy place to live for those homeless population deemed eligible to step to the next phase to end their homelessness. The Step-up Program is a major reward for the who people are sick and tired of living in the river bottoms. These classes will start with high school GED to interview prep and everything in between. This step in the program will try to get them to be independent and gain confidence. Giving shelter, food, medical services and education to boost the confidence of the homeless individuals are components of the step-up program.

Conclusion

With projected increased state funding local communities like Sutter County can identify and design, fund implement and evaluate homeless projects. Public, private and non-profit sectors can work together to reduce the pain felt by the homeless. The pay-off for partnership collaboration is that a losing battle can be changed to a winning campaign. California citizens, public officials, business and non-profit agency leaders must work together to find a holistic solution. Housing and resource shortages have resulted in an increasing homeless population. Forging collaborative partnership among community leaders to find a solution that works best is essential. To solve the homelessness problem in Sutter County, community partners must work together to find the ways and means to reduce the housing shortage and provide mental health services for the homeless. Leaving it solely to the government is not the correct solution. Private, non-profit and public sectors must collaborate efforts and resources to collectively solve homelessness in Sutter County.

REFERENCES

Center on Budget and Policy Priorities. Updated February 12, 2019. *Chart Book: The Legacy of the Great Recession.* Retrieved from https://www.cbpp.org/research/economy/chart-book-the-legacy-of-the-great-recession.

Johnstone, Melissa. *Frontiers in Psychology.* June 1, 2015. Discrimination and well-being amongst the homeless: the role of multiple group membership. Retrieved from https://www.ncbi.nlm.nih.gov/pmc/articles/PMC4450171/.

Kusisto, Laura. (2019, March 27). *The Wall Street Journal.* A decade after the housing bust, the exurbs are back. Retrieved from http://www.msn.com/en-us/money/realestate/a-decade-after-the-housing-bust-the-exurbs-are-back/ar-BBVfdCq?ocid=mailsignout.

Legislative Analyst's Office. (2018, October 2). California Spending Plan. Retrieved from https://lao.ca.gov/Publications/Report/3870/8.

Manning, R. M., & Greenwood, R.M. (2019, February 7). Recovery in Homelessness: The Influence of Choice and Mastery on Physical Health, Psychiatric Symptoms, Alcohol and Drug Use, and Community Integration. *Psychiatric Rehabilitation Journal.* Retrieved from http://dx.doi.org/10.1037/prj0000350.

Rossi, PH. (1990, August). The old homeless and the new homelessness in historical perspective. Department of Sociology, University of Massachusetts, Amherst. Retrieved from https://www.ncbi.nlm.nih.gov/pubmed/2221566.

Smith, Kevin. *Pasadena Star.* (August 28, 2019). California needs to build a staggering number of homes and we are way behind. Retrieved from https://www.pasadenastarnews.com/2017/01/04/california-needs-to-build-a-staggering-number-of-homes-and-we-are-way-behind/.

Tran, Tracy. Solutions for Change. (2019, July 10). Governor Jerry Brown's New Homelessness Budget Plan. Retrieved from http://solutionsforchange.org/governor-jerry-browns-new-homelessness-budget-plan/.

United States Interagency Council on Homelessness. (2018, January). California Homelessness Statistics. Retrieved from https://www.usich.gov/homelessness-statistics/ca/.

12. Strengthening Homelessness Public-Private Partnerships in Washington State*

JASON YERGLER

The issues surrounding and contributing to homelessness in the United States are numerous, highly nuanced, and stem from a variety of causes. The multifaceted problem where homelessness exists affects everyone in the communities. Due to that omnipresent level of impact, it is not surprising that massive sums of resources are allocated to combating the causes of homelessness and supporting individuals currently homeless or at-risk of homelessness.

The City of Seattle and King County began to seriously prioritize the homelessness problem as a policy area in 2005 with the creation of a 10-year plan focused on ending homelessness in King County ("Timeline: Understanding Seattle's homeless issues," 2018). All Home, previously the Committee to End Homelessness in King County (CEH), was established to oversee the implementation of the 10-year plan and included members from government organizations, private business, and non-profit organizations (All Home Strategic Plan, 2015). All Home issued a report on the impact of the 10-year plan in 2015 citing both a reduction in total homeless individuals of almost 40,000 and also that nearly 10,000 people are still experiencing homelessness in King County, with almost 40 percent of that population unsheltered (All Home Strategic Plan, 2015).

Starting in 2016 several reports were published focusing on homelessness in Seattle/King County and how homelessness has been addressed by various city and county agencies as well as All Home. The reports universally recognized that the homelessness problem in King County/Seattle is multifaceted and requires a more comprehensive, unified, and coordinated response from all agencies involved.

A poll was conducted by *The Seattle Times* in 2019 highlighting attitudes of Seattleites towards homelessness and how effective the city's response has been. The polling data indicated distrust towards the ability of city leaders, yet strong support existed for continued efforts to address homelessness. Interesting highlights from the polling data indicate only a small portion of respondents thought that homelessness was completely unsolvable (14 percent), over half of the respondents indicated that all levels of government should be doing much more to address homelessness (54 percent), and over

---

*Published with permission of the author.

a third (35 percent) thought the business community should also be doing "much more to address homelessness" (Coleman and Davila, 2019).

There are many agencies providing the government's homeless response in Seattle and King County. The main agencies organized within the jurisdiction of the City of Seattle include the Seattle Office of Housing and the Seattle Human Services Department. The main agencies housed in the jurisdiction of King County include the King County Department of Community and Human Services and the institutions that share jurisdiction include the Seattle and King County Department of Public Health and the King County and Seattle Public Housing Authorities.

All Home is the Seattle/King County version of the U.S. Department of Housing and Urban Development's Continuum of Care (CoC) program. The CoCs "are geographically based groups of organizations that establish, plan, and coordinate local homeless assistance" (Continuum of Care Program, 2012). Each geographic area CoC is funded by the HUD and mandated to address homelessness. The relationships between and among local and regional agencies are characterized by a high degree of overlap as city, county, and All Home share responsibilities to outline policy goals and establish the strategic vision. King County agencies bear most of the responsibility regarding operational support including management of the HMIS (Homeless Management Information System). In terms of funding allocation, the City of Seattle and King County agencies both share responsibility to manage as well as track performance outcomes of service contracts. All Home is the recipient of HUD grants and is primarily a coordinating body for allocating funding to homeless agencies and partners.

Due to the large scope of the homelessness response and the lack of coordination among relief providers, several key responsibility areas experience overlap. A disjointed relationship exists between service providers and has been identified as a factor that decreases the effectiveness and efficiency of the homelessness response. Future Laboratories, a consulting firm commissioned by Seattle and King County, issued a report in 2018 which identified the organizational structure of homeless response providers in Seattle and King County as contributing to "minimized efficacy across systems and stunted progress toward ending homelessness in the region … [multiple agencies] cannot hold primary responsibility for the same thing" (HRS, 2018).

The Puget Sound Business Journal published a report in 2017, *The Price of Homelessness*, focused on the financial impact of the homelessness issue in the Greater Puget Sound area. The report included an estimation of the total annual spending of the Greater Puget Sound region towards addressing the homelessness problem of around $1 billion annually and found a widespread lack of communication between all types of organizations operating on this issue. A specific finding described the lack of data both shared and available associated to the homelessness problem. Emily Parkhurst, Editor in Chief of the PSBJ, found that there appeared to be space on this specific front for the numerous local technology companies to partner with homelessness organizations. Parkhurst offers that, "[w]e are paying far too high a price for homelessness … and we have the ability to fix this … it will take a coordinated effort by government, nonprofit, and business leaders to make any headway" ("The Price of Homelessness," 2017).

Dr. Patrick J. Fowler co-authored two journal articles to determine how to best design CoC governance structures and homelessness solutions that are based on coordination between systems. In "Capability Traps Impeding Homeless Services: A Community Based System Dynamics Evaluation" Fowler and colleagues discovered a lack of evidence-based research regarding best practices for designing CoCs. Due to the complexities of coordinating/delivering homeless services across public, private, and non-profit organizations, CoCs may inadvertently contribute to overextending the ability to provide service and therefore result in low quality service to homeless populations seeking assistance. Despite the lack of evidence-based prescriptions, Fowler and co-authors offer well founded suggestions to public administrators highlighting the importance of mitigating against negative potentialities of partnership endeavors involving multiple homelessness service providers. These include ensuring that outcome goals are based on a realistic measure of a service providers operational capacities so that goals are achievable and target populations receive high quality service. In Fowler and colleagues' 2019 article, "Solving Homelessness from a Complex Systems Perspective: Insights for Prevention Responses" they observed the potential for complex systems to inform a better approach to preventing homelessness. Fowler and colleagues offer, "[c]omplex systems provide a critical perspective on the delivery of coordinated responses to homelessness…[c]omplex systems are composed of multiple interacting agents that produce nonlinear patterns of behaviors, and they continually adapt and evolve in response to conditions within the system" (Fowler, Hovmand, Marcal, Das, 2019, pg. 475). Complex system principles, such as operational flexibility, responsiveness to data trends, and the ability to provide tailored solutions to multiple stakeholders, should be considered when public administrators are exploring collaborative opportunities between homelessness service providers.

Citing Marsh (2013), Denhardt and Denhardt find that "public servants must join with their counterparts in nonprofit and private business in order to solve problems that are simply too large in scope and cross too many boundaries to be tackled by any single organization" (Denhardt and Denhardt, 2015, pg. 85). It is an accurate assessment that collaboration between all sectors and areas of society is necessary to effectively address entrenched issues that permeate all sectors and areas of society. Further, the current status of the efforts to address homelessness in Seattle and King County should be modeled after this idea.

Seattle and King County are home to many successful technology and other business sector companies such as Amazon, Microsoft, Zillow, Expedia, Starbucks, T-Mobile, and others. These private companies offer operational capacities and expertise that if leveraged could help improve the effectiveness of Seattle's and King County's homelessness response and prevention efforts. It should not be surprising that efforts towards addressing homelessness have not been as effective as planned because although the governmental structures in these service areas share similar responsibilities and a vision/mission, they also feature low levels collaboration and coordination. Effective collaboration is practical must-have when agencies partner together so that the negative aspects of partnership, such as redundancy and overlap, can be avoided.

The following recommendations were provided for consideration to the stakeholders associated to the homeless response in Seattle and King County:

1. City and county administrators should design a governance structure that coordinates all agencies conducting any major type of homelessness response, such as the agencies mentioned earlier.

2. All Home is well positioned to serve as the primary coordinating body for Seattle and King County's homelessness response.

3. Close or at least shrink the communication gap concerning sharing operation and performance data between and among homelessness agencies and organizations in the Seattle and King County area.

4. Engage, encourage, and leverage local technology companies to contribute their technical knowledge and expertise to help solve homelessness in the Seattle and King County area. For example, an Atlanta based non-profit homelessness support organization, Open Doors, partnered with Salesforce to create an application that allows social workers to quickly find available housing units that accept subsidy programs. City and county leaders should pursue similar collaborations with the abundance of local technology knowledge.

5. Honor the patience of the citizens of Seattle in a meaningful way. As the Seattle Times poll indicated, the public is still very much engaged in this issue in constructive ways. Therefore, city and county administrators should electronically publish progress on major homelessness projects currently underway and planned so that the public can remain engaged in a healthy and supportive way.

Homelessness is a complex issue that Seattle and King County leaders can attest. Despite the difficulties in permanently addressing the issue, research and technological advancements are providing new ways to conceptualize the best approach to homelessness which seems to be a collaboration between public, private, and non-profit partners.

References

All Home. (2015). All Home Strategic Plan. Retrieved from http://allhomekc.org/wp-content/uploads/2015/09/All-Home-Strategic-Plan.pdf

Continuum of Care Program, 24 C.F.R. Part 578 (2012).

Davila, V., & Coleman, V. (2019, January 12). In new poll on homelessness, Seattle area favors compassion but distrusts politicians. Retrieved from https://www.seattletimes.com/seattle-news/homeless/homeless-poll-results/.

Denhardt, J. V., & Denhardt, R.B. (2015). *The New Public Service: Serving, Not Steering* (4th ed.). New York: Routledge/Taylor & Francis Group.

Fowler, P. J., Hovmand, P. S., Marcal, K. E., & Das, S. (2019). Solving Homelessness from a Complex Systems Perspective: Insights for Prevention Responses. *Annual Review of Public Health*, *40*, 465–486. https://doi.org/10.1146/annurev-publhealth-040617-013553 HRS. (2018). Retrieved from https://hrs.kc.future.com/.

Fowler, P. J., Wright, K., Marcal, K. E., Ballard, E., & Hovmand, P.S. (2019). Capability Traps Impeding Homeless Services: A Community-Based System Dynamics Evaluation. *Journal of Social Service Research*, *45*(3), 348–359. https://doi.org/10.1080/01488376.2018.

The Puget Sound Business Journal. (2017, December 17). The Price of Homelessness. Retrieved from https://www.bizjournals.com/seattle/digital-edition?issue_id=7436

Timeline: Understanding Seattle's homeless issues. (2018, December 19). Retrieved from https://mynorthwest.com/1030524/timeline-seattle-homeless/

13. Cities Have a New Target for Ending Homelessness: Landlords*

J.B. Wogan

Families wait years to get off the government's waiting list for a rental voucher, sometimes while living in a homeless shelter. When they finally get that housing aid, they often struggle to find landlords willing to rent to them.

Most landlords screen out people who have a criminal background, poor credit or a history of evictions, making it difficult for voucher holders to find somewhere to live, even when they can afford rent. In fact, it's common for people to lose their vouchers—which have expiration dates—after months of unsuccessful searching for a home.

To ease landlords' worries and house more of the homeless, a growing number of cities are offering to reimburse landlords for certain losses—unpaid back rent or repairs for tenant-caused damages—that result from accepting applicants who have rental vouchers.

"Many, many communities are doing this, and it's out of necessity," says Elisha Harig-Blaine, who works on affordable housing issues at the National League of Cities. "They simply can't get people placed into housing with these subsidies."

Boston and the District of Columbia announced their own "housing guarantee" or "risk mitigation" programs.

In Boston, the city will reimburse landlords for up to $10,000 in unpaid back rent or property damages that go beyond normal wear and tear. In D.C., a nonprofit is raising $500,000 in private funds to cover up to $5,000 in landlord costs per tenant. In both places, program staff will be available to address landlord complaints and provide case management for the tenants.

The question is, will that be enough to convince landlords to accept tenants who pay with rental vouchers?

In many of the cities that have these programs, affordable housing is hard to find, but renters with clean criminal and financial backgrounds are not.

"At the end of the day, real estate is a business. These landlords want to do the right thing, but we're talking about their livelihood," says Harig-Blaine, who has attended landlord recruitment events in nine communities across the country.

Landlords, he says, don't want to deal with missed payments or other trouble that might come with renting to someone who was recently homeless.

*Originally published as J.B. Wogan, "Cities Have a New Target for Ending Homelessness: Landlords," *Governing*, October 24, 2017. Reprinted with permission of the publisher.

Nevertheless, local officials in D.C.—which is getting 800 new residents every month and has some of the country's highest rents—are optimistic.

"Rather than [renting] to the millennial who is just moving in from some other part of the country," Neil Albert, president and executive director of the DowntownDC Business Improvement District, the nonprofit raising the money, told *Governing*. Albert thinks the risk funds will spur landlords to "weigh our needs and give equal consideration" to voucher holders.

There is no official number of landlord assistance programs, according to the U.S. Interagency Council on Homelessness, but they exist in Denver, Fargo, N.D.; Marin County, Calif.; Orlando, Fla.; Portland, Ore.; and Seattle-King County, Wash, which started one of the first almost a decade ago. Some states, such as Minnesota and Oregon, offer them as well.

Before launching its program, Boston researched them in other cities and found that participating landlords rarely had to use the risk funds, according to Boston's Department of Neighborhood Development. In 2016, in Seattle and King County, for example, participating landlords filed mitigation claims for only 15 percent of the renters covered by the program. Data on how many landlords participate in each city and how many people are housed through such programs, however, is not readily available.

D.C. officials, though, expect demand for the risk funds to be higher in their city.

"We think it will be a little different here in D.C. We think people will actually use this fund," says Albert, adding that if it results in more units being rented to voucher-holders, then "that's a great problem to have."

One difference between the Boston and D.C. landlord programs is the funding and management structure. In Boston, the city is putting up the risk funds and managing its landlord relations on a two-year pilot basis. In D.C., a nonprofit business improvement district is raising funds—mostly from developers—and a local housing nonprofit is administering the program. That's because landlords and property managers in D.C. pushed for a privately managed fund that could provide reimbursements faster than a government agency, says Albert.

More than 5 million Americans receive some kind of rental voucher from the state or federal government, according to the Center on Budget and Policy Priorities. In general, households must be below the federal poverty line or make less than 30 percent of the area median income to qualify for housing assistance. Because the program is not an entitlement, less than a quarter of all eligible families receive housing assistance, and many households wait years before a voucher becomes available.

Landlord assistance programs are trying to address a chicken-and-egg problem, says Laura Zeilinger, D.C.'s director of human services. Landlords want renters who have jobs and earn a steady income. But stable housing is usually the first step to helping people get and keep a job. She's hoping that landlords in D.C. will waive income requirements in their applications.

"Housing is an important foundation for people to be able to work and to achieve their potential," she says. "It's a really difficult thing for people to do while living in a shelter environment."

14. No Questions Asked*

DAVID KIDD

David Higgins, homeless for years, is bent over a dark green plastic trash bin, the kind you see curbside in every city and town in America. His eyes are closed and his head almost touches the rim as his fingers reach for something at the bottom. But it isn't trash. It's his own pair of perfectly good running shoes. This particular container is one of 500 numbered bins, arranged in neat rows on a wide area of gravel and concrete. The containers are storage closets for residents of the Courtyard, a homeless resource center in Las Vegas.

Higgins has come back to the Courtyard to collect the last of his possessions. After living at the resource center since August, he got a job and his own place to live. "I've had problems with alcohol," he says. "I'm still dealing with it."

The Courtyard is unlike most homeless shelters in the country in several important ways. It allows guests, as they are called, to store their belongings in the bins. It allows them to have pets. It lets couples come in together. Most striking of all, it admits people who show up drunk or high. "You have to allow them to come in with their drugs and alcohol," says Las Vegas Mayor Carolyn Goodman. "But they can't sell it. They can't be buying it. If they're high, we'll help them."

Goodman, like the residents of the Courtyard, knows that denying access to alcoholics and drug addicts can pose problems for people living on the streets. "I had an intoxicated gentleman try to rape me and hit me in the mouth and knocked my two bottom teeth out," says Julia Laymance, a Courtyard resident for the past six months. Kathi Thomas-Gibson, the director of community services for the city, says that "people come here because if they stay on the street they get beat up, mugged and abused. There has to be a safe place so folks can make a decision about what next step to take. If you're out there, you're just in survival mode."

At the Courtyard Homeless Resource Center, there are no beds. Overnight guests, typically around 200 of them, sleep on mats laid along the ground outside. No food is served except on rare special occasions. What the Courtyard does offer is easy access to services that include securing ID cards, getting medical help and finding a job.

Traditional shelters and other places to stay and eat exist not far away. Catholic Charities is across the street. The Salvation Army and the Shade Tree shelter for women and children are also close. They are not competitors to the Courtyard. "Our partners are full every night," says Thomas-Gibson. "There are beds for 500 men across the street.

*Originally published as David Kidd, "No Questions Asked," *Governing*, April 2019. Reprinted with permission of the publisher.

Where do the women go? Where do the people with pets go? Where do same-sex couples go? Same thing for the Salvation Army. They're full. So you add it all together you've got maybe a thousand beds. We've got 6,000 people on the streets."

One thing that draws homeless people to the Courtyard is the policy toward possessions. Most providers will insist that people give up their belongings in order to access services, a meal or a place to sleep for the night. "If everything you own is in two shopping bags ... or however you're trying to maintain a semblance of your former life, we say you don't have to leave it outside," says Thomas-Gibson. "You can bring it inside."

The Courtyard sits alongside North Las Vegas Boulevard, a half-mile up the road from the Neon Museum, the resting place of the once-glittering signage of the city's storied past. The most prominent feature of the Courtyard is an abandoned three-story motel of the same vintage as the museum, but devoid of any charm. Until the city purchased the property, it was used by a homeless youth center. A vacant church was demolished to make room for the hundreds of storage bins. The steeple was spared and sits alone in a distant corner of the lot.

Guests' possessions are kept in 500 locked, numbered bins that are neatly arranged in rows on the Courtyard's property.

The empty motel's ground floor is open and paved, presumably once used to keep parked cars out of the elements. The space is now occupied by pallets of bottled water, a kennel and homeless guests seated at picnic tables, reading, talking, sleeping or playing with their pets.

While one side of the abandoned motel is up against Las Vegas Boulevard, the other looks down on an open expanse of dirt and concrete. A few forlorn trees punctuate the otherwise barren space. An open shed protects a few more tables and benches where people stand guard over their phones while charging them. Large red rocks provide seating for those who would rather take their chances with the elements. Beyond the courtyard itself is a tent-covered outdoor basketball court, also with picnic tables. Next door, a former funeral home serves as the shelter's office space and provides storage.

The campus perimeter is ringed with fencing. Guests may come and go, but they must use the one and only entry point. Armed security personnel are always visible everywhere on the property. It's hard to find someone with anything negative to say about the security staff. "They treat you like a human being," says Laymance. "They joke with you." Outside the gate, Metro Police routinely stop to question individuals loitering on the street to keep guests from being taken advantage of as they come in and out.

Besides the fence and security personnel, perhaps the most important feature of the Courtyard is a row of 10 Port-a-Potties that are cleaned every day, along with hand-washing stations near the entrance. Goodman says her first order of business upon opening the Courtyard in 2017 was sanitation. "The biggest thing for me were the stupid Port-a-Potties. Safety first and sanitation. They go hand in hand," she says, slapping the top of her desk. "There are certain basic needs and we have to be able to provide them."

Armed personnel are visible everywhere on the property. "They treat you like a human being," one guest says of the security staff.

All of this, the old motel, the converted funeral home offices and the basketball court, will soon be gone, replaced with a brand-new facility with expanded offerings for the homeless. But no matter how inviting the Courtyard may be now, there are still many homeless people who won't step foot in the Courtyard or any other shelter.

On a chilly late-winter Tuesday, three white vans pull up to a deserted, trash-strewn lot not far from the Courtyard grounds. As they do every day, the vans have brought members of the Multi-Agency Outreach Resource Engagement Team (MORE) to look for people in need. They try to coax them into the Courtyard. If they won't come in, it is hoped they will at least agree to get help with services. The MORE team always works in tandem with law enforcement officials.

In this lot, a tent city the length of a football field has been set up beside a cement drainage ditch. Train tracks run along the other side. Piles of trash, shopping carts and all manner of debris define individual encampments. It is quiet except for the sounds of small planes buzzing overhead. Stopping at every makeshift dwelling, a Las Vegas city marshal leans in. "Hey, folks inside the tent, we have service providers out here if you want to talk to them." Sometimes a muffled "no" comes from within, but usually there is silence. Once in a while someone will come out to talk.

Two women in bright green MORE vests ask a disheveled young man some questions while the marshal stands a few yards off to the side. "It sounds like you had a pretty shitty childhood. Have you talked to someone? Maybe a little depression? Anxiety?"

"No, it takes a lot to bring me down."

"Do you have a learning disability?"

"Dyslexia."

"Are you currently running from something? Do you have any pets with you?" The women try to convince him to come to the Courtyard, but he won't. He says he's at least thinking of spending the night at a conventional shelter, and he eventually agrees to meet them again in the morning.

"You can't make people take services," says staffer Jason Arroyo of MORE. "But you can try, try, try."

The MORE team, which always works in tandem with law enforcement, try to convince homeless people to come to the Courtyard.

To visit the Courtyard headquarters, guests must submit to a search by a security guard in a short hallway adorned with missing person flyers. The largest room is divided into a small number of cramped offices and cubicles, each staffed by someone with a specific responsibility to help obtain IDs, arrange for medical assistance, deal with insurance, get transportation or find a job.

In a tiny corner office, case manager Jakki Wells is questioning a guest with a head injury. "Has anybody threatened you or tried to harm you? Have you tried to threaten or hurt anybody in the last year? Have you been attacked or beaten up in the last year? What happened to your head?"

"Don't touch it. It's gonna hurt."

"You fell? Did somebody beat you up?"

"No," is all he can answer.

"You did, you've got a big gash on your head right now. Is there anybody that thinks you owe them money?"

Less than two feet away, another staffer is arranging for a young woman to get a bus ticket home to her mother in Seattle. Every day several guests take advantage of a program offering free rides home. After showing that someone expects them on the other end, they are handed a ticket and a bag lunch and sent on the 20-minute walk to the bus station. "It doesn't bother me if it's tonight or tomorrow morning. But I would prefer today," says the hopeful passenger. "I don't have any money now because I gambled it all away. Yesterday I slept outside underneath an awning."

Many of the staff and volunteers at the Courtyard have their own history of homelessness and addiction that helps them identify with the Courtyard's guests. Wells has been clean for 29 years. "I'm very proud of my own accomplishment," she says. But her empathy for the homeless and addicted doesn't mean she's a pushover. Her expression turns to exasperation if she thinks someone is trying to manipulate her. "They're not bad people," she says of the guests. "They're just in bad situations."

Although this is the desert, temperatures are close to freezing and a light rain is falling on a February afternoon. Groups of people huddle under blankets at the tables beneath the old motel. Suddenly, the area is bathed in a red glow as heat lamps mounted in the ceiling are turned on. A chorus of "Thanks, Mark," goes up, directed at Mark Sommerfeld, manager of the Courtyard's physical plant.

He has turned on the lamps sooner than he was supposed to.

Buddy and Krystal are part of the group thankful for the heat lamps. They have been staying at the Courtyard for three of the eight months they've been married. Buddy, 34, says he's had two heart attacks and is quick to tell you about his dislocated shoulder. L-O-V-E is tattooed across the fingers of one hand and H-A-T-E across the other. "I was a bad drug user," he says. "Now I smoke weed." Krystal, 27, is pregnant with twins. They stay here because they can be together at night. "We may sleep on mats," Buddy says. "But at least I'm not too far from my wife."

The Courtyard lets couples stay together. Buddy and Krystal have been there for three of the eight months they've been married.

Dogs, cats and birds are welcome to spend the night in the Courtyard's kennel. There is one more animal in residence this week, but no one who's seen it can agree what it is. Chipmunk and prairie dog are the most popular guesses. A volunteer from an organization dedicated to helping animals and their owners makes regular appearances to donate pet food, clean pens and help the homeless care for their animals.

Las Vegas and surrounding Clark County have the eighth-largest homeless population among all of the country's metropolitan areas. Two thirds of the region's 6,000-plus homeless population are unsheltered. To address the need, the Courtyard sprang from modest beginnings two years ago on vacant land purchased by the city. "When I came here, this place was nothing. It was a mess," says staffer Steve Rehberger. After the Port-a-Potties were installed, a security staff was added, along with a rented trailer for any interested service providers. Bottled water was handed out during hours of operation, initially 6 a.m. to 6 p.m.

As the project began to take off, says Rehberger, "all the politicians and the mayor came, nonprofits wanted to come and do services—it just turned into a mini courtyard."

Steve Quackenbush was one of those living on the street at the time and recalls the early days. "Three cases of water, 10 guests. I came over and was just relaxing on a bench and I saw there was trash that needed to be dumped. So I was trying to help out and started dumping trash. I'd come every day." His enthusiasm for work eventually earned him a paid position.

Will Kight came from similar circumstances, having met Quackenbush at Catholic Charities. "Being part of the homeless population makes it easy to relate," he says. Kight now does public speaking on behalf of the Courtyard. "I want to see it to completion," he says.

The Courtyard provides a safe and sanitary place to stay so that guests can focus on more than just day-to-day existence.

The Courtyard is not the only low-barrier facility in the United States. Other cities have their own versions of an alcohol-tolerant one-stop shop for homeless services. The most elaborate and well-established is in San Antonio. Largely funded by a retired oil executive, Haven for Hope has 60 nonprofit partners on its $100 million, 23-acre campus, which includes open-air sleeping and dormitories for 850 people.

The size and funding model of the San Antonio campus make it difficult to replicate. But delegations from several other cities, including members of the Courtyard team, have made multiple trips to the private, nonprofit facility looking for ideas. "We took our team down to see San Antonio because we knew we were going to adapt elements of what they were doing," says Thomas-Gibson, the city's director of community services. "You can't adopt, pick it up whole and plop it here, but you can adapt certain aspects. The folks who work here needed to see that in action."

Rehberger has commandeered someone's office and is spreading the architect's plans for the new Courtyard across a desk. "We're going to be able to sleep 500 people," he says. "There's going to be heat and cooling. We're going to have 15 or 16 permanent showers, with bathrooms. No more Port-a-Potties." Plans also call for a large covered dayroom for watching TV, playing games or just staying dry when it rains. There will be new office space for service providers, a kennel and a laundry. The city plans to begin construction on the new facility in the fall.

But all of this is coming at a price. In the past few months, the anticipated cost of building the new facility has almost doubled to $15 million. "The issue, as with everything in life and everything in government in particular, is how do you fund it?" says Goodman. "Not only how do you fund it but how do you sustain it? There has to be an ongoing stream of income to do all the wonderful things. There is no free. You have to pay for it." But the mayor is mindful of the larger effects of the city's homeless policy. "It does affect all of us," she says. "It affects tourism. It affects business. It affects schools. It affects safety. It affects everything."

In the end, what may be most important is that the Courtyard gives people a chance to focus on moving forward instead of just surviving. "This is a population that has chronic issues and we need to be able to intervene," the mayor says. "If you don't allow them to come in with their [alcohol or drugs] and everything else, they're not coming."

15. Five Questions
for Mayor Richard J. Berry*

BETH VELASQUEZ

"The community I serve has seen fit to step up and tackle some of the most difficult issues that we've faced for generations in America and we're making a big difference. We're really shining as a city that's compassionate. We have some programs that are the best in the nation for addressing homelessness."

—Richard J. Berry, mayor of Albuquerque, New Mexico

According to the U.S. Department of Housing and Urban Development, homelessness among veterans in Albuquerque has reached the level of "functional zero" (which is a housing measure for, essentially, having fewer homeless people living on the streets than in some form of housing). According to the U.S. Conference of Mayors, unsheltered homelessness in Albuquerque dropped by 80 percent between the years 2009 and 2016.

Among the reasons for this accomplishment is There's a Better Way, a work program Albuquerque Mayor Richard J. Berry launched in 2015 after seeing a man holding a sign that read, "Want a Job. Anything Helps."

"We're trying to give people a better option than standing on a street corner panhandling," he explains. "So now we actually go out with a van and offer to hire them to do day work."

The participants are paid $9 an hour, which is slightly higher than the city's $8.80 minimum wage, and are provided lunch and overnight shelter if needed. "We've cleaned up more than 400 city blocks and picked up more than 120,000 pounds of weeds and trash, so our beautiful city looks even better," says Berry.

Another program of note is the Heading Home Project, which has been able to house more than 650 chronically homeless individuals since 2011, the year Berry founded the work. By housing the chronically homeless, Albuquerque is saving money—$5 million by early 2017—because when people have housing they are off the streets and out of the crisis situations that require more extensive, and costly, city services.

News of Albuquerque's success has inspired cities including Chicago, Seattle, Denver and Dallas to adopt the day-work program. Berry has fielded interest from officials in Calgary, Canada, and Melbourne, Australia, too.

---

*Originally published as Beth Velasquez, https://www.aarp.org/livable-communities/livable-in-action/info-2017/wwl-work-albuquerque-mayor-richard-berry.html (September 27, 2017). Reprinted with permission of the publisher.

Prior to serving as mayor of New Mexico's largest city (population: 560,000, about 20 percent of whom are age 60 or older), Berry was elected twice as a representative to the New Mexico State Legislature. Before that, he owned an Albuquerque-based construction company. Berry's second term as mayor ended on December 1, 2017.

Creating programs to make Albuquerque a more livable and age-friendly community began early in your administration and seemed to be a priority. Was this by design or something that grew out of other areas?

It was and is a priority. We believe that Albuquerque is already a very age friendly city and that we are going to continue to get better as time goes on. But we know that what we do has to be intentional. We want to make sure we're overlaying policy with the notion that we are a livable age friendly community. Our directors have done a wonderful job coming together—whether by planning capital improvement projects or making decisions about what streets we build, what we do with sidewalks, what we do with bike paths, what we do with senior centers, what we do with our multigenerational centers. We need to make sure that we're putting age-friendliness and livability in place in whatever we do.

We also created ABQ Together, which is our dialogue about the city's future. We've brought leaders together—from business, nonprofits, academia, houses of worship, the media, as well as institutional and government sectors—to create a new age friendly blueprint for Albuquerque.

What does a livable community look like to you?

First of all, a livable community is a community for everyone—meaning people of all ages can participate in what's going on. They can live here, they can work here, they can be active and well, and that there are resources, places and infrastructure that allows them to do that.

We want to make sure we're concentrating on the human element and providing our citizens with the support they need. We want a community without barriers, as much as that's possible. One barrier, for example, is transportation. Transportation in general is just important. Infrastructure in general is important. Bridges and highways need to work.

Right now we are installing what will be the best-of-its-kind public transit system in America—the Albuquerque Rapid Transit (ART) line. We're making it so people can get where they need to go by using public transit. We're incorporating accessibility into service routes and transportation stops. There are really several reasons why ART is so important.

#1: It's an economic driver. Independent studies show we could add upwards of $2 billion worth of new investments up and down the corridor. We can already document $300 million since we started construction.

#2: It's a mobility issue and if you're a two-income couple and both of you work, and one of you can take public transportation, well, that's like a $9,000 raise for your family, since that's about what it costs to own and maintain a vehicle and drive it each year.

Having a rapid transit line creates what Albuquerque doesn't have much of right now, which we'd like more of, and that's an urban corridor. We have an urban core but we don't have an urban corridor. We've already changed the zoning to allow for more density, so if someone wants to live along the transit line and not have a vehicle anymore, they can. Or people with cars who don't feel like driving all the time don't have to drive. There's a population, including folks age 50-plus, that want to live in the urban core now. We're creating a place where livability can happen.

Albuquerque does already have a spectrum of transit services. We provide a half-million rides a year through our Sun Van services. We have bus services that connect with other main bus lines. And we're working on developing partnerships with ride sharing programs, which as a service have made a tremendous impact on people's lives.

We've also added another airline to the ranks that serve us as well as a number of direct flights to some popular cities, including San Francisco, San Diego and New York City. In addition, we've brought in some world class consultants to make sure we're super walkable as well.

In addition to There's a Better Way, the Heading Home Project and ART, what other programs have you implemented?

We run Launch to Learn, one of the best summer learning programs. We have more than 40 local partners, so when our kids get out of school in the spring, they have an opportunity to spend their summer in a way that allows them to lead and learn when they get back in the classroom in the fall.

For kids that are living in poverty, Launch to Learn enables them to get their immunizations, have dental work done and get their hair cut. The program helps ensure that the kids have new shoes on their feet and new clothes to wear when they go back to school.

Launch to Learn is, of course, about reading and literacy, which creates a tremendous opportunity for folks to jump in and volunteer as a summer tutor. So people who want to help the community and help the next generation, we have lots of opportunities for doing that.

You've earmarked resources into developing and expanding the city's multi-generational centers. What are multigenerational centers and how do they fit into livable communities?

I've talked to many, many people who say they are amazed at the quantity and quality of services for seniors in the city of Albuquerque. We built our first multi-generational center in 2002. The city recently opened the North Domingo Baca Multigenerational Center and we're in the process of purchasing property for a new multigenerational center in the northwest quadrant of our city. That won't happen while I'm the mayor but we're putting the foundations in place.

These really are wellness centers, and it's important that they're multi-generational. One success story is the "Teeniors" program. We get our tech savvy teens and young adults to come together at our multigenerational centers with their smart devices, just one-on-one navigating the landscape of new technologies that changes every day.

The centers also act as a place for the communities to gather and discuss and make decisions. That's where we go out and have a lot of our public meetings.

Your time as mayor ends this year. What would you like your "livability legacy" to be?

That we got better, that we were already good, but we went from good to great. It's a good to great story. I believe that the city of Albuquerque has one of the most robust departments of senior affairs in the country. We have taken a community that already cares about these issues, a community that has had a 50-year commitment of being a city for people all ages, and we've launched a new era of making it even better.

One of the things you learn as a mayor is that you rely on the work that came before you, and others will rely on the work I've done.

I'll be 55 when I get out of office, and maybe it's a little bit of selfishness on my part, but I think we underutilize the 50-plus population in the United States. I run into people all the time who would do more if they knew about the opportunities out there. Folks in this category bring a breath of experience, lots of life lessons and a lot of wisdom. I know that my wife, Maria, and I, if we're blessed with a lot of years, we'd like to be active and engaged. I'm so happy we live in a city that will allow us to do that.

16. Empty Space*

MICHAEL SILLIMAN

On February 23, 2018, Mayor Muriel Bowser ceremonially declared Washington, D.C., had reached 700,000 residents. D.C. had a population of 693,972 as of the most recent official U.S. Census on July 1, 2017. The city is adding a net gain of about 800 residents a month either through birth or immigration (about equal parts domestic and international). A recent population trends report by the Office of Planning shows that between the years of 2000 and 2015 D.C. added 100,000 people—and the growth is not done yet.

The Metropolitan Washington Council of Governments (COG) is projecting D.C. proper will surpass one million residents by 2045. While this is only a projection and one that has received some criticism lately, the growth D.C. and many other urban areas around the country continue to experience is putting pressure on governments and communities to meet the housing need. Housing affordability is the number one issue facing D.C. residents. While this pressure is at every level of the housing market, it disproportionately affects D.C.'s most vulnerable residents, pushing those that cannot afford to live in high-rise glass boxes on the Wharf or Georgetown single-family homes to the suburbs.

Some think our cities are too full. Residents complain about the growing pains of construction next door and car traffic in the suburbs. Because of these inconveniences, some residents try to block new developments and changes to the comprehensive plan that would encourage more density. However, as was pointed out on Greater Greater Washington, "shouting 'go back where you came from' at prospective residents, or halting construction of new houses, won't stop greater Washington's population growth." The reality is our cities will continue to grow, and it is up to its public officials to plan this growth to be inclusive and smart.

Growth is not good or bad, but it is inevitable—the good news is, D.C. can handle more people. According to this U.S. Census Bureau chart, D.C. held more people than current levels from about 1940 to 1975, reaching a population peak of 900,000 in 1943 and 1946. A new report from D.C. Policy Center concludes that building more apartments in Northwest and investing in more amenities in Southwest and Northeast would help solve D.C.'s affordable housing shortage. A WAMU writeup of the report explained:

"A wide-ranging analysis of the city's housing supply, the report released Tuesday morning shows that the dominance of single-family homes in amenities-rich neighborhoods, coupled with a lack of amenities in denser neighborhoods, is putting D.C.'s

*Originally published as Michael Silliman, "Empty Space," *PA Times*, https://patimes.org/empty-space/ (April 16, 2018). Reprinted with permission of the publisher.

housing market in a pressure cooker. Addressing those key issues could increase housing supply and drive down prices, opening the city to a wider range of incomes, says the study's author, economist Yesim Sayin Taylor."

D.C. does not have a max capacity. When people say D.C. is full, what they should be saying is that supply is not keeping up with demand. The city is failing to meet the housing demand and failing to meet the basic moral responsibility of protecting its citizens. It would also be wrong to assume the resources needed to meet these demands are unattainable or would require an unattractive style of development. A person experiencing homelessness costs the city considerable resources in homeless services, hospitalizations and the justice system which can offset providing housing for that same person.

When it comes to density, a lot of people assume that means developers coming in and building ugly high-rise condo buildings. However, you can walk around any neighborhood in D.C. and find vacant rowhouses. Empty parking spaces and garages are overgrown with weeds behind houses filled with carless millennials. The lack of affordable housing does not correlate with lack of space; there are many methods that D.C. could use to encourage occupancy rates and land usage. These methods can include lifting restrictive zoning on lot sizes allowing for subdividing, allowing single family homes to add accessory dwelling units, better using city resources (like D.C.'s Vacant to Vibrant program) to encourage private fine grain infill affordable developments, or implementing a land value tax that links property taxes with land usage. The city must meet the housing demand by leveraging every possible resource and method. A D.C. of one million people does not have to mean displacement.

17. Not Just a Place to Live*

From Homelessness to Citizenship

MICHAEL ROWE *and* CHARLES BARBER

Twenty years ago, Jim lived under a highway bridge in New Haven, Connecticut. He was in his 50s and had once been in the Army.

After an honorable discharge, he bounced from one job to another, drank too much, became estranged from his family and finally ended up homeless. A New Haven mental health outreach team found him one morning sleeping under the bridge. His neon yellow sneakers stuck out from underneath his blankets.

The team tried for months to get Jim to accept psychiatric services. Finally, one day, he relented. The outreach workers quickly helped him get disability benefits, connected him to a psychiatrist and got him a decent apartment.

But two weeks later, safe in the apartment, Jim said he wanted to go live under the bridge again. He was more comfortable there, where he knew people and felt like he belonged, he said. In his apartment he was cut off from everything.

As researchers in mental health and criminal justice at Wesleyan and Yale universities, we have been studying homeless populations in New Haven for the past 20 years. In that moment, when Jim said he wanted to leave what we considered the safety of an apartment, the outreach team, which co-author Michael Rowe ran, realized that, while we were capable of physically ending a person's homelessness, assisting that person in finding a true home was a more complicated challenge.

Helping the most marginalized people in society feel comfortable in a new and alien environment, where they were isolated from their peers, required a different approach that went beyond finding them a place to live.

The people we worked with needed to see themselves—and be seen as—full members of their neighborhoods and communities. They needed, in other words, to be citizens.

Record Number of Homeless Deaths

Fueled by the opioid crisis, high housing costs and extreme weather, homelessness and its fatal costs are on the rise.

*Originally published as Michael Rowe and Charles Barber, "Not Just a Place to Live: From Homelessness to Citizenship," *The Conversation*, https://theconversation.com/not-just-a-place-to-live-from-homelessness-to-citizenship-97170 (June 4, 2018). Reprinted with permission of the publisher.

The U.S. Department of Housing and Urban Development estimates an increase in the homeless population in 2017 for the first time in seven years, with more than half a million Americans lacking permanent shelter.

In addition, in cities across the country, there has been a surge in deaths of homeless individuals. In 2017, New Orleans saw a record 60 homeless deaths, a 25 percent rise over two years. Denver saw an estimated increase of 35 percent over 2016, while Rapid City, South Dakota, with a population of only 75,000, saw five deaths of homeless individuals just since December.

Complicating matters, about 25 percent of the homeless population is severely mentally ill. Many are deeply distrustful of shelters and the service system, sometimes refusing to engage in services even when their lives are at stake.

We believe our research might provide a hopeful answer for the increasing number of homeless Americans whose lives are in jeopardy on the streets of our cities.

From Outcasts to Insiders

Jim's story, and other similar ones, led us on a 20-year quest to create a formal mechanism to enhance a sense of belonging and citizenship among society's outsiders.

Aristotle said that to be a citizen is to participate in the political life of a city. Much later, Alexis de Tocqueville linked citizenship to civic participation.

We defined citizenship as the strength of a person's connection to the "Five Rs"—the rights, responsibilities, roles and resources that society confers on people through its institutions, as well as one's relationships to and with friends, neighbors and social networks.

Fifteen years ago, we got a small grant and created the Citizens Project in New Haven for people with mental illness and criminal histories, including major felonies. Often, they had histories of homelessness. The six-month program meets twice a week at a soup kitchen.

There are four months of classes on the Five Rs of citizenship, covering pragmatic topics such as the capacity to effectively advocate for oneself, public speaking and conflict resolution. A community advocate and peer mentors—people with mental illnesses who are now doing well—teach, support and counsel participants, or "students," as well as provide them with living, breathing proof that people can indeed change.

Then students undertake a meaningful project in the community, such as training police cadets how to approach people living on the streets in a nonthreatening manner. Graduations are held at City Hall, with family, friends and public officials cheering on.

The results?

There were statistically significant reductions—55 percent—in alcohol and drug use among citizenship program participants (as compared to 20 percent reduction in the control group). Additionally, participants' self-reported indicators of quality of life—such as satisfaction with daily activities and with their employment for those who secured jobs—were significantly higher in the citizenship group than the control groups. We have published the results in peer-reviewed articles and a book, Citizenship and Mental Health.

Criminal charges decreased, as they did in the control group, which received "usual" mental health care. Perhaps most important, each class of students became a supportive community in itself. Participants have taken seriously their new role as students, one that many had not embraced before.

Over the period in which we have conducted the citizenship project, homelessness overall in New Haven has decreased, likely through many factors, including perhaps our own work.

Citizenship Approach Spreading

Interestingly, however, anxiety and depression increased at various points among our participants. Perhaps the challenge of the intervention had an impact on students. Perhaps also the courage to change brought with it a vulnerability to difficult thoughts and feelings: grief over lost opportunities, lost friends, or lost dreams, even while their quality of life increased.

The project has run for years now, graduating hundreds. We've received funding from federal and state government. A state-wide social service agency is making their primary focus the enhanced citizenship of its 6,000 clients. Citizenship projects, based on our model, have been launched at a state forensic hospital in Connecticut and internationally in mental health programs in Quebec, Scotland, and soon, Spain and New Zealand.

It seems our citizenship program born 20 years ago is now coming of age. The intervention is inexpensive and follows a straightforward manual. The costs of doing nothing are certainly higher.

And Jim? He did pretty well for a while, then one day ranted enough about a public official that it had to be reported as a threat. Though exonerated, he fired his treatment team and refused all help once again. The Citizens Project had apparently arrived too late to help him.

The stakes of full membership in society are indeed high as we undertake this work for people on the margins. But our graduates—as they are recognized at City Hall by the mayor, as they train the police, as they serve on boards of homeless shelters where they once lived—say that seeing themselves as citizens helps.

And when we see the smiles on our graduates' faces, or when they talk about their new employment, or when they talk about their joy in getting away from drugs and alcohol, we know that their new-found citizenship helps others, too.

18. Care Not Cash Program for the Homeless in San Francisco, California*

DaVina Flemings *and* Rachel D. McGuffin

Homelessness is a visible and controversial social problem that most metropolitan and small pockets of suburban cities grapple with on a daily basis. A significant number of homeless individuals and families live on the street because they have no permanent housing and no access to emergency shelters. This societal crisis has also tremendously impacted tourism in certain main cities, as some tourists refrain from visiting those high concentrated areas where homeless people reside. A decline in the tourist industry has led to negative impacts on the local economy, not to mention the amount of discord sown between the homeless and the local population.

The state of California continues to contend with housing the homeless. This population reached 134,000 in 2017, an increase by 13.7 percent, and is recorded as the largest spike in the nation (Smith, 2018). Starting in the 1970s, homelessness erupted in cities across the western state, especially in San Francisco. Non-profit coalitions such as the Coalition on Homelessness (COH), as well as municipal actors enacted legislation and organized donations over the decades, some of which have seen marginal success, while others drained funds with little results. Thus, at the turn of the century, it became imperative for the municipal government to find a solution to house the homeless.

Care Not Cash Initiative

In the November 2002 election, voters passed the Care Not Cash Program (Proposition N) in San Francisco Municipality, which significantly altered how General Assistance was provided to single homeless adults. Homeless people who received cash aid from the City's County Adult Assistance Program (CAAP) phased into the Care Not Cash Program over a seven-month period. After which, those homeless CAAP clients were offered shelter in lieu of the cash benefits received through CAAP. The intention of this program was to target those homeless individuals who represent the "chronically" homeless, which were defined as people who did not have a permanent residence in more than one year (National Alliance to End Homeless, 2019).

---

*Published with permission of the authors.

In 2004, the Department of Human Services became responsible for offering support services such as identifying affordable permanent housing, mental and substance abuse counseling, in place of receiving cash aid estimated at $349 per month. This living stipend of $349 was cut to roughly $69 per month. A Human Services Care Fund was established to fund the housing projects, the source of this capital originating from a decline in caseloads and reduced cash grants. Since its implementation, the fund has totaled roughly $13.5 million annually (Shaw, 2009). This annual sum is dedicated to the non-profit development, operation, and maintenance of the permanent support housing units.

The Care Not Cash Program stirred up a great deal of political controversy. Program implementation was originally delayed as a result of multiple legal court battles from homeless advocates, legal advocates and community leaders opposed to the welfare reform. Program implementation did not begin until May 2004 when a judge finally overturned a superior court decision to throw out Care Not Cash. Mr. Sellstrom, an attorney representing a homeless woman and a nurse, explained some of the reasons why his clients filed lawsuits against the City in 2005, stating: "the Proposition N initiative is very misleading." The proposition as it stood in 2004, reduced welfare benefits for Care Not Cash recipients from $349 to $50 per month and placed them in a homeless shelter and not permanent housing (Sellstrom Interview, 2005).

What Worked

In November 2002, two years before the passing of Care Not Cash, the City and County of San Francisco's Annual Homeless Count Report indicated that approximately 8,640 people were declared homeless, an 18 percent increase since the previous year (Mayor's Office on Homelessness, 2002). After a year of the program's implementation, the homeless count was down to 6,248 people, a 28 percent decrease since the last count in 2002 (Fagan, 2005). Furthermore, the Newsom Administration of San Francisco reported that of the 6,248 count, 2,655 were actually homeless people living on the streets, which was a 41 percent drop from the 4,535 count in 2002 (Fagan, 2005).

On May 3, 2005, the Department of Human services reported that nearly 800 CAAP recipients had been "moved into supportive housing and general assistance rolls for the homeless have been slashed by 73 percent" (Coalition on Homelessness, 2005). Skip forward almost a decade later, and some permanent supportive housing complexes reported over 90 percent of tenants stay in the apartment once they gain access to it, which touts to the success of not only getting people housing, but helping them stay housed (Hart, 2014). In 2015, the Mayor's office released a statement declaring 11, 362 people had been placed in permanent supportive housing since the program's implementation in 2004 (Knight, 2015).

A survey was given to 64 participants in the Care Not Cash Program in April 2005 with the purpose of gathering and analyzing the feedback received by the participants regarding the program's effectiveness. Approximately 35 percent of the respondents reported that they had been homeless for over six months before they were placed in temporary shelter. When asked if the program has assisted them with finding permanent housing, only 34 percent of the respondents have been placed in permanent housing. The survey results indicated that approximately 50 percent of the respondents believed that their transition into Care Not Cash had been an effective preventative measure in keeping them from a homeless situation (Flemings, 2005).

What Didn't Work?

Over ten years has passed since the program's implementation, and Care Not Cash continues to garner mixed results from different parties in San Francisco. Reports from 2018 placed the homeless population around 7,499 which shows no discernable decline from 8,640 in 2002. Homeless advocacy groups and certain community leaders who strongly opposed Care Not Cash have also fired back against many positive updates from the municipal government, citing mainly that those who used Care not Cash benefits were only placed in temporary and not permanent housing.

Harkening back to the survey conducted in 2005, nearly 66 percent of the respondents stated that the program had not assisted them with finding permanent housing. When asked if they had become employed since joining Care Not Cash, approximately 52 percent of the have not obtained employment while 48 percent said they are employed. 45 percent believed that the program did not provide them with the assistance to keep from returning to the streets. Once more, based on the statistical data collected, the "savings" Occupational Health Services generated by reducing the cash aid of CAAP recipients appears to have no equity. In other words, the program reduces cash aid of 2.5 CAAP clients to permanently house one CAAP recipient (Flemings, 2005).

The program ran into a myriad of problems over the past decade, including an imbalance of housing supply to homeless population demand, low turnover rates for occupants, compartmentalized referral systems that lead to long waiting periods, and lack of caseworkers to handle the influx of homeless cases. There are nearly 3,000 units scattered across San Francisco, which averaged out to roughly 100 homeless people per one case worker. This imbalanced ration greatly diminished the support each case worker could give to every tenant. The pool of applicants qualified for Care not Cash outgrew the number of housing slots available by 2013. With a pool of roughly 700 candidates, only 30 slots opened per month, and the selection process had to be handled by case workers already overloaded with work (Hart, 2014).

Supervisor Daly was very involved with the issues concerning the development of the Proposition N initiative. He, along with several other supervisors was extremely opposed to some of the policy language set within the initiative. When asked what specifically about the Care Not Cash program he finds problematic, Supervisor Daly replied, "the financial mechanism utilized is not good enough to subsidize housing." He mentioned that it costs 2.5 CAAP benefits to pay for permanent housing for one person, which equates to $1000 per month. Basically, Supervisor Daly inferred that the Care Not Cash program was "robbing Peter to pay Paul" and not necessarily housing all of the CAAP recipients. The COH also cited the following flaws: shelter instability/empty shelter beds, shelter displacement, missed food and medical provision, and undocumented immigrants displaced from shelter system.

Recent Developments

Among the problems previously listed, perhaps the largest impediment to housing this population lies in the archaic and overburdened referral/caseworker system. In order to combat this issue as well as many others, in 2016, Mayor Edwin M. Lee announced the establishment of the Department of Homelessness and Supportive Housing (HSH).

The sole purpose of this consolidated department was to prevent and end homelessness within San Francisco (HSH, 2019). The HSH works intimately with the Department of Public Health, The Human Services Agency, and many others to connect homeless people with housing and services via the pioneered Coordinate Entry Form System. This system is operated by the Episcopal Community Services, a non-profit organization who provides access points and online services covering the process from selection to referrals for transitional housing. Since 2016, HSH has engaged over 6,000 homeless people with outreach initiatives and has housed 7,000 formerly homeless with permanent supportive housing—not to mention the 5,000 plus who have been sheltered through this program (HSH, 2019).

Other methods were also employed to tackle the large amount of temporary homeless structures set up around San Francisco. Specifically, Proposition Q passed in 2016 by Mayor Ferrell, which allowed local enforcement to provide twenty-four-hour notice to tent dwellers, offering them a shelter bed for temporary housing. If the person refused, the police were authorized to return twenty-four hours later to tear down the tent. This aggressive approach was met with resistance by the Coalition on Homelessness (COH), as this organization purported that this new policy actually caused an increased number of phone calls and complaints regarding temp encampments (Reisenwitz, 2018). Another complaint of this Proposition detailed that if the person accepted the temporary shelter bed, they would be forced to give up all their outdoor equipment, leaving them defenseless to battle the elements after their inevitable discharge from the shelter (Reisenwitz, 2018).

Lastly, in addition to the HSH in 2016, the Homeless Coordinating and Financing Council was created in 2017 to oversee the implementation of the Housing First Approach. This approach dictated that anyone experiencing homelessness should be connected to a permanent home as quickly as possible based solely on hierarchy of needs. In other words, barriers such as sobriety, drug use, or criminal history should not be considered when finding permanent housing for the chronically homeless. The Care Not Cash Proposition still falls under the Housing First umbrella as it specifically provides supportive permanent housing in San Francisco. In order to become compliant under the Housing First Approach, Care Not Cash must accept tenants regardless of their sobriety or use of substances and selection must take into account other criteria besides "first come, first served," such as vulnerability to early mortality and/or chronicity of homelessness.

Recommendations

The following should be conducted in order to ensure the Care Not Cash Program is compliant with Housing First:

1. The Department of Homelessness and Supportive Housing in conjunction with the Mayor's Office should audit the existing program and ensure CAAP recipients are not receiving reduced cash aid until they have been placed in a permanent supportive housing unit.

2. If certain shelters are reserving beds specifically for CAAP recipients, then the policy should be revised to include a "deadline for arrival" so if they do not show up on time, the bed can go to someone who needs it.

3.   A working group should be formed between the Coalition on Homelessness, the Department of Homelessness and Supportive Housing, and the Mayor's Office to normalize communication between parties and provide an official grievance process.

4.   A consulting firm should be hired to conduct an unbiased study on the total funds spent on this program and the amount of the population who have been permanently housed as a result. A comprehensive analysis will help shed light on any areas of the policy that are falling short of its original intent, and keep it relevant for San Francisco.

References

Coalition on Homelessness (2005). The Forgotten: A Critical Analysis of Homeless Policy in San Francisco. Retrieved from: http://www.cohsf.org/wp-content/uploads/2019/03/The-Forgotten.pdf.

Department of Homelessness and Supportive Housing (2019). Retrieved from: http://hsh.sfgov.org/.

Fagan, K. (2005). Fewer homeless people on streets of San Francisco / 28% drop since fall of '02, but other counties report higher numbers. Retrieved from: https://www.sfgate.com/news/article/Fewer-homeless-people-on-streets-of-San-Francisco-2730156.php.

Flemings, D. (2005). San Francisco's Care Not Cash Program for the Homeless: An Evaluation of Care Not Cash Transitioning the Chronically Homeless to Permanent Housing. Retrieved from Golden Gate University.

Hart, A. (2014). Promise of Supportive Housing for Homeless Faces Reality of Short Supply. Retrieved from: https://sfpublicpress.org/news/2014-10/promise-of-supportive-housing-for-homeless-faces-reality-of-short-supply.

Homeless Count Report (2002). Mayor's Office on Homelessness. Retrieved from www.sfgov.org.

Knight, H. (2015). A decade of homelessness: Thousands in S.F. remain in crisis. Retrieved from: https://www.sfchronicle.com/archive/item/A-decade-of-homelessness-Thousands-in-S-F-30431.php.

National Alliance to End Homelessness (2019). Chronically Homeless. Retrieved from: https://endhomelessness.org/homelessness-in-america/who-experiences-homelessness/chronically-homeless/.

Reisenwitz, C. (2018). Farrell Can't Sweep Homelessness Under the Rug–Unintended Consequences. Retrieved from: https://www.thebaycitybeacon.com/politics/farrell-can-t-sweep-homelessness-under-the-rug--/article_d41691be-6854-11e8-b643-971dd1ef3150.html.

Sellstrom, Oren. Telephone interview. April 8, 2005.

Shaw, R. (2009). The real story of care not cash. Retrieved from: http://beyondchron.org/the-real-story-of-care-not-cash/.

Smith, D. (2018). Gavin Newsom's approach to fixing homelessness in San Francisco outraged activists. And he's proud of it. Retrieved from: https://www.latimes.com/politics/la-pol-ca-gavin-newsom-homelessness-san-francisco-20181023-story.html.

19. Tackling Homelessness in San Francisco*

SAN FRANCISCO DEPARTMENT
OF HOMELESSNESS AND SUPPORTIVE HOUSING

Mission

Through the provision of coordinated, compassionate, and high-quality services, the Department of Homelessness and Supportive Housing strives to make homelessness in San Francisco rare, brief, and one time.

The City and County of San Francisco's Department of Homelessness and Supportive Housing (HSH) launched on July 1, 2016. HSH combines key homeless serving programs and contracts from the Department of Public Health (DPH), the Human Services Agency (HSA), the Mayor's Office of Housing and Community Development (MOHCD), and the Department of Children Youth and Their Families (DCYF). This consolidated department has a singular focus on preventing and ending homelessness for people in San Francisco.

Overview

HSH provides assistance and support to homeless and at-risk youth, adults and families to prevent imminent episodes of homelessness and end homelessness for people in San Francisco. Services including outreach, homelessness prevention, emergency shelter, drop-in centers, transitional housing, supportive housing, short-term rental subsidies, and support services to help people exit homelessness.

Goals

A strategic planning process will take place during HSH's first year of operation to determine the long-term goals and benchmarks to which HSH will be accountable. The Department's big picture goals are:

- End homelessness for 8,000 people in the next 4 years
- Reducing the length of time people spend homeless

---

*Public document originally published as San Francisco Department of Homelessness and Supportive Housing, "Tackling Homelessness in San Francisco," http://hsh.sfgov.org/.

- Reducing street homelessness
- Developing a strategy and plan for addressing homelessness in SF

Priorities

- Housing First—a system focused on permanent housing and a rapid re-housing model
- Building on the culture of client-centered services within the City's system of care & housing
- Continuing to move toward a fully coordinated system with transparency in the housing placement process
- Ending homelessness for people who have been homeless the longest

HSH Frontline Services Teams

Homeless Outreach Team

The San Francisco Homeless Outreach Team (SFHOT) works to engage and stabilize the most vulnerable homeless individuals by placing them into shelter and housing. To make these placements SFHOT works in small teams to provide outreach and care management to homeless people living on the streets of San Francisco who have severe illnesses. Services are provided by teams with expertise in the complex issues that are barriers to stability for this population.

Outreach Services:
Skilled teams working a neighborhood beat provide practical support, information and referral, and in-depth assessment and case management for the most vulnerable and at risk.

Case Management:
Stabilizes individuals by addressing the numerous day-to-day and long-term problems related to homelessness.

Provides shelter beds and stabilization rooms within the severely limited resources available.

Works to connect each person with shelter and housing

Develops a stabilization plan for each of the individuals SFHOT works with to reduce the harms of homelessness.

Street Medicine:
Medical staff joins outreach services to help transition people living on the streets into shelter and housing. The street medicine team provides healthcare using an adapted patient centered medical home model. The street medicine team assess patients and establish care for chronic conditions such as medical, mental health, substance use, and cognitive disorders. Additionally, the team provides health care services in shelter and Navigation Centers.

Encampment Resolution Team

HSH is committed to addressing encampments, not through criminalization, but by connecting people living on the streets with services and housing, partnering with other City departments to address the conditions on the streets. To effectively and compassionately address encampments, the City has created the Encampment Resolution Team (ERT). The ERT is a specialized team of outreach staff. During resolution, ERT collaborates closely with encampment residents, neighbors, property owners and other city departments to close encampments and assist remaining people to connect with residential programs.

HSH is committed to addressing encampments following standards it has created, consistent with recommendations by the U.S. Interagency Council on Homelessness. These include:

1. Planning and implementing an encampment resolution strategy that includes input from all stakeholders, including homeless people and residents impacted by encampments.

2. Collaborating across sectors and systems including partnering closely with the Department of Public Works, Department of Public Health, Police Department, and the community

3. Providing intensive and persistent outreach and engagement through the Homeless Outreach and Encampment Resolution Teams to ensure people from encampments do not return to the streets.

4. Creating low-barrier pathways to services and housing for those prioritized for immediate assistance through Navigation Centers and Resource Centers

5. Collecting input from the community and documenting outcomes from our efforts in order to continuously improve our response to unsheltered homelessness.

6. Preventing encampments from re-forming in previously addressed areas through sustained engagement by City agencies, site activation, physical changes to the site, and community engagement.

HSH Programs and Services

Adult Coordinated Entry System

The Department of Homelessness and Supportive Housing has launched Adult Coordinated Entry and its community Access Points. Access Points are localized community gateways into San Francisco's Homelessness Response System, which is the overall system of programs and housing opportunities for adults experiencing homelessness.

Operated by Episcopal Community Services (ECS), the non-profit service provider for Adult Coordinated Entry, Access Points are designed to provide access, determine eligibility, conduct problem solving and assessments, and perform housing referrals for San Francisco adults experiencing homelessness. Families with children are served via Family Coordinated Entry.

Family Coordinated Entry

The Department of Homelessness and Supportive Housing has launched Family Coordinated Entry and its community Access Points: Central City Access Point and

Bayview Access Point. Access Points are localized community gateways into San Francisco's Homelessness Response System, which is the overall system of programs and housing opportunities for families experiencing homelessness.

Operated by non-profit service providers, Access Points are crucial to the function of the Coordinated Entry process, which is designed to assess, prioritize, and match families experiencing homelessness to housing problem solving, shelter, housing opportunities, and other services in San Francisco.

Coordinated Entry for Youth

The Department of Homelessness and Supportive Housing has launched Coordinated Entry for Youth and its community Access Points. Access Points are localized community gateways into San Francisco's Homelessness Response System, which is the overall system of programs and housing opportunities for youth ages 18–24 experiencing homelessness.

The non-profit service providers for Coordinated Entry for Youth is operated by two leads, Larkin Street Youth Services and Huckleberry Youth, and in partnership with Homeless Youth Alliance, LYRIC, The SF LGBT Center, 3rd Street Youth Center and Clinic. Access Points are designed to provide access, determine eligibility, conduct problem solving and assessments, and perform housing referrals for San Francisco youth experiencing homelessness.

Outreach and Homelessness Prevention

San Francisco Homeless Outreach Team (SFHOT) connects unsheltered San Franciscans with services, medical care, and shelter to help them move off the streets and stabilize their lives. SFHOT utilizes a multidisciplinary approach to serve people living on the streets. To request homeless outreach please call 311.

Homelessness Prevention programs provide financial assistance to individuals and families at imminent risk of becoming homeless to maintain their housing or find suitable alternative housing before becoming homeless.

Homeward Bound reunites homeless individuals living in San Francisco with family and friends willing and able to offer ongoing support to end the cycle of homelessness.

Eviction Prevention provides services that include funds to pay back rent to prevent eviction, one-time rental assistance, security deposit funds to move into permanent housing, legal services, counseling, and other support services.

Transitional Housing Programs

Transitional Housing provides people with significant barriers to housing stability with a place to live and intensive social services for up to two years while they work toward self-sufficiency and housing stability.

If you are a homeless veteran, family or youth, transitional housing may help you move from the street to permanent housing. People using transitional housing may stay in the housing for six months to two years and receive intensive services such as education, job training and placement, substance abuse counseling, parenting classes and child care services. They usually pay 30 percent of their income for services and housing. Transitional housing is provided by nonprofit partners of the Department of Homelessness and Supportive Housing. To apply, contact these agencies directly at the phone numbers listed below.

Emergency Shelter

Interfaith Winter Shelter Program: Spaces are reserved on a first come, first served basis each Sunday. The reservation ticket will allow the guest a seven-night stay. Two meals will be served to shelter guests each night.

Adult Shelter System provides short-term emergency shelter for up to 90 days to adults experiencing homelessness in San Francisco. The current adult shelter system has 1,203 shelter beds for adults over the age of 18.

Shelter reservations for one night and weekend stays are made starting at 4:30 p.m. at the resource centers listed below, and must be made in person. These sites are also where individuals can set up a profile in the reservation system and there are phones to connect with 311.

Adult Permanent Supportive Housing

HSH administers locally and federally funded supportive housing to provide long-term affordable housing with on-site social services to people exiting chronic homelessness. San Francisco's adult supportive housing programs offer housing to very low-income homeless adults and couples without custody of children. Some of the units in this portfolio are in SRO hotels that have been renovated by their owners and are managed by non-profit organizations that provide property management and supportive services. Other housing in this portfolio is provided in apartment buildings that offer housing to adults that meet the specific eligibility requirements of each building.

Homeless Adults without children seeking permanent supportive housing can be referred to the San Francisco Continuum of Care Coordinated Entry Pilot. Referral must be made by a third party and may not come directly from the person seeking housing.

For supportive housing that is not included in the Coordinated Entry Pilot program, HSH does not take applications directly from clients. Referrals to vacancies come from HSH-selected programs serving homeless adults, city-funded shelters, and the County Adult Assistance Programs (CAAP) office for homeless clients receiving benefits such as General Assistance. Referrals are made only when there is a vacancy as there is no waiting list.

Direct Access to Housing (DAH) is one of HSH's permanent supportive housing programs for adults without custody of children. DAH provides permanent supportive housing for adults experiencing homelessness who are low-income San Francisco residents with special needs. A "low threshold" program that accepts adults into permanent housing directly from the streets, shelters, hospitals and long-term care facilities, DAH strives to help tenants stabilize and improve their health outcomes despite co-occurring mental health diagnoses, alcohol and substance use, and/or complex medical conditions.

DAH does not accept self-referrals and is closed to new community referrals.

• *B. States* •

20. California Housing Crisis*

Damon Conklin

"Shelter solves sleep. Housing solves homelessness."
—Governor Gavin Newsom

California is experiencing an extreme housing shortage. No community, city or sector of our economy is immune to its impact.

Several factors create the disparity between the supply and the demand. California's population is growing at a steady rate and it's expected to balloon from the current 39 million residents to 50 million by 2050.

According to the California Housing and Community Development Department, over the last decade, California has seen around 80,000 new homes built each year, far short of the projected need of 180,000 new homes needed annually (CHCDD, 2019).

In total, California's supply is about 4 million units short of demand with more than 80 percent of units unaffordable or unavailable for Californians living with extremely low income (defined as less than 30 percent of the area median income). This pressure is even more extreme for the 2.2 million low-income renter households competing for an existing inventory of 664,000 affordable housing rental units, resulting in a gap of 1.54 million units. While homelessness in America is declining, it is rising in California where more than one-third of the nation's 553,000 homeless reside.

Approximately one million households spend more than 50 percent of their income on rent, leaving them vulnerable to homelessness when their rent is increased or a large unforeseen bill comes due. Low-cost rental options for Californians, such as single room occupancy rooms, have evaporated as most were converted to high-end rentals for investment purposes.

As a result, this stagnant inventory of affordable housing causes prices in the state to have ballooned.

In response, Governor Gavin Newsom called for 3.5 million units of affordable housing to be built by 2025. To put this ambitious goal into context, California's highest level of housing production for a single year was in 1960 when 363,000 homes were built—less than half of what the governor is calling for annually.

---

*Published with permission of the author.

Costs

The cost of housing in California is the highest of any state in the nation, and the pace of change has far outstripped that in other parts of the county. According to the U.S. Census, in 1970 the median price of a single-family home in California was $23,600 or $3,000 more expensive than the U.S. average; now it is 250 percent more expensive. Further widening this gap, individual and family incomes during the same period have increased at a much slower pace (1970 at $58,000). Despite some ups and downs over the past several decades, today's real average wage (that is, the wage after accounting for inflation) has about the same purchasing power it did nearly 50 years ago (Bureau of the Census, 1972).

California's higher than average costs for housing are a result of a combination of pressures that have disrupted and imbalanced the cost per unit of housing. These pressures include: high development fees, entitlement fees, local zoning restrictions, which increase the base price for housing in California, California Environmental Quality Act (CEQA) litigation, which deters developers from pursuing large housing developments and inclines them instead towards smaller projects that can be shoe-horned with the exemptions of CEQA, other regulatory mandates, which further increase the cost and challenges of building homes that consumers want; and policymaking bodies at all levels of government lacking the political will to seriously examine and address these problems.

According to the **Legislative Analyst's Office**, "a collection of factors drive California's high cost of housing. First and foremost, far less housing has been built in California's coastal areas than people demand. As a result, households bid up the cost of housing in coastal regions. In addition, some of the unmet demand to live in coastal areas spills over into inland California, driving up prices there too. Second, land in California's coastal areas is expensive. Homebuilders typically respond to high land costs by building more housing units on each plot of land they develop, effectively spreading the high land costs among more units. In California's coastal metros, however, this response has been limited, meaning higher land costs have translated more directly into higher housing costs. Finally, builders' costs—for labor, required building materials, and government fees—are higher in California than in other states. While these higher building costs contribute to higher prices throughout the state, building costs appear to play a smaller role in explaining high housing costs in coastal areas" [pg. 10].

The Drivers of Construction Costs

Construction costs are just one part of the housing cost equation. It takes a lot of money to build housing reserved for lower-income Californians—roughly $330,000 per unit, by some estimates and much higher in coastal regions ($700,000 in San Francisco) (Carlisle, 2019). Costs layer on top of one another throughout the development process from planning to construction (material and labor) to inspection (regulatory and permitting)—and not all construction costs are in control of local decision-makers. Macroeconomic conditions (including the cost of capital), labor market cycles and lack of skilled subcontractors and trade policies (that influence the price of materials) all influence the cost of building. In total, the cost of construction increases on average 1 percent per month each year (Elka, 2018).

Construction costs are also driven by local decisions and processes that are within the control of city agencies. Industry experts (Kim et al., 2014) identify several local drivers of rising construction costs: city permitting processes, design and building code requirements, workforce regulations and ordinances, procurement (small and local business) requirements, and environmental regulations. Such examples include, development fees—charged to builders as a condition of development—are outsized in California—about $22,000 per single-family home, compared to about $6,000 in the rest of the country.

Workforce Gap

The rebounding housing market has meant more housing starts and more apartment buildings breaking ground, but construction employment never fully recovered from the Great Recession. Subsequently, a persistent labor shortage is driving up costs and cutting into margins for these projects, adding to significant economic pressure for developers to focus on luxury units. While these units can turn a higher profit, they are built at the expense of affordable housing, rather than in addition to it.

In the long term, members of the construction industry worry about a pipeline problem: the average age of those in the building trades hovers in the mid–40s, and many industry and union leaders are struggling to attract younger workers and potential apprentices to job training programs. As a result, for every five construction workers preparing for retirement, only one apprentice is in line to replace them. Without significant investment in education and workforce training, the labor shortage will continue to be a drain on the housing industry's growth.

CEQA

Signed in 1970, the California Environment Quality Act (CEQA) requires a study regarding the environmental impact of any major construction project prior to approval of the project. CEQA is heralded by environmentalists as supplying the strongest environmental protections in the country (mitigating "impacts on parking, traffic, air and water quality, endangered species, and historical site preservation") resulting in greater data for informed decision making, many contend that CEQA has been weaponized to delay or even block projects from evening moving forward by tying them up in costly litigation.

Between 2004 and 2013, California's 10 largest cities took about two and a half years on average to approve housing projects that required an environmental impact report, according to the Legislative Analyst's Office (LAO, 2015).

As part of his aggressive rollout of the state budget and initiatives to address housing affordability, Governor Newsom noted that the state's current ranking of 49th out of 50th in home production "isn't cutting it" and when he convened labor and the real estate industry to discuss a compromise to streamline CEQA, Newsom quipped, "We are past the point of absurdity with some of the abuses we are seeing" (Politico, 2019).

However, in a letter sent to legislators and Gov. Gavin Newsom, more than 100 environmental and labor groups signed off on a desperate urging to protect the regulation and build upon its provisions.

The supporters argue that CEQA encourages sustainable development and is helping California reach climate change goals. "CEQA plays a vital role in both preserving

California's unparalleled natural resources and protecting the rights of residents to weigh in on the land use decisions that most affect them," the letter read. "Development interests have long complained about California's flagship environmental law. Now they are trying to blame CEQA for the state's housing crisis. However, CEQA did not cause the housing crisis, and weakening CEQA will not solve it. Rather, if implemented properly, CEQA can be an effective tool in helping to address California's housing problems by encouraging sustainable development" (Planning and Conservation League, 2019). If correct, then why did lawmakers fast track CEQA review to expedite several sporting and entertainment venues to be constructed throughout the state?

Local Government

Restrictive zoning codes are often an effective tool in the fight against new construction and, frequently, densification, helping to suppress housing supply even as demand rises. Whether by limiting the height of new buildings or deciding that large apartment buildings need a minimum number of parking spots, these restrictions make construction more difficult and more expensive. California cities like Los Angeles and San Francisco are known for impeding new construction through these methods, which has contributed to the state's severe housing shortage.

The rapid rise of these types of regulations—and the corresponding "not in my backyard," or NIMBY, sentiments among residents and landowners—has increased property values, added to the cost of housing, and made it harder for workers to chase opportunity by moving into fast-growing areas with high concentrations of open jobs. While beneficial for existing homeowners who see the value of their houses rise due to a lack of supply, such restrictive practices hurt the wider economy.

California local governments have very little power, because the state—and the voters via statewide ballot initiatives—have taken it away from them via Proposition 13 and other tax-limiting measures. Local Government's best tool for economic development—redevelopment—was taken away from them during the Great Recession.

Despite this, the state keeps adding to the growing list of unfunded mandates placed on local jurisdictions. Most famously in the past decade, the state addressed prison overcrowding by pushing offenders to local jails. The results of the emptying of the prisons—and "realignment" of responsibility onto local governments—can be seen in the explosion of homeless Californians on our streets.

Even worse, under the state's tax and budget system, housing rarely benefits municipalities as it commands high costs for the provision of municipal services but produces little in the way of sales tax revenues. Many cities with an overabundance of housing—most notably, San Jose—are desperate for industrial, commercial and retail development that produces more tax dollars.

While more than 90 percent of the state's 539 cities and counties comply with the state housing supply law, known formally as the "housing element" (Fowler et al., 2019). The housing element law requires cities and counties to zone land for new development sufficient to accommodate new residents (no requirement to facilitate construction). Nevertheless, many cities and counties have exacerbated the housing shortage by creating barriers to new housing construction and now are being threatened by lawsuits by the state for not meeting the housing element.

State law provides additional powers and duties for cities and counties regarding land use. The Planning and Zoning Law requires every county and city to adopt a general plan that sets out planned uses for all the area covered by the plan. A general plan must include specified mandatory "elements," including a housing element that establishes the locations and densities of housing, among other requirements. Cities' and counties' major land use decisions—including most zoning ordinances and other aspects of development permitting—must be consistent with their general plans. The Planning and Zoning Law also establishes a planning agency in each city and county, which may be a separate planning commission, administrative body, or the legislative body of the city or county itself. Cities and counties must provide a path to appeal a decision to the planning commission and/or the city council or county board of supervisors.

State Government

The California Legislature has enacted a variety of statutes to facilitate and encourage the provision of housing, particularly affordable housing and housing to support individuals with disabilities or other needs. Among them is the Housing Accountability Act (HAA), enacted in 1982 in response to concerns over a growing rejection of housing development by local governments due to NIMBY sentiments among local residents. The HAA restricts a local agency's ability to disapprove, or require density reductions in, certain types of residential projects. The HAA limits the ability of local governments to reject or render infeasible housing developments based on their density without a thorough analysis of the economic, social and environmental effects of the action. Specifically, when a proposed development complies with objective general plan and zoning standards, including design review standards, a local agency that intends to disapprove the project, or approve it on the condition that it be developed at a lower density, must make written findings based on substantial evidence that the project would have a specific, adverse impact on the public health or safety and that there are no feasible methods to mitigate or avoid those impacts other than disapproval of the project.

In 2019, Governor Newsom signed his first budget with over $2 billion going to housing and homelessness causes, including $650 million in one-time funds for cities to spend on shelters, provide emergency rental assistance and support other homeless services. For context, if the $2 billion were to be spent solely on constructing housing units, 6,000 homes would be built.

Rent Control

With some renters citing significant increases in rents, many policymakers have pointed to rent stabilization or "rent control" policies, along with tenant protection and relocation assistance, to provide renters with greater stability and reassurance of their housing needs.

In 2018, California voters issued their mandate to reject Proposition 10 that sought to lift restrictions on local governments by imposing rent control ordinances (protections afforded by Costa Hawkins Act of 1995). Independent academic experts agree, and as evidenced by cities who have adopted rent stabilization policies, rent control significantly impedes construction of and investment in rental housing, exacerbates the housing crisis, making it significantly harder for middle class families to afford a place to live.

In 2019, despite the voters rejecting Prop 10 the year prior, the governor called for and the Legislature passed a "rent cap" measure blended with various tenant protections which was modeled after what Oregon had passed earlier the same year.

Conclusion

California needs both public and private investment, as well as land use solutions to address critical housing challenges. Funding programs alone cannot address California's housing needs and land use policy changes, such as those discussed above, are now more critical today than ever before. However, even with drastic changes in land use policy to increase supply, the needs of certain populations cannot be met by the private market alone.

Policymakers might wish to consider adopting a set of state and local policies to ignite and encourage new development and construction of multi-family, while providing means-tested subsidies targeted towards those units dedicate towards lower-income housing, such proposals include:

- Adopt a sliding fee scale structure based on the ratio of units to proposed for Area Market Income (AMI) that fall below 50%;
- Temporarily waive property tax assessments for newly constructed workforce housing projects that are built and house a percentage of tenants who qualify below 50% AMI;
- Eliminate inclusionary zoning in lieu-fee requirements to encourage economic investment and allow for a wider range of housing types to be considered;
- Adopt a transit-oriented community loan program that aligns local affordable housing development programs to maximize matching funds from state housing programs;
- Provide expedited permitting (to allow construction to being immediately) at no cost to the applicant when the number of units in a proposed project exceeds specific percentages for very-low income and low-income units; and
- Including a pre-zoning and pre-entitlement program if a project meets density and design guidelines, is located within a disadvantaged community and is within ½ mile of transit. Projects would be eligible for streamlined permitting, long-term fee deferrals for affordable housing development City-wide, fee reductions and density bonuses.

Building new housing is the only way to solve California's housing crisis. In order to build this needed housing, politicians must have the courage and political will to ensure a statutory and regulatory environment that not only allows predictability, but also must ignite and incentivize private investment in the construction of affordable housing.

REFERENCES

Addressing a Variety of Housing Challenges-California Department of Housing and Community Development. http://www.hcd.ca.gov/policy-research/housing-challenges.shtml.

Bureau of the Census. Social and Economic Statistics Administration, U.S. Department of Commerce; Housing Characteristics for States, Cities, and Counties, August 1972.

Carlisle, Patrick. "Housing Affordability in the San Francisco Bay Area." *Compass*, 2019. Retrieved from: https://www.bayareamarketreports.com/trend/bay-area-housing-affordability.

Elka, Torpey. "Careers in construction: Building opportunity," Career Outlook, U.S. Bureau of Labor Statistics, August 2018.

Fowler, Adam, Hoyu Chong, Stephanie Leonard, Marcia Perry, Collen Kredell, and Noel Perry. Next 10 & Beacon Economics: Missing the Mark: Examining the Shortcomings of California's Housing Goals, 2019. Retrieved from: https://www.next10.org/sites/default/files/california-housing-goals-2019-3.pdf.

Kim, Jin-Lee, Martin Greene, and Sunkuk Kim. *Journal of Construction Engineering and Management.* Cost Comparative Analysis of a New Green Building Code for Residential Project Development | Journal of Construction Engineering and Management. Vol. 140, No. 5, 2014. Retrieved from: https://ascelibrary.org/doi/full/10.1061/(ASCE)CO.1943-7862.0000833.

Planning and Conservation League. A letter to the Members of the Legislature and Governor Newsom, 2019. Retrieved from: https://www.pcl.org/media/prior-p/Pro-CEQA-letter-to-legislature-and-governor-April-2019-3.pdf.

Taylor, Mac. California's High Housing Costs: Causes and Consequences, Legislative Analyst Office, March 2015.

White, Jeremy B., et al. "NEWSOM Dishes on HOUSING, RENT CONTROL—State Senate GOP Picks GROVE—CENSUS Decision Praised—KHANNA in Dem Tech Dispute—BREED's New Homelessness Push." *Politico*, 16 Jan. 2019. Retrieved from: https://www.politico.com/newsletters/california-playbook/2019/01/16/newsom-dishes-on-housing-and-rent-control-census-decision-praised-khanna-in-dem-tech-dispute-breeds-new-homelessness-push-377275.

21. California's Housing Future*

Challenges and Opportunities

CALIFORNIA DEPARTMENT OF HOUSING
AND COMMUNITY DEVELOPMENT

Home is the foundation for life. It's where we raise families, feel safe and secure, rest and recharge. Our options for where we live have far-reaching impacts in our lives—from our job opportunities to our physical and mental health, from our children's success in school to our environmental footprint.

With California's desirable climate, diverse economy, and many of the nation's top colleges, the State continues to experience strong housing demand; however, housing construction is constrained by regulatory barriers, high costs, and fewer public resources.

Some of the housing challenges facing California include:

- **Not enough housing being built:** During the last ten years, housing production averaged fewer than 80,000 new homes each year, and ongoing production continues to fall far below the projected need of 180,000 additional homes annually.
- **Increased inequality and lack of opportunities:** Lack of supply and rising costs are compounding growing inequality and limiting advancement opportunities for younger Californians. Without intervention, much of the new housing growth is expected to be focused in areas where fewer jobs are available to the families that live there.
- **Too much of people's incomes going toward rent:** The majority of Californian renters—more than 3 million households—pay more than 30 percent of their income toward rent, and nearly one-third—more than 1.5 million households—pay more than 50 percent of their income toward rent.
- **Fewer people becoming homeowners:** Overall homeownership rates are at their lowest since the 1940s.
- **Disproportionate number of Californians experiencing homelessness:** California is home to 12 percent of the nation's population, but a disproportionate 22 percent of the nation's homeless population.
- **Many people facing multiple, seemingly insurmountable barriers—beyond**

*Public document originally published as California Department of Housing and Community Development, "California's Housing Future: Challenges and Opportunities," http://www.hcd.ca.gov/policy-research/specific-policy-areas/index.shtml (2019).

just cost—in trying to find an affordable place to live: For California's vulnerable populations, discrimination and inadequate accommodations for people with disabilities are worsening housing cost and affordability challenges.

While the state's housing challenges appear overwhelming, California's housing crisis is a solvable issue. With focus and continued support, California can begin to reverse the course.

Challenges

California's housing future includes five key challenges regarding housing affordability:

1. Housing supply continues to not keep pace with demand, and the existing system of land-use planning and regulation creates barriers to development.
2. The highest housing growth is expected in communities with environmental and socio-economic disparities.
3. Unstable funding for affordable home development is hindering California's ability to meet California's housing demand, particularly for lower-income households.
4. People experiencing homelessness and other vulnerable populations face additional barriers to obtaining housing.
5. High housing costs have far-reaching policy impacts on the quality of life in California, including health, transportation, education, the environment, and the economy.

Options for Addressing Housing Challenges

Options for advancing the discussion about how to address the cost of housing fall into three broad categories, with specific potential actions falling under each:

1. Reforming land use policies to advance affordability, sustainability, equity.
2. Addressing housing and access needs for vulnerable populations through greater inter-agency coordination, program design, and evaluation.
3. Investing in affordable home development and rehabilitation, rental and homeownership assistance, and community development.

Specific Policy Areas

The California Department of Housing and Community Development's (HCD's) policy work is built on the notion that housing is the foundation for life and opportunity. Housing affordability and homelessness have far-reaching impacts that affect other important issues facing Californians, including health, education, transportation, economic well-being, and climate change.

- Housing and Health
- Housing and Education

- Housing and Transportation
- Housing and Economic Well-Being
- Housing and Climate Change

Housing programs (administered by HCD and other California departments and agencies) are increasingly viewed as a platform to achieve multiple policy goals; for example, the Veterans Housing and Homelessness Prevention program connects the needs of veterans and people experiencing homelessness. Providing homes and supportive services for people who experienced homelessness has been shown to improve health outcomes while also reducing local and state healthcare spending.

Another example is the Affordable Housing and Sustainable Communities program, which connects housing with environmental and transportation goals. Increased collaborations across these issues to share knowledge and leverage resources can improve housing programs while addressing multiple state policy objectives.

Focusing on People, Place, and Funding

Much of HCD's policy work focuses on people, place, and funding.

People

Addressing housing and access needs for vulnerable populations through thoughtful coordination, housing program design and evaluation

While millions of Californians struggle to find an affordable place to live, HCD's policy work pays particular attention to specific populations that face additional challenges in finding affordable homes, including:

- People experiencing homelessness
- Veterans
- Native American Tribes
- Farmworkers
- People with disabilities

Related policy issues include:

- Fair Housing
- Accessibility and Universal Design

Place

Strengthening land-use policies to advance affordability, sustainability and equity

Land-use policies and planning are more than just tools to increase housing affordability. These processes also drive the type and location of housing, which can translate into the ability for families to access neighborhoods of opportunity, where children can attend higher-performing schools, where there is a greater availability of jobs that afford entry to the middle-class, and where people have convenient access to transit and services.

As California prioritizes equity and reducing greenhouse gases, the focus has turned to more-compact development that reduces sprawl (and many of its negative environmental and health consequences); however, targeting development to specific areas can put pressure on limited land and result in higher costs for a variety of reasons (infrastructure limitations, demand for limited land, etc.). The true costs of sprawl are much higher when taking into account health impacts, environmental damage, and lost productivity, but these costs are often "hidden" from housing prices.

Accessory Dwelling Units

HCD provides technical guidance to cities with sample ordinances and other resources and guidance.

Funding

Effectively administering public funds (federal and state) in affordable-home development and rehabilitation, rental and homeownership assistance, and community development.

California needs both public and private investment, as well as land use solutions to address critical housing challenges and ensure access to jobs in neighborhoods of opportunity for those living here today and the generations to follow. Land-use regulations can be modified to increase housing supply; encourage development of more affordable housing; and prime the housing market to build a variety of housing types located near jobs, transportation, high-performing schools, hospitals, and other services.

However, even with drastic changes in land-use policy to increase supply, a large number of Californians will always remain priced out of both the ownership and rental housing market. Public investment in housing programs will remain necessary to meet the needs of those who struggle the most to keep roofs over their heads.

HCD administers both federal and state housing funds through its grants and funding programs.

22. California's Housing First Policy*

CALIFORNIA DEPARTMENT OF HOUSING
AND COMMUNITY DEVELOPMENT

People Experiencing Homelessness

On a single night in 2016, more than 118,000 people experienced homelessness in California—22 percent of the entire nation's homeless population. California also has the highest number of unaccompanied youth, veterans and chronically homeless in the United States, with nearly one-third of the nation's youth, nearly one-fourth of the nation's homeless veterans, and more than one-third of the nation's chronically homeless residents. Most of California's homeless population resides in major metropolitan areas; however, homelessness impacts communities of all sizes and people experience homelessness throughout all regions of the state.

The availability of affordable homes is an important part of addressing California's housing needs, but many households bear additional challenges. For example, a person exiting homelessness may not have the credit or rental history required to rent an apartment, even if they have financial assistance, or they may need a variety of services to help them transition and stabilize.

Even with federal Housing Choice Vouchers that assist with rent, many households are still unable to find affordable homes. In many high-cost markets, the amount of rent a federal Housing Choice Vouchers will cover is capped based on the Federal Housing and Urban Development (HUD) Fair Market Rent, which can fall significantly below the market rent. This, combined with too few available rentals and landlords who are unwilling to accept vouchers at all, is exacerbating the problem.

In addition to policy work on homelessness, HCD administers the following programs:

- Emergency Solutions Grant program
- Supportive Housing Multifamily Housing program
- Veterans Housing and Homelessness Prevention program
- No Place Like Home
- Homeless Youth Multifamily Housing program

Following two-and-a half years of work, in 2016, HCD released a redesigned state Emergency Solutions Grant program (ESG). The updated program better aligns with the

*Public document originally published as California Department of Housing and Community Development, "California's Housing First Policy" http://www.hcd.ca.gov/policy-research/specific-policy-areas/homelessness. shtml#.

federal Homeless Emergency Assistance and Transition to Housing Act and increases coordination of state investment, federal investment, and local systems that address homelessness. HCD shared the redesigned program's changes via roundtable meetings with regional bodies that coordinate homelessness efforts (continuums of care) and webinars. HCD prepared the 2016 ESG application and rating tool for scoring the applications. In May 2016, HCD released an ESG NOFA for approximately $20 million, and subsequently, made awards in September 2016 (FY 2016–17).

The Business, Consumer Services and Housing Agency assists and educates consumers regarding the licensing, regulation, and enforcement of professionals and businesses in California.

The Governor's Reorganization Plan No. 2 of 2012 provided for the consolidation of entities that license industries, business activities, and professionals. This consolidation will improve service, consistency and efficiency by facilitating shared administrative functions and expertise in areas such as automated systems, investigative practices, and licensing and legal processes.

Mission of the Council

The Homeless Coordinating and Financing Council was created in 2017 to oversee the implementation of Housing First policies, guidelines, and regulations to reduce the prevalence and duration of homelessness in California. The Council's mission is to develop policies, identify resources, benefits, and services to prevent and work toward ending homelessness in California.

By July 1, 2019, agencies and departments administering State programs in existence prior to July 1, 2017, shall collaborate with the Council to revise or adopt guidelines and regulations that incorporate the core components of Housing First if the existing guidelines and regulations do not already incorporate the core components of Housing First.

Homeless Coordinating and Financing Council Members

The Council consists of up to nineteen members, representing ten state agency heads or their designees, seven members appointed by the Governor representing statewide organizations and homeless advocacy groups, one stakeholder appointed by the Senate Committee on Rules, and one stakeholder appointed by Speaker of the Assembly.

The Council may also invite stakeholders, individuals who have experienced homelessness, members of philanthropic communities, and experts to participate in meetings, or provide information to the Council as needed.

California's Housing First Policy?

Housing First is an approach to serving people experiencing homelessness that recognizes a homeless person must first be able to access a decent, safe place to live, that does not limit length of stay (permanent housing), before stabilizing, improving health, reducing harmful behaviors, or increasing income. Under the Housing First approach, anyone experiencing homelessness should be connected to a permanent home as quickly as possible, and programs should remove barriers to accessing the housing, like requirements for sobriety or absence of criminal history. It is based on the "hierarchy of need": people must access basic necessities—like a safe place to live and food to eat—before being able to achieve quality of life or pursue personal goals. Finally, Housing First values choice not only in where to live, but whether to participate in services. For this reason, tenants are not required to participate in services to access or retain housing.

What Type of Housing Is Considered Housing First?

Programs using Housing First generally fall into two categories:

- Supportive housing, which is an apartment made affordable through long-term rental assistance, paired with intensive services promoting housing stability.
- Rapid re-housing, which connects a family or individual to an apartment affordable through short- to medium-term rental assistance, along with moderate services designed to allow that household to increase their income sufficiently to be able to afford the apartment over the long term.

While Housing First recognizes housing is a necessary precursor to treatment, Housing First does not mean "housing only." On the contrary, Housing First acknowledges social services and care coordination are necessary elements of housing stability and quality of life.

Core Components of Housing First Under California Law

In 2016, the California Legislature passed Senate Bill 1380 (Mitchell). It required all housing programs to adopt the Housing First model.[1] The legislation defined Housing First with these "core components":

- Tenant screening and selection practices promote accepting applicants regardless of their sobriety or use of substances, completion of treatment, or participation in services.
- Applicants are not rejected on the basis of poor credit or financial history, poor or lack of rental history, criminal convictions unrelated to tenancy, or behaviors that indicate a lack of "housing readiness."

Housing providers accept referrals directly from shelters, street outreach, drop-in centers, and other parts of crisis response systems frequented by vulnerable people experiencing homelessness.

- Supportive services emphasize engagement and problem solving over therapeutic goals and service plans that are highly tenant-driven without predetermined goals.
- Participation in services or program compliance is not a condition of housing tenancy.
- Tenants have a lease and all the rights and responsibilities of tenancy.
- The use of alcohol or drugs in and of itself, without other lease violations, is not a reason for eviction.

- Funding promotes tenant selection plans for supportive housing that prioritize eligible tenants based on criteria other than "first-come-first-served," including, but not limited to, the duration or chronicity of homelessness, vulnerability to early mortality, or high utilization of crisis services.
- Case managers and service coordinators are trained in and actively employ evidence-based practices for engagement, including motivational interviewing and client-centered counseling.
- Services are informed by a harm-reduction philosophy that recognizes drug and alcohol use and addiction as a part of tenants' lives, where tenants are engaged in nonjudgmental communication regarding drug and alcohol use, and where tenants are offered education regarding how to avoid risky behaviors and engage in safer practices, as well as connected to evidence-based treatment if the tenant so chooses.
- The project and specific apartment may include special physical features that accommodate disabilities, reduce harm, and promote health and community and independence among tenants.

EVIDENCE BASIS

The federal and State government recognize Housing First as an evidence-based practice. In fact, a settled and growing body of evidence demonstrates—

- Tenants accessing Housing First programs are able to move into housing faster than programs offering a more traditional approach.[2]
- Tenants using Housing First programs stay housed longer and more stable than other programs.[3]
- Over 90% of tenants accessing Housing First programs are able to retain housing stability.[4]
- In general, tenants using Housing First programs access services more often, have a greater sense of choice and autonomy, and are far less costly to public systems than tenants of other programs.[5]

NOTES

1. Codified as California Welfare & Institutions Code § 8255.

2. Gulcur, L., Stefancic, A., Shinn, M., Tsemberis, S., & Fishcer, S. Housing, Hospitalization, and Cost Outcomes for Homeless Individuals with Psychiatric Disabilities Participating in Continuum of Care and Housing First programs. 2003.

3. Tsemberis, S. & Eisenberg, R. Pathways to Housing: Supported Housing for Street-Dwelling Homeless Individuals with Psychiatric Disabilities. 2000.

4. Montgomery, A.E., Hill, L., Kane, V., & Culhane, D. Housing Chronically Homeless Veterans: Evaluating the Efficacy of a Housing First Approach to HUD-VASH. 2013.

5. Tsemberis, S., Gulcur, L., & Nakae, M. Housing First, Consumer Choice, and Harm Reduction for Homeless Individuals with a Dual Diagnosis. 2004; Perlman, J. & Parvensky, J. Denver Housing First Collaborative: Cost Benefit Analysis and Program Outcomes Report. 2006.

23. Rhode Island First State to Pass Homeless Bill of Rights*

Darby Penney

In 2012, Rhode Island became the first U.S. state to pass a Homeless Bill of Rights (the text follows), thanks to the leadership of the Rhode Island Homeless Advocacy Project (RIHAP). RIHAP is an organization led by people who have experienced homelessness or are currently experiencing homelessness. Founded by the late John Joyce, who drafted the original bill, RIHAP worked in collaboration with allies in the state legislature, the Rhode Island Coalition for the Homeless (RICH), the state chapter of the American Civil Liberties Union (ACLU), the Interfaith Coalition to Reduce Poverty, and other community organizations to pass the legislation on June 20, 2012. The bill prohibits discrimination based on housing status, stating, "No person's rights, privileges, or access to public services may be denied or abridged solely because he or she is homeless. Such a person shall be granted the same rights and privileges as any other resident of this state."

Promoting the Bill

While the language may sound deceptively simple, the ramifications are far-reaching, according to Jim Ryczek, executive director of RICH. "The bill is both an educational tool to raise awareness of the ways in which people experiencing homelessness have been discriminated against and a legal tool to enforce people's rights," he said. In the tradition of civil rights legislation generally, the goal of the bill was to stop discriminatory practices against a vulnerable group of people by ending discriminatory behavior. The intent of the legislation was not to single out any specific group engaging in discriminatory practices, but rather to provide comprehensive protections against discrimination for people and families experiencing homelessness within all areas of the public sector.

The campaign for passage of the bill also served as a way to educate legislators and the public about the reality of life for people experiencing homelessness. "Working in partnership with RIHAP members, we developed flyers and talking points for advocates to use in lobbying their legislators and speaking to the press," Ryczek said. "We focused on explaining that people were asking for equal rights, not 'special rights.' In our lobbying

*Public document originally published as Darby Penney, "Rhode Island First State to Pass Homeless Bill of Rights," https://www.samhsa.gov/homelessness-programs-resources/hpr-resources/rhode-island-homeless-bill-rights (August 12, 2019).

and conversations with the media, we highlighted the experiences of discrimination faced by individuals in our community. We all learned much more about what it feels like to experience homelessness in Rhode Island," Ryczek explained. "Much of that knowledge is uncomfortable to sit with and unsavory to acknowledge."

Efforts in Other States

Other jurisdictions have since passed homeless bills of rights, including the states of Connecticut and Illinois in 2013. Illinois' Bill of Rights for the Homeless contains language similar to Rhode Island's, focusing on ensuring that people who are homeless have the same rights and privileges as all other residents, including the right to use public spaces such as sidewalks, parks, and transportation; equal treatment by government agencies, including the right to vote; and a right to confidentiality and reasonable expectation of personal property. Connecticut's law is similar, but also explicitly prohibits "harassment or intimidation from law enforcement officers."

According to the National Coalition for the Homeless (NCH), legislation establishing homeless bills of rights is currently being considered in California, Delaware, Minnesota, Missouri, Oregon, Puerto Rico, Tennessee, and Vermont, as well as in the cities of Baltimore, Maryland, and Madison, Wisconsin. The need for such protective legislation is made more urgent by legislation in localities across the country that effectively criminalize people who are experiencing homelessness by targeting them for their lack of housing and not for their behavior, according to NCH. This includes laws that prohibit feeding people in public places; sleeping in cars, tents, or public spaces; or panhandling.

In Rhode Island, one of the arguments made by opponents of the Homeless Bill of Rights was that it would unleash a flood of lawsuits. This has not happened, according to Jim Ryczek of RICH. In fact, not a single action has been brought under the provisions of the law to date, and RICH encourages Rhode Islanders who feel they have been discriminated against to consider filing a claim. Ryczek offers the following advice to advocates in other jurisdictions: "The laws are important because we currently have no other recourse in our fight to stop discrimination against people experiencing homelessness. Even if few lawsuits are brought, it is vital that these laws are in place to keep the issue visible."

State of Rhode Island
Title 34 Property
CHAPTER 34–37.1
Homeless Bill of Rights

§ 34–37.1–1. Short title.

This chapter shall be known and may be cited as the "Homeless Bill of Rights." History of Section.
(P.L. 2012, ch. 316, § 1; P.L. 2012, ch. 356, § 1.)

§ 34–37.1–2. Legislative intent.

(1) At the present time, many persons have been rendered homeless as a result of economic hardship, a severe shortage of safe, affordable housing, and a shrinking social safety net.

(2) Article 1, Section 2 of the Rhode Island State Constitution states in part, that "All free governments are instituted for the protection, safety, and happiness of the people. All

laws, therefore, should be made for the good of the whole; and the burdens of the state ought to be fairly distributed among its citizens. No person shall be deprived of life, liberty or property without due process of law, nor shall any person be denied equal protection of the laws."

(3) Concordant with this fundamental belief, no person should suffer unnecessarily or be subject to unfair discrimination based on his or her homeless status. It is the intent of this chapter to ameliorate the adverse effects visited upon individuals and our communities when the state's residents lack a home.

History of Section.

(P.L. 2012, ch. 316, § 1; P.L. 2012, ch. 356, § 1.)

§ 34–37.1–3. Bill of Rights.

No person's rights, privileges, or access to public services may be denied or abridged solely because he or she is homeless. Such a person shall be granted the same rights and privileges as any other resident of this state. A person experiencing homelessness:

1. Has the right to use and move freely in public spaces, including, but not limited to, public sidewalks, public parks, public transportation and public buildings, in the same manner as any other person, and without discrimination on the basis of his or her housing status;

2. Has the right to equal treatment by all state and municipal agencies, without discrimination on the basis of housing status;

3. Has the right not to face discrimination while seeking or maintaining employment due to his or her lack of permanent mailing address, or his or her mailing address being that of a shelter or social service provider;

4. Has the right to emergency medical care free from discrimination based on his or her housing status;

5. Has the right to vote, register to vote, and receive documentation necessary to prove identity for voting without discrimination due to his or her housing status;

6. Has the right to protection from disclosure of his or her records and information provided to homeless shelters and service providers to state, municipal and private entities without appropriate legal authority; and the right to confidentiality of personal records and information in accordance with all limitations on disclosure established by the Federal Homeless Management Information Systems, the Federal Health Insurance Portability and Accountability Act, and the Federal Violence Against Women Act; and

7. Has the right to a reasonable expectation of privacy in his or her personal property to the same extent as personal property in a permanent residence.

History of Section.

(P.L. 2012, ch. 316, § 1; P.L. 2012, ch. 356, § 1.)

§ 34–37.1–4. Damages and attorneys' fees.

In any civil action alleging a violation of this chapter, the court may award appropriate injunctive and declaratory relief, actual damages, and reasonable attorneys' fees and costs to a prevailing plaintiff.

History of Section.

(P.L. 2012, ch. 316, § 1; P.L. 2012, ch. 356, § 1.)

§ 34–37.1–5. Definitions.

For purposes of this chapter, "housing status" shall have the same meaning as that contained in § 34–37–3.

History of Section.

(P.L. 2012, ch. 316, § 1; P.L. 2012, ch. 356, § 1.)

§ 34–37.1–6. Homeless persons with service animals—Homeless shelters.

Nothing in this chapter shall be construed to prohibit persons from entering a homeless shelter while in possession of a service animal as defined in the "Americans with Disabilities Act" (28 C.F.R. § 35.136) and the state and federal "fair housing acts."

History of Section.

(P.L. 2018, ch. 214, § 1; P.L. 2018, ch. 297, § 1.)

• *C. Federal* •

24. HUD Reports Homelessness Unchanged in U.S. in 2018*

U.S. DEPARTMENT OF HOUSING AND URBAN DEVELOPMENT

Homelessness in the U.S. remained largely unchanged in 2018, according to the latest national estimate by the U.S. Department of Housing and Urban Development (HUD). HUD's 2018 Annual Homeless Assessment Report to Congress found that 552,830 persons experienced homelessness on a single night in 2018, an increase of 0.3 percent since 2017. Meanwhile, homelessness among veterans fell 5.4 percent and homelessness experienced by families with children declined 2.7 percent nationwide since 2017.

As in previous years, there is significant local variation in the data reported from different parts of the country. Thirty-one (31) states and the District of Columbia reported decreases in homelessness between 2017 and 2018 while 19 states reported increases in the number of persons experiencing homelessness.

"Our state and local partners are increasingly focused on finding lasting solutions to homelessness even as they struggle against the headwinds of rising rents," said HUD Secretary Ben Carson. "Much progress is being made and much work remains to be done but I have great hope that communities all across our nation are intent on preventing and ending homelessness."

"Communities across the country are getting better and better at making sure that people exit homelessness quickly through Housing First approaches," said Matthew Doherty, executive director of the U.S. Interagency Council on Homelessness. "We know, however, that a lack of housing that people can afford is the fundamental obstacle to making further progress in many communities."

HUD's national estimate is based upon data reported by approximately 3,000 cities and counties across the nation. Every year on a single night in January, planning agencies called Continuums of Care (CoCs) along with tens of thousands of volunteers, seek to identify the number of individuals and families living in emergency shelters, transitional housing programs, and in unsheltered settings. These one-night "snapshot" counts, as well as full-year counts and data from other sources (U.S. Housing Survey, Department of

---

*Public document originally published as U.S. Department of Housing and Urban Development, "HUD Reports Homelessness Unchanged in U.S. in 2018 with Notable Declines Among Veterans and Families with Children," https://www.hudexchange.info/news/hud-reports-homelessness-unchanged-in-u-s-in-2018-with-notable-declines-among-veterans-and-families-with-children/ (December 17, 2018).

Education), are crucial in understanding the scope of homelessness and measuring progress toward reducing it.

Key Findings of HUD's 2018 Annual Homeless Assessment Report

On a single night in January 2018, state and local CoCs reported:

- 552,830 people were homeless representing an overall 0.3 percent increase from 2017 but a 13.2 percent decrease since 2010. This small increase is due to two factors: a 2.3 percent increase of unsheltered homelessness and nearly 4,000 persons staying in emergency shelters set up in areas impacted by Hurricanes Harvey, Irma, Maria, and Nate; western wildfires; and other storms and events.
- Most homeless persons (358,363) were located in emergency shelters or transitional housing programs while 194,467 persons were unsheltered.
- The number of families with children experiencing homelessness declined 2.7 percent since 2017 and 29 percent since 2010.
- On a single night in January 2018, 37,878 veterans experienced homelessness, a decline of 5.4 percent (or 2,142 persons) since January 2017. The number of female veterans dropped nearly 10 percent since 2017. Overall, Veteran homelessness in the U.S. declined by 49 percent since 2010.
- 88,640 individuals experienced long-term homelessness in 2018, an increase of 2.2 percent over 2017 levels though chronic homelessness declined by 16.4 percent (or 17,422 persons) since 2010.
- The number of unaccompanied homeless youth and children in 2018 is estimated to be 36,361, a 5.1 percent decline since 2017. In 2017, HUD and local communities launched a more intense effort to more accurately account for this important, difficult-to-count population. HUD is treating 2017 as a baseline year for purposes of tracking progress toward reducing youth homelessness.

Family Homelessness

HUD's latest national estimate notes a continuing decline in family homelessness in the U.S. In January of 2018, there were 56,342 family households with children experiencing homelessness, a 29 percent decline since 2010. These declines are largely a consequence of HUD's policy shift from supporting higher cost transitional housing to rapid rehousing programs across the country. Following HUD's guidance and best practices, local planners are increasingly using rapid rehousing to move families into permanent housing more quickly and at lower cost. Communities are also implementing more prevention activities to help families avoid needing shelter as well as more robust coordinated entry efforts. Taken together, these Housing First models have proven to be a more effective and efficient response to help families experiencing temporary crisis as well as those enduring the most chronic forms of homelessness.

Veteran Homelessness

Veteran homelessness in the U.S. is nearly half of what was reported in 2010. In 2017 alone, the number of homeless veterans declined by 5.4 percent and homelessness experienced by female veterans dropped by nearly 10 percent. These declines are the result of intense planning and targeted interventions, including the close collaboration between HUD and the U.S. Department of Veterans Affairs (VA). Both agencies jointly administer the HUD-VA Supportive Housing (HUD-VASH) Program, which combines permanent HUD rental assistance with case management and clinical services provided by the VA. In 2018, more than 4,400 veterans, many experiencing chronic forms of homelessness, found permanent housing and critically needed support services through the HUD-VASH program. An additional 50,000 veterans found permanent housing and supportive services through the VA's continuum of homeless programs.

Chronic Homelessness

Long-term or chronic homelessness among individuals with disabilities grew by 2.2 percent since 2017 though is 16.4 percent below the levels reported in 2010. This longer trend is due in part to a concerted effort to make more permanent supportive housing opportunities more available for people with disabling health conditions who otherwise continually cycle through local shelters or the streets. Research demonstrates that for those experiencing chronic homelessness, providing permanent housing, coupled with appropriate low-barrier supportive services, is the most effective solution for ending homelessness. This Housing First approach also saves the taxpayers considerable money by interrupting a costly cycle of emergency room and hospital, detox, and even jail visits.

HUD Programs

Continuum of Care (CoC) Program

The Continuum of Care (CoC) Program is designed to promote communitywide commitment to the goal of ending homelessness; provide funding for efforts by nonprofit providers, and State and local governments to quickly rehouse homeless individuals and families while minimizing the trauma and dislocation caused to homeless individuals, families, and communities by homelessness; promote access to and effect utilization of mainstream programs by homeless individuals and families; and optimize self-sufficiency among individuals and families experiencing homelessness.

Emergency Shelter Grants Program

The HEARTH Act revised the Emergency Shelter Grants Program to create the Emergency Solutions Grants (ESG) Program. The Emergency Shelter Grants provided funds under the first allocation of FY 2011 funds and earlier fiscal years. ESG recipients and subrecipients use Emergency Shelter Grants Program funds to rehabilitate and operate emergency shelters and transitional shelters, provide essential social services, and prevent homelessness.

Housing Opportunities for Persons with AIDS

The Housing Opportunities for Persons with AIDS (HOPWA) Program is the only Federal program dedicated to the housing needs of people living with HIV/AIDS. Under the HOPWA Program, HUD makes grants to local communities, States, and nonprofit organizations for projects that benefit low-income persons living with HIV/AIDS and their families.

Pay for Success (PFS) Permanent Supportive Housing (PSH) Demonstration

The Department of Justice (DOJ) and HUD are partnering to advance Pay for Success (PFS), a new, promising model for financing services that can attract additional, non-traditional sources of funding. The Consolidated Appropriations Act, 2014 (Pub. L. 113–76) and the Consolidated and Further Continuing Appropriations Act, 2015 (Pub. L. 113–235) authorized DOJ to make funds available for a PFS initiative implementing the PSH model for a population continuously cycling between the criminal justice system and homeless services. DOJ and HUD entered into an interagency agreement that designates HUD as the agency responsible for implementing the PFS Demonstration, and through this NOFA, HUD is making $8,679,000 available.

What is Pay for Success? PFS is an innovative financing model that leverages philanthropic and private dollars to provide assistance up front, with the government paying after they generate results. Unlike programs structured around processes rather than measurable results, PFS provides greater flexibility for state, local and tribal governments to implement evidence-based solutions, carefully test promising innovations, and scale programs that work.

Title V–Federal Surplus Property for Use to Assist the Homeless

Title V of the McKinney-Vento Homeless Assistance Act, Public Law 101–645 (42 U.S.C. 11411), enables eligible organizations to use unutilized, underutilized, excess, or surplus federal properties to assist persons experiencing homelessness.

Eligible applicants are states, local governments, and nonprofit organizations. Properties, including land and buildings, are made available strictly on an "as-is" basis. No funding is available under Title V. Leases are provided free of charge and range from 1 to 20 years, depending on availability. Successful applicants may use the Title V properties to provide shelter, services, storage, and other benefits to persons experiencing homelessness.

Each Friday, HUD publishes a Suitability Determination Listing on the HUD Exchange identifying available unutilized, underutilized, excess, and surplus properties.

Base Realignment and Closure Program

The Base Realignment and Closure Program (BRAC) is a community-based process that balances the need for economic and other redevelopment while addressing the needs of people experiencing homelessness at base closure and realignment sites. Under this program, HUD reviews base redevelopment plans and offers technical assistance to the communities in the vicinity of the military installation.

HUD Veterans Affairs Supportive Housing Program

An essential tool towards ending veteran homelessness, HUD-VASH is a joint program between HUD and the U.S. Department of Veterans Affairs (VA). HUD provides housing choice vouchers and VA provides case management and outreach. This program targets veterans who are currently homeless.

25. Ending Chronic Homelessness through Employment and Housing Projects*

U.S. DEPARTMENT OF LABOR

The U.S. Department of Labor (DOL) works to foster, promote, and develop the welfare of the wage earners, job seekers, and retirees of the United States; improve working conditions; advance opportunities for profitable employment; and assure work-related benefits and rights. The DOL's Office of Disability Employment Policy (ODEP) is the only non-regulatory federal agency that promotes policies and coordinates with employers and all levels of government to increase workplace success for people with disabilities.

ODEP was authorized by Congress in the Department of Labor's FY 2001 appropriation. Recognizing the need for a national policy to ensure that people with disabilities are fully integrated into the 21st-century workforce, the Secretary of Labor delegated authority and assigned responsibility to the Assistant Secretary for Disability Employment Policy. ODEP is a subcabinet level policy agency in the Department of Labor.

Mission: ODEP's mission is to develop and influence policies and practices that increase the number and quality of employment opportunities for people with disabilities.

To fulfill this mission, ODEP promotes the adoption and implementation of ODEP policy strategies and effective practices—meaning those that ODEP has developed and/or validated—that will impact the employment of people with disabilities. ODEP's approach is to drive systems and practice changes by disseminating ODEP policy strategies and effective practices, sharing information, and providing technical assistance to government agencies, service providers and non-governmental entities, as well as public and private employers. Through these activities, ODEP contributes to the achievement of: DOL's Strategic Goal 1: Support the ability of all Americans to find good jobs, and Strategic Objective 1.3: Develop evidence-based policies, practices, and tools to foster a more inclusive workforce to increase quality employment opportunities for individuals with disabilities.

Vision: A world in which people with disabilities have unlimited employment opportunities.

ODEP and its partners within DOL, the Veterans Employment and Training Service

---

*Public document originally published as U.S. Department of Labor, "Ending Chronic Homelessness through Employment and Housing Projects," https://www.dol.gov/odep/programs/homeless.html (2019).

(VETS) and the Employment and Training Administration (ETA), in cooperation with the Department of Housing and Urban Development (HUD), funded on September 29, 2003, for a potential five year effort, projects to increase and improve employment opportunities for chronically homeless individuals with disabilities through a local partnership with HUD housing providers. The goal of the DOL cooperative agreements is to enable persons who are chronically homeless to achieve employment and self-sufficiency, thereby preventing unnecessary institutional placements. The DOL awards to the communities listed below are supplemented by parallel HUD permanent housing grants. These demonstration grants will begin or expand the delivery and implementation of "customized employment" strategies for homeless individuals with disabilities so that they may live, work, and fully participate in their communities.

Chronic Homelessness Project Sites

Portland, Oregon

Worksystems, Inc. will organize a coalition of 17 local organizations, including faith-based organizations, from the housing, disability, employment, employer and veteran communities, to coordinate permanent housing services with customized employment services in an effort to end the cycle of chronic homelessness for individuals within the Portland community. The key operational component of this project will be the Community Services Team (CST), which will use a strength-based assessment and treatment plans and motivational interviewing to engage individuals in self-determined service planning. The CST will deliver a full array of services in a facilitative manner, eliminating obstacles. Customized employment strategies such as job carving, micro-enterprise development, individual development accounts (ITA's) and peer mentors will be the hallmarks of this effort.

Boston, Massachusetts

The Boston Private Industry Council will organize a coalition of local organizations from the housing, disability, employment, employer and veteran communities in a combined effort to coordinate permanent housing services with customized employment services so as to end the cycle of chronic homelessness for individuals within the Boston community. Through an extensive collaboration, the project will create a blend of housing and employment services that will be presented in a seamless and coordinated fashion, providing ease of access to consumers. The integration of housing and support services with customized employment services will help program participants to move more effectively towards self-sufficiency. The project will build a continuum of employment services. This effort will increase connections and capabilities of the One-Stop Career Centers and of other service systems to serve persons with disabilities who are chronically homeless.

San Francisco, California

Under the leadership of the Private Industry Council of San Francisco, Inc., this award will help the community implement the concept of offering "vocationalized" housing to a representative number of targeted individuals, in order to begin to create a culture of work with the hope of ending the cycle of chronic homelessness for individuals within the San Francisco community by offering new strategies for servicing this rapidly growing population. This effort will seek to better combine and coordinate the multiple services and agencies that deliver vocationalized housing in an effort to improve both the involvement of the area's workforce development system, including the area One-Stop Career Centers, and the employment options for the chronically homeless.

Indianapolis, Indiana

Under this award, the Indianapolis Private Industry Council, Inc. will create a new "System of Care" approach designed to combine and coordinate the various service delivery partners, including in the employment and housing areas, in a way which offers the consumer no wrong doors for entry into the system. This approach will also organize a process that includes housing.

26. Home, Together*

The Federal Strategic Plan to Prevent and End Homelessness

U.S. Interagency Council on Homelessness

The USICH

The U.S. Interagency Council on Homelessness (USICH) leads national efforts to prevent and end homelessness in America. We drive action among the 19 federal member agencies that comprise our Council and foster the efficient use of resources in support of best practices at every level of government and with the private sector.

USICH is statutorily charged with developing and regularly updating a national strategic plan to prevent and end homelessness. Home, Together is the strategic plan adopted by the Council for Fiscal Years 2018–2022.

It mandates USICH to work with its federal partners and the interagency working groups they manage to implement this Plan. USICH will lead and support federal activities aligned with the Plan's Objectives and Strategies, partner with states and communities to implement the most effective practices, and assess the Plan's impact to further strengthen our actions and outcomes.

Home. Because we know that the only true end to homelessness is a safe and stable place to call home.

Home enables our families, friends, and neighbors—indeed, everyone in our nation—to have a platform from which they can pursue economic opportunity. Having a home provides people with better chances for succeeding in school and advancing their careers. It also allows them to take care of their health, build strong families, and give back to their communities.

But far too many people experience homelessness in our country, limiting their ability to pursue these opportunities.

Together. Because the causes of homelessness are complex, and the solutions are going to take all of us working together, doing our parts, strengthening our communities.

Thriving communities need enough housing that is affordable and equitably available to people across a full range of incomes—from young adults just starting out to seniors who want to spend their remaining years feeling secure. Quality educational and career opportunities, child care, health care, substance abuse and mental health services,

---

*Public document originally published as U.S. Interagency Council on Homelessness, "Home, Together: The Federal Strategic Plan to Prevent and End Homelessness," https://www.usich.gov/home-together/.

and aging services can help individuals and families build strong social networks, pursue economic mobility, and strengthen their overall well-being. These services, and other federal, state, and local programs, must be well-coordinated among themselves, and with the business, philanthropic, and faith communities that can supplement and enhance them.

Together, We Are Making Progress

The problem of homelessness can seem daunting—it is estimated that on any given night more than 550,000 people are experiencing homelessness in America. The good news is that states and communities, with the support of the federal government and the private sector, are making progress, using best practices and building the coordinated responses that are necessary to reduce and ultimately end homelessness in America.

Driven by federal, state, and local actions, and by public and private partnerships, point-in-time data shows an estimated 13 percent fewer people were experiencing homelessness in 2017 compared to 2010, and there were 17 percent fewer people who were unsheltered, sleeping on our sidewalks, in our parks, and in other unsafe environments.

For some targeted groups, communities have made even greater progress. For example, since 2010, there are 46 percent fewer Veterans and 27 percent fewer families with children experiencing homelessness. And we've reduced chronic homelessness—homelessness among people with disabilities who have been without a home for long or repeated periods of time—by 18 percent.

In addition, since the release of federal criteria and benchmarks in 2015 to measure progress for ending homelessness among Veterans, more than 60 communities across more than 30 different states have effectively ended Veteran homelessness. And three communities have achieved the federal criteria and benchmarks for ending chronic homelessness.

These achievements show that ending homelessness is possible. And we know that it's possible in all kinds of places—big cities, suburbs, small towns, and across entire states.

Working Together Is What Works

We are making this progress because communities are focused more than ever on the ultimate solution to homelessness: Home. And they are doing this work by breaking down silos and working together in profoundly new ways. To help people find the stability of home, communities are embracing Housing First practices, through which people experiencing homelessness are connected to permanent housing swiftly and with few to no treatment preconditions, behavioral contingencies, or other barriers.

Communities are also developing coordinated homelessness service systems so that people who need help are identified quickly, their needs and strengths are assessed, and they can be matched to the appropriate local housing and services opportunities and social supports. Through housing interventions like supportive housing and rapid re-housing, individuals and families are connected to the tailored array of community services that can help them stay and succeed in their home and pursue economic advancement.

Our Path Home

While our progress is promising, we also know that we have much more work to do, and many more challenges that we must face together. Beyond the critical work to make sure there is enough housing for everyone, we must also focus more attention on preventing people from falling into homelessness in the first place and on diverting people from entering emergency shelter if they have other stable options available.

We also have an urgent need for strategies to address the immediate crisis of unsheltered homelessness—especially in communities with high-cost housing markets—and homelessness in rural communities, where housing and services are scarce. We must also address the racial inequities and other disparities in the risks for, and experiences of, homelessness. And we must be clear that exiting homelessness is not the end point for people, it is a starting place from which they can pursue employment, education, community involvement, and other goals.

These are difficult challenges, but momentum is on our side. We know where we are going and we know how we are going to get there: Home, Together.

Our Shared National Goals

Through the hard work of communities around the country, we now have proof of something that we didn't before—that ending homelessness is achievable. Home, Together builds upon what we have learned from states and communities over time, and lays out the strategies we know we must advance at the federal level in order to support and accelerate state and local progress.

Home, Together has one fundamental goal, a goal shared across federal, state, and local partners: to end homelessness in America.

But the people who experience homelessness are diverse—in their experiences, in their challenges, in their household compositions, in their ages, in many other ways—and we must tailor and target our strategies and actions to reflect that diversity.

Therefore, the Plan sets important population-specific goals as well:

- To end homelessness among veterans
- To end chronic homelessness among people with disabilities
- To end homelessness among families with children
- To end homelessness among unaccompanied youth
- To end homelessness among all other individuals

Achieving these shared goals is not possible through federal action alone—it requires strategic focus, effort, and investments from both the public and the private sectors and across all levels of government.

Achieving these goals as a nation means achieving these goals in all our communities, communities that are also diverse—in their demographics, in their needs, in their geographic characteristics, in their progress to date, in their resources, in their infrastructure, in their housing markets, and in many other ways. Some communities have already succeeded at achieving some of these sub-goals, others are on the cusp of major successes, and many are striving hard to make progress but face very significant challenges.

Therefore, the Plan does not set uniform timeframes. Rather, federal partners will continue to work with communities, and provide tools and information, that will enable them to set their own ambitious goals, tailored to their local conditions, and grounded in their local data.

With a few exceptions, the Objectives and Strategies outlined in this Plan are not population-specific. In the implementation of the Plan, USICH will work with its federal partners, through established inter-agency working group structures, to plan, implement, and assess the impact of specific activities to drive progress toward the population-specific sub-goals. Those activities will also be attentive to the specific needs of other subpopulations of people, such as older adults, people with disabilities, or people with substance use disorders, including opioid use disorders, who are represented across the population goals identified above.

Objectives

To end homelessness, every community needs to be able to implement a systemic response that ensures homelessness is prevented whenever possible or, if it can't be prevented, it is a **rare, brief, and one-time experience**. And that systemic response must endure for the long term. The plan's objectives are:

1. Ensure Homelessness is a Rare Experience

- Objective 1.1: Collaboratively Build Lasting Systems That End Homelessness
- Objective 1.2: Increase Capacity and Strengthen Practices to Prevent Housing Crises and Homelessness

2. Ensure Homelessness is a Brief Experience

- Objective 2.1: Identify and Engage All People Experiencing Homelessness
- Objective 2.2: Provide Immediate Access to Low-Barrier Emergency Shelter or other Temporary Accommodations to All Who Need It
- Objective 2.3: Implement Coordinated Entry to Standardize Assessment and Prioritization Processes and Streamline Connections to Housing and Services
- Objective 2.4: Assist People to Move Swiftly into Permanent Housing with Appropriate and Person-Centered Services

3. Ensure Homelessness is a One-Time Experience

- Objective 3.1: Prevent Returns to Homelessness through Connections to Adequate Services and Opportunities

4. Sustain an End to Homelessness

- Objective 4.1: Sustain Practices and Systems at a Scale Necessary to Respond to Future Needs

Defining Success

Achieving these goals is grounded in a shared vision of what it means to end homelessness: that every community must have a systemic response in place that ensures homelessness is prevented whenever possible, or if it can't be prevented, it is a rare, brief, and one-time experience. That means that every community must have the capacity to:

- Quickly identify and engage people at risk of and experiencing homelessness.
- Intervene to prevent people from losing their housing and divert people from entering the homelessness services system.
- Provide people with immediate access to shelter and crisis services without barriers to entry if homelessness does occur.
- Quickly connect people experiencing homelessness to housing assistance and services tailored to their unique needs and strengths to help them achieve and maintain stable housing.

To help communities to assess their progress toward achieving this vision, USICH and our federal partners have developed qualitative criteria and quantitative benchmarks that provide states and communities a clear road map for assessing how well their local systems are designed and implemented, for measuring the effectiveness of those systems, and for determining if they have achieved the goals.

Measuring Our Progress

To drive and track progress against the federal Strategies outlined in Home, Together, USICH and its federal partners will develop and utilize an annual performance management plan with specific target actions, milestones, and deadlines. USICH will also use multiple performance measures to assess the overall impact of the implementation of Home, Together.

USICH will focus on changes in the following key measures:

- The number of people experiencing sheltered and unsheltered homelessness at a point in time in the annual Point-in-Time count, including Veterans, people experiencing chronic homelessness, families with children, unaccompanied youth, and all individuals.
- The number of states reporting increases versus decreases in the number of people experiencing sheltered and unsheltered homelessness within annual Point-in-Time counts.
- The number of Continuums of Care reporting increases versus decreases in the number of people experiencing sheltered and unsheltered homelessness within annual Point-in-Time counts.

- The number of people, including Veterans, people experiencing chronic homelessness, families with children, unaccompanied youth, and all individuals, spending time in emergency shelter and transitional housing annually.
- The number of children and youth, including both students in families and unaccompanied students, identified as experiencing homelessness at some point during the school year.
- The number of communities, states, and Continuums of Care that have achieved each population-specific goal.

These assessments will be used to inform future revisions to the Plan and its Objectives and Strategies, and USICH will provide an annual report on its effort to the President and to Congress.

Areas of Increased Focus

While our progress is promising, we also know that we have much more work to do, and many more challenges that we must face together. Areas of increased focus include:

- Increasing Affordable Housing Opportunities
- Strengthening Prevention and Diversion Practices
- Creating Solutions for Unsheltered Homelessness
- Tailoring Strategies for Rural Communities
- Helping People Who Exit Homelessness Find Employment Success
- Learning from the Expertise of People with Lived Experience

Driving Increased Progress

Home, Together provides a framework for federal interagency working groups to plan, implement, and assess the impact of their efforts and investments into ending homelessness. Communities can also use the plan to identify and implement their own strategic activities and align their efforts with federal agencies and other partners.

U.S. Interagency Council on Homelessness members:

- Department of Agriculture
- Department of Commerce
- Department of Defense
- Department of Education
- Department of Energy
- Department of Health and Human Services
- Department of Homeland Security
- Department of Housing and Urban Development
- Department of the Interior
- Department of Justice
- Department of Labor
- Department of Transportation
- Department of Veterans Affairs

- Corporation for National and Community Service
- General Services Administration
- Office of Management and Budget
- Social Security Administration
- U.S. Postal Service
- White House Faith and Opportunity Initiative

27. The White House Housing Development Toolkit*

Executive Summary

THE WHITE HOUSE

Over the past three decades, local barriers to housing development have intensified, particularly in the high-growth metropolitan areas increasingly fueling the national economy. The accumulation of such barriers—including zoning, other land use regulations, and lengthy development approval processes—has reduced the ability of many housing markets to respond to growing demand. The growing severity of undersupplied housing markets is jeopardizing housing affordability for working families, increasing income inequality by reducing less-skilled workers' access to high-wage labor markets, and stifling growth domestic product (GDP) growth by driving labor migration away from the most productive regions. By modernizing their approaches to housing development regulation, states and localities can restrain unchecked housing cost growth, protect homeowners, and strengthen their economies.

Locally constructed barriers to new housing development include beneficial environmental protections, but also laws plainly designed to exclude multifamily or affordable housing. Local policies acting as barriers to housing supply include land use restrictions that make developable land much more costly than it is inherently, zoning restrictions, off-street parking requirements, arbitrary or antiquated preservation regulations, residential conversion restrictions, and unnecessarily slow permitting processes. The accumulation of these barriers has reduced the ability of many housing markets to respond to growing demand.

Accumulated barriers to housing development can result in significant costs to households, local economies, and the environment.

- Housing production has not been able to keep up with demand in many localities, impacting construction and other related jobs, limiting the requisite growth in population needed to sustain economic growth, and limiting potential tax revenue gains.
- Barriers to housing development are exacerbating the housing affordability crisis, particularly in regions with high job growth and few rental vacancies.

*Public document originally published as The White House, "The White House Housing Development Toolkit: Executive Summary," https://www.whitehouse.gov/sites/whitehouse.gov/files/images/Housing_Development_Toolkit%20f.2.pdf, (September 2016).

- Significant barriers to new housing development can cause working families to be pushed out of the job markets with the best opportunities for them, or prevent them from moving to regions with higher-paying jobs and stronger career tracks. Excessive barriers to housing development result in increasing drag on national economic growth and exacerbate income inequality.
- When new housing development is limited region-wide, and particularly precluded in neighborhoods with political capital to implement even stricter local barriers, the new housing that does get built tends to be disproportionally concentrated in low-income communities of color, causing displacement and concerns of gentrification in those neighborhoods. Rising rents region-wide can exacerbate that displacement.
- The long commutes that result from workers seeking out affordable housing far from job centers place a drain on their families, their physical and mental well-being, and negatively impact the environment through increased gas emissions.
- When rental and production costs go up, the cost of each unit of housing with public assistance increases, putting a strain on already-insufficient public resources for affordable housing, and causing existing programs to serve fewer households.
- Modernized housing regulation comes with significant benefits.
- Housing regulation that allows supply to respond elastically to demand helps cities protect homeowners and home values while maintaining housing affordability.
- Regions are better able to compete in the modern economy when their housing development is allowed to meet local needs.
- Smart housing regulation optimizes transportation system use, reduces commute times, and increases use of public transit, biking and walking.
- Modern approaches to zoning can also reduce economic and racial segregation, as research shows that strict land use regulations drive income segregation of wealthy residents.

Cities and states across the country are interested in revising their often 1970s-era zoning codes and housing permitting processes, and increasingly recognize that updating local land use policies could lead to more new housing construction, better leveraging of limited financial resources, and increased connectivity between housing to transportation, jobs and amenities.

This toolkit highlights actions that states and local jurisdictions have taken to promote healthy, responsive, affordable, high-opportunity housing markets, including:

- Establishing by-right development
- Taxing vacant land or donate it to non-profit developers
- Streamlining or shortening permitting processes and timelines
- Eliminate off-street parking requirements
- Allowing accessory dwelling units
- Establishing density bonuses
- Enacting high-density and multifamily zoning
- Employing inclusionary zoning
- Establishing development tax or value capture incentives
- Using property tax abatements

PART III

Services, Innovations and Challenges

• A. Affordability and Inclusion •

28. Key Findings on Housing Affordability*

INTERNATIONAL CITY/COUNTY MANAGEMENT ASSOCIATION

Housing affordability in the United States has been a widely discussed topic since the end of the Great Recession. Driven in part by rising costs associated with high demand, and in part by slow or stagnant wage growth, the need to develop affordable housing options is quickly becoming a higher priority for many communities. Our research snapshot highlights four key findings on housing affordability impacting local governments across the country.

More than one in three American households are housing cost-burdened. In 2014, about 35 percent of American households were housing cost-burdened, spending more than 30 percent of household income on housing. Among renters in particular, almost half of all households were housing cost-burdened *(Source: U.S. Census Bureau)*.

Housing affordability is increasingly cited among local leaders as a barrier to economic development. The lack of affordable housing options can impact not only a community's quality of life, but also its ability to grow, attract, and retain businesses. The proportion of local governments identifying housing affordability as an economic development barrier has more than doubled since 2009. About 14.1 percent of local governments responding to ICMA's *2009 Economic Development Survey* indicated that high housing costs represented a barrier to economic development. A follow-up survey conducted in 2014 revealed that 30.6 percent of responding governments saw high housing costs as either a "medium" or "high" barrier to economic development.

Local governments fund a large proportion of housing affordability programs. Understanding the impact that housing affordability can have on the economy as well as on a community's quality of life, local leaders have been pursuing a variety of initiatives to expand housing options for residents of all income levels. While the federal and state governments continue to be the primary source of funding for housing affordability initiatives, local governments are also making significant investments. ICMA's 2015 Survey of Local Government Sustainability Practices found that among communities with

*International City/County Management Association, "Key Findings on Housing Affordability," *PM Magazine*, https://icma.org/articles/article/key-findings-housing-affordability (May 20, 2016). Originally published in the May 2016 issue of *Public Management (PM)* magazine and copyrighted by ICMA, the International City/County Management Association (icma.org); reprinted with permission.

a housing affordability program, 41.2 percent of these programs were supported by local government funding.

Communities of all sizes and in all regions are economically impacted by housing affordability challenges. While densely populated metropolitan areas, such as Los Angeles, San Francisco, Washington, DC, and New York City, receive much national attention for their high housing costs, ICMA's survey results demonstrate that communities of all sizes and in all regions of the country are economically impacted by a lack of affordable housing. In many smaller communities, demand may not be driving higher housing costs, but residents may be housing cost-burdened nonetheless because of low income levels.

29. Affordable Housing Development*

TOWN OF BEDFORD, MASSACHUSETTS

The Town of Bedford has achieved a strategically planning and executing a program of affordable housing development over the past 14 years. During this period, the inventory of actual affordable units increased 161 percent and units under the State of Massachusetts system for monitoring units increased by 336 percent.

Bedford (2008 pop. of 13,315) is located 15 miles northwest of Boston with an area of almost 14 square miles. Unlike many suburban communities, Bedford almost doubles in size during the day. Approximately 25,000 people work at the various commercial, industrial, and institutional facilities, giving Bedford one of the highest jobs to homes ratios in Massachusetts—five to one. Despite this, a strong sentiment exists to preserve the small-town colonial character while maintaining diversity. As housing prices soared in the 1990s and early 2000s and large homes replaced small homes, many residents agreed that strategies were needed to provide more affordable housing directed toward modest incomes, ensuring that such households could reside here and enjoy the many benefits of this special community.

Owing to the rising cost of housing, many residents were finding it difficult to remain in Bedford. Several groups were particularly at risk of losing their place in the community: residents who grew up in the town; long-term residents, especially the elderly, who were less able to maintain their large homes; military personnel and their families from Bedford's Hanscom Air Force Base not desiring to live on base; and employees of the town and local businesses.

The State of Massachusetts, through its General Laws Chapter 40B, has set a goal for all municipalities to have at least 10 percent of their housing classified as affordable, as defined by state standards. Communities failing to reach the goal are susceptible to override of local zoning if a developer chooses to include affordable housing as part of his/her development proposal. In such cases, the developer files a "comprehensive permit" application with the locality and, if denied the permit, may appeal to the state to override of the local zoning provisions. Communities often lose control of the development process in such situations and residents (including abutters) become extremely dissatisfied with the result. The best way to avoid such an eventuality is to achieve the 10 percent goal in accordance with local preferences by laying out a plan to meet affordable housing needs in a manner acceptable to the community's own vision.

Surprisingly, reaching the goal of 10 percent affordable housing has been elusive. By

*Public document originally published as Town of Bedford, Massachusetts, "Affordable Housing Development," https://www.bedfordma.gov/town-manager/pages/affordable-housing (2019).

2019, only 51 of the 351 municipalities in the state have reached the goal, even though the law was adopted in 1970. After Bedford's efforts, it now ranks fourth in the state with 18.3 percent affordable units, highest among suburban municipalities. Of the three communities ahead of Bedford, one is a small rural community with a very low number of housing units overall; the other two (Boston and Holyoke) are large urban cities.

Although Bedford first set a goal to address affordable housing needs in its 1970 Comprehensive Plan by calling for completion of a detailed housing plan, little occurred until the Comprehensive Plan was again updated in 1985, followed by the Town's first Housing Plan adopted in 1986. That plan called for the creation of a non-profit housing corporation as an early step towards meeting its goals.

Richard Reed was appointed as the Town Administrator (later Town Manager) in 1988. He learned in his first year that Town officials and citizens wanted to make progress in the Town's affordable housing goals but had not been well organized for the task. Until 1990, Bedford actually had three committees, each of which was involved with differing aspects of housing. None were staffed; there was some difficulty in attracting citizens to serve; and the committees were not effective. At that time, of the 4,588 total housing units in Bedford, 200 (4.36 percent) were considered.

Reed recommended that the committees meet together under one umbrella. The committees began meeting as one in 1991 and became known as the Bedford Housing Partnership. Reed assigned then-Assistant to the Town Administrator (now Assistant Town Manager) Joanna Nickerson to provide staff support. With the limited number of staff in Bedford, all affordable housing activity has been staffed through the Town Manager's Office.

At the recommendation of Reed and Nickerson, the next significant step was the formation of a non-profit Bedford Housing Trust in 1994, a non-governmental organization exempt from real property state procurement laws. To ensure consistency with Town affordable housing goals, the Trust's Articles of Incorporation established that all Bedford Housing Partnership members appointed by Selectmen would automatically be members of the Trust. Membership in the Trust was also open to the general public. With all the organizational components then in place, the critical momentum had been established to ensure progress would be made toward the Town's affordable housing goals.

In 1995, the first owner-occupied single-family unit development with affordable units was built, resulting in ten homes for moderate income families. Because the Town was concerned with the imbalance between employment and housing, a developer agreed to donate $365,000 to the Bedford Housing Trust for the development of affordable housing in the community as part of the mitigation package for a new office complex permitted in 1997. This funding enabled the Trust to begin efforts to develop affordable units on its own. Also, when the Town was considering a rental housing development proposal, it was able to negotiate a $200,000 contribution from the developer for smaller scale affordable housing initiatives elsewhere in the community.

With the progress the Town was making, the State Department of Housing and Community Development certified in 2000 that Bedford was well on its way to meeting its housing goals.

As momentum grew with the early successes, citizens became more supportive of the Town officials' efforts. In 2001, Bedford was the very first community in the state to accept Massachusetts's Community Preservation Act (CPA). This act provides matching state funding for affordable housing, open space acquisition, and historic preservation projects, provided the Town's voters agreed to impose up to a 3 percent surcharge on Town property tax bills. These funds have provided a valuable resource for affordable housing development.

Seeking additional financial resources, and upon the recommendation of the Housing Partnership and staff, in 2002 Bedford joined the Metro West HOME Consortium, a regional municipal affordable housing consortium receiving funding from the U.S. Department of Housing & Urban Development. This federal program exists to expand the supply of decent, affordable housing for low- and very low-income families. Later in 2002, as a sign of confidence in Bedford's commitment to affordable housing, a state-funded agency, the Massachusetts Housing Partnership awarded Bedford a $1 million grant for the development of affordable family unit rental housing. The Town pledged a vacant parcel of land obtained many years earlier through tax foreclosure for the development. The Town entered into a long-term lease with a developer after a competitive procurement process overseen by Town Manager Reed.

In 2004, the State signaled further approval of Bedford's efforts by approving its updated plan for affordable housing production. This approval provided the ability for Town boards to forestall adversarial comprehensive permit applications as the Town continued to make progress in meeting its goals on its own terms.

Results show that Bedford has realized its affordable housing goals and continues to have a strong commitment to affordable housing. Since 1995, Bedford has added 284 units to its existing 176 units for a total of 460 affordable units, representing 9.8 percent of the Town's total housing inventory (based on the 2000 U.S. Census). By state guidelines used to calculate affordable housing levels, the Town had 873 units representing 18.3 percent. These units are dispersed throughout the Town in a manner that does not overburden any one neighborhood.

Also, affordable units are Two projects that are worthy of special note are the VA SRO units for homeless and the Habitat for Humanity project. The SROs have allowed previously homeless veterans to live in Bedford in one-room units; the Habitat projects will eventually provide eight owner-occupied, LEEDS-certified, housing units utilizing a $600,000 grant from the Town. This increased number of affordable units has been achieved in a way that meets the housing needs of Bedford and also preserves the small-town character while increasing the diversity of our town. Bedford has shown its commitment to affordable housing through a variety of strategies. Exceeding the state's 10 percent subsidized housing goal was an important milestone, but Bedford will continue to create affordable housing units.

Acquired in 2018 is Bedford Village which was built in 1973 developed through a partnership among federal, state, and private entities to preserve affordable housing units. Located in suburban Boston's Route 128 corridor, Bedford Village consists of 96 one-, two-, and three-bedroom households in 10 residential buildings set on 10.3 acres. The property enjoys close proximity to retail centers, medical facilities, civic institutions and local schools. The main beneficiaries are seniors and families.

These homes provide affordable options to low-income individuals as well as those earning 80 percent of median area income. They are greatly needed in Bedford, where the lack of restricted housing limits rental options for low-income families. POAH is preserving and increasing the number of income-restricted apartments at Bedford Village, whose affordability would have otherwise expired at the end of the state's 13A subsidy program from the 1970s.

Using a combination of Federal Low Income Housing Tax Credits, bonds from MassHousing, and local Community Preservation Act funds, Bedford Village has been renovated with new roofs, windows, select kitchen and bath updates, and low-flow fixtures.

"Most pleased of all were the residents of Bedford Village—some of whom have lived in their apartments for more than 40 years—who are now assured that their rents will remain affordable. Bedford Village provides affordable options to low-income individuals as well as to those earning 80 percent of median area income. Housing of this type is greatly needed in Bedford. As a recent housing survey revealed, rising real estate prices make it virtually impossible for low to moderate income individuals to live in town."

REFERENCE

Bergin, Dot (2018). "Bedford Village Celebrates New Ownership and Continuing Affordability." *The Bedford Citizen*, June 1, 2018.

30. Perceptions of and Barriers to Affordable Housing in Virginia*

THE CENTER FOR PUBLIC POLICY AT VCU'S WILDER SCHOOL

More than three in four Virginians (78 percent) see housing affordability as a problem in America today, and almost half (47 percent) see it as a very serious problem, according to a 2019 statewide poll by the Center for Public Policy at Virginia Commonwealth University's L. Douglas Wilder School of Government and Public Affairs.

The poll, conducted through landline and cellphone from June 9–19, is a random sample of 816 adults in Virginia with an overall margin of error of 3.43 percentage points.

The poll also found that a sizable minority (34 percent) of respondents said that they or someone they knew had been evicted, foreclosed upon, or lost their housing in the past five years. When asked about perceptions of future housing costs, the majority of respondents felt that the average rent in their area would increase (69 percent), as would the average home price in their area (67 percent). Thirty percent of respondents said that they have had to take on an additional job or work more at their current job in order to make their housing payments in the past three years.

Though concerning, these findings are not necessarily surprising; in 2018, a *New York Times* article detailed high rates of evictions in multiple cities in Virginia. While this issue is being taken seriously by Virginia's policymakers, government agencies and nonprofits, there is still work to be done. The following sections discuss a few aspects of affordable housing and provide information regarding barriers to home ownership as well as the impact of housing costs on various groups. As policymakers work to address issues related to affordable housing, it may be beneficial to consider some of these topics.

Limited budget, poor credit score and lack of down payment are noted as primary obstacles to home ownership. Sixty percent of respondents reported that they own their home, while 35 percent rent and six percent live with their parents or in some other arrangement. When those who rent or live with parents (41 percent of the total sample) were asked whether they aspire to own a home, 70 percent said yes, 22 percent said no and eight percent said that they did not know. This group also was asked about obstacles to buying a home; the primary barriers are as follows:

---

*Originally published as the Center for Public Policy at VCU's Wilder School, "Perceptions of and Barriers to Affordable Housing in Virginia," *PA Times*, https://patimes.org/perceptions-of-and-barriers-to-affordable-housing-in-virginia/ (July 28, 2019). Reprinted with permission of the publisher.

- Limited housing options available within their budget (22 percent).
- A poor credit history (18 percent).
- A lack of a down payment (15 percent).
- Existing debt (11 percent).

Minorities and those with lower levels of education are more likely to spend more than 30 percent of their monthly income on housing. Respondents also were asked how much of their monthly income went to mortgage or rent. A commonly used measure of affordability is spending less than 30 percent of total income on housing. Using that measure, 35 percent of the respondents said they spend more than 30 percent of their total monthly income on rent or mortgage, 45 percent said they spent less than 30 percent and 16 percent said they did not know.

Level of education and income also played a significant role in a respondent spending more than 30 percent on housing. A majority of those making under $50,000 (52 percent) said that they spend more than a third of their income on housing. Those with an income of $100,000 or more were likely to spend less than 30 percent on housing (71 percent). Likewise, more than half of college graduates (57 percent) spend less than 30 percent, while only 38 percent of those with a high school education or less said the same. Those with a high school education or less also were more likely to say they did not know (23 percent). Minorities were more likely to spend more than 30 percent on housing (46 percent) compared to only 29 percent of whites. Democrats were more likely to spend more than 30 percent on housing (44 percent), Republicans were more likely to spend less (55 percent) and independents were more evenly split (36 percent spend less than 30 percent and 31 percent spend more than 30 percent).

Moving forward. Fortunately, policymakers in Virginia are working to address these issues and to support the creation of affordable housing in the commonwealth. As Delegate Lamont Bagby stated, "Every Virginian deserves a safe place to call home.... By supporting more affordable housing, we can address the devastating impacts of Virginia's high eviction rates."

More information about this and other polls may be found on the Wilder School Commonwealth Poll website.

The Center for Public Policy aims to advance research and training that informs public policy and decision-making to improve our communities. We provide diverse public-facing services including leadership development and training, economic and policy impact analysis, survey insights and program evaluation to clients in state and local governments, nonprofit organizations, businesses and the public, across Virginia and beyond.

31. Snapshot*

The Current State of Housing Affordability in California

CALIFORNIA DEPARTMENT OF HOUSING AND COMMUNITY DEVELOPMENT

A fundamental purpose of this report is to assess California's housing needs. This section details the State's projected housing needs through 2025, demographic trends, current housing characteristics, and housing costs and affordability. As this section will show, California has severe housing issues for both rental and homeownership in terms of both supply and affordability. There is a shortfall of more than one million rental homes affordable to extremely and very low-income households and California's home-ownership rate has declined to the lowest rate since the 1940s. In addition, California needs more than 1.8 million additional homes by 2025 to maintain pace with projected household growth.

About 1.8 Million New Homes Needed by 2025. From 2015–2025, approximately 1.8 million new housing units are needed to meet projected population and house-hold growth, or 180,000 new homes annually. The California Department of Housing and Community Development (HCD), in consultation with the California Depart-ment of Finance, determines the State's housing need for a 10-year period, based upon Department of Finance population projection and demographic household formation data.

Past Production. California's housing needs are influenced by a number of fac-tors that include both the size of the population (sheer number of people), but more importantly, the characteristics of that population (e.g., age, ethnicity, household size). Other characteristics also affect whether California has enough housing to meet the needs of the population, including the percentage of people who have disabilities, per-centage of farmworkers whose work is seasonal, and percentage of people experiencing homelessness.

Demographic Trends Drive Housing Needs. California has a diverse and growing population. Understanding the State's changing and unique demographics can inform housing policy decisions

Population. California's 39 million people live in 13 million households across 58

*Public document originally published as California Department of Housing and Community Development, "California's Housing Future: Challenges and Opportunities," https://www.hcd.ca.gov/policy-research/plans-reports/docs/SHA_Final_Combined.pdf (February 2018).

counties and 482 cities. The graphic below shows the percentage of the total population that lives in each county. The State's cities and counties range greatly in population. While there are three cities with more than one million residents, there are 107 cities with less than 10,000 residents. The largest population concentration is in Southern California.

32. Mapping as Citizen Engagement in the Fight for Affordable Housing*

Michael Silliman

The housing supply is being squeezed from every angle, leaving behind millions of Americans to fend for themselves and citizen engagement groups try to find solutions. The United States is surprisingly underdeveloped, particularly in key areas near transit and rapidly growing urban centers. The type of housing being built is not flexible in usage nor serves the greatest citizen concerns such as family, workforce and affordable housing options. Moreover, subsidized and rent-controlled housing units are expiring in cities like Washington, D.C. and San Francisco, as these are being flipped to market rate units faster than new affordable housing can be politically willed into creation.

The scope of this problem and who is most affected is alarming.

According to the rental housing advocacy organization Make Room USA, nearly 11 million Americans, including 2 million seniors, can barely pay their rent each month. The DC Fiscal Policy Institute says, "The scale of this problem in DC is enormous. Some 26,000 households are both extremely low-income and spending more than half their income on rent. Nearly one of every five children in the District faces such situations."

Even worse, homelessness in cities like Atlanta, Los Angeles and Seattle shows:

1. This is a national problem; and,
2. It has only been getting worse over the last decade since the peak of the housing crash in 2008.

As a response, as small as it may feel in the face of this national affordable housing crisis, citizens in communities across the country are starting to organize; creatively documenting and telling the stories of this new housing crisis and the inequality it is creating, as well innovative ways to build for everyone. One of the tools these citizen engagement groups are using is collecting open sourced data and mapping.

The first example is a group of volunteers for a civic tech organization called Code for D.C. that came together to build an online tool to find and track current affordable housing. The tool, Housing Insights, documents every affordable housing unit in Washington, D.C. along a whole dataset of variables from zoning and number of units to subsidy program and ownership type. Affordable housing activists (full transparency: this

---

*Originally published as Michael Silliman, "Mapping as Citizen Engagement in the Fight for Affordable Housing," *PA Times*, https://patimes.org/mapping-as-citizen-engagement-in-the-fight-for-affordable-housing/ (July 16, 2018). Reprinted with permission of the publisher.

includes some groups I am a part of), are using this tool to organize around and support vulnerable housing projects.

Another example comes from Matthew Desmond, a sociologist and Pulitzer Prize winner who authored *Evicted, Poverty and Profit in the American City*. Desmond has worked with students at Princeton University to create The Eviction Lab, the first nationwide database of evictions—a platform where you can create custom maps, charts and reports of eviction statistics in your neighborhood. "The lab has collected 83 million records from 48 states and the District of Columbia," and, "Desmond estimates that 2.3 million evictions were filed in the U.S. in 2016" (NPR). This is powerful information at the fingertips of laypeople, public servants, and politicians alike.

Yet another example of civic mapping in the housing space is Prologue DC, which is a public history project documenting the historic segregation of D.C.'s housing, primarily focusing on racially restrictive housing covenants, which had a dramatic impact on the development of the nation's capital decades before government-sanctioned redlining policies were implemented in cities across the country. They are telling the story of D.C.'s racial housing history using GIS mapping. Check out their interactive map stories here.

However, mapping the historical racial issues and the current affordability crisis is not for the sole purpose of telling the stories of those most affected. Another example, which is still only theatrical from my understanding, is the idea to create a map of affordable housing opportunities. Retaining the current affordable housing is not enough. So where are the best places to build new or convert old buildings into affordable housing? A group in D.C., again that I am a part of, has started to think about doing just this. Pouring over property tax data to find city-owned land, vacant properties, and searching for underutilized spaces, we have started to build a list. Other cities, such as Cleveland, have done just this. What would it take to turn this into a full-scale, nationwide project? What would a model for turning these opportunities into reality look like? Could a group of concerned citizens, of public servants and administration wonks, pull this off?

33. Inclusionary Housing*

A Policy Whose Time Has Come

DEBORAH BAILEY

How we live in America is changing. While incomes remain flat for most working people, the cost of housing has continued to rise. It's difficult for many hard working-class and professionals to rent or buy homes at price points they can afford, in the cities and communities in they teach or work as police officers, firefighters and civil servants. Inclusionary housing is a concept and public policy decision whose time has come for America's cities and counties.

Part of the legacy of the Great Recession, government announcements of 4.9 percent unemployment rates just don't get people that excited about "Livin' in America." If unemployment rates under 5 percent are supposed to represent full employment in America, then it's time to peep underneath the curtain to see how fully employed people are living these days.

Employed... But Hardly Keeping a Roof Over My Head

According to the U.S. Department of Housing and Urban Development (HUD), more than 12 million Americans are now paying more than 50 percent of their household income on the rent or mortgage. Remember that old formula you learned growing up that good personal budgeting meant spending no more than 30 percent of your household income on housing. Well that formula has gone out the high-priced window for one-third of American households who are paying more than the 30 percent of their monthly income on housing.

HUD has developed the official title of "cost burdened households" for those of us paying upward of 30 percent of household income on housing and "severely cost burdened" for the poor souls anteing up more than half of their income for a place to lay their heads at night.

Basic Affordable Housing in Today's Economy

Inclusionary housing/zoning ordinances are local legislative tools that help balance the housing market and make it more affordable for middle and lower wealth income

*Originally published as Deborah Bailey, "Inclusionary Housing: A Policy Whose Time Has Come," *PA Times*, https://patimes.org/inclusionary-housing-policy-time/ (September 9, 2016). Reprinted with permission of the publisher.

persons. In the last quarter of the 20th century, inclusionary housing legislation was primarily used to ensure a developer set aside a certain number or percentage of their units for low-wealth residents.

But as we continue our so-called economic recovery from the Great Recession of 2008, many full-time working professionals cannot afford the price of housing stock. The average price of rent in the United States in August 2016 was $1,120, with $1,300 for a two-bedroom unit. In New York, the most expensive rental market, the one-bedroom price shoots up to $3550. Given these prices, what are the prospects for a middle-income family?

According to Dietderich's landmark article on Inclusionary housing policy, there are a variety tools that cities can use to regulate the housing market. But all of them involve a developer either voluntarily setting aside a certain percentage of units for a planned development below market rate or having to abide by legal ordinances that mandate the set aside percentages and/or the terms of opting out of the set-aside program.

Inclusionary housing is of course, not without controversy. For example, Baltimore currently has ordinances that compensate developers for building affordable units. Other cities, like San Jose, California, have a highly controversial law that requires units be built at the developer's cost.

Today, more than 200 cities across the U.S. have inclusionary housing ordinances, and 170 such ordinances in the state of California alone where the state Supreme Court has ruled in favor of a citywide, mandatory inclusionary housing ordinance for San Jose, California. The Court let stand San Jose's inclusionary housing ordinance that required developers building housing projects of more than 20 units to include 15 percent of for-sale housing units at below market rate housing or pay an in-lieu fee.

The Future for Our Cities

The U.S. Supreme Court declined to hear a challenge to San Jose's mandatory inclusionary housing ordinance signaling that for now, inclusionary housing ordinances are on safe ground.

A HUD study examined two of the wealthiest counties in America—Montgomery County, Maryland and Fairfax County, Virginia—determined their Inclusionary housing policies had a positive impact for families. Both of these communities have had inclusionary housing policies in place for more than 30 years. They are examples that over time, inclusionary housing does not lead to our greatest fears of urban decline. Instead, it points us to our greatest hopes—communities that work for citizens from all walks of life.

• B. Health •

34. Sacramento County Reducing the Number of Mentally Ill Homeless*

SAMANTHA CARR *and* ALAN R. ROPER

During 2007 and 2008, research was conducted on the correlation between the severely mentally ill people who are suffering from chronic homelessness, and Sacramento County's newly implemented programs ability to increase or decrease the amount of mentally ill persons who are without homes. The research was conducted in completion of a graduate degree and used primary interview data from subject matter experts on mental health and homeless services in the County of Sacramento. The researcher revisited the original study in 2019 (over ten years later) to evaluate impact and evolution of programs, services and outcomes.

The initial research showed a definitive correlation between programs that focus directly on solving housing, treatment, and rehabilitation as well as other resource issues among mentally ill persons and programs which are proactive in reducing system and funding fragmentation as being the most successful in lowering the amount of mentally ill homeless that are on the streets. Recommendations from that study included maintaining the existing Community Services and Supports (CSS) programs structure. Additionally, recommendations included thoroughly evaluating the service providers program outcome measures and other data and to keep an agreed upon timeline of when outcomes should be achieved on a continual basis. Additional recommendations included reassessing the effectiveness of the mentally ill homeless program (Pathways) if the outcome measure of having all mentally ill homeless persons in permanent supportive housing is not met within five years after implementing the program.

This chapter focuses on the correlation between the severely mentally ill people who are suffering from chronic homelessness, and Sacramento County's programs ability to reduce the amount of mentally ill persons who are without permanent residence.

Background of the Problem

Sacramento County has continually strived over the years to lower the homeless rate of its citizens by focusing on various factors and implementing changes through new policies. One area that has still not been explored in depth is the homeless rate of the mentally ill and how this growing problem can be effectively addressed. The Division

---

*Published with permission of the authors.

of Mental Health Services in Sacramento County has been providing mental health services for homeless adults with serious and persistent mental illness since the late 1980s. Because the needs of the mentally ill adults are sometimes co-occurring, meaning a mental disorder as well as some form of drug addiction that needs to be treated, the services provided can often become multi-faceted and complex.

In early November 2004, California voters passed Proposition 63, or The Mental Health Services Act (MHSA), to aid in adequately meeting the needs of children, adults, and older adults with serious mental illness, and reduce the long-term adverse impact resulting from untreated and under treated mentally ill individuals. When it became state law in 2005, MHSA placed a 1 percent tax on the adjustable gross income of those in California who earn $1 million or more.

The County of Sacramento and City of Sacramento promised a collaboration to end chronic homelessness in 10 years, with a key focal point of addressing new strategies to reduce homelessness among the mentally ill. Adopted unanimously by the City Council and the County Board of Supervisor in September 2006, the Ten-Year Plan described its mission as preventing, and eventually eliminating chronic homelessness by providing permanent housing and coordinated services to help individuals achieve maximum self-sufficiency.

Findings from 2007–2008

The research showed a definitive correlation between having programs that focus directly on solving housing, treatment, and rehabilitation as well as other resource issues among the mentally ill persons and programs which are proactive in reducing system and funding fragmentation as being the most successful in lowering the amount of mentally ill homeless that are on the streets. The implication of these findings demonstrated that the County of Sacramento's capability to effectively achieve these goals on a consistent basis will determine their success rate.

The research methodology used the major assumption that Sacramento County's new mental health programs would be effective in reducing the amount of severely mentally ill who are chronically homeless. This assumption was contingent upon implementing a structure to the program that will reduce system and funding fragmentation and reduce barriers of stabilization, enabling the mentally ill homeless population to obtain permanent housing.

Recommendations included keeping the Community Services and Supports (CSS) programs structured as they currently were, thoroughly evaluating the service providers program outcome measures and other data and to keep an agreed upon timeline of when outcomes deliverables should be achieved on a continual basis. Other recommendations included reassessing the effectiveness of the mentally ill homeless program (Pathways) if the outcome measure of having all mentally ill homeless persons in permanent supportive housing was not met within five years after implementing the program.

Reflections 10 Years Later

It was the researcher's assumption that Sacramento County would be successful in combating this important societal issue of caring for the severely mentally ill who experience chronic homelessness if they appropriate their core resources to three key areas: housing, recovery, and rehabilitation through treatment for mental illness. Along with these key areas, ensuring a service care model that would make certain to reduce and possibly eliminate system and funding fragmentation would be ideal.

Sacramento Steps Forward, a non-profit organization, holds a biennial census, a Point-in-Time Count (PIT), of people who are experiencing homelessness, as defined by the U.S. Department of Housing and Urban Development, on a single night in January. The count includes people who are in emergency shelters and those who are unsheltered. Hundreds of volunteers are strategically placed throughout the county to count the number of people living on the streets and in temporary sheltered housing, including homeless shelters, automobiles, RV's and tents. The data collected is analyzed by California State University, Sacramento, and put into a biannual report, which is then shared with Sacramento County as a resource to determine where to allocate funds and deploy resources.

The PIT Count representing the past number of years of homelessness, with those individuals who are considered chronic homeless and/or mentally ill homeless, and the percentage change in each year that the PIT Count was conducted. The data shows the gradual increase of homeless population within Sacramento County. Even during 2011 where there was a drop, 2013 shows a continued progression of more homeless than previous years, which continues into 2019. Similarly, the percentage between the number of chronic homeless and mentally ill homeless within the entire homeless population increased by a standard deviation of little more than 15 percent throughout the last ten years. Beginning in 2011, the Federal definition of chronic homeless also began to include homeless families, and the family being included in the chronically homeless definition was allowed if the adult head of household met the criteria. This was a new element for the PIT volunteers to try and capture but stated in their reports that there were no families that fit the definition in Sacramento County until 2013.

In the original research conducted in 2007–2008, the researcher included in their methodology that the industry standard for the definition of chronic homelessness as it pertained to the mental health community was defined as, "an unaccompanied individual with a disabling condition who has either been continuously homeless for a year or more, or has had at least four episodes of homelessness within the past three years."

That definition was reviewed, and in late 2015, HUD changed the official definition of "Chronic Homelessness" as individuals who must meet two conditions, one pertaining to the length of time an individual has been homeless and the other to suffering from one of a potential group of disabilities. Specifically, a chronically homeless person:

- Has been continuously homeless for over a year; or has had four (4) or more episodes of homelessness in the past three (3) years.
- And they have a physical, developmental or mental disability that hinders their ability to maintain gainful employment.

Because of this new definition and assessments, the PIT volunteers who counted the homeless starting in 2017 show that homeless numbers for Sacramento County increased to nearly 77 percent from 2015, and the amount of chronically homeless and mentally ill homeless combined climbed to 31 percent. It should also be noted that counting homeless persons sleeping in places not meant for human habitation is inherently difficult and we can assume that not every unsheltered person was in fact counted.

In the 10+ years of doing the biannual count of Sacramento homeless, Sacramento Steps Forward issued a press release in June 2019 citing 2019 as their "most comprehensive and accurate snapshot of homelessness." They cite that there have been major improvements to the survey that is used, invariably more demographic questions, there are more volunteers that now cover twice the area than they used to, and the volunteers now count the homeless for two nights instead of just one as previously done.

Besides improving the plan of action to count the homeless in the most efficient manner, Sacramento County has also continued to follow the recommendations that were provided in the previous research 10 years ago. Namely, Sacramento has continued to fund community-based plans for support services and programs that are structured with the proven Assertive Community Treatment (ACT) approach. The County has done thorough evaluations on the service providers in the community to ensure the outcome measures are being met within the agreed timeline.

They have also put policies in place to fix the fragmentation in parts of the system, making it more seamless for the chronically homeless demographic to find resources quickly to get off the street. In the table above, results from 2019 show that while the number of homeless went up 19 percent, the percentage of chronically homeless lowered 1 percent. Sacramento Mayor Darrell Steinberg, who during the original research was a State Senator authoring funding bills for the mentally ill homeless, applauded the 2019 numbers in a press release Sacramento Steps Forward put out in June 2019, saying "This change shows that our strategy of targeting the most chronically homeless with services and shelter is beginning to work."

Lastly, the program that Sacramento County relied heavily on to be a changing force for this demographic, (Pathways), continues to be a great community asset that the County has partnered with, albeit restricted by resources. The program, which is under Turning Point Community Programs, has been a considerable resource in initial assessments for mental illness, being a community advocate for the mentally ill, lowering the relapse rate of the chronically homeless they currently service, and finding permanent supportive housing for this demographic. The recommendation to access their outcomes every five years has been done, and while they have not eliminated all the mentally ill homeless problem within 5 years, they are a first stop for this demographic within the Sacramento community.

Conclusions

Although Sacramento County has made every effort to push resource allocations including but not limited to personnel, and funding, the amount of mentally ill homeless who are chronically homeless continues to climb. There are several plausible reasons for this, which have no bearing on how efficient or inefficient the County has been with their intentions:

1. HUD's new definition of chronically homeless includes individuals and families that would not normally be counted within that demographic, essentially raising the number.

2. The Point in Time (PIT) Count now includes more days for counting the homeless in Sacramento County, and has a wider canvas within the County line, which has increased the number of homeless counted.

3. The County has experienced a slower rate of development with housing strategies and permanent supportive housing that have fluctuated with the general housing market in California over the past 10 years. Less permanent housing along with the increase of chronically homeless has created a bottleneck effect.

Expectations for Sacramento County still remain the same as they did back in 2007–2008; that the results of the 2007–2008 research will be used within Sacramento County as a compelling suggestion to maintain the improvements that have moved the County from the status quo of mental health support services to a more organized, community participated, client driven, and wholly transformed mental health support services. Likewise, that the original and updated research data be used by counties similar to Sacramento as a reference when taking a proactive stance in changing their current homeless and mental health policies, resource allocations, etc.

35. How Funding to House the Mentally Ill and the Homeless Is a Financial Gain, Not Drain*

Carol Caton

As Congress considers the federal budget proposal for fiscal year 2018 to reduce funding for services to poor and homeless Americans, programs with proven cost-effectiveness should not be on the chopping block. One such program is supportive housing for homeless people with severe mental illness.

Supportive housing, funded and coordinated by several different federal agencies and nonprofits, provides homeless people who have severe mental illness with housing coupled with treatment and support services. There is no increase in net public cost compared to street and shelter living.

While it may appear that paying for supportive housing is a drain on the federal budget, research has shown that ending homelessness for the severely mentally ill saves taxpayers money.

Because funding comes from several different agencies, it is hard to know specifically from the president's budget plan how deep the cuts to supportive housing could be. Yet we do know that the president has proposed cuts in funding to Housing and Urban Development by 13 percent and to Health and Human Services by 19 percent. Both these agencies provide significant funding for supportive housing.

I research mental illness and homelessness. Cutting funds to house the homeless would cost us more money than it would save.

Supportive Housing and the Homeless Mentally Ill

Since the 1980s, homelessness has plagued cities and towns across the country. Today, more than a half-million people in the U.S. are homeless. One in every three homeless people suffers from a mental illness, which is often compounded by multiple health problems and substance abuse.

The homeless mentally ill are likely to remain undomiciled and without treatment

---

*Originally published as Carol Caton, "How Funding to House Mentally Ill, Homeless Is a Financial Gain, Not Drain," *The Conversation*, https://theconversation.com/how-funding-to-house-mentally-ill-homeless-is-a-financial-gain-not-drain-74914 (May 3, 2017). Reprinted with permission of the publisher.

for long periods of time. This brings a high social and economic cost to society. Disabled by mental illness and unable to work, these individuals have little hope of exiting homelessness without public assistance.

Beset with extreme poverty and disability, their inability to work renders them heavily dependent on the largesse of government agencies for disability income, housing support and health care.

The challenges facing homeless people in general are daunting. Security, privacy and creature comforts are in short supply. The daily burden of being homeless involves finding ways to assuage exhaustion and hunger, and to sidestep the violence and victimization that regularly occurs in life on the streets. An estimated 14 to 21 percent of homeless people are victims of crimes, compared to about 2 percent of the general population.

Supportive housing, started in the early 1980s, has shown to make a big difference. Unlike the temporary respite provided by crisis shelters, it provides access to permanent housing, mental health treatment and support from mental health professionals to guide the adjustment from homelessness to stable residence in the community.

Supportive housing tenants must have a behavioral health condition that qualifies them for a federal disability income. Residents pay one-third of the cost of rent and utilities with their disability income (about $733 per month). The balance is covered by a housing subsidy provided through private or governmental sources. In some cases, eligibility for a housing subsidy is based on duration of street and shelter living.

The Numbers Tell the Story

In concert with the federal plan to "End Chronic Homelessness in Ten Years," supportive housing has helped to reduce chronic homelessness by 35 percent between 2007 and 2016.

At an annual cost ranging from $12,000 to nearly $20,000 per unit, permanent supportive housing is expensive, but it is substantially less than the annual cost of a stay in a homeless shelter, jail or prison, or psychiatric hospital.

Some of the funding comes from the federal government, including from the Department of Housing and Urban Development's Continuum of Care and from Section 8 housing subsidies. The Department of Health and Human Services and the Department of Veterans Affairs also provide funding.

States including New York, California, Washington and Connecticut have helped to fund housing for people with mental illness, as have some city and county governments.

Other sources of funding include low-income housing tax credits, private foundations and charitable donations to nonprofit housing providers. The Affordable Care Act Medicaid expansion program provides Medicaid reimbursement for services provided to individuals in supportive housing.

And the Winner Is … Everyone

Controlled trials conducted in the United States and Canada have found the majority of people who have had access to supportive housing remain housed for a year or more, showing greater housing stability than that among comparison subjects. In addition, individuals in supportive housing not only stayed longer but also had a reduction in subsequent homelessness and decreased use of emergency departments and hospitals.

Cost offset studies show that supportive housing leads to less use of costly public services.

A landmark analysis of administrative data from multiple public service systems examined the impact of supportive housing placement on 4,679 individuals and their use of the public shelter system, public and private hospitals, and correctional facilities. The study found that persons placed in supportive housing experienced significant reductions in use of homeless shelters, hospitals and time incarcerated. In fact, public service cost reductions following housing placement nearly offset the cost of the housing itself.

Significantly, supportive housing is nearly half the average cost per year of $35,578 for a chronically homeless person. Part of the reason is that stable housing resulted in a shift in service use from expensive crisis services to less costly community-based care.

Strong and compelling evidence indicates that supportive housing is a "win-win" for both the homeless mentally ill and the holders of the public purse. It offers people with mental illness safe and adequate housing and greater access to treatment, essential elements in their recovery. And it can lead to greater cost-efficient use of public services.

Currently there are not nearly enough supportive housing units to house the thousands of individuals with severe mental illness who are currently unstably housed or are at risk of falling into homelessness.

It would not make economic sense to cut funding for a cost-effective intervention that provides a solution to homelessness. Rather, what we need now is the public will to bring supportive housing to scale so that the most fragile among us might achieve stable residence in the community. They, too, deserve the opportunity for personal fulfillment and involvement in mainstream society.

36. California Hospitals See Massive Surge in Homeless Patients*

Phillip Reese

Homeless patients made about 100,000 visits to California hospitals in 2017, marking a 28 percent rise from two years earlier, according to the most recent state discharge data.

More than a third of those visits involved a diagnosis of mental illness, according to the Office of Statewide Health Planning and Development. By contrast, 6 percent of all hospital discharges in California during that time involved a mental health diagnosis.

Health officials and homeless advocates attribute the trend to the surging number of people living homeless in California in recent years. From 2015 to 2017, the state's homeless population grew by about 16 percent, to 134,000, according to point-in-time reports compiled by the U.S. Department of Housing and Urban Development. Those figures cover only a single day, and homeless advocates argue far more Californians experience homelessness at some point over the course of a year.

Many researchers say California's skyrocketing housing costs have helped drive the overall spike in homelessness. Studies also indicate that more than a quarter of people living on the streets are dealing with mental illness.

Besides mental illness, a disproportionate number of homeless were hospitalized for treatment of HIV infections, alcohol and drug addictions, skin disorders, burns, drug overdoses and traumatic injuries.

Bottom of Form

"The folks who are living in the streets are sicker than the general public," said Christie Gonzales, director of behavioral health operations for WellSpace Health.

WellSpace Health provides respite care to homeless patients in the Sacramento region after they are discharged from the hospital. "We tend to see more of them with injuries and trauma, co-occurring with alcohol and drug problems," Gonzales said.

Los Angeles County saw the most discharges involving homeless patients in 2017,

*Originally published as Phillip Reese, "California Hospitals See Massive Surge in Homeless Patients," *Kaiser Health News*, https://khn.org/news/california-hospitals-see-massive-surge-in-homeless-patients/ (April 2, 2019). This KHN story first published on California Healthline, a service of the California Health Care Foundation. Kaiser Health News is a nonprofit news service covering health issues. It is an editorially independent program of the Kaiser Family Foundation that is not affiliated with Kaiser Permanente.

with 35,234, followed by San Diego, Sacramento, Orange and San Francisco counties. The number of homeless patients treated in L.A. County grew by about 7,500 from 2015 to 2017, the largest numerical increase in the state. (That is largely due to the county's size; the percentage growth in L.A. County homeless discharges was similar to the state average.)

Among places with at least 5,000 hospital discharges in 2017, the counties with the highest proportion of discharges involving homeless patients were San Francisco, Yolo, Santa Cruz and Humboldt. In all four counties, homeless discharges made up at least 4 percent of all hospital discharges.

"There is no housing out here," said Nicole Ring-Collins, who manages a winter shelter program for Mercy Coalition of West Sacramento in Yolo County. "It is so expensive."

Providers who work with homeless people say it is no surprise they end up hospitalized at disproportionate rates. Living in deep poverty can lead to health problems. Many homeless people are driven to the streets by health issues, particularly mental illness and drug addiction. Most of their inpatient health care is paid for through Medi-Cal, the state-federal insurance program for the poor, or Medicare, the government insurance program for seniors and people with disabilities.

"When folks are forced to live outside with no shelter, the trauma they experience can result in more medical issues," said Noel Kammermann, executive director of Loaves and Fishes, a homeless services agency in Sacramento.

Often, people living homeless do not see the doctor until they have a serious problem, Kammermann said. That lack of preventive care can lead to hospital stays. And living on the streets makes it all the more challenging to follow post-discharge instructions for rehabilitation and recovery.

"You heal better at home," said Peggy Wheeler, a vice president at the California Hospital Association. Homeless patients struggle after discharge when they "have to go right back out to the street for a wound that needs to heal or medicine that needs to be taken on a regular schedule," she added.

Hospitals across the state are working to provide respite care to the homeless after discharge, similar to the collaborative program at WellSpace in the Sacramento region, Wheeler said. Hospitals design such programs to lower readmission rates.

The homeless "are more vulnerable to other things because they don't have a home to go to convalesce," said Trina Gonzalez, director of community integration at UC Davis Health. "We want to make sure they are connected to the appropriate follow up care."

37. Finding Homeless Patients a Place to Heal*

Ana B. Ibarra

After they amputated the second toe on John Trumbla's right foot last summer, doctors sent him to a nursing home because he still needed medical care—but not necessarily a hospital bed.

The proud, burly Army veteran resisted at first, but he didn't have a choice. Before his hospitalization at Santa Clara Valley Medical Center in California, Trumbla, 56, and his wife had been homeless, crashing in his boss's construction shop or living out of their station wagon.

Trumbla spent six months at the nursing home, Skyline Healthcare Center, while social workers sought housing vouchers and scouted rental leads. But nothing panned out. When he finally left Skyline in mid–February, he stayed at a motel for a night before heading back to his boss's shop.

"We might just have to leave this area. I don't want to, but I also don't want to live on the streets," Trumbla said from his bed at Skyline in early February, citing the San Francisco Bay Area's astronomical rents.

Skyline allocates 15 beds to the Santa Clara hospital for patients who are homeless or have no one to care for them at home. It's part of a year-old partnership born of necessity. Santa Clara Valley Medical Center, like many other hospitals in the state, has struggled to find suitable accommodations for a growing number of homeless patients who need follow-up medical attention after they're discharged, said Dr. Raymond Chan, co-director of the hospital's program at Skyline.

In Santa Clara County, the number of homeless patient discharges from hospitals jumped 42 percent from 2015 to 2017, according to data from the Office of Statewide Health Planning and Development.

Statewide, hospitals discharged homeless patients nearly 100,000 times in 2017, a 28 percent increase over 2015. The discharges include 2,608 deaths in hospitals from 2015 to 2017.

As hospitals contend with the dramatic growth in homeless patients, they must comply with a new state law, implemented in January, which requires them to

*Originally published as Ana B. Ibarra, "Finding Homeless Patients a Place to Heal," *Kaiser Health News*, https://khn.org/news/finding-homeless-patients-a-place-to-heal/ (April 3, 2019). Kaiser Health News is a nonprofit news service covering health issues. It is an editorially independent program of the Kaiser Family Foundation that is not affiliated with Kaiser Permanente. This story first published on California Healthline, a service of the California Health Care Foundation.

provide homeless patients a meal, clothes and vaccine screenings before discharging them.

Hospitals also must try to find the patients a bed at a safe destination, offer them transportation there and document the steps they have taken to do so.

If a hospital cannot find a bed for a patient, or if the patient refuses help, he can go to a location of his choice, including back to the streets.

The requirements expand on July 1. Starting then, hospitals will have to keep a log of the homeless patients they discharge and where they go, among other mandates.

Legislators passed the law in response to reports that hospitals were dumping homeless patients on the streets with little more than their hospital gowns. One Sacramento woman who had undergone a double mastectomy was sent to a Salvation Army shelter after her discharge, only to find there were no available beds. She had to sleep in her car, The Sacramento Bee reported.

Several California hospitals have settled lawsuits in response to such allegations.

But finding a suitable place for each patient isn't as easy as calling a shelter and securing a cot. There simply aren't enough places—or, in some cases, the right places—to send these individuals, hospitals say.

Some patients need more follow-up care and monitoring than might be available in a basic shelter.

"We knew that the challenge for our hospitals would be what to do with patients who require services when there are few programs, spaces and beds available for post-acute care," said Peggy Wheeler, vice president of rural health at the California Hospital Association, which initially opposed the legislation.

If appropriate settings aren't available for homeless patients who need to heal from a wound or require follow-up treatment, some of them may stay in the hospital longer than necessary, Wheeler said.

"This puts hospitals in a situation where they don't have a bed available for someone who does need acute care," she said.

Homeless patients with complex medical needs are especially difficult to place in rural communities because of a lack of adequate services, said Brenda Robertson, care management regional director for Adventist Health hospitals in central California.

"Most shelters will not accept a patient on oxygen, and a subset of younger, aggressive behavioral health patients are not appropriate to be placed in a skilled nursing facility amongst frail elders," Robertson said.

Many of these patients need transitional care where they can rest and recover before being on their own again, she said. "But in central California there really isn't much."

Bigger cities have more resources—but also more homeless patients.

In 2018, the nonprofit National Health Foundation opened a 62-bed facility in downtown Los Angeles for discharged hospital patients who need less intensive medical oversight than a nursing home provides. Patients at that facility have access to case managers who arrange for transportation and food and try to find them permanent housing.

Area hospitals often reserve beds at the facility for discharged homeless patients, said Jennifer Bayer, vice president of external affairs at the Hospital Association of Southern California. At least one health plan also leases beds there for its enrollees.

In San Jose, Santa Clara Valley Medical Center sent 55 patients, including Trumbla, to Skyline Health Care Center in the first 10 months of the partnership, said Dr. Huy Ngo, who oversees the program along with Chan. Medical services for those patients are primarily covered by Medi-Cal, the state's Medicaid program for low-income residents.

During that period, Skyline discharged 42 of the patients, the majority into long-term housing programs or to family members and friends, said Ngo. Of those, six were readmitted to the hospital—a low number for this population, Ngo said.

That was encouraging, he said, but "we know 15 beds don't even begin to meet the needs" of the homeless population in Santa Clara County.

The homeless count in 2017 showed 7,394 homeless people in the county, with the majority in San Jose.

A month after his discharge, Trumbla still lives in his boss's shop. But his toe has healed, and he credits the six months at the nursing home for helping him control his diabetes. He planned to start working again in construction.

But his wife, Manda Upham, is now in a hospital because of chronic obstructive pulmonary disease and congestive heart failure, Trumbla said. It's possible she might be transferred to a hospital outside of San Jose.

"More hospitals and no housing in sight yet," Trumbla lamented. "It's getting complicated again."

38. The Homeless Are Dying in Record Numbers on the Streets of L.A.*

Anna Gorman *and* Harriet Blair Rowan

A record number of homeless people—918 in 2018 alone—are dying across Los Angeles County, on bus benches, hillsides, railroad tracks and sidewalks.

Deaths have jumped 76 percent in the past five years, outpacing the growth of the homeless population, according to a Kaiser Health News analysis of the coroner's data.

Health officials and experts have not pinpointed a single cause for the sharp increase in deaths, but they say rising substance abuse may be a major reason. The surge also reflects growth in the number of people who are chronically homeless and those who don't typically use shelters, which means more people are living longer on the streets with serious physical and behavioral health issues, they say.

"It is a combination of people who are living for a long time in unhealthy situations and who have multiple health problems," said Michael Cousineau, a professor at the Keck School of Medicine of the University of Southern California. "There are more complications, and one of those complications is a high mortality rate. It's just a tragedy."

Nearly 53,000 people were homeless in L.A. County in 2018, according to a point-in-time count of homeless residents, an increase of about 39 percent since 2014. The majority were not living in shelters.

The homeless population has also grown nationwide, but there is no national count of homeless deaths.

The Los Angeles County Department of Medical Examiner-Coroner considers someone homeless if that person doesn't have an established residence, or if the body was found in an encampment, shelter or other location that suggests homelessness.

Based on that criteria, the coroner reported 3,612 deaths of homeless people in L.A. County from 2014 to 2018.

A detailed look at the numbers reveals a complex picture of where—and how—homeless people are dying.

---

*Originally published as Anna Gorman and Harriet Blair Rowan, "The Homeless Are Dying in Record Numbers on the Streets of L.A." *Kaiser Health News*, https://khn.org/news/the-homeless-are-dying-in-record-numbers-on-the-streets-of-l-a/ (April 24, 2019). Kaiser Health News is a nonprofit news service covering health issues. It is an editorially independent program of the Kaiser Family Foundation that is not affiliated with Kaiser Permanente. This story first published on California Healthline, a service of the California Health Care Foundation.

One-third died in hospitals and even more died outside, in places such as sidewalks, alleyways, parking lots, riverbeds and on freeway on-ramps.

Male deaths outnumbered female deaths, but the percentage of homeless women who died increased faster than that of men. And although black people make up fewer than one-tenth of the county's population, they accounted for nearly a quarter of the homeless deaths.

"We need to take action now," said the Rev. Andy Bales, CEO of the Union Rescue Mission, a homeless shelter on L.A.'s skid row. "Otherwise next year it's going to be more than 1,000."

Substance Abuse

Drugs and alcohol played a direct role in at least a quarter of the deaths of homeless people over the past five years, according to the analysis of the coroner's data. It likely contributed to many more, including some whose deaths were related to liver and heart problems.

The coroner's cause of death determination "doesn't necessarily tell the whole story," said Brian Elias, the county's chief of coroner investigations, who called the increase "alarming."

A person who is homeless may get an infection on top of a chronic disease on top of a substance abuse disorder—and all of those together lead to bad outcomes. "It's a house of cards," said Dr. Coley King, a physician at the Venice Family Clinic.

Raymond Thill was just 46 when he died of what his wife, Sherry Thill, called complications related to alcoholism. The couple had been homeless for many years before moving into a small apartment in South Los Angeles shortly before his death.

Thill said her husband often drank vodka throughout the day and had been in and out of the hospital because of liver and other health problems. He tried rehab and she tried taking the alcohol away. Nothing worked, she said.

"His mind was set," she said. "So I took care of him."

In the end, Thill said, cirrhosis left her husband jaundiced, swollen and unable to keep food down.

King treated Raymond Thill and said he is convinced that Thill would have lived longer if he'd been off the streets earlier.

"This shouldn't be happening," especially when many deaths could have been prevented with better access to health care and housing, said David Snow, a sociology professor at the University of California–Irvine. "If you are on the streets, you are not getting the attention you need."

"Ready for Bad Luck to Happen"

Homeless residents in Los Angeles also died from the same ailments as the general population—heart disease, cancer, lung disease, diabetes and infections. But they did so at a much younger age, said Dr. Paul Gregerson, who treats homeless residents as chief medical officer for JWCH Institute clinics in the Los Angeles area.

A stressful lifestyle, lack of healthy food and exposure to the weather contribute to an early death, he said. "If you are homeless, your body ages faster from living outside," Gregerson said.

In Los Angeles County, the average age of death for homeless people was 48 for women and 51 for men. The life expectancy for women in California in 2016 was 83 and 79 for men—among the best longevity statistics in the nation.

Over the five-year period in L.A. County, there also was a sharp increase in deaths of younger adults who were homeless. For instance, the deaths of adults under 45 more than doubled.

The data does not include information about mental illnesses, which Elias of the coroner's office said could be a contributing factor in some of the deaths.

Stephen Rosenstein, 59, was walking across the street in Panorama City, an L.A. neighborhood, when a car struck and killed him one night, said his sister, Cindy Garcia. He had spent years bouncing from the streets to shelters to board-and-care homes, she said.

Rosenstein had been diagnosed with schizophrenia and manic depression, Garcia said, and often resisted help—behavior she attributed to his mental illness. "Most people would want to have a roof over your head," she said. "He just fought it all the way."

Rosenstein's cause of death was listed as "traumatic injuries." Deaths by trauma or violence were common among the homeless in the period analyzed: At least 800 people died from trauma, and of those, about 200 were shot or stabbed.

"They are ready for bad luck to happen," King said.

39. "Medieval" Diseases Flare as Unsanitary Living Conditions Proliferate*

Anna Gorman

Jennifer Millar keeps trash bags and hand sanitizer near her tent, and she regularly pours water mixed with hydrogen peroxide on the sidewalk nearby. Keeping herself and the patch of concrete she calls home clean is a top priority.

But this homeless encampment off a Hollywood freeway ramp is often littered with needles and trash and soaked in urine. Rats occasionally scamper through, and Millar fears the consequences.

"I worry about all those diseases," said Millar, 43, who said she has been homeless most of her life.

Infectious diseases—some that ravaged populations in the Middle Ages—are resurging in California and around the country and are hitting homeless populations especially hard. Los Angeles experienced an outbreak of typhus—a disease spread by infected fleas on rats and other animals—in downtown streets. Officials briefly closed part of City Hall after reporting that rodents had invaded the building.

People in Washington state have been infected with *Shigella* bacteria, which is spread through feces and causes the diarrheal disease shigellosis, as well as *Bartonella quintana,* which spreads through body lice and causes trench fever.

Hepatitis A, also spread primarily through feces, infected more than 1,000 people in Southern California in the past two years. The disease also has erupted in New Mexico, Ohio and Kentucky, primarily among people who are homeless or use drugs.

Public health officials and politicians are using terms like "disaster" and "public health crisis" to describe the outbreaks, and they warn that these diseases can easily jump beyond the homeless population.

"Our homeless crisis is increasingly becoming a public health crisis," California Gov. Gavin Newsom said in his State of the State speech in February, citing outbreaks of hepatitis A in San Diego County, syphilis in Sonoma County and typhus in Los Angeles County.

"Typhus," he said. "A medieval disease. In California. In 2019."

---

*Originally published as Anna Gorman, "'Medieval' Diseases Flare as Unsanitary Living Conditions Proliferate," *Kaiser Health News*, https://khn.org/news/medieval-diseases-flare-as-unsanitary-living-conditions-proliferate/ (March 12, 2019). Kaiser Health News is a nonprofit news service covering health issues. It is an editorially independent program of the Kaiser Family Foundation that is not affiliated with Kaiser Permanente.

The diseases have flared as the nation's homeless population has grown in the past two years: About 553,000 people were homeless at the end of 2018, and nearly one-quarter of homeless people live in California.

The diseases spread quickly and widely among people living outside or in shelters, fueled by sidewalks contaminated with human feces, crowded living conditions, weakened immune systems and limited access to health care.

"The hygiene situation is just horrendous" for people living on the streets, said Dr. Glenn Lopez, a physician with St. John's Well Child & Family Center, who treats homeless patients in Los Angeles County. "It becomes just like a Third World environment where their human feces contaminate the areas where they are eating and sleeping."

Those infectious diseases are not limited to homeless populations, Lopez warned. "Even someone who believes they are protected from these infections are not."

At least one Los Angeles city staffer said she contracted typhus in City Hall last fall. And San Diego County officials warned in 2017 that diners at a well-known restaurant were at risk of hepatitis A.

There were 167 cases of typhus from Jan. 1, 2018, through Feb. 1, 2019, up from 125 in 2013 and 13 in 2008, according to the California Public Health Department.

Typhus is a bacterial infection that can cause a high fever, stomach pain and chills but can be treated with antibiotics. Outbreaks are more common in overcrowded and trash-filled areas that attract rats.

The typhus outbreak began last fall when health officials reported clusters of the flea-borne disease in downtown Los Angeles and Compton. They also have occurred in Pasadena, where the problems are likely due to people feeding stray cats carrying fleas.

In February 2019, the county announced another outbreak in downtown Los Angeles that infected nine people, six of whom were homeless. After city workers said they saw rodent droppings in City Hall, Los Angeles City Council President Herb Wesson briefly shut down his office to rip up the rugs, and he also called for an investigation and more cleaning.

Hepatitis A is caused by a virus usually transmitted when people come in contact with feces of infected people. Most people recover on their own, but the disease can be very serious for those with underlying liver conditions. There were 948 cases of hepatitis A in 2017 and 178 in 2018 and 2019, the state public health department said. Twenty-one people have died as a result of the 2017–18 outbreak.

The infections around the country are not a surprise, given the lack of attention to housing and health care for the homeless and the dearth of bathrooms and places to wash hands, said Dr. Jeffrey Duchin, the health officer for Seattle and King County, Wash.

"It's a public health disaster," he said.

In his area, Duchin said, he has seen shigellosis, trench fever and skin infections among homeless populations.

In New York City, where more of the homeless population lives in shelters rather than on the streets, there have not been the same outbreaks of hepatitis A and typhus, said Dr. Kelly Doran, an emergency medicine physician and assistant professor at NYU School of Medicine. But Doran said different infections occur in shelters, including tuberculosis, a disease that spreads through the air and typically infects the lungs.

The diseases sometimes get the "medieval" moniker because people in that era lived in squalid conditions without clean water or sewage treatment, said Dr. Jeffrey Klausner, a professor of medicine and public health at UCLA.

People living on the streets or in homeless shelters are vulnerable to such outbreaks because their weakened immune systems are worsened by stress, malnutrition and sleep deprivation. Many also have mental illness and substance abuse disorders, which can make it harder for them to stay healthy or get health care.

On a February afternoon, Saban Community Clinic physician assistant Negeen Farmand walked through homeless encampments in Hollywood carrying a backpack with medical supplies. She stopped to talk to a man sweeping the sidewalks. He said he sees "everything and anything" in the gutters and hopes he doesn't get sick.

She introduced herself to a few others and asked if they had any health issues that needed checking. When she saw Millar, Farmand checked her blood pressure, asked about her asthma and urged her to come see a doctor for treatment of her hepatitis C, a viral infection spread through contaminated blood that can lead to serious liver damage.

"To get these people to come into a clinic is a big thing," she said. "A lot of them are distrustful of the health care system."

On another day, 53-year-old Karen Mitchell waited to get treated for a persistent cough by St. John's Well Child & Family Center's mobile health clinic. She also needed a tuberculosis test, as required by the shelter where she was living in Bellflower, Calif.

Mitchell, who said she developed alcoholism after a career in pharmaceutical sales, said she has contracted pneumonia from germs from other shelter residents. "Everyone is always sick, no matter what precautions they take."

During the hepatitis A outbreak, public health officials administered widespread vaccinations, cleaned the streets with bleach and water and installed hand-washing stations and portable toilets near high concentrations of homeless people.

But health officials and homeless advocates said more needs to be done, including helping people access medical and behavioral health care and affordable housing.

"It really is unconscionable," said Bobby Watts, CEO of the National Health Care for the Homeless Council, a policy and advocacy organization. "These are all preventable diseases."

• C. Substance Abuse •

40. Addicted to Homelessness*

JOHANNA L. WONG *and* WILLIE L. BRITT

Substance use disorder and homelessness appear to be correlated. In 2013, 80 percent of unsheltered homeless individuals in San Mateo County, California, had at least one disability.

About 72 percent cited their disability as "drug or alcohol problems" (HOPE, 2013, p. 13). In 2013, 22 percent of this population comprised the emergency housing clientele of Safe Harbor Shelter. 62 percent of total clients served voluntarily exited the shelter within 90 days of seeking temporary housing services and did not receive transitional housing services (Brown & Rodriguez, personal communication, October 4, 2013).

In order to assess the effectiveness of substance abuse services provided at Safe Harbor Shelter, the curriculum of those services was examined, literature was reviewed and analyzed, existing clients were surveyed, and the Substance Abuse Case Manager, Associate Directors of Safe Harbor Shelter, and Director of Programs and Services of Samaritan House were interviewed. Recommendations were made to guide future programming and treatment strategies.

The study evaluated the correlation between homelessness and substance use disorder, and the curriculum of substance abuse services provided by Safe Harbor Shelter of Samaritan House, a non-profit organization within San Mateo County. The treatment philosophies of 12-Steps and Harm Reduction and their effectiveness were compared in efforts to possibly diversify the treatment services provided and empower this population to live healthier lives and sustain permanent housing upon exiting the shelter. As previously stated, it was anticipated that results of the study could be used to guide programming and treatment strategies provided by Safe Harbor Shelter of Samaritan House to better serve clients with substance use disorder.

In 1974, Public Health Nurse Cora Clemons and her associates created Samaritan House in partnership with the City of San Mateo, to provide referrals for people who needed basic social services. By 1985, Samaritan House became a Core Service Agency for the entire County of San Mateo and began providing free and direct services, acting as a safety net for low income families offering food, shelter, clothing, medical and dental care, counseling, and worker resources with the goal of promoting client self-sufficiency. Safe Harbor Shelter of Samaritan House is a 90-bed emergency homeless shelter located in South San Francisco, California. It provides temporary and transitional housing services to unsheltered homeless adults 18 years and older from San Mateo County and

---

*Published with permission of the authors.

operates in collaboration with the County of San Mateo Human Services Agency. In fiscal year 2012 and 2013, it had $9 million operating budget and employed 41 full-time, 31 part-time, and seasonal employees. Since its establishment, Samaritan House has met its performance measures with the Department of Housing and Human Services Agency of San Mateo County. Hence, the county continues to negotiate and contract with this agency without interruption (Samaritan House, 2013, "Financials," para. 1).

There were an estimated 7,151 homeless people in San Mateo County on an annual basis (HOPE, 2013, p. 3). The latest report prepared by the San Mateo County Human Services Agency, Center on Homelessness (2013), notes an increase of 12 percent of unsheltered homeless individuals and an increase of 6 percent of sheltered homeless individuals within the county since 2011 (Hope, 2013, p. 4). The 2013 homeless census determined that there were 2,281 homeless people in San Mateo County on the night of January 23, 2013:

- 1,299 unsheltered homeless people (living on streets, in vehicles, in homeless encampments) and,
- 982 sheltered homeless people in emergency shelters, transitional housing, motel voucher programs, and institutions: residential treatment, jails, and hospitals
- Hidden Homeless, defined as homelessness not easily measured, such as individuals who are living in structures not meant for human habitation or individuals who are living with friends or relatives that are unstably housed and at risk of becoming homeless (HOPE, 2013, pp. 3–12).

Treatment Philosophies: 12-Steps versus Harm Reduction

It is important to define the difference between harm reduction and clean and sober as options of controlling or abstaining from alcohol and drug abuse. According to the International Harm Reduction Association, harm reduction, "refers to policies, programs, and practices that aim primarily to reduce the adverse health, social and economic consequences of the use of legal and illegal psychoactive drugs without necessarily reducing drug consumption. Harm reduction benefits people who use drugs, their families and the community" (International Harm Reduction Association, 2010, "Definition," para. 5).

The term clean and sober is derived from the disease model of addiction. It proposes that people addicted to alcohol and other drugs have a chronic disease that can never be cured but can be arrested. The ideal treatment for anyone with this disease is total abstinence. Anyone who still uses in any quantity continues to trigger the intense cravings for their drugs of choice, which can only be suppressed by using more drugs or complete abstinence. Some organizations that support the disease model of addiction are Alcoholics Anonymous, Narcotics Anonymous, and the American Medical Association (Larimer, Marlatt, & Witkiewitz, 2012, pp. 63–68).

To date, the data regarding effective treatment for individuals with substance use disorder has not unequivocally demonstrated the effectiveness 12-step facilitation approaches for reducing substance abuse, dependence, or problems (Johnson, 2010, p. B3). The main challenge in obtaining success rates of 12-step groups is the emphasis on *anonymity* of group members at the level of press, radio, and films (Basic Text of Narcotics Anonymous, 2008).

As a result of having anonymity at the core of their foundation, none of the 12-step groups or fellowships will provide or release any form of representative samples of success or failure rates at any time. Twelve-step (12-step) facilitation groups are modeled around the principles of 12-step fellowships, which originated with Alcoholics Anonymous in 1935, in Akron, Ohio (Alcoholics Anonymous, Big Book, 2014).

In the mid–1980s harm reduction emerged as a treatment philosophy. G. Alan Marlett, PhD, "conducted pioneering work on understanding and preventing relapse in substance abuse treatment and was a leading proponent of the harm reduction approach to treatment of addictive behaviors" (Marlatt, Larimer, & Witkiewitz, 2012, p. vii). The purpose of harm reduction is to empower individuals to manage their high-risk behavior, incrementally and reduce harm affiliated with substance abuse without necessarily reducing the amount of use. "Harm reduction means meeting individuals where they are with outreach services such as methadone maintenance, needle exchange, condoms, medical referral, and information on drug treatment" (Richardson, 1998, p. 81). In their 2012 book, *Harm Reduction: Pragmatic Strategies for Managing High-Risk Behaviors*, Marlatt, Larimer, and Witkiewitz present harm reduction as a humane and compassionate alternative to the punitive "zero-tolerance" approach to individuals with substance use disorder. Harm reduction philosophy includes practices previously discussed of cognitive behavioral therapy and motivational enhancement therapy which support client empowerment. The seven characteristics of this treatment philosophy include:

1. Meeting the client as an individual
2. Starting where the client is at in their behavior
3. Assuming that the client has strengths that can be supported
4. Accepting small incremental changes as steps in the right direction
5. Not holding abstinence, or any other preconceived notions as a necessary precondition of the treatment before getting to know the individual
6. Developing a collaborative, empowering relationship with the client
7. De-stigmatizing substance users [Marlatt et al., 2012, pp. 39–40].

Harm reduction is "more of an attitude than a fixed set of rules or regulations." This attitude has influenced various fields: public health, prevention, intervention, education, peer support, and advocacy (Marlatt et al., 2012, p 6). The [President] Obama administration redefined drug policy from a war on drugs to a public safety and a public health concern. Despite the influence of harm reduction on public policy, this movement has not "lessened the confusion and controversy surrounding what constitutes harm reduction" (Marlatt et al., 2012, p 4).

Results, Conclusion, and Recommendations

The results of the case study analysis indicate that despite entering and exiting treatment, individuals with substance use disorder experienced high rates of recidivism and relapse. Additional prevalent life problems experienced were unemployment, homelessness and mental health disorders. There is a correlation between substance abuse and homelessness, but assessing direct causation was not established in this study.

Despite the differences in philosophies of treatment offered at any time, an individual's willingness and ability to modify his/her behavior and thought process will continue only after an individual has the desire and motivation to do so. Treatment, of any kind, offers education, information, and resources to assist clients with substance use disorder make healthier choices and improve their quality of life.

Despite a perceived difference between the practice of harm reduction and being clean and sober, it appears that these two types of treatment options seek to offer the same solution: to reduce the negative consequences that result from abusing drugs and alcohol, with the goal of complete abstinence as a choice. Both practices leave that choice to the individual and based on the data appear to be equally effective. The main difference between these two treatment philosophies is that 12-steps suggest complete abstinence, while harm reduction offers complete abstinence on its continuum of harm reduction practices.

Based on the findings of this study, it appears that most of the clients surveyed were interested in receiving additional mental health services and 12-step meetings onsite. Of greatest importance were the goals of obtaining employment and stable housing while at the shelter. As a result of these discoveries, to maximize the programming operations of Safe Harbor Shelter, the following strategies were recommended as a part of organizational improvement.

1. Associate Directors of Safe Harbor Shelter implement three total weekly in-house recovery meetings, consisting of one meeting from Narcotics Anonymous, Alcoholics Anonymous, and LifeRing by July 1, 2014. Upon final approval from the Director of Programs and Services, implementation efforts would be conducted and defined upon contacting the organizations of Narcotics Anonymous, Alcoholics Anonymous, and LifeRing. Incorporating these in-house meetings would diversify the frequency and philosophies of substance abuse services offered for residents with a history of substance use disorder.

2. Associate Directors of Safe Harbor Shelter implement one life skills group, one evening per week, focused on job searching techniques and effective resume construction by July 1, 2014. This group would be conducted in the likeness of a class session and would allow for open discussion, lecture, and individual attention. The duration of this group would be sixty minutes. Upon final approval from the Director of Programs and Services of Samaritan House, implementation efforts would be defined by Associate Directors of Safe Harbor Shelter. This life skills group would provide all residents of Safe Harbor Shelter the critical skills for job searching and obtaining stable employment.

3. Associate Directors of Safe Harbor Shelter design and implement formal trainings with the Harm Reduction Therapy Center in San Francisco for all staff of Safe Harbor Shelter concerning the philosophy and strategies of Harm Reduction by October 1, 2014. Sixteen total hours of training would be recommended yearly, and trainings would take place semi-annually. Upon evaluation and approval by the director of programs and services of Samaritan House, implementation efforts would be conducted by the Associate Directors of Safe Harbor Shelter. Trainings and education regarding the philosophy of harm reduction for all staff would emphasize client-centered services and create an urgency of doing more with less, as a performance measure. This would assist in identifying and analyzing the strengths, weaknesses, opportunities, and threats encountered by Safe Harbor Shelter of Samaritan House as a *business* and non-profit organization. Client-centered services

and adopting an urgency of doing more with less, would improve the agency's overall strategic operations in efforts to effectively and efficiently carry out its mission and goals.

References

Basic Text of Narcotics Anonymous (6th ed.). (2008) Chatsworth, CA: Narcotics Anonymous World Services.

Big Book of Alcoholics Anonymous (4th ed.). (2001) New York City: Alcoholics Anonymous World Services.

County of San Mateo. (2013). San Mateo County 2013 Homeless Census and Survey. Housing Our People Effectively (HOPE): Ending Homelessness in San Mateo County.

International Harm Reduction Association. (2010). What is Harm Reduction? A position statement from the International Harm Reduction Association. Retrieved October 15, 2013, from http://www.ihra.net/.

Johnson, Bankole A. (2010, August 8).12 Steps to Nowhere. *The Washington Post.* p. B.3. Retrieved March 6, 2014 from http://search.proquest.com/docview/740264605?accountid=25283.

Larimer, M., Marlatt, A., and Witkiewitz, K. (2012). *Pragmatic Strategies for Managing High-Risk Behaviors.* New York: Guilford Press.

Richardson, D. (2000). Harm Reduction: Pragmatic Strategies for Managing High-Risk Behaviors. *Psychiatric Rehabilitation Journal,* 24(1), 81–82. Retrieved March 9, 2014 from http://search.proquest.com/docview/204740924?accountid=25283.

Samaritan House. (2013). Safe Harbor. Retrieved September 29, 2013, from http://samaritanhousesanmateo.org.

Wong, J.L. (2014) Addicted to Homelessness: An Examination of Substance Abuse Treatment Philosophies and Their Effectiveness on the Prevalent Life Problem of Homelessness. Unpublished master's capstone, Golden Gate University, San Francisco, California.

41. Homelessness Programs and Resources*

SUBSTANCE ABUSE AND MENTAL HEALTH SERVICES ADMINISTRATION

The Substance Abuse and Mental Health Services Administration (SAMHSA) is the agency within the U.S. Department of Health and Human Services that leads public health efforts to advance the behavioral health of the nation. SAMHSA's mission is to reduce the impact of substance abuse and mental illness on America's communities.

SAMHSA's grant programs and services support efforts for ending and preventing homelessness among people with mental and/or substance use disorders.

Stable housing is a critical component of recovery. SAMHSA's homelessness programs and resources work to end homelessness by improving access to treatment and services that support health and wellness. It is well documented that untreated behavioral health conditions can contribute to issues such as unemployment that make it difficult to find and keep stable and affordable housing. As reported by the Office of National Drug Control Policy, approximately 30 percent of people experiencing chronic homelessness have a serious mental illness, and around two-thirds have a primary substance use disorder or other chronic health condition.

SAMSHA's homelessness programs support many types of behavioral health treatments and recovery-oriented services. These services include:

- Outreach
- Case management
- Treatment for mental and/or substance use disorders
- Enrollment in mainstream benefits such as Medicaid and the Supplemental Nutrition Assistance Program (SNAP)
- Peer support services
- Employment readiness services

Programs primarily target people experiencing homelessness who have been underserved, or who have not received any behavioral health services. Most of these programs support people who experience chronic homelessness.

SAMSHA's homelessness programs include discretionary and formula grants. In

---

*Public document originally published as Substance Abuse and Mental Health Services Administration, "Homelessness Programs and Resources," https://www.samhsa.gov/homelessness-programs-resources/grant-programs-services (March 28, 2019).

addition, the SSI/SSDI Outreach, Access, and Recovery (SOAR) program helps increase access to disability income benefits for eligible adults who are experiencing or at risk for homelessness.

SAMHSA's Projects for Assistance in Transition from Homelessness (PATH) program is a formula grant that funds community-based outreach, mental and substance use disorder treatment services, case management, assistance with accessing housing, and other supportive services.

Case Management

Case management is one of the primary services offered to individuals and families experiencing homelessness. The National Association of State Mental Health Program Directors (NASMHPD) defines case management as "a range of services provided to assist and support individuals in developing their skills to gain access to needed medical, behavioral health, housing, employment, social, educational, and other services essential to meeting basic human services." This also includes providing "linkages and training for the patient served in the use of basic community resources and monitoring of overall service delivery."

Case managers work with people and families experiencing homelessness and those who are at risk of homelessness. Case managers identify households of greatest risk and determine the type of support needed to prevent homelessness. They also help clients develop independent living skills, provide support with treatment, and serve as the point of contact between clients and people in their social and professional support systems. To be successful, case managers need the right skills and adequate community knowledge.

Self-Care for Providers

Working with individuals and families experiencing homelessness can be rewarding. However, helping clients with the challenges they may face can also be extremely demanding. Homeless service providers may often feel a sense of sadness, powerlessness, and anger during the course of their work. Tension often exists between feeling inspired by the work and feeling frustrated about the things outside of one's control. To provide clients the best care and services, providers must also take care of themselves.

Housing and Shelter

Poverty, unemployment, and lack of affordable housing are commonly recognized causes of homelessness. These risk factors can be exacerbated by personal vulnerabilities such as mental and substance use disorders, trauma and violence, domestic violence, justice-system involvement, sudden serious illness, divorce, death of a partner, and disabilities.

Housing and shelter programs can help address the root causes of homelessness through a range of essential recovery support services, including mental and substance use disorder treatment, employment, and mainstream benefits. Types of housing and shelter programs include:

Emergency shelters are often where people experiencing economic shock first turn for support through a wide range of services.

Transitional housing typically involves a temporary residence of up to 24 months with wrap-around services to help people stabilize their lives.

Permanent supportive housing offers safe and stable housing environments with voluntary and flexible supports and services to help people manage serious, chronic issues such as mental and substance use disorders.

Providing permanent supportive housing on a housing first basis—without requiring transitional steps or demonstrated sobriety—is effective for people experiencing chronic homelessness. People with a serious mental illness, substance use disorder, or co-occurring mental and substance use disorder have demonstrated similar or better housing stability and substance use, compared to those placed in housing with pre-requisites. Large-scale studies demonstrating the benefits include the Collaborative Initiative to End Chronic Homelessness and HUD-VA Supportive Housing Program.

Research shows interventions to prevent homelessness are more cost effective than addressing issues after someone is already homeless. The longer a person is homeless, the harder and more expensive it becomes to re-house this person. Rapid rehousing helps people move from emergency/transitional shelter or on the street into stable housing as fast as possible. It also connects people with supportive, community-based resources that help them maintain housing.

The success of this strategy is noted in this example from a research report: Only 10 percent of families exiting the Department of Housing and Urban Development's Rapid Re-housing for Homeless Families Demonstration sites returned to homelessness.

Other strategies showing evidence of effectiveness for preventing homelessness include:

Programs that help stabilize households by providing food support, such as food stamps and programs for free school breakfast and lunch.

Programs seeking to increase the supply of affordable housing in America, such as the Housing Trust Fund.

Benefits advocacy, which helps people find public and entitlement benefits such as Social Security Disability Insurance (SSDI), veterans' benefits, food stamps, childcare assistance, Medicaid, and low-income energy assistance.

Discharge planning for people released from institutional care (e.g., hospitals, psychiatric care, substance abuse treatment centers, foster care, military service, jail, prison).

Case management that focuses on determining clients' needs for housing assistance, helping them find and get housing, and securing other resources needed to maintain housing stability (e.g., health insurance, childcare services, medical treatment, psychological services, food, clothing).

Employment

Employment can play an important role in recovery. People with histories of homelessness, including those with disabilities, often want to work given the opportunity and support to do so. When people who previously experienced homelessness are placed in housing, many develop feelings of isolation. Employment not only provides income but offers a structured activity with a sense of purpose and accomplishment. Also, employment promotes membership in the community and social inclusion.

With support, employment is possible for many people experiencing homelessness, including those with mental or substance use disorders. In Los Angeles' "Skid Row," a study offered housing and employment supports to people with serious mental illness who had experienced chronic homelessness. About one in four found competitive employment (a job not reserved for people with disabilities). However, the employment supports were the key. People in the study's comparison group, meaning they received housing alone, were half as likely to obtain competitive employment.

The following are helpful tips for case managers and employment specialists for helping clients pursue employment:

- Set and support vocational goals
- Help clients determine their strengths and weaknesses
- Identify the resources clients need to be successful
- Support clients in developing their job skills
- Match clients with appropriate job opportunities

Trauma

Homelessness is traumatic. People experiencing homelessness often live with a multitude of personal challenges, such as the sudden loss of a home or adjusting to conditions of shelter life. Some people, particularly women, may have histories of trauma, including sexual, psychological, or physical abuse. Most families who are experiencing homelessness are headed by single women, and these women experience posttraumatic stress disorder, depression, and substance use at a rate higher than the national average.

Within the larger society, people experiencing homelessness often are marginalized, isolated, and discriminated against. Additionally, they are highly vulnerable to violence and victimization, and re-traumatization becomes a distinct possibility. Given these concerns, it is important to understand the linkages between trauma and homelessness, and the impact on ensuring quality care.

Social Inclusion

People experiencing homelessness have lost the protection of a home and their community. They are often marginalized and isolated within the larger society. Also, people with mental and/or substance use disorders frequently face challenges in building and maintaining social connections. They may fail to seek out treatment for fear of discrimination or feel unworthy of help. Helping people experiencing homelessness overcome these beliefs and participate in treatment is a key step in recovery.

Social inclusion offers opportunities to re-engage with the community and form positive relationships. Consumer involvement is the practice of integrating people with lived experience of homelessness into staff and leadership roles at homeless service agencies. Consumers may provide peer support as role models and resources for other services. Peer support creates a sense of belonging for both the individual providing the service and those receiving the support.

Youth

Approximately 30 percent of people experiencing homelessness are younger than age 24, according to the Department of Housing and Urban Development's (HUD) 2018 annual report on Continuum of Care Homeless Assistance Programs Homeless Populations and Subpopulations. The growth of homelessness among youth and young adults, as well as their unique circumstances and needs, prompted HUD to establish 2017 as a baseline year for tracking progress toward ending youth homelessness.

The trauma of homelessness, even short term, can have a major effect on a youth's future development. Children who experience homelessness have significantly higher rates of emotional, behavioral, and immediate and long-term health problems. They often struggle with self-esteem, which puts them at risk for substance use, suicide, and other negative outcomes. They have numerous academic difficulties, including below-grade level reading, high rate of learning disabilities, poor school attendance, and failure to advance to the next grade or graduate. Four out of five children who are experiencing homelessness have been exposed to at least one serious violent event by age 12.

Risk factors associated with adult homelessness—mental and substance use disorders, poverty, and lack of educational employment opportunities—are often also true for youth homelessness. But, service delivery for individuals under the age of 24 experiencing homelessness must also consider other risk factors. Family conflict and "aging out" of the foster care or juvenile justice systems may play a significant role in a youth's experience with homelessness. According to the report Missed Opportunities: Homeless Youth in America, one in 10 young adults (ages 18–25), and at least one in 30 adolescents (ages 13–17), experience some form of homelessness unaccompanied by a parent or guardian over the course of a year. Unaccompanied youth can find it difficult to find a place to live and someone willing to rent them a room. Parenting teens experiencing homelessness face their own unique challenges.

Furthermore, youth who identify as lesbian, gay, bi-sexual, transgender, or queer or questioning (LGBTQ) disproportionately experience homelessness. They are at high risk for family rejection, physical assaults and sexual exploitation in shelters and on the streets, trauma, and mental and substance use disorders. Providing safe, supportive, and welcoming environments for LGBTQ youth is essential for reaching this vulnerable population.

• *D. Veterans* •

42. Ending Veteran Homelessness*

U.S. Department of Veterans Affairs

VA is committed to ending Veteran homelessness, community by community. Our work in collaboration with large and small localities proves that—through their leadership, cooperation and evidence-based practices—it's possible to ensure that every Veteran has a home.

Here's what national, state and local leaders are saying about these successes:

"We've re-tooled programs and systems to be more coordinated and overall more effective at finding our most vulnerable Veterans, triaging their needs, and then navigating them to the most appropriate housing resources and supportive services."—**Little Rock, AR, Mayor Mark Stodola, Dec. 14, 2018**

"Today, we say with certainty that Miami-Dade is treating its Veterans with the respect they deserve."—**Miami-Dade County Mayor Carlos A. Gimenez, Aug. 2, 2018**

"It is because of this relentless community-wide effort that we have reached such a significant and immeasurably impactful goal."—**Norman, OK, Mayor Lynne Miller, Feb. 27, 2018**

"It's certainly an accomplishment that we don't take lightly. It's something that certainly puts our local VA and its great staff on the map nationally. It also is a real compliment to the City of Beckley."—**Beckley, WV, Mayor Rob Rappold, Feb. 8, 2018**

"Five hundred eighty-seven individuals and their families are in a much better position because of the work that was done between federal, state, county and city government together with those that were on the ground carrying out the mission."—**Pittsburgh, PA, Mayor Bill Peduto, Nov. 21, 2017**

"One of the things we recently did was we took the opportunity to combine the Coordinated Council for Homelessness so there could be one single voice. We need to do a better job of tracking and caring for people and not caring what side of the state line they are on."—**Kansas City, KS, Mayor Mark Holland, Nov. 20, 2017**

---

*Public document originally published as U.S. Department of Veterans Affairs, "Ending Veteran Homelessness," https://www.va.gov/HOMELESS/endingVetshomelessness.asp (January 22, 2019).

"I want to express my sincere thanks to all of our partners and the providers who made this possible. It means so much to me to know that we have been able to help the women and men who risked it all in service to their country."—**Atlanta, GA, Mayor Kasim Reed, Nov. 6, 2017**

"The County staff has shown a great dedication to helping Veterans and ending homelessness. More than 170 Veterans Affairs Housing Vouchers have been provided in Kent County in recent years. I'm proud of the work they've done to help reach Functional Zero."—**Kent County, MI, Board Commissioner Tom Antor, Sept. 26, 2017**

"The plans ensure that when homelessness does occur, it is rare, brief, and non-recurring," said Carla Solem, Continuum of Care Coordinator. "[I]t is evidence that the CoCs have plans in place to assure Veteran[s] is sheltered immediately, housed rapidly and supported in a manner that reduces the likelihood that he or she will ever become homeless again."—**Northwest & West Central Minnesota Continuum of Care Coordinator Carla Solem, Aug. 24, 2017**

"Lowell has identified every homeless Veteran by name and has a support system in place to ensure, whenever possible, that no Veterans are sleeping on the streets…. Every Veteran has access to permanent housing, and the community has a capacity to ensure that Veteran homelessness when it occurs is rare, brief and nonrecurring."—**Lowell, MA, Mayor Edward Kennedy, Aug. 23, 2017**

"[T]he idea that anyone who has worn our country's uniform spends their nights sleeping on the ground should horrify us. Our veterans fought for our freedom and they deserve our help when they need it most."—**Allentown, PA, Mayor Ed Pawlowski, July 10, 2017**

"This designation is a significant achievement for the city of Akron and the Continuum of Care, and a milestone in our fight to end Veterans' homelessness in this community."—**Akron, OH, Mayor Daniel Horrigan, May 26, 2017**

"We have made homelessness in our community rare, brief and non-reoccurring."—**Charlotte County, FL, Homeless Coalition's CEO, Angela Hogan, Mar. 30, 2017**

"The Nashua community takes care of our people, and the elimination of Veteran homelessness is an example of that caretaking."—**Nashua, NH, Mayor Jim Donchess, Mar. 24, 2017**

"[W]hat has been so powerful about the work of ending Veteran homelessness, and the reason we're actually seeing the end of it here in Minnesota and other places around the country, is that they set this goal at the federal level, and it was a bipartisan goal."—**Minnesota State Director to Prevent and End Homelessness, Cathy ten Broeke, Mar. 23, 2017**

"Veterans who have served our country should not … be forced to sleep in parking garages, shelters, cars, or on street corners—**unfortunately, that is a reality in too many cities across the country. But over the last two years, Chattanoogans have banded together to say, 'Not in our city.'"—Chattanooga, TN, Mayor Andy Berke, Feb. 9, 2017**

"It is my prayer that all that we accomplish in working to eradicate homelessness for Veterans, would be transformational in their lives and allow them to transition into society as productive citizens who enjoy a good quality of life."—**Shreveport, LA, Mayor Ollie Tyler, Jan. 5, 2017**

"La Crosse signed on to the national effort, as part of the Mayor's Challenge, to work together and provide permanent housing for our homeless Veterans and it is awe-inspiring to see this dream realized. We are so fortunate to live in such a caring, compassionate, and hard-working community."—**La Crosse, WI, Mayor Tim Kabat, Dec. 19, 2016**

"This is what it looks like when a community comes together to get things done. We can change lives."—**Hales, Multnomah County, OR, Chair, Deborah Kafoury, Dec. 10, 2016**

"I'm proud today, that Portland is the first West Coast city to receive official designation in meeting the…. Mayors Challenge to End Veterans Homelessness. This would not have been possible without our government, nonprofit, faith and private sector partners' complete dedication to this work. With continued commitment, I know our community can reach our goal to provide permanent, affordable housing to every Portlander who needs it."—**Portland, OR, Mayor Charlie Hales, Dec. 10, 2016**

"If you are a veteran in DeKalb County and need a place to live, we will help you."—**DeKalb County, GA, iCEO, Lee May, Dec. 9, 2016**

"Together, the City of Dayton, Montgomery County, and our community partners have worked to ensure that every veteran has access to permanent housing. Targeted collaboration among our partners has streamlined a community process that ensures that any veteran in the Dayton community, who needs assistance, receives a rapid connection to housing resources."—**Dayton, OH, Mayor Nan Whaley, Nov. 28, 2016**

"Even one homeless veteran is one too many. That's why this week I was thrilled to announce that—after more than a year's work with our local, state and federal partners—we have effectively ended veteran homelessness in our state. Thank you to everyone who has made it possible to get our veterans the help they need and deserve. Showing them the same level of commitment they made to our country will help keep Delaware moving forward."—**Governor's Weekly Message: Ending Veteran Homelessness in Delaware, Nov. 16, 2016**

"This is the story of many hands and heads working together to achieve a common goal. I thank and commend our County staff and our community partners for sharing my passion and my vision for ending Veterans Homelessness. We did it. And we did it together."—**Middlesex County, NJ, Freeholder Director, Ronald G. Rios, Nov. 4, 2016**

"All cities in Volusia County need to come together and collaborate with the county.… If you rapidly house people … we see stability over the long term. About 85 percent don't return to homelessness."—**Volusia County/Daytona Beach, FL, Executive Director of the Office on Homelessness with Florida Department of Children and Families, Erik Braun, Nov. 4, 2016**

"We accepted that challenge, we delivered, and I can announce proudly today that we have essentially ended veteran homelessness in our community."—**Buffalo, NY, Mayor Byron Brown, Nov. 4, 2016**

"In most cases, folks who've been homeless make tremendous tenants. They're very grateful for the housing and they take care of their apartments very well."—**Adviser to the Mayor of Boston for the Initiative to End Chronic Homelessness, Laila Bernstein, Oct. 5, 2016**

"It's important that we reflect on victories when we have them and our victory on effectively reaching the end of chronic Veteran homelessness … is a cause for celebration."—**Orlando, FL, Mayor Buddy Dyer, Sept. 23, 2016**

"We got to this community win today in a classic Austin way. We were innovative, creative and determined. There was great work already being done when this initiative started, but these efforts weren't quite getting the job done all the way. We needed a new way, new partners, and a wider and renewed commitment."—**Austin, TX, Mayor Steve Adler, Aug. 19, 2016**

"The men and women who have so bravely served our country deserve more than just our deepest gratitude. They deserve to live securely and prosperously in our communities. That security starts with a roof over their heads."—**Bergen County, NJ, Executive, James J. Tedesco III, Aug. 4, 2016**

"Along with my partners in government, we have ensured that every homeless Veteran seeking shelter on Long Island has been housed, and that any Veteran or active-duty military personnel who may be in need in the future will receive immediate shelter."—**Nassau County (Long Island, NY) Executive Edward P. Mangano, July 15, 2016**

"Our community is one that stands with one another, especially those who sacrifice their lives for the very freedoms we enjoy today."—**Hattiesburg, MS, Mayor Johnny DuPree, June 15, 2016**

"This is an important victory in our ongoing efforts to make our Parish the best place for veterans to live, work and raise a family. However, we must remain committed to keeping homelessness among veterans rare, brief and non-recurring."—**Terrebonne Parish, LA, President Gordon Dove, June 3, 2016**

"Our Veterans fought for us, and now it's time to fight for them."—**Rochester, NY, Mayor Lovely Warren, May 18, 2016**

"In January 2015, I pledged my commitment to the Mayors Challenge to End Veteran Homelessness. Together, the City of San Antonio, our business sector led by USAA, and our non-profit partners have achieved the goal of effectively ending veteran homelessness in our community."—**San Antonio, TX, Mayor Ivy R. Taylor, May 13, 2016**

"We embrace our responsibility to provide our Veterans with the services and supports they need, with housing at the top of that list."—**Lynn, MA, Mayor Judith Flanagan Kennedy, Mar. 17, 2016**

"Any veteran who is experiencing or is at risk of homelessness in Des Moines and Polk County has access to a safety net of resources and services."—**Supervisor for Central Iowa's Department of Veterans Affairs, Jennifer Miner, Mar. 17, 2016**

"We work[ed] really hard to achieve this goal."—**Executive director of the Berks Coalition, PA, Sharon Parker, Feb. 18, 2016**

"You need someplace to brush your teeth and clean your clothes and bathe, so you can look presentable when you're out interviewing for a job."—**Fayetteville, NC, Mayor Nat Robertson, Jan. 16, 2016**

"I am so proud of our City staff and immensely grateful for their efforts in combating homelessness among Veterans in Riverside."—**Riverside, CA, Mayor Rusty Bailey, Jan. 7, 2016**

"This effort has been a team effort. Biloxi and Gulfport are receiving this designation because of strong partnerships with the Biloxi Veterans Administration, the Biloxi Housing Authority, the Mississippi Housing Authority Region VIII in Gulfport, and community partners that include Oak Arbor, Hancock Resource Center, and Voices of Calvary Ministries who have received federal funds to assist veterans and their families across the Coast."—**Biloxi, MS, Mayor Andrew Gilich, Dec. 31, 2015**

"As the lead agency for the Harrison County HOME Consortium, Gulfport has partnered with Biloxi, Back Bay Mission and Gulf Coast Housing Initiative in the construction of eight new apartments designated for our veterans. This benchmark for veterans is crucial, however, we must build on this work to create solutions for the overall problem and causes of homelessness which persists in our communities."—**Gulfport, MS, Mayor Billy Hewes, Dec. 31, 2015**

"The brave women and men who valiantly protected our nation abroad should never be left without a home. Today, we have ensured that those in the veteran community who have struggled to find and remain in housing time and time again will have a stable place to call home. I'm grateful to the city agencies, federal partners and the City Council, who all worked tirelessly together to make this pledge a reality."—**New York City Mayor Bill de Blasio, Dec. 30, 2015**

"We are proud of this recognition and the work we have done, yet we know that our efforts to end homelessness among veterans will continue in the days and years ahead. We are resolved to make sure that homelessness among veterans will remain infrequent and short-lived."—**Albany, NY, Mayor Kathy Sheehan, Dec. 22, 2015**

"Montgomery County now has a coordinated and efficient system, which has been developed with our community partners to ensure that every veteran in our County has access to the supports needed to move quickly from homelessness to permanent housing. Providing a stable home for our veterans is simply the right thing to do for those who have sacrificed so much for our country."—**Montgomery County, MD, Councilman George Leventhal, Dec. 18, 2015**

"Too often, veterans find themselves struggling with issues like homelessness and poverty and that is a shame. For those who gave so much of themselves to this Nation, there is no reason why they should be left out in the cold. Today, I am happy to report that homelessness among veterans in Philadelphia is now rare, brief and non-recurring. In other words, Philadelphia has effectively ended veteran homelessness for those who want a home."—**Philadelphia Mayor Michael Nutter, Dec. 17, 2015**

"Every Veteran has a name. Every person has a story. When we make their story part of our story and our life and our work, we're able to get people housed, we're able to manage that list, we're able to make the connections to solve that problem."—**Rockford, IL, Mayor Larry Morrissey, Dec. 15, 2015**

"I'm excited that the [mayors] have supported and stood behind this, and as a community, we all can achieve this. Does that mean that we still have some work to do down the road? Absolutely."—**Chief of Social Work Service at the VA Southern Nevada Healthcare System, Josh Brown, Dec. 8, 2015**

"The problem of Veteran homelessness has been a shadow hanging over our country and our community for far too long. But we can finally say that, working with this coalition, we have built a collaborative system that within 30 days will enable us to house the few remaining homeless Veterans in Santa Fe, and, moving forward, any Veteran who becomes homeless in the future will be housed within 30 days."—**Santa Fe, NM, Mayor Javier M. Gonzales, Nov. 12, 2015**

"On a day when we remember those who fought and died for our nation, I am proud to proclaim that Virginia is leading the way in the fight to end veteran homelessness. This is an important victory in our ongoing efforts to make our Commonwealth the best place on earth for veterans to live, work and raise a family. However, we must remain committed to keeping homelessness among veterans, and, all Virginians, rare, brief and non-recurring. This successful effort will serve as the launching pad for our next goal of functionally ending chronic homelessness among all Virginians by the end of 2017."—**Virginia Gov. Terry McAuliffe, Nov. 11, 2015 (Veterans Day)**

"It's the nature of it where you have to go through each individual and see what their unique features are and then work through issues like housing, drugs and mental health problems."—**Schenectady, NY, Mayor Gary McCarthy, Nov. 11, 2015 (Veterans Day)**

"It means we have a process put in place to identify and find services for Veterans to make sure they are not homeless, or slip into homelessness."—**Syracuse, NY, Mayor Stephanie Miner, Nov. 11, 2015 (Veterans Day)**

"Achieving this milestone is a testimony to the hard work of the people and organizations that have been working tirelessly to house our homeless veterans. Given this success, I have no doubt that we will succeed in meeting our ultimate goal of ending chronic homelessness for all in our community."—**Winston-Salem, NC, Mayor Allen Joines, Oct. 27, 2015**

"Providing homeless veterans a path to proper housing opportunities is a fulfillment of a responsibility to those who answered the call to defend our freedoms. I am incredibly proud of the effort undertaken by our city and our community partners in assisting veterans here in the City of Troy and I look forward to our continued efforts to provide these important services to those who served our country."—**Troy, NY, Mayor Lou Rosamilia, Sept. 26, 2015**

"We established this bold goal to end homelessness among our veterans, not because it's good for our economy and makes communities stronger, but because it's morally right. Ending chronic veteran homelessness is just another step forward and another marker of progress towards reaching our goal of ending all veteran homelessness by the end of this year."—**Connecticut Gov. Dannel P. Malloy, Aug. 27, 2015**

"Our pledge is that if a Veteran presents as homeless, they do not spend a single night on the street."—**Saratoga Springs, NY, Mayor Joanne Yepsen, July 29, 2015**

"Ending veteran homelessness is important for one simple reason: Veterans fought for our freedom and our way of life, and it is now our turn to fight for them."—**Las Cruces, NM, Mayor Ken Miyagishima, July 2015**

"Houston is there for our heroes, and just like on the battlefield, we will leave no one behind. From regular provider coordination meetings and aligning local and federal resources, to dedicated street outreach teams and a coordinated assessment system that identifies, assesses, refers and navigates homeless veterans to housing, the Houston region has come together as a team to transform our homeless response system to effectively end veteran homelessness."—**Houston Mayor Annise Parker, June 1, 2015**

"New Orleans is now the first major city in the nation to answer the call … to end Veteran homelessness—and we did so one year earlier than the federal goal. We owe our Veterans our eternal gratitude for their service and sacrifice to this nation, and making sure they have a place to call home is a small but powerful way we can show our appreciation."—**New Orleans Mayor Mitch Landrieu, Jan. 7, 2015**

43. VA National Center on Homelessness Among Veterans*

U.S. Department of Veterans Affairs

About Us

The mission of the National Center on Homelessness among Veterans is to promote recovery-oriented care for Veterans who are homeless or at risk of homelessness. The Center is designed to improve the lives and treatment services of Veterans who are homeless and who have mental health, substance use disorders, medical illness, cognitive impairment or other psychosocial treatment needs.

Background on VHA's National Center on Homelessness Among Veterans (the Center)

The primary goal of the National Center on Homelessness Among Veterans (the Center) is to develop, promote, and enhance policy, clinical care research, and education to improve and integrate homeless services so that Veterans may live as independently and self-sufficiently as possible in a community of their choosing.

The Department of Veterans Affairs has been providing direct and specialized services for homeless Veterans for over 20 years. Beginning in 1987 with 43 pilot programs, which provided street outreach and residential community services, VA Homeless Programs have developed and expanded to be the largest integrated provider of homeless services in the country.

VA has enhanced these efforts by committing to the Five-Year Plan to End Homelessness among Veterans by 2015, part of the larger Federal Strategic Plan to Prevent and End Homelessness, Opening Doors. Strategies for achieving the plan's goal are to increase leadership, collaboration and civic engagement; increase access to stable and affordable housing; increase economic security; improve health and stability; and improve homeless crisis response. The Center has been a significant contributor to this Federal goal.

The Center works in collaboration with VHA's Homeless Programs Office, network directors, network homeless coordinators, national professional associations, and community partners as well as with their academic partners from the University of

*Public document originally published as U.S. Department of Veterans Affairs, "VA National Center on Homelessness Among Veterans," https://www.va.gov/homeless/nchav/about-us/about-us.asp (May 18, 2018).

Massachusetts Medical School, University of Pennsylvania, and the University of South Florida to: The Center will support the development of a network of excellence with the scope and vision that will enable it to have substantial impact within the host VAMCs, the VISNs, and across the Nation. In coordination with the national office and host-site academic affiliates, the University of Pennsylvania and the University of South Florida, Louis de la Parte Florida Mental Health Institute, the Center will have an impact along several dimensions of the delivery of care for Veterans who are homeless. These include but are not limited to:

- Develop of new empirical knowledge and policy that can be directly applied to improve services for Veterans who are homeless;
- Develop of quality management strategies that promote timely access to evidence-based services and/or emerging best practices;
- Develop education for a broad target audience of providers with the ultimate goal of enhancing the delivery of high-quality services to homeless Veterans and their dependents.
- Serve as a national resource for policy development, program implementation, education, research and the care of Veterans who are homeless; and
- Establish ongoing efforts to identify potential areas for federal, state and local as well as non-profit and faith-based collaboration in service integration and training.

The Center embraces and practices ICARE, the core values of the U.S. Department of Veterans Affairs.

- Integrity: Act with high moral principle. Adhere to the highest professional standards. Maintain the trust and confidence of all with whom I engage.
- Commitment: Work diligently to serve Veterans and other beneficiaries. Be driven by an earnest belief in VA mission. Fulfill my individual responsibilities and organizational responsibilities.
- Advocacy: Be truly Veteran-centric by identifying, fully considering, and appropriately advancing the interests of Veterans and other beneficiaries.
- Respect: Treat all those I serve and with whom I work with dignity and respect. Show respect to earn it.
- Excellence: Strive for the highest quality and continuous improvement. Be thoughtful and decisive in leadership, accountable for my actions, willing to admit mistakes, and rigorous in correcting them.

These core values are the basic elements of how we go about our work. They define "who we are" and form the underlying principles we use every day in our service to Veterans.

Rural Veterans and Homelessness

When the initiative to eradicate Veteran homelessness was launched in 2009, efforts and resources were focused in urban areas, where the problem was most visible. But poverty and housing problems are also major issues in rural settings. On June 22, 2017, the Center hosted its fifth Homeless Evidence and Research Synthesis virtual symposium where researchers, clinicians, service providers, and advocates discussed what homelessness and risk look like in rural areas, the particular needs and challenges of Veterans, and how the VA is addressing them. Go to the Center website for links to the webinar online and a list of questions and answers posted in the chatroom during the presentations. Written proceedings from the event will be available on the Center website in August.

Center Research Affiliates

The Center affiliated researcher group was established in 2016 to expand the scope and breadth of the Center's research portfolio and place it in greater alignment with the priorities and needs of field staff and leadership within the Homeless Programs Office. This is a secondary affiliation that provides an opportunity to collaborate with like-minded investigators within VA and the Center on homeless-related projects, apply for intramural funding for operations focused rapid response analyses, and participate in ongoing cyber-seminars, research-in-progress presentations, and hosted conferences. You can find more information about the research group on the Center website.

Publications

The special issue in *Psychological Services* (Vol. 14, Issue 2) "Homelessness Among Veterans, Other Adults, and Youth" features many authors affiliated with the National Center on Homelessness among Veterans and is guest edited by Jack Tsai, PhD Center Research Affiliate and Thomas O'Toole, MD, Center Director. For a list of these and other published articles, go to the Center website.

44. Veteran Homelessness in Monterey County[*]

WILLIAM BARE *and* MICKEY P. MCGEE

There is a disproportionately large amount of homeless veterans in the United States. Homelessness levels among our veteran population are three times more than the rate among non–veteran homeless. "Every night, we estimate up to 40,000 Veterans do not have a dependable place to sleep, and are considered 'chronically homeless' per the U.S. Interagency Council on Homelessness in Aug 4, 2017, and National Coalition for Homeless Veterans in February 2019. On a single night in January 2018, just over 37,800 Veterans were experiencing homelessness. On the same night, just over 23,300 of the Veterans counted were unsheltered or living on the street. Between 2017 and 2018, there was a 5.4 percent decrease in the estimated number of homeless Veterans nationwide" (https://www.va.gov/HOMELESS/pit_count.asp). This number is a significant decrease from the estimated 107,000 in 2010, but nonetheless begs the question: why does the United States allow any veteran to be homeless?

Compounding the problem, on any given day, almost 1.5 million veterans are at—or below—the poverty level according to the National Veterans Foundation (Sep 10, 2015). After pledging to give their lives in defense of the nation, don't we owe it to each veteran to keep them from living on the streets, in vehicles, encampments, and shelters? (*Veterans Today*, Sept. 2, 2013). Many believe our nation should to do more to help veterans in their post-military lives. Attending to the veteran homeless is an important moral issue. This paper provides recommendations on what and how our government and populace should address and resolve it.

In 2010, then–President Barack Obama made a promise and put in place programs to reduce veteran homelessness to zero in five years (USICH, Sept. 7, 2017). That ambitious goal was unmet in 2015; but renewed and refocused initiatives continue, with $188 million of VA grants announced to aid hundreds of programs across the country to provide daily housing for Veterans (National Coalition for Homeless Veterans [NCHV], Sep 13, 2017). Since 1994, approximately $2 billion has been awarded to private organizations to realize housing solutions that get veterans off the street and geared towards productive, self-sustaining lives. Another $1 billion has been issued in the last five years towards veteran homelessness prevention (U.S. Department of Veterans Affairs, May 3, 2017). The public should continue to take responsibility for sustaining this substantial commitment.

During his second Inaugural Address in the final months of the Civil War, President

---

[*]Published with permission of the authors.

Abraham Lincoln proclaimed, "let us strive on to finish the work we are in, to bind up the nation's wounds, to care for him who shall have borne the battle and for his widow, and his orphan." These words are a call-to-arms and are etched on plaques outside the entrance of the Department for Veterans Affairs. Their credo, "To care for him who shall have borne the battle and for his widow, and his orphan," has stood the test of time and is a strong reminder of the national commitment to assist our veterans (VA, Origin of the VA Motto, n.d.). Consequently, having a homeless veteran problem is a point of public shame to many. However, many programs and resources are being devoted to tackle the issue, and success is being realized in Monterey County through a combination of public and private collaborations.

Developments reveal the homeless veteran problem is being reduced across the board at national, state, and local levels, but much work remains. Although progress is being broadly realized, challenges remain daunting for further reducing the problem:

1. **Specific challenges for individual homeless veterans**. What makes the situation for homeless veterans different than that of other homeless? Many have regular income, have had job experience and training, and have a higher level of education that their age peers. However, one glaring statistic offers a likely explanation: over 80 percent of homeless veteran suffer from some form of mental illness (VA, Homeless Veterans: Mental Illness, n.d.). Affordable housing is the big issue for most homeless, and for veterans is no exception. In the 2017 Monterey homeless census, the largest obstacle to permanent housing was by far affordability (as per 73 percent of responders) (Coalition of Homeless Service Providers, 2017 Homeless Census). Communities can do better to provide affordable housing, especially for low-income individuals, especially veterans who have guaranteed income. Other factors that need to be addressed to ensure transitional or permanent housing include sobriety. employment, medical support, and secured benefits.

2. **Measuring the effectiveness of national, state, and local programs**. Measures are showing positive results from a national-level prioritization on ending veteran homelessness. Since 2010, In fact, 3 states and 51 communities have already declared victory in erasing veteran homelessness to the extent possible (VA, Ending Veteran Homelessness, n.d.). From 2015 to 2017, homelessness in Monterey County increased by 23 percent; however, the Coalition of Homeless Service Providers reported a 22 percent decrease in the number of homeless veterans in the county (CHSP, 2015 PIT Census & Survey, 2015; and CHSP 2017 Survey). The agency attributes that to a national effort to help veterans through the Supportive Services for Veteran Families rapid re-housing and homeless prevention funding, as well as the joint HUD-VA Supportive Housing program.

3. **Ineffectiveness of state programs**. Part of the problem to assist homeless veterans is the lack of "affordable housing" in most parts of California. Monterey County is no exception. In addition to a lack of affordable housing, many landlords are reluctant to rent to homeless or even low-income veterans on subsidies, for fear those subsidies. However, in the last three years there have been promising developments that have trickled down to Monterey County.

- **California Veterans (CalVet) leadership, and California Housing and Community Development (HCD) funding opportunities.** In 2014, California redirected $600,000,000 of bond monies previously identified for veterans mortgage payments, to go to new construction and housing rehab of veteran communities. Monterey County was able to get $5.9 million of that to build a singular project for affordable housing for veteran families (personal communication, November 2015).

- **Economic development at the State and municipal levels is key for solving veteran homelessness.** The development of affordable housing has become a priority in Sacramento. More than 130 bills were introduced into the Legislature in 2017, with major success—several bills were passed that are already having significant impact to the Central Coast and Monterey County (Marino, 2017). California Senate Bill (SB) 3 in particular will be a boost to veteran housing. SB3, the Veterans and Affordable Housing Bond Act of 2018, seeks to direct $1 billion for affordable housing directly for veterans, which will benefit the large veteran population of Monterey County (Marino, 2017). According to Jan Lindenthal of MidPenn Housing, these bills could "double the number of [affordable housing] projects MidPenn is doing in the region" (Marino, 2017).

Recommendations. The United States sent Americans to war. In return, it is only fitting that it should also provide permanent housing for homeless veterans. The U.S. government is rightly contributing an enormous amount of resources into ending veteran homelessness. Monterey County also needs to strongly echo and support this effort. Some community-level successes have occurred but the problem remains. At the local level, there may not be official mandate to address this issue; it is a moral one. Veterans who pledged their lives and fortunes to defend this country must certainly be cared for with same amount of devotion, no matter the sacrifice. Monterey County is working to help solve the large homeless veteran population. The large Monterey County veteran population is committed and encouraging local governments for solutions. Solving the homeless veteran problem in Monterey County includes:

1. Remain engaged with U.S. Congressman Panetta (D-20), U.S. Senators Harris and Feinstein, California State Assemblyman Mark Stone and other local elected officials of Monterey County to push for continued initiatives to support homeless veterans and affordable housing.

2. Remain engaged with the VA at District and Federal level to ensure existing and potential programs are in compliance and focused on same goals as ever-changing national efforts.

3. Remain engaged with HUD at District and federal level to ensure existing and potential programs are in compliance and focused on same goals as national efforts.

4. Remain engaged with NCHV to promote funding/solutions in Central California.

5. Remain engaged with California CalVet leadership, and Cal Housing and Community Development (HCD) funding opportunities.

6. Remain engaged with Monterey County Veterans Affairs Office and ensure non-profit/community/municipal efforts are tied into county goals and initiatives.

7. Ensure CHSP is at forefront of developing opportunities at state and federal level to support affordable housing and VA/Federal funding which also requires municipal-level support.

8. Establish independent council of Trustees for Veterans Affairs made up

of senior retired military officials that can espouse need for attention to important veteran issues (such as homelessness).

9.   United Veterans Center of Monterey County take lead for homeless veteran issues and provide regular updates to cities and County. Provide leadership to various non-profits with recommended COAs.

Conclusion. As a society, we should be doing all we can to assist veterans who come upon difficult times in their post-military lives. It is debatable whether veteran homelessness is self-inflicted, or is a result of their military service. No matter—this is a solvable problem. Millions of dollars are coming into Monterey County to address the issue. The concern is twofold: (1) Clarify a need and justify federal and state support; and, (2) apply those resources in an effective manner and make a difference. This is the issue for Public Administrators in the County.

Public administrators should consider there are many initiatives in place to address the matter of homelessness in their area of jurisdiction. Progress is being made in Monterey County through a vast collaborative effort that includes the federal, state, county, city, and an array of non-profits and concerned citizens who are motivated to ensure veterans in need are taken care of. Even though the homelessness veteran population can be a geographical-transitory issue on this peninsula and within Monterey County, there are appropriate steps that can be taken by elected and non-elected officials at the County, City, and non-profit levels. It is possible to make a difference. The lives that pledged to defend this nation are depending on us.

References

Broom, C.A., Jackson, M., Harris, J.L. *Performance Measurement: Concepts and Techniques*. Washington, D.C.: American Society for Public Administration, 2002.
Denhardt, J.V., & Denhardt, R.B. (2015). The New Public Service: Serving, Not Steering. Armonk, NY: M. E. Sharpe, 2011.
Herrera, James (Nov. 13, 2015). "Patriot Housing Program in Seaside Providing Affordable Housing for Veterans," *Monterey Herald*; retrieved from http://www.montereyherald.com/article/NF/20151113/NEWS/151119901, 28 Sept. 2017.
National Coalition for Homeless Veterans. 2015 Annual Report.
2013 Monterey County Homeless Point-in-Time Census & Survey (Final). http://www.chspmontereycounty.org/CensusPage/2013%20Monterey%20County%20Homeless%20Report_FINAL3_7.3.13.pdf.
2015 Monterey County Homeless Point-in-Time Census & Survey–Comprehensive Report. http://www.chspmontereycounty.org/wp-content/themes/chsp/img/Final-MC-2015-Census-Report.pdf.
2017 Monterey County Homeless Census & Survey–Comprehensive Report. http://www.chspmontereycounty.org/wp-content/themes/chsp/img/2017-Monterey-County-Census-Report.pdf.
U.S. Department of Veterans Affairs; https://www.va.gov/homeless/.
United States Interagency Council on Homelessness. "Ending Veteran Homelessness." 4/8/17.
United States Interagency Council on Homelessness. https://www.usich.gov/.

45. Monterey Programs Focused on Supporting Homeless Veterans and Their Families*

Kurt Schake *and* Mickey P. McGee

The U.S. Department of Housing and Urban Development-VA Supportive Housing (HUD-VASH), a collaborative program, combines HUD housing vouchers with VA supportive services to help veterans who are homeless and their families find and sustain permanent housing. Through public housing authorities, HUD provides rental assistance vouchers for privately owned housing to veterans who are eligible for VA health care services and are experiencing homelessness. VA case managers may connect these veterans with support services such as health care, mental health treatment and substance use counseling to help them in their recovery process and with their ability to maintain housing in the community. Among VA homeless continuum of care programs, HUD-VASH enrolls the largest number and largest percentage of veterans who have experienced long-term or repeated homelessness. As of April 8, 2018, HUD has allocated more than 87,000 vouchers to help house veterans across the country.

The Homeless Providers Grant and Per Diem (GPD) Program supports state, local and tribal governments and nonprofits organizations. These organizations receive capital grants and per diem payments to develop and operate transitional housing and/or service centers for veterans who are homeless. VA funds an estimated 600 agencies that provide over 14,500 beds for eligible veterans. Grantees work closely with an assigned liaison from the local VAMC. The VA GPD liaison monitors the services the grantees offer to Veterans and provides direct assistance to them. Grantees also collaborate with community-based organizations to connect veterans with employment, housing and additional social services to promote housing stability. The maximum stay in this housing is up to 24 months, with the goal of moving veterans into permanent housing.

Supportive Services for Veteran Families (SSVF) is aimed at supporting very low-income veterans who are homeless or at imminent risk of becoming homeless. Services may include deposit assistance, rental assistance, veteran outreach, transportation assistance, case management services, assistance obtaining VA and other benefits. SSVF provides case management and supportive services to prevent the imminent loss of a veteran's home or identify a new, more suitable housing situation for the individual and his or her family or to rapidly re-house veterans and their families who are homeless and

---

*Published with permission of the authors.

might remain homeless without this assistance. Through referrals and direct outreach, nonprofit agencies and community cooperatives use SSVF funding to quickly house veterans and their families who are homeless and keep others from slipping into homelessness by providing time-limited supportive services that promote housing stability. Case management includes help securing VA and other benefits such as educational aid and financial planning.

The Monterey County Veterans Transition Center (VTC)

The mission of the VTC is to provide services for homeless veterans and their families in the Monterey Bay Area. By providing veterans with transitional housing and case management programs, VTC creates short- and long-terms solutions to homelessness and gives them the tools they need to help themselves become employable, productive members of the community. VTC has a 19-year record of success and continues to achieve the VA's Service Intensive Model Required Minimum Performance Metrics/Targets. VTC seeks to exceed those targets as follows: Service-Intensive Transitional Housing Planned Performance Matrix: Discharge to permanent housing 75 percent; employment of individuals at discharge 60 percent; and negative exits will be less than 20 percent.

The VTC has provided transitional housing since 1998 when it received 23 buildings via the Fort Ord Reuse Authority (FORA) via the McKinney Act. It took about five years to rehabilitate the buildings. Currently there are 20 buildings dedicated to housing veterans and in some cases family members. VTC is able to walk each client through the process of securing permanent housing through the HUD-VASH office and referrals to Supportive Services for Veteran Families (SSVF). The VTC provide beds for 70 veterans and, in some cases, their family members. Funding for housing comes from the following programs (number of beds provided in parenthesis): VA Grant Per Diem Program, Veterans who are currently homeless, often find themselves on the street, living in their cars or in other areas not meant for human habitation (4); VA Emergency Rapid Rehousing (4); Residential Services; and Permanent Supportive Non-HUD-VASH Vouchers (4); HUD-VASH Permanent and/or until they exceed income qualifications, homeless Veterans and their families (8); VA Transitional Housing/Clinical (14); VA Service Intensive Transitional Housing (30); VA Transitional Housing Bridge (14).

Case managers evaluate the benefits a veteran is receiving when they enter into a VTC program and make sure that all earned benefits are being collected. If there is a deficiency, the veteran and case manager work together for the veteran to start receiving all unpaid earned benefits. VTC case managers provide formerly homeless veterans the tools necessary to achieve successful independence in society. The program is designed to place an emphasis on veteran accountability through a strong partnership between a client and their case manager. Veterans enrolled in VTC programs work to establish short-term goals that accumulate to reach larger program goals. Clients also work with their case managers to address any employment barriers and have the opportunity to improve their marketable job skills at VTC's Job Development and Education Center (JDEC), work one-on-one on their resume and job interview skills and take advantage of VTC partnerships with multiple employment agencies.

The Veterans Transition Center can refer veterans to an agency who can assist with short-term temporary financial assistance with rent, moving expenses, security and utility deposits, child care, transportation, utility costs, and emergency expenses. Agencies may also provide a variety of services including housing and credit counseling, housing advocacy, legal assistance, moving assistance, and representative payee services.

Job Development Center

- Increasing skills and helping veterans become employment-ready is crucial to become active members of the community. The newly expanded JDC can assist 100 veterans per year, provide training areas, classes, skills assessments, and other tools that will help a veteran succeed. Through the VET+PREP! program, VTC currently offers assistance with job placement, quarterly job fairs, job skills training, and skills assessment.
- Upon entering the program, all veterans are assessed and are provided with an Individualized Service Plan, taking into consideration their specific skill set, interests, and past employment experience. From there, they are provided with assistance in job interview training, resume writing, and job skills classes. Other services provided by VET+PREP! include basic skills and literacy workshops; remedial education and GED assistance; life skills and financial literacy workshops; classroom and vocational workshops; employment uniform and equipment subsidies; specialized and/or certification courses, and other formal training programs deemed appropriate to benefit the veteran.

Public-private partnership was working very well. Key stakeholders in the region to include the National Coalition of Homeless Veterans, the federal government departments (HUD, HHS, VA), the State of California, the County of Monterey, the cities of the Monterey Bay Area and many others contribute funding and serve on local committees to raise and donate money to help solve problems (see the VTC website for a full listing of community supported and sponsors, https://www.vtcmonterey.org/).

Community supporters and sponsors work together to collaborate and communicate on how best to serve and solve the problems faced by the Homeless Vet Population and their families in Monterey County.

There is a need for a common definition of homelessness was needed to help decipher the various federal, state and local funding application requirements. The biggest challenge for the VTC is operating funds, especially to pay for case work staffing. Funding by supporting sponsors provides specific dollars for the Homeless Vets and their families however, other grants do not cover much of the labor costs for staff support to assist an ever-growing homeless vet population.

46. An Assessment of Homeless Veteran Programs in Sacramento County*

BENEDICT SERAFICA *and* MICKEY P. MCGEE

Veteran homelessness is an ongoing problem in the United States. Homeless veterans were among the general homeless population as early as the Reconstruction Era. At the end of Civil War, thousands of veterans wandered the country and some went homeless. In 1932, approximately 15,000 homeless and disabled veterans barricaded Washington, D.C., demanding for benefits. It was during time that homeless veterans were considered to be part of the so-called Bonus Army (Block, 2007). In 1987, the number of homeless veterans increased rapidly to approximately 300,000. In 2007, Iraq and Afghanistan combat veterans started to be recognized in homeless shelters. And by 2009, the Veterans Affairs reported that about 154,000 veterans were homeless, and about "one-third of all homeless adults are veterans ... nearly half of homeless veterans (47 percent) served in Vietnam and one third were stationed in a war zone" (Jannson, 2010, p. 72).

A 2009 point-in-time survey conducted by the U.S. Department of Housing and Urban Development predicted that more than 634,000 individuals were either in a sheltered or unsheltered homeless state, and around 111,000 of these individuals were chronically homeless (U. S. Department of Housing and Urban Development, 2010). Schinka et al. (2013) wrote that more than "15% of the homeless population are 51 years of age and older, and the numbers of homeless over the age of 65 are expected to increase dramatically, doubling by 2050."

In 2011, the VA also reported that 14 percent were homeless adult males and 2 percent from homeless adult females, and "both groups were over represented within the homeless population compared to the general population" (Metraux et al., 2013, p. 4). From 2012–2016, the overall population of homeless veterans in the United States was over 39,000. Homelessness among female veterans is also a nationwide dilemma. Women who have served in the United States military are "three to four times more likely to become homeless than are non-veteran women, though the reasons for this are not clearly understood" (Gamache, Rosenheck, & Tessler, 2003). A study conducted by Dr. Donna Washington and colleagues from the Women's Health and Equity at the VA Greater Los Angeles Health Services Research and Development Center of Excellence (2010) indicated that women are considered to be at a high risk among the homeless

---

*Published with permission of the authors.

181

population (Washington, Yano, McGuire, Hines, Lee, and Gelberg, 2010, p. 82). They also noted that "homeless women veterans likely present different needs with respect to privacy, gender related care, treatment for physical and sexual trauma, housing support, and care for dependent children" (p. 82).

There are numerous reasons or risk factors explaining veteran homelessness and non-veterans. Service members who served in the conflicts in Iraq and Afghanistan for more than ten years expressed concern with regards to their well-being when they returned back to the society (Metraux et al., 2013, p. 255). Some of these factors concern personal issues and unavailability of secured and affordable housing. According to Cunningham, et al., almost "half a million veterans pay their income for rent and more than half of them have incomes below the federal poverty level" (Cunningham, Henry, and Lyons, 2007). The HUD emphasized that, "for every one hundred men living by themselves with incomes below the federal poverty level, twelve are likely to be in the sheltered homeless population over the course of a year compared to four of every one hundred women living alone in poverty" (Department of Housing and Urban Development, 2009).

There are 113,000 homeless individuals living in California, the highest number of homeless veterans of any state and is "home to nearly 26 percent of all homeless veterans in the United States" (Blanton, 2013, p. 1). The City of Sacramento is second only to the City of Los Angeles for highest homeless population in California (Sacramento Steps Forward, 2015). Rebecca Blanton, a senior policy analyst from the California Research Bureau specified that the County of Los Angeles alone accounts for 10 percent of homeless veterans in America (2013, p. 11). The HUD 2012 Continuum of Care Homeless Population Sub-count revealed that, "California is home to 4,512 veterans living in temporary housing or shelters and 11,949 veterans living on the streets or in places unintended for human habitation" (Blanton, 2013, p. 11). In Sacramento County, over 2,659 individuals experience homelessness, and approximately 5,200 individuals will eventually become homeless in a year (Sacramento Steps Forward, 2015). The Sacramento County & Incorporated Cities Homeless Count reported that, there is "roughly one third of Sacramento County's homeless population is unsheltered" (Sacramento Steps Forward, 2015, p. 3).

In 2012, the Veterans Affairs (VA) and the Department of Housing and Urban Development (HUD) projected that the growing number of homeless veterans in the United States was around 62,619. Approximately 25 percent of homeless veterans were located in California. California is home to the highest number of homeless veterans than any other state. The Housing Unit and Development 2012 Continuum of Care Homeless Population Sub-count revealed that, "California is home to 4,512 veterans living in temporary housing or shelters and 11,949 veterans living on the streets or in places unintended for human habitation" (Blanton, 2013, p. 11). Service members transitioned from military to civilian life find it difficult to secure employment and housing.

There are programs and services provided to support veterans, programs such as housing assistance, health care, employment services, etc. However, "many of our nation's veterans particularly those with low incomes still face challenges finding affordable and stable housing and supportive services" (Sturtevant, Brennan, Viveiros, Handelman, 2015, p. 1). HUD and VA joined forces to create a housing program that would help veterans and their families find secure housing—the HUD and VA Supportive Housing (HUD-VASH). HUD-VASH has been "an effective tool for combating veteran homelessness and affordability challenges" (Sturtevant et al., 2015, p. 4). The HUD-VASH program provides housing assistance through HUD Section 8 Housing Choice Vouchers along with case management with the help of the Veterans Affairs.

According to the National Alliance to End Homelessness, approximately 70,000 HUD-VASH certificates have been allocated to Public Housing Authorities across the country since 2008 (2015). An assessment regarding the effectiveness of the HUD-VASH program reveals an increase in employment and income and the total amount of days to house a homeless person. Moreover, the HUD-VASH program "has been found to have a one-year cost savings of approximately on $6,000 per participant on health services" (Byrne, Roberts, Culhane, & Kane, 2014).

The presence of strong leadership, sheer-determination, and partnership among federal, state and local programs were vital in the development of key strategies used to help end veteran homelessness in their community. Some of these key strategies are described below:

Mayors Challenge to End Veteran Homelessness. This program was initiated by former first lady Michelle Obama as a challenge for all mayors and other state and local leaders across the country to help ensure every veteran is provided a house they can call home (USICH, 2016, p. 1). The goal of this strategy was to enlist every mayor in the country to set a deadline for his/her community, designate an effective leader, organize weekly meeting with major agencies such as the Veterans Affairs, and other key financial contributors with the goal of "developing an integrated landlord strategy, and addressing current state/city laws and regulations that are barriers towards housing Veterans" (Bond, 2016, p. 3).

Implementing a Housing First System Orientation and Response (USICH, 2016, p. 1). Communities were encouraged to consider a Housing First System orientation and response to guarantee homeless veterans that are relocating into permanent housing get the proper treatment they deserved. The United States Interagency Council on Homelessness stated that not all veterans have great credit, are substance free nor are they clear of a criminal record (2016, p. 1). These past faults should not be deterrents in helping place the homeless veterans. Those working with the different programs should be adequately trained to deal with people of different backgrounds, including those with substance abuse, criminal records, and the like. It is vital that these past faults not be hindrances in helping veterans get out of homelessness (USICH, 2016, p. 1).

The City of Philadelphia's 2013 initiative Rapid Results Veteran Bootcamp gave veterans a goal of obtaining housing within 100 days as well as bettering the efforts for other additional housing options. This campaign was funded by the HUD and focused on streamlining the process from identifying homeless veterans to getting them placed in proper housing. The cooperation between the Philadelphia Housing Authority and the VA staff was successful and became an example to other communities. The early success showed that housing homeless veterans in a timely and efficient manner was possible with the right amount of cooperation and team effort (Culbertson et al., 2015, p. 2).

The analysis of data collected for this article reveals the following findings:

- Programs such as permanent housing must be implemented in Sacramento County to house veterans that are experiencing homelessness and at the same time keep them off the streets;
- Programs created to support and reduce the veteran homelessness population are not supported by the homeless individuals;

- Most homeless veterans who seek services such as food vouchers, medical health care, and bus passes from the Veterans Affairs were only there for that type of services only. Many of the homeless veterans do not choose to pursue housing and prefer to remain on the streets.
- Most homeless veterans prefer to stay homeless;
- Most homeless veterans with pets would rather spend living in homeless camp than settling in housing where their pets are not allowed, such as housing provided by the Veterans Affairs and other housing agencies;
- Many of the homeless veterans prefer to keep things as status quo because that is the life that they know and are accustomed;
- Some of the homeless veterans prostitute themselves for food.

The County of Sacramento was provided with recommendations based on best practices from homelessness programs from other cities and regions to help reduce the population of homeless veterans:

Encourage Public/Private Landlords as Partners. The Department of HUD, public and private sector housing industries, as well as rental property owners should collaborate to collectively reduce veteran homelessness.

Develop and Increase Connections to Employment and Education Services. The County of Sacramento, the Department of VA, Volunteers of America and other homeless agencies that provide support to homeless individuals in general must organize, promote and administer additional stand downs in the form of job training and educational programs. Stand-downs provide homeless veterans with opportunities for skill and job training and educational programs, food, clothing and other resources to come off the streets. more skills training.

REFERENCES

Blanton, R. (2013). "Overview of veterans in California." California State Library. Retrieved from: https://www.library.ca.gov/crb/13/13-020.pdf.
Byrne, T., Roberts, C., Culhane, D., & Kane, V. (2014), Estimating cost savings associated with HUD-VASH placement. See also http://www.endhomelessness.org/library/entry/fact-sheet-veteran-homelessness.
Cunningham, M., Henry, M., & Lyons, W. (2007) Vital mission. See also https://www.usich.gov/resources/uploads/asset_library/BkgrdPap_Veterans.pdf.
Gamache, G., Rosenheck, R., Tessler, R. Overrepresentation of women veterans among homeless women. *Am J Public Health*. 2003 Jul; 93(7):1132–6.
Jansson, Bruce S. (2010). *Becoming an Effective Policy Advocate*. Boston: Cengage Learning.
Metraux, S., Clegg, L., Daigh, J., Culhane, D., & Kane, V. (2013). Risk Factors for Becoming Homeless Among a Cohort of Veterans Who Served in the Era of the Iraq and Afghanistan Conflicts. U.S. National Library of Medicine. National Institutes of Health. PubMED.Gov Retrieved from: https://www.ncbi.nlm.nih.gov/pubmed/24148066.
Sacramento Steps Forward. (2015). 2015 point-in-time homeless count report. Sacramento County & Incorporated Cities. Retrieved from: http://sacramentostepsforward.org/wp-content/uploads/2015/07/SSF2015PITReport-July162015_CoverMemo.pdf.
U.S. Department of Housing and Urban Development. (2010). The 2009 annual homeless assessment report to Congress. Washington, DC: Office of Community Planning and Development. Available at http://www.hudhre.info/documents/5thHomelessAssessmentReport.pdf.
Washington, Donna L., M.D., M.P.H., Yano, Elizabeth M, PhD., M.S.P.H., McGuire, James, PhD., M.S.W., Hines, Vivian, M.S.W., A.C.S.W., Lee, M., PhD., & Gelberg, Lillian, M.D., M.S.P.H. (2010). Risk factors for homelessness among women veterans. *Journal of Health Care for the Poor and Underserved, 21*(1), 81–91. Retrieved from http://0-search.proquest.com.library.ggu.edu/docview/220588734?accountid=25283.

47. Homeless Vets with Families*

An Untold Part of Veterans' Struggles

Roya Ijadi-Maghsoodi

In 2010, the Obama administration announced the ambitious goal of ending homelessness among veterans. Over 2016, the number of veterans who are homeless dropped 30 percent in Los Angeles County. Nationwide, veteran homelessness fell by almost 50 percent since 2009.

Yet statistics are only part of the story. What is missing from federal and state statistics, the media and the minds of many Americans, is the story of homeless veteran families.

Through my work as a researcher and physician caring for women and homeless veterans, I see these families. I hear about their struggles to find housing in safe neighborhoods instead of skid row, where their children are exposed to violence and drug use.

Overlooking Veterans with Families

Families are often missed when volunteers head out to count homeless individuals. Veterans with families often stay with friends, known as doubling up. Or, forced to fragment, parents send kids to stay with family while they go to a shelter.

Plus, some females who are homeless and the head of their household don't identify as veterans. They may not be eligible for Veterans Affairs (VA) benefits or are unclear about available services. Some may not seek care at the VA due to mistrust, harassment or past military sexual trauma.

Providers, policymakers and the public need to understand that homelessness among the families of men and women who have served our nation may be invisible. But it is significant.

Limited studies point to higher rates of veteran family homelessness than expected from the counts. Nineteen percent of families served by Supportive Services for Veteran Families in the FY 2015 had at least one child. A study of veterans receiving VA homeless services by Tsai and colleagues showed that nine percent of literally homeless male veterans—those living on the streets or uninhabitable locations—and 18 percent of unstably housed male veterans had children in their custody.

---

*Originally published as Roya Ijadi-Maghsoodi, "Homeless Vets with Families: An Untold Part of Veterans' Struggles," *The Conversation*, http://theconversation.com/homeless-vets-with-families-an-untold-part-of-veterans-struggles-77539 (May 26, 2017). Reprinted with permission of the publisher.

A striking 30 percent of literally homeless female veterans, as well as 45 percent of unstably housed female veterans, had children in their custody.

Causes of Homelessness

What contributes to homelessness among veteran families?

First, homelessness among women veterans is rising. Eleven percent of military personnel who served in Operation Iraqi Freedom/Operation Enduring Freedom (OIF/OEF) were women, the largest number involved in combat operations in U.S. history.

Women veterans are more likely to be mothers and mothers at a younger age than civilians, and more likely to receive lower income than male veterans.

They face high rates of trauma, especially military sexual trauma, a known risk for homelessness.

And, strikingly, women veterans are up to four times more likely to be homeless than civilian women.

Male veterans returning from OIF/OEF tend to be younger and may have young families. As of 2010, 49 percent of deployed service members had children. They also have a higher prevalence of PTSD, compared to veterans of other wars. This is thought to be associated with an increased risk for homelessness.

To make matters worse, our country is in the grips of an affordable housing crisis. In California, we have only 21 homes available for every 100 extremely low-income households. And every day, families face discrimination searching for housing due to their race or ethnicity, being a veteran or using a voucher.

What Homeless Veteran Families Need

These families are at high risk. Decades of research show that children in homeless families are at risk for physical and mental health problems, academic delay and of becoming homeless themselves as adults—creating a second generation of homelessness. Many homeless veteran families are resilient but face additional stressors of reintegrating into civilian society and coping with parents who may have PTSD and traumatic brain injuries.

Our team has been conducting interviews to understand the needs of veteran families who are homeless. We also formed a work group of recently homeless veteran parents.

We are finding that, although veterans are often satisfied with their own health and mental health services at the VA, many parents feel alone when it comes to their family.

Many veterans are overwhelmed by PTSD and depression, as well as the search to find housing and a job. They worry about the toll on their family. Yet they find few resources for their family within the VA, such as family therapy, and need help finding needed health and mental health care for their spouse and children in the community.

Parents need more help connecting to resources for their families in the community, clearer information about the social services available to veteran families and more emotional support as parents.

Moving Forward

We need to change the conversation when we talk about homeless veterans. We need to talk about homeless veteran families.

These families are in our communities, the children are attending public schools, their parents are trying to work multiple jobs or attend college and many receive care in our VA and community clinics.

Within the VA, we need to consider the whole family and provide more connection to the community to help families succeed. At the VA Greater Los Angeles Healthcare System West Los Angeles Medical Center, a new family wellness center will open as a collaborative effort between UCLA and the VA. The center will serve as a hub to strengthen veteran families, through services such as family and couple resilience programs, parenting skills workshops and connection to community services. More efforts are needed to engage families who may need it most.

Beyond the VA, we need enhanced understanding and empathy for veteran families with homelessness within the community. This involves greater understanding of the needs of these children in schools. We should also find ways to help veteran families dealing with PTSD integrate into the community after being homeless.

And most of all, we need to increase access to affordable housing in safe neighborhoods for these families.

The recent wars may seem over for many Americans, but they are far from over for our homeless veteran families. We owe it to them to do better.

48. At Some Veterans Homes, Aid-in-Dying Is Not an Option*

JoNel Aleccia

California voters passed a law two years ago that allows terminally ill people to take lethal drugs to end their lives, but controversy is growing over a newer rule that effectively bans that option in the state's eight veterans homes.

Proponents of medical aid-in-dying and residents of the Veterans Home of California-Yountville—the largest in the nation—are protesting a regulation passed in 2017 by the California Department of Veterans Affairs, or CalVet, that requires that anyone living in the facilities must be discharged if they intend to use the law.

That's a position shared by most—but not all—states where aid-in-dying is allowed. As more U.S. jurisdictions consider whether to legalize the practice, the status of terminally ill veterans living in state-run homes will loom large.

"It would be a terrible hardship, because I have no place to go," said Bob Sloan, 73, who suffers from congestive heart failure and other serious cardiac problems. He said he intends to seek medical aid-in-dying if doctors certify he has six months or less to live.

"I'm not going to be a vegetable," said Sloan, a Vietnam War–era veteran who moved into the Yountville center five years ago. "I'm not going to end up living in so much pain it's unbearable."

A CalVet official said the agency adopted the rule to avoid violating a federal statute that prohibits using U.S. government resources for physician-assisted death. Otherwise, the agency would jeopardize nearly $68 million in federal funds that helps run the facilities, said June Iljana, CalVet's deputy secretary of communications.

California is not alone. Three other states where aid-in-dying is legal—Oregon, Colorado and Vermont—all prohibit use of lethal medications in state-run veterans homes.

In Montana, where aid-in-dying is allowed under a state Supreme Court ruling, officials didn't respond to multiple requests about whether veterans would be able to use the law in the residences. However, Dr. Eric Kress, a Missoula physician who prescribes the lethal medication, says he has transferred patients to hospice, to relatives' homes, even to extended-stay hotels to avoid conflict.

In Washington, D.C., where an aid-in-dying law took effect last summer, the Armed

*Originally published as JoNel Aleccia, "At Some Veterans Homes, Aid-in-Dying Is Not an Option," *Kaiser Health News*, February 13, 2018. Kaiser Health News is a nonprofit news service covering health issues. It is an editorially independent program of the Kaiser Family Foundation that is not affiliated with Kaiser Permanente. KHN's coverage of these topics is supported by John A. Hartford Foundation and the SCAN Foundation.

Forces Retirement Home won't assist patients in any way. Those who wish to use the law would be referred to an ethics committee for individual consideration, spokesman Christopher Kelly said in an email.

Only Washington state has a policy that allows veterans to remain in government-run residences if they intend to ingest lethal medications. At least one veteran has died in a state-run home using that law, said Heidi Audette, a spokeswoman for the state's Department of Veterans Affairs.

Paul Sherbo, a spokesman for the U.S. Department of Veterans Affairs, said the choice is up to the states.

"VA does not mandate how states comply with federal law," Sherbo said in an email. "There are a number of ways individual states can choose to handle such situations and still be in compliance."

To date, none of the 2,400 residents of California's veterans homes has formally requested medical aid-in-dying, said Iljana. That includes the more than 900 residents of the Yountville center, located about 60 miles north of San Francisco.

"We would respectfully and compassionately assist them in transferring to a hospice, family home or other location," Iljana said in an email. "We will readmit them immediately if they change their minds."

But Kathryn Tucker, executive director of the End of Life Liberty Project, an advocacy group that supports aid-in-dying, said that CalVet is interpreting the federal regulations too broadly and denying terminally ill veterans the right to choose a "peaceful death" through medical assistance.

"Nothing exists in the federal statute's language that would prohibit a resident from receiving aid-in-dying services at state homes, so long as they are not provided using federal funds or employees," she said.

Ed Warren, head of the Allied Council, a group representing veterans at the Yountville site, co-signed a letter to CalVet officials protesting the ruling.

"My point of view is that it is inhumane to expect people in the last stages of dying to go through the hullabaloo of leaving their homes," he said.

In Washington state, a 60-year-old man diagnosed with terminal chronic obstructive pulmonary disease, or COPD, died in June 2015 after ingesting lethal drugs at the Washington Soldiers Home in Orting, where he lived.

"It was all done very much in the open," said Chris Fruitrich, a volunteer with the group End of Life Washington, which assisted the man.

There has been no indication that the policy jeopardizes the nearly $47 million the agency receives each year in federal funds, said Audette, the state VA spokeswoman.

In California, additional protests have centered on allegations that CalVet suppressed information about the aid-in-dying law.

Critics at the Yountville home contend that CalVet passed the discharge rule quietly, with little public input. Then the agency refused to broadcast a public meeting about medical aid-in-dying on KVET, the center's state-run, closed-circuit television station.

Iljana said the broadcast of the Aug. 21 meeting, led by Tucker and Dr. Robert Brody, also a supporter of aid-in-dying, violated state rules that prohibit using public resources to promote political causes.

"Free speech is great and criticizing the government is great, but not using the government's own resources and paid staff to advocate for a change in the law," Iljana wrote in an email to prohibit the broadcast.

That decision, however, prompted Jac Warren, 81, who has been KVET's station manager for eight years, to resign in protest, citing censorship.

"What is at issue is whether a state may completely suppress the dissemination of concededly truthful information about entirely lawful activity," Warren wrote in an email to CalVet.

The hour-long meeting, attended by about 50 people, was not propaganda, Tucker said, but "an educational event with information provided by an attorney and a physician who both specialize in their respective fields in end-of-life care."

Bob Sloan, who works as an engineer at KVET for a $400 monthly stipend, disagreed with the decision not to broadcast the meeting on the system that serves residents of the Yountville home.

Sloan said he knows other residents who would like to be able to use California's aid-in-dying law if their illnesses progress.

"The only other option that people have in this state is committing suicide," he said. "If I can't find some way of doing it legally, I'll do it illegally."

49. "They Deserve It"*

In Foster Homes, Veterans Are Cared for Like Family

PATRICIA KIME

With the motto "Where Heroes Meet Angels," a small Veterans Affairs effort pairs vets in need of nursing home care with caregivers willing to share their homes.

Ralph Stepney's home on a quiet street in north Baltimore has a welcoming front porch and large rooms, with plenty of space for his comfortable recliner and vast collection of action movies. The house is owned by Joann West, a licensed caregiver who shares it with Stepney and his fellow Vietnam War veteran Frank Hundt.

"There is no place that I'd rather be. ... I love the quiet of living here, the help we get. I thank the Lord every year that I am here," Stepney, 73, said.

It's a far cry from a decade ago, when Stepney was homeless and "didn't care about anything." His diabetes went unchecked and he had suffered a stroke—a medical event that landed him at the Baltimore Veterans Affairs Medical Center.

After having part of his foot amputated, Stepney moved into long-term nursing home care at a VA medical facility, where he thought he'd remain—until he became a candidate for a small VA effort that puts aging veterans in private homes: the Medical Foster Home program.

The $20.7 million-per-year program provides housing and care for more than 1,000 veterans in 42 states and Puerto Rico, serving as an alternative to nursing home care for those who cannot live safely on their own. Veterans pay their caregivers $1,500 to $3,000 a month, depending on location, saving the government about $10,000 a month in nursing home care. It has been difficult to scale up, though, because the VA accepts only foster homes that meet strict qualifications.

For the veterans, it's a chance to live in a home setting with caregivers who treat them like family. For the Department of Veterans Affairs, the program provides an option for meeting its legal obligation to care for ailing, aging patients at significantly reduced costs, since the veterans pay room and board directly to their caregivers.

Cost-effectiveness is but one of the program's benefits. Stepney and Hundt, 67, are in good hands with West, who previously ran a home health care services company. And

*Originally published as Patricia Kime, "'They Deserve It': In Foster Homes, Veterans Are Cared for Like Family," *Kaiser Health News*, May 30, 2018. Kaiser Health News is a nonprofit news service covering health issues. It is an editorially independent program of the Kaiser Family Foundation that is not affiliated with Kaiser Permanente. KHN's coverage of these topics is supported by the SCAN Foundation and John A. Hartford Foundation.

they're in good company, watching television together in the main living room, going to elder care twice a week and sitting on West's porch chatting with neighbors.

West, who considers caring for older adults "her calling," also savors the companionship and finds satisfaction in giving back to those who spent their young lives in military service to the U.S.

"I took care of my mother when she got cancer and I found that I really had a passion for it. I took classes and ran an in-home nursing care business for years. But my dream was always to get my own place and do what I am doing now," West said. "God worked it out."

The Medical Foster Home program has slightly more than 700 licensed caregivers who live full time with no more than three veterans and provide round-the-clock supervision and care, according to the VA. Akin to a community residential care facility, each foster home must be state-licensed as an assisted living facility and submit to frequent inspections by the VA as well as state inspectors, nutritionists, pharmacists and nurses.

Unlike typical community care facilities, foster home caregivers are required to live on-site and tend to the needs of their patients themselves 24/7—or supply relief staff.

"It's a lot of work, but I have support," West says. "I try to make all my personal appointments on days when Mr. Ralph and Mr. Frank are out, but if I can't, someone comes in to be here when I'm gone."

VA medical foster home providers also must pass a federal background check, complete 80 hours of training before they can accept patients, plus 20 hours of additional training each year, and allow the VA to make announced and unannounced home visits. They cannot work outside the home and must maintain certification in first aid, CPR and medicine administration.

But one prerequisite cannot be taught—the ability to make a veteran feel at home. West has grown children serving in the military and takes pride in contributing to the well-being of veterans.

"It's a lot of joy taking care of them," she said of Stepney and Hundt. "They deserve it."

To be considered for the program, veterans must be enrolled in VA health care; have a serious, chronic disabling medical condition that requires a nursing home level of care; and need care coordination and access to VA services. It can take up to a month to place a veteran in a home once they are found eligible, according to the VA.

The veterans also must be able to cover their costs. Because medical foster homes are not considered institutional care, the VA is not allowed to pay for it directly. The average monthly fee, according to the VA, is $2,300, which most veterans cover with their VA compensation, Social Security and savings, said Nicole Trimble, Medical Foster Home coordinator at the Perry Point VA Medical Center in Maryland.

Pilot Program Takes Off

Since 1999, the Department of Veterans Affairs has been required to provide nursing home services to veterans who qualify for VA health care and have a service-connected disability rating of 70 percent or higher, or are considered unemployable and have a disability rating of 60 percent or higher.

The VA provides this care through short- or long-term nursing home facilities, respite care, community living centers on VA hospital grounds, private assisted living facilities and state veterans' homes.

Shortly after, the VA Medical Center in Little Rock, Ark., launched an alternative—a pilot program that placed veterans in individual homes, at an average cost to the VA of roughly $60 a day, including administration and health care expenses, compared with upward of $500 a day for nursing home care.

And because veterans who are enrolled in the Medical Foster Care program must use the VA's Home-Based Primary Care program, which provides an interdisciplinary team of health professionals for in-home medical treatment, the program saves the VA even more. One study showed that the home-based care has yielded a 59 percent drop in VA hospital inpatient days and a 31 percent reduction in admissions among those who participate.

More than 120 VA medical centers now oversee a Medical Foster Home program in their regions, and the VA has actively promoted the program within its health system.

It also has attracted bipartisan congressional support. In 2013, Sen. Bernie Sanders (I–Vt.) introduced a bill to allow the VA to pay for medical foster homes directly.

In 2015, former House Veterans Affairs Committee chairman Rep. Jeff Miller (R–Fla.) introduced similar legislation that would have allowed the VA to pay for up to 900 veterans under the program.

And in May, Rep. Clay Higgins (R–La.) raised the issue again, sponsoring a bill similar to Miller's. "Allowing veterans to exercise greater flexibility over their benefits ensures that their individual needs are best met," Higgins said in support of the program.

A Guardian "Angel"

Foster care has been a blessing for the family of Hundt, who suffered a stroke shortly after his wife died and was unable to care for himself. Hundt's daughter, Kimberly Malczewski, lives nearby and often stops in to visit her dad, sometimes with her 2-year-old son.

"I'm not sure where my father would be if he didn't have this," she said. "With my life situation—my husband and I both work full time, we have no extra room in our house, and we have a small child—I can't take care of him the way Miss Joann does."

Trimble, whose program started in 2012 and has five homes, said she hopes to expand by two to three homes a year. The VA will remain meticulous about selecting homes.

"There is a strict inspection and vetting process to be a medical foster home," Trimble said. "We only will accept the best."

It also takes a special person to be an "angel," as the caregivers are referred to in the program's motto, "Where Heroes Meet Angels."

Stepney and Hundt agree West has earned her wings. On a cruise to Bermuda, she brought Stepney and Hundt along.

For Hundt, it was the first time he'd been on a boat. And Stepney said it was nothing like the transport ships he and his fellow troops used in the late 1960s: "Well, I've gotten to travel, but it was mainly two years in Vietnam, and there weren't any women around."

When asked why she brought the pair along, West said caregiving is "a ministry, something you really have to like to do."

"And you know how the saying goes," she said. "When you like what you do, you never work a day in your life."

50. Tiny Home Villages for Homeless Veterans*

RACHEL D. MCGUFFIN

In the early 2000s, U.S. citizens began turning to smaller accommodations, some as tiny as 250 square feet, in response to the appeal of minimalist living and the ever-rising real estate prices. Major television networks broadcasted a myriad of shows, *Tiny House Nation, Tiny House Hunting*, and others, providing a glimpse into the popularity of these micro-homes among Americans, as this way of life offered freedom from mortgage payments with little cost up front. Around 2010, local non-profit organizations and governments began seeing the potential benefits of these tiny home villages in response to housing the chronically homeless population, especially for veterans.

The National Coalition for Homeless Veterans (NCHV) reported in 2018 estimates of 40,000 homeless veterans slept on the street on any given night, and roughly 30 percent of them were younger veterans of recent wars (Caseley, n.d.). Public and private entities pooled funds and enabled developers to design, build, and maintain housing options to get these veterans off the street and into communities, where they could be housed and provided with the care they needed to integrate back into society. Tiny Home "Veteran Villages" have already been successfully established in Missouri and California, while others are under current consideration in the Californian cities of Monterey, Bakersfield, and San Jose.

The Tiny Home Community—Why It Works for Veterans

Tiny home villages provide a tailored environment that is highly favorable to veterans attempting to transition from military life to the civilian world. Firstly, the twenty-five to fifty home villages offer the veteran a community of like-minded individuals who have endured similar experiences and can provide a strong sense of camaraderie. More importantly, the veteran has autonomy over the level of integration into this community and can always retreat back to their safe space if needed. Veterans who have deployed or undergone a stressful, traumatic event are supported within the military, but the transition into the private sector often tests their coping mechanisms and resiliency. Many do not have the support system to combat the post traumatic stress disorder that regularly accompanies deployments. The Veterans Community Project, a successful

---

*Published with permission of the author.

non-profit run Veteran Village in Kansas City, Missouri, emphasizes the need for incremental approach to re-integration and the support it provides: Going from extreme isolation to extreme socialization can be very overwhelming and cause unwanted outcomes. We believe that handing the veteran the keys to their own home and letting them socialize at their own pace is one key to a successful outcome (Veteran's Community Project, 2019).

Secondly, the tiny house is constructed with the specific needs of a person who has undergone severe trauma in the past. For example, the bed is placed directly across from the door, there are few windows (or points of vulnerability) placed in the home, and the windows are small and located high up on the walls (Veterans' Community Project website, 2019). The smaller space enables them to feel in control of the situation, while the stand-alone structure encourages freedom and autonomy over their living space. In the Kansas City Veterans Village, the 2-by-4 beams were engraved by local citizens with supportive and encouraging messages to the veterans to add that extra layer of inclusion.

On top of the sense of community and layout of the housing structures, supportive care is also provided tailored to veterans and their needs. The layout of the village ideally is circular or constructed in parallel lines of houses, equipped with a common room, outdoor seating, and access to professional case managers. These managers coordinate individual and group counseling, access to healthcare through the Veteran's Affairs Department, professional development, and employment facilitation. The ultimate goal of a Veterans Village is to provide transitionary housing, thus the services provided are all anchored on helping the veteran transition and find steady employment within a year or two.

As of 2019, two veteran village models have been successful in housing and transitioning veterans into the civilian sector. The Veterans Village Project in Kansas City, Missouri, sits on a five-acre plot that was developed into 49 tiny homes to provide transitional housing services for Veterans. Chris Stout, one of the founders of the non-profit organization, who had deployed to Iraq and Afghanistan, got the idea from watching one of the many televised shows for tiny homes (Gross, 2018). The Veterans Village comes equipped with a community center, linkage to employment agencies, and a range of counseling options. Rent is subsidized by the Housing and Urban Development (HUD) Veterans Affairs (VA) Supportive Housing Program, and the remaining costs are covered by donations, local government funding, and grants. Henry Owens, a 32-year-old Navy Veteran claimed the Veterans Village Project saved his life, as he was sleeping in a park before moving into the village, a park where his friend was shot and killed not two day after Owens moved in (Gross, 2018).

The Michael Wolff/John Zane Veterans Village built in Sonoma County, California, welcomed 14 veterans in March 2019. Contractor Michael Wolff, a marine veteran, purposely underbid for the construction of this project and worked through wildfires and rain for two years to bring it to fruition (Ban, 2019). The Community Housing of Sonoma County was able to pool both private and public funds to complete construction on the village, and with the HUD-VASH program, veterans were provided homes along with access to supportive services. Each tiny home is compliant with the Americans with Disabilities Act, and bids are awaiting approval for the installation of solar panels (Ban, 2019). Supervisor Shirley Lane explains the reasoning behind the county's choice to go with a tiny home village as opposed to other housing options: "It's hard when the veterans move in off the street, they need a lot of privacy and support about changing their life so radically" (Ban, 2019).

Tiny Homes vs. Other Transitional Housing for the Homeless

More urban areas in the U.S. are beginning to explore this type of transitional housing model for their homeless population because it is cheaper than building and maintaining traditional shelters, takes less time, and is considered more humane and private than other options. The 10 tiny house villages funded by the Low Income Housing Institute in Seattle Washington reported just how much lower the cost could be: $25,000 to build each house, with an annual budget of $60,000 to $500,000, depending on the size of the village, which would include maintenance fees, land permits, and provision of services (Lee, 2019). This couple hundred thousand dollar budget is much more doable than the $2 billion spent annually by New York City on homeless shelters, or the $650 million L.A. would need to construct and maintain a new homeless shelter (Palta, 2018).

Traditional transitional housing for the homeless requires a hybrid of public and private cooperation for funding, construction, and maintenance; however, this is not the case for tiny home villages. One man by the name of Elvis Summers in L.A. decided to open a crowdfunding project with no overhead to help build tiny homes for veterans. He raised over $100,000 via crowdfunding websites, and has built over 49 homes, all of which can be found on donated land (Lapidus, 2017). As his project gained popularity in the local community, middle school classes and other veterans began reaching out to help him build the houses. The same phenomenon is now happening in Monterey, CA, where Monterey Peninsula College is working in concert with the Veterans Transition Center to pilot the construction of zero-net pocket houses (Herrara, 2018). These tiny homes are self-sufficient for electricity and water, allowing a total off the grid lifestyle. The Veterans Transition Center wants to employ homeless veterans in the construction of the site as the advantage is twofold—build the community and also teach the individuals marketable skills.

Tiny home villages also provide a humane approach to transitional housing. Sources in Seattle report that shelters must often turn away couples or those with mixed gender children because they would be housed separately, breaking up the family (Lee, 2018). Four walls, equipped with a bed and bathroom, provides a greater sense of security than a bed in an open, often crowded space. Veterans especially need this sense of security, as they are operating full in survival mode with PTSD symptoms by the time they are placed in transitional housing. The layout of this transitional housing model encourages a sense of community by providing a balanced amount of personal and shared space, which is almost non-existent in shelter models.

Potential Problems

Building tiny home villages for veterans encounters a slightly different set of problems than villages built solely for the chronically homeless. For example, the rate at which developers or supporters encounter the "not in my back yard" mentality is drastically less, because there is generally an undercurrent of support for those who have served the country. That being said, the two biggest problems which are also shared by traditional tiny home villages for the homeless include funding and preventing stagnation where those inside the village never successfully find permanent housing.

Funding and gaining approval for land usage has proven troublesome, especially in more expensive states like California. The village mentioned earlier in this chapter in Sonoma County, California, took two years longer than originally projected to build because of funding constraints that happened with those years' natural disasters. Eighty homeless people in San Jose, California, were scheduled to move into a tiny home village built on leased land from the California Department of Transportation, but that move has been suspended as arguments about liability sprouted between the municipal government and the leaser (Deruy, 2019).

Other tiny home villages, like Lichton Springs in Seattle, Washington, have been shut down due to the negative impact on local society coupled with the failure in helping these tiny home residents find permanent housing. Of the 58 residents living the village, 39 had been there for over a year (Davila et al., 2018). Some potential causes of this failure include the lack of sustained care management within the community, the allowed use of drugs and alcohol, and the lack of support from local businesses in hiring chronically homeless individuals. There was also the issue of the tiny houses and their construction, as each only took up one hundred and twenty square feet and had no plumbing.

Recommendations

In order to ensure tiny home villages for homeless veterans succeed as a transitional housing model, the developers and stakeholders must not only adopt best practices from the Veterans Community Project, they must also take into account the following recommendations.

1. Conduct extensive research into local homelessness issue and diversify stakeholders accordingly. Funding and development can take many forms: non-profit organizations with government assistance, crowdfunding coupled with individual or church assistance, or any mixture in between. Avoid leasing issues by capitalizing on unused commercial land or church property.

2. Employ support from local businesses and veterans for construction of the project. This has been successful in Bakersfield, California, where plumbing, concrete, roofing, and electrical parts have been donated by local businesses for their tiny home veterans' village (Mayer, 2018).

3. Ensure a career development pipeline is in place to maintain the integrity of the transitional housing model. Veterans who are placed in these tiny home villages need specific, concrete goals to work towards, covering aspects like physical/mental health, finances, social integration, and career skill development.

4. Maintain local support by interacting with local media, businesses, non-profit organizations, and social events. Help close the gap of isolation by integrating these homeless veterans throughout society; this can be done by organizing volunteer events and promoting participation in job fairs or communal projects.

References

Ban, C. (2019). Sonoma County houses veterans in tiny homes. Retrieved from: https://www.naco.org/articles/sonoma-county-houses-veterans-tiny-homes.

Caseley, L. (n.d.). Veterans' tiny house village is finally giving heroes the care they deserve. Retrieved from: https://www.littlethings.com/tiny-house-veteran-village.

Davila, V. & Greenstone, S. (2018). A tiny house village for the homeless will close its doors in Seattle. Retrieved from: https://www.governing.com/topics/health-human-services/tns-seattle-tiny-house-home-homeless.html.

Deruy, E. (2019). San Jose: Tiny homes delayed amid site negotiations. Retrieved from: https://www.mercurynews.com/2019/07/15/san-jose-tiny-homes-delayed-amid-site-negotiations/.

Gross, N. (2018). Think small? This initiative offers tiny houses to homeless vets. Retrieved from: https://rebootcamp.militarytimes.com/news/transition/2018/10/19/think-small-new-initiative-offers-tiny-houses-to-homeless-vets/.

Herrara, J. (2018). Multi-story permanent veterans housing project coming together for VTC in Marina. Retrieved from: https://www.montereyherald.com/2018/06/15/multi-story-permanent-veterans-housing-project-coming-together-for-vtc-in-marina/.

Lapidus, F. (2017). School children help build tiny home for homeless veteran. Retrieved from: https://www.voanews.com/episode/schoolchildren-help-build-tiny-home-homeless-veteran-3760436?fbclid=IwAR04IsDELErLyYekqtyIMiOv8CYAIrhaorVimgdgD8avEQp9In2KD2Vc2fE.

Lee, S. (2019). Tiny house villages in Seattle: an efficient response to our homelessness crisis. Retrieved from: https://shelterforce.org/2019/03/15/tiny-house-villages-in-seattle-an-efficient-response-to-our-homelessness-crisis/.

Mayer, S. (2018). If it works, this tiny homes plan for homeless vets will likely be duplicated. Retrieved from: https://www.bakersfield.com/news/if-it-works-this-tiny-homes-plan-for-homeless-vets/article_587a882a-ccbe-11e8-a321-b73fa063df1f.html.

Palta, R. (2018). Here's what it would cost to shelter every homeless person—and why LA will never do it. Retrieved from: https://laist.com/2018/06/22/heres_what_it_would_cost_to_shelter.php.

Veterans Community Project (2019). Retrieved from https://www.veteranscommunityproject.org.

Xie, J. (2017). 10 tiny house villages for the homeless across the U.S. Retrieved from: https://www.curbed.com/maps/tiny-houses-for-the-homeless-villages.

• E. Seniors •

51. How the Homeless Population Is Changing[*]

It's Older and Sicker

Margot Kushel

On any given night in the United States, according to the Department of Housing and Urban Development, over half a million people are without a home. That number may have decreased nationwide in the past few years, but California remains on the forefront of the problem, accounting for 20 percent of the country's homeless in 2014.

With the winter's freezing temperatures and El Niño's massive rainstorms, what to do about the thousands living in our city streets has been making headlines on both the East and West coasts.

What policymakers and the general public need to recognize is that the homeless are aging faster than the general population in the U.S. This shift in the demographics has major implications for how municipalities and health care providers deal with homeless populations.

In the early 1990s, only 11 percent of the adult homeless population was aged 50 and over. That percentage was up to 37 by 2003. Today half of America's homeless are over 50.

In fact, people born in the second half of the baby boom (1955–1964) have had an elevated risk of homelessness compared to other age groups throughout their lives.

So how have people aged 50 and over become homeless? And what happens to them and their health after they are homeless?

These are the questions my research team, funded by the National Institute on Aging, has been asking 350 participants in a study we've been conducting since July 2013 in Oakland, California.

Oakland's Older Homeless

Our results have shown that a large proportion of the older homeless population in Oakland first became homeless late in life, and once they become homeless, their health declines precipitously.

*Originally published as Margot Kushel, "How the Homeless Population Is Changing: It's Older and Sicker," *The Conversation*, https://theconversation.com/how-the-homeless-population-is-changing-its-older-and-sicker-50632 (January 8, 2016). Reprinted with permission of the publisher.

Oakland, like most places in the U.S., has a problem with housing costs, particularly for older adults. In the United States, more than 30 percent of renters and 23 percent of homeowners aged 50 and older spend more than half of their household income on rent. This makes it hard to pay for food and medicine and puts them at high risk of becoming homeless.

California has the highest housing costs of any large state, and they are rising faster than elsewhere. It is not surprising that Oakland has a large homeless population.

The common perception of homelessness is that it is a problem that afflicts only those with mental health and substance use problems. But this description doesn't describe the experience of older adults, particularly those who first experienced homelessness late in life.

For the most part, these are men and women who worked throughout their lives in low-skill, low-wage jobs. They are also disproportionately people of color: Oakland's population is 28 percent African American, but 80 percent of our study participants are.

The stories they have told us follow a similar pattern. One of our participants spoke of the shock of losing his job after 27 years: "I had lost my job and just could not … find another one. So in that 27 years, you know, I worked, you know, paid bills, and pretty much tried to enjoy … the things that life gives you when you go out and earn. But when I became homeless it was like a little, it was like a little shock at the time."

Another described losing his housing after being evicted when his wife had had a stroke and his daughter went back on her promise to let them stay: "After we moved out of the place, turned in the keys and everything we went over to her house and she said, 'Y'all can't stay here.' And I said, 'I got $9 in my pocket … at least let your mother spend the night because we don't have enough money to get a motel room.' She said, 'No.' So that was the beginning."

Their lives became derailed by job loss, illness, a new disability, the death of a loved one or an interaction with the criminal justice system. Often, it was a combination of these factors that led to homelessness.

The other half of the older homeless we surveyed had been homeless on and off for years. Much of this time was spent cycling through jails, prisons and hospitals.

For these people, life has been difficult from their childhood.

One participant described how abuse had caused him to flee his family, beginning a lifetime of homelessness: "'Next time you, if you run away, I'll beat you with a car chain or I'm going to throw you out the window.' […] Then I looked out the window and said—we lived on the 13th floor—I said, 'I ain't playing with this man.' He went to work, I had whatever I had on me, I was out the door."

In many cases, participants' drug and alcohol abuse started early, as did mental health problems.

Shared Health Problems

All our study participants, whether newly homeless or homeless for many years, faced challenges with their health once they lost their home.

As research shows, homeless people in their 50s and 60s have similar or worse health problems than people in the general population who are in their 70s and 80s.

There are many causes for this discrepancy. High rates of smoking, alcohol and drug use; poor access to health care, poor nutrition and high stress are just some of the factors that take their toll.

People who are homeless also have a hard time getting medical care. They may qualify for public insurance, but they often don't have the wherewithal to get to a clinic or to contact a health provider. Others prioritize obtaining food and shelter or don't seek health care because of shame around being homelessness or fear of how health care providers will treat them.

When the homeless population was made up of a majority of younger adults, health care providers focused on treating substance use and mental health disorders, traumatic injuries and infections, many of which could be treated with short-term care.

Now, with an older homeless population, health care providers have the difficult task of managing chronic diseases like diabetes and heart and lung disease.

People with chronic diseases need to make repeated visits to their health care provider and adhere to complicated medication regimens, specific diets and physical routines. None of these are easy to stick to, but doing so becomes almost impossible for people who are homeless.

Add to this high rates of cognitive impairment (problems with memory, information processing and following directions), functional impairment (the ability to manage daily tasks such as dressing, bathing, toileting), mobility impairment (the ability to walk), and deteriorating hearing and vision.

These problems further complicate the older homeless person's ability to manage chronic diseases, access services and exit homelessness.

It is hardly surprising that only about one in five of our participants were housed one year after we first met them.

Systemic Change Needed

The point our study highlights is that the systems set up in the 1980s were not designed to serve an aging population.

Cognitive impairment, for example, makes it difficult to follow through with instructions to come to appointments, fill out complicated paperwork for disability benefits or housing applications, or adhere to treatment regimens.

People with mobility impairments are not able to walk miles between service providers, carrying their belongings with them. People at high risk of falls are not well served by bunk beds or by bathrooms in shared facilities that do not have grab bars and slip-resistant floors.

Shelter and housing providers are grappling with the need to provide clients with personal care assistants to enable them to handle activities of daily living, like bathing and dressing. They are reporting difficulty with clients whose cognitive impairments make them unable to understand or follow rules.

Many Medicaid programs will cover the costs of personal care via the Home and Community Based Services Program, which is designed to keep Medicaid recipients living at home and in the community instead of in expensive institutional care.

However, it is nearly impossible to arrange these services for people living in temporary shelters or in the street.

While there are few data, our study suggests that many older homeless adults will require nursing home placement, some of which could have been avoided with housing and home-based services.

Two years into our study, many of our participants have already spent extended time in nursing facilities.

Death on the Street

We have known for years that homeless people are likely to die prematurely.

When the homeless population was younger, these deaths were mostly attributable to substance use, violence and infectious diseases.

Older homeless adults die at a rate four to five times what would be expected in the general population but die from different causes than do younger homeless adults. They die from the same causes as do other people—heart disease and cancer—but they do so 20 to 30 years earlier.

In the course of our two-year study, for example, 14 of our 350 participants have died. Others are very ill and, we fear, will die soon.

To put it bluntly, as a society, we face the specter of older adults dying on the streets. So, what is to be done?

Our argument is that there is no one-size-fits-all solution.

An individual who has spent 30 years rotating between institutional care and the streets requires different services than a 54-year-old man who has become homeless for the first time after a period of extended unemployment.

To solve the problem of homelessness among older Americans, we will have to find answers to two questions.

How do we adapt existing programs for homeless adults to meet the needs of an aging population?

And possibly even more intractable but fundamental: how do we stop older people from losing their homes?

52. Housing Policy Solutions to Support Aging with Options[*]

SHANNON GUZMAN, JANET VIVEIROS
and EMILY SALOMON

The phrase "home is where the heart is" captures the sentiments of many older adults when it comes to making choices about where they live as they age. Seventy-eight percent of adults ages 45 and older surveyed in 2014 stated that they would prefer to remain in their homes indefinitely as they age. Should they find themselves unable to do so, 80 percent of the people surveyed agreed with the statement, "What I'd really like to do is remain in my local community for as long as possible."[1] Social connections with friends and neighbors, familiarity with local amenities, and proximity to services and even doctors are among the many things that may be lost when an older adult has to move from his or her community.

Population projections indicate that by 2030, one in five people will be age 65 or older.[2] Communities must prepare for the housing and service needs of older adults. Local decision makers and other community stakeholders can act now to put policies in place that will address challenges that community members may face as they age.

Implementing policies that tackle issues of housing affordability, accessibility, and supportive services is a key action local officials can take to improve community livability and support people at all life stages.

What Is Aging In Place?

"Aging in place" describes older adults living independently in their current residence or community for as long as possible. Policies to promote aging in place often provide services and supports in the home, but the ability to age in place is also determined by the physical design and accessibility of the home, as well as community features such as the availability of nearby services and amenities, affordable housing, and transportation options. The AARP report "Aging in Place: A State Survey of Livability Policies and Practices" highlights examples of states and local want to age in their homes and communities.[3]

---

[*]Originally published Shannon Guzman, Janet Viveiros, and Emily Salomon, "Housing Policy Solutions to Support Aging with Options," AARP Policy Institute, https://www.aarp.org/content/dam/aarp/ppi/2017/06/housing-policy-solutions-to-support-aging-with-options.pdf (July 2017). Reprinted with permission of the publisher.

Studies have found that aging in place can lead to better health outcomes, life satisfaction, and self-esteem, compared with aging in a nursing home.[4] In addition, aging in place is typically more affordable than moving to an assisted living facility or nursing home. For example, the median annual cost for a private room in an assisted living facility exceeded $43,000 in 2016, and a semi-private room in a nursing facility was nearly twice as costly.[5] By comparison, the average annual costs for a home health aide working 30 hours a week is much lower, at $31,000.[6]

Aging with Options: Housing Challenges and policy solutions

Following are some of the principal obstacles to aging in homes and communities, along with potential solutions for meeting those challenges.

CHALLENGE: The population of older adults is rapidly rising and expected to reach 20 percent of the U.S. population by 2030. Many communities are lagging behind in supporting policies and programs that will address the needs, including housing, of older adults.

A MetLife survey, from 2011, found that many municipalities and counties across the country are struggling to set policies and provide services for older adults who wish to remain in their communities as they age.[7] Survey respondents indicated that their greatest challenges were providing housing- and transportation-related programs and services to older adults due to financial constraints as a result of the Great Recession.[8]

Additionally, the findings reveal that the majority of jurisdictions are not considering the needs of older adults when developing strategic and long-term community plans. Localities are failing to include the voices of older adults in their community planning activities and reflecting their needs in strategic plans.[9] Neglecting older adults may put localities at a disadvantage both in preparing for the health and well-being of their communities as residents age and in losing older adults' knowledge and experience that they may bring to discussions about shaping the future of their neighborhoods.

SOLUTION: Local jurisdictions can use programs such as the AARP Network of Age-Friendly Communities or similar initiatives to address the housing and other needs of all residents regardless of age.

AARP is the U.S. affiliate for the World Health Organization's Age-Friendly Cities and Communities program.[10] When communities join the AARP Network of Age-Friendly Communities (AFC), they commit to take programmatic and policy actions to improve the lives of their residents at every life stage. Since 2012, over 170 communities (cities, counties, and towns) have joined the AFC, covering a population of more than 65 million people.[11]

The initiative's framework highlights the importance of key community characteristics that support the ability of community members to remain independent and active participants in community life as they age. These characteristics cover the built environment, amenities, and services across several areas called domains. These include housing, transportation, health, civic participation, and education, among others, that have an impact the health and well-being of residents.[12] For example, an age-friendly community has affordable options for households with varying income levels and has homes with design features to accommodate people with limited mobility.

Member jurisdictions engage community members, local organizations, and businesses to develop an action plan that prioritizes strategies to address their locality's critical and unique challenges and to align their actions with these valued community features.[13]

The collaboration between local leaders and residents is important not only to obtain the diverse perspectives of each party, but also to begin forming coalitions that can work together toward solving their most pressing issues.

Each community is different and has its own unique set of assets and challenges, especially when considering the needs of people as they age. Local leaders can make crucial decisions today that can have a positive impact on older adults' lives now and in the future by taking steps toward being more age friendly. The AFC is one program, among several others, such as Grantmakers in Aging's AGEnda grants, helping communities do so successfully.[14]

CHALLENGE: As people age, some will need assistance with daily tasks.

Many older adults develop chronic conditions and mobility challenges that make it difficult to care for themselves and their home. The older the members of a household, the more likely they are to have a disability. Older and low-income individuals are at greatest risk of developing a disability.[15] Having a disability or chronic condition can make it difficult for older adults to complete activities of daily living such as bathing, dressing, or eating, as well as instrumental activities of daily living such as cooking, shopping, and managing medications on their own.

If older adults' health and mobility change and they need assistance with these activities, they are faced with a decision on how to get the help they need in order to live safely. They may rely on family members to serve as caregivers, hire personal care assistants to help them in their homes, or move to an assisted living or nursing facility. However, most older adults would prefer to age in their home or community instead of an assisted living or nursing facility; moreover, the costs of these facilities can pose financial hardships.

SOLUTION: Offering supportive services at home or close by in the community can help older adults continue to live safely in their homes.

Supportive services can include a variety of forms of help, ranging from personal care assistance to medication management, that are focused on aiding individuals in completing daily tasks and managing their health and well-being. In urban communities, supportive service programs offered in home and community settings can take the form of collaborations between housing providers and health providers who understand the important role of stable housing in supporting health and well-being. In New York State, the Office for the Aging funds Naturally Occurring Retirement Community Supportive Service Programs (NORC-SSP) in multifamily buildings having a concentration of older adults. The program provides supports and services to facilitate aging at home and in communities.

The success of many of these programs at supporting aging is in part the result of the cooperation of housing providers who promote participation. Housing providers also share information on the well-being of residents with health care provider partners so they can better tailor services to individuals' needs.

Since its inception, NORC-SSP in New York State have served over 19,000 adults ages 60 or older.[16] Around the country, similar home- and community-based programs are offered in senior and community centers in suburban and rural communities by social service agencies and health provider networks.

In fact, contrary to common assumptions, quality support isn't just an option for cities. Whether older adults rent or own, or live in a high-rise building in the city or a single-family home in a rural community, a variety of models are available for offering services that support healthy aging.[17] Some programs offer services onsite in multifamily buildings or through home visits, while other programs are based in central and accessible community centers.

Local governments can facilitate the development and expansion of new and existing home- and community-based supportive service programs by offering grants to fund programs to ensure that services are affordable to low-income older adults. They can also support programs by making space available at low or no cost in community centers so that programs can operate in central and accessible locations. State governments also play an important role by funding supportive service programs for aging through grants from various sources.

CHALLENGE: An older adult's home is not physically accessible or requires burdensome or expensive upkeep.

Structural barriers, such as narrow doorways and the absence of a first-floor bathroom, can make it difficult for older adults with mobility limitations to meet their daily needs and engage in routine activities.

A home's age and size have implications for the amount of time and effort required to keep it well maintained, up to local building codes, and accessible to an aging individual. Older homes (which are often where older individuals may reside if they have lived there a long time) typically require more maintenance than newer homes and can pose a barrier to aging in place. Residents may be unable to manage upkeep or improve accessibility because of physical or financial restrictions.

SOLUTION: Existing homes can be modified to improve accessibility and safety for older residents, while communities can implement innovative programs to enable such improvements.

A simple modification might be installing handrails to make it easier to use stairs; a more complex modification might involve adding a bedroom on a home's first floor or widening doorways to accommodate a wheelchair. Modifications such as grab bars and railings make homes more accessible and can reduce the risk of falls needing medical treatment, a prevalent cause of injury among older adults, by about 20 percentage points.[18]

Local governments can take numerous steps to support home modifications for older adults, including adopting expedited permitting and review policies, certifying home improvement contractors that specialize in aging-in-place modifications, and allocating resources from housing trust funds or other revenue streams to subsidize the cost of home modifications for income-eligible residents.[19]

Home modifications can be a viable option to enable homeowners to remain in their homes as they age; however, renters are generally at a disadvantage because they have less control over the features of their homes. Accessibility requirements of the Fair

Housing Act do not apply to buildings with fewer than four units, so older renters in single-family homes, duplexes, and other small structures can often face hardships as a result. Although the Fair Housing Act permits renters with disabilities in single-family homes to make "reasonable modifications" to improve accessibility in their homes, they must do so at their own expense,[20] which can present a challenge for those with limited financial resources.

Communities can provide assistance to landlords to make modifications that accommodate the needs of their tenants. In Boston, for example, landlords who rent to older adults or people with disabilities are eligible to apply for the Metropolitan Boston Housing Partnership's zero- and low-interest home modification loans. The program issued nearly 2,000 home modification loans between 2000 and 2013.[21]

In the case of new construction, jurisdictions should consider building codes that require accessibility features to accommodate residents as they age, thus reducing the prevalence of barriers and minimizing the need for future home modifications.

CHALLENGE: In many communities, the existing housing stock does not offer a range of choices for older adults wishing to remain in their community by moving to homes that are smaller or closer to transit, shops, places of worship, and other destinations.

Almost 60 percent of adults over age 50 live in single-family detached homes.[22] Those homes may be too large, too expensive, and too automobile dependent for many residents. Restrictive zoning laws and other land-use policies or strong NIMBY (not in my backyard) sentiment can make it difficult for developers to build multifamily housing, accessory dwelling units (ADUs), or other, often smaller, more affordable and accessible alternatives to single-family homes.

Meanwhile, land-use policies that separate homes from services and amenities can make aging more difficult for people who want to remain in their homes and communities. For example, health care and social service facilities that are permitted only in areas far from where many older adults live can make it difficult for them to receive the care they need, especially if public transportation services are inadequate and driving is not an option.

SOLUTION: Local governments can revisit their zoning policies and encourage a mix of housing types and affordability levels to accommodate older adults and others interested in multifamily housing.

For example, communities can rezone areas to accommodate more compact residential development near transit stops and in mixed-use, walkable communities—increasing accessibility for older adults who are unable or choose not to drive. By coordinating this development with their affordable housing policies, communities can ensure that a portion of these units are affordable to low- or moderate-income households.

Another possibility is to promote the use of ADUs, which are self-contained residential units located either within a single-family home or on the same property. Many local communities have adopted ADU policies. The city of Santa Cruz, California, for example, developed "ADU Plan Sets Books," which include ADU plans designed by architects and a homeowner manual for how to plan, design, and obtain permits for an ADU.[23] Since ADUs are built on existing properties rather than on the fringe of the community, they are more commonly located near city amenities and bus routes. They also tend to be smaller and more affordable than stand-alone units.

CHALLENGE: As older adults age, incomes often do not keep pace with housing costs.

Housing costs in excess of what older adults can afford may also present a barrier to aging in place, particularly for those with limited financial resources. Nearly one-third of adults between the ages of 50 and 80 spend more than 30 percent of their income on housing costs, while almost 40 percent of adults 80 years or older spend more than 30 percent of their incomes on housing.[24] Spending more than 30 percent of income on housing may reduce the available funds that families have for other vital household expenses. Although both owners and renters are susceptible to housing cost burdens, the two groups face very different affordability challenges.

More than 80 percent of households headed by adults 65 or older own their homes.[25]

Historically, housing affordability problems for older homeowners could be traced to rising property taxes, utility costs, or costly property insurance. Recently, however, challenges have evolved, particularly with so many Americans relying on their homes as a key financial asset. The Great Recession during the past decade and the subsequent collapse in the housing market impacted many older homeowners when property values tumbled. The depressed housing prices in many markets contributed to the decline in the net wealth (primarily home equity) of low-income older home owners. Between 2007 and 2010, the median net wealth of low-income homeowners ages 50 and older fell by about 30 percent.[26] This loss of wealth poses a major challenge to homeowners who were planning on using the proceeds of the sale of their home to pay for health care or supportive services that they may need as they age.

For renters, hundreds of thousands of government-subsidized units affordable to low- and moderate-income households are at risk of being lost as their landlords reach the end of their required affordability periods.[27] Historically affordable rental homes, particularly those that lack government subsidies, are also at risk of becoming less so as they are upgraded, or as homeowners displaced by foreclosure increase demand (and rents) for low-cost rental housing. Thus, growing competition and rising rents may make it difficult for older adults to remain in their communities.

SOLUTION: Whether renting or owning, older adults can benefit from programs that increase or preserve the stock of affordable housing units and reduce costs for existing units.

Localities have a wide variety of policy tools at their disposal to produce and preserve affordable housing for older adults. Jurisdictions should consider developing a comprehensive housing strategy to assess both the supply of and demand for affordable units targeted to older adults and to coordinate housing policies to meet the needs of the community. In some jurisdictions, for example, it may be appropriate to create a housing trust fund and use the revenue to increase the affordable stock. In others, states and localities may wish to prioritize efforts to preserve the affordability of subsidized rental housing by maintaining or adding subsidies, refinancing existing debts, or taking other rental preservation steps. In communities with an ample supply of moderately priced units, tenant-based rental subsidies may be the right solution to alleviate cost burdens for older adults. Because housing affordability problems are often multidimensional, a coordinated series of complementary policy solutions that cut across industries is likely the needed strategy in many communities.

Many states seek to reduce housing costs for older adults by providing tax relief to current residents. One example is a homestead exemption, authorized by states and administered by localities, which reduces the portion of a property's assessed value that is subject to taxation. Another example is a property tax deferral program that allows older homeowners to postpone payment of all or part of their property taxes until death or the sale of their property.[28]

To date, 33 states and Washington, DC, use such "circuit breakers" to reduce the property tax burden of homeowners, and many also extend the program to renters.[29] Although renters do not pay property taxes directly, renter circuit breakers offer a tax credit to income- or age-eligible households based on the assumption that property tax is implicitly part of their monthly rent payment. Credits range from 6 to 25 percent of the total rent paid.[30] In Maryland, the state's circuit breaker property tax relief program targets low-income homeowners and renters, including people with disabilities. In 2014, 80 percent of the more than 49,000 tax credits issued to older adult homeowners ages 60 and over in the state had an average value of $1,219.[31] Maryland's tax credit program for renters is open to older adults ages 60 and older, people with disabilities, and households with children. In that same year, the average tax credit for renters in Maryland was $307.[32]

By supporting both policies that expand the availability of affordable housing and those that reduce the housing cost burden for residents, states and localities can provide comprehensive solutions to address the affordable housing needs of older adults.

Federal Policy to Expand Home- and Community-Based Services

Some provisions of the Affordable Care Act (ACA) have the potential to expand aging-in-place options by better connecting low-income older adults with supportive services. The ACA creates options and incentives for states to offer more home- and community-based supportive service programs to Medicaid enrollees in order to reduce overall Medicaid long-term care spending. In 2013, older adults made up approximately 9 percent of the Medicaid enrollees but accrued 21 percent of total Medicaid expenditures.[33]

This policy direction helps states serve more Medicaid enrollees through home- and community-based services, which are both more cost effective and better aligned with the personal preferences of people who want to age at home instead of in institutional settings. These changes make it possible for states to significantly expand the number of people they serve in home- and community-based settings, making it easier for more low-income older adults to age in place. Potential action to repeal or remove aspects of the ACA could hinder the ability for states to provide the services to those who desire to stay in their homes and communities as they age.

Notes

1. Linda Barrett, *Home and Community Preferences of the 45+ Population 2014* (Washington, DC: AARP Research Center, September 2014).

2. Rodney Harrell, Jana Lynott, and Shannon Guzman, *Is This a Good Place to Live? Measuring Community Quality of Life for All Ages* (Washington, DC: AARP, April 2014).

3. Nicholas Farber, Douglas Shinkle, Jana Lynott, Wendy Fox-Grage, and Rodney Harrell, *Aging in Place: A State Survey of Livability Policies and Practices* (Washington, DC: National Conference of State Legislatures and AARP, December 2011).

4. Jordana Maisel, Eleanor Smith, and Edward Steinfeld, "Increasing Home Access: Designing for Visitability" (Washington, DC: AARP, August 2008); Janet Viveiros and Maya Brennan, "Aging in Every Place:

Supportive Service Programs for High and Low Density Communities" (Washington, DC: The National Housing Conference, 2014).

5. Genworth 2016 Cost of Care Survey, conducted by CareScout, April 2016, accessed November 3, 2016, https://www. genworth.com/about-us/industry-expertise/cost-of-care.html.

6. AARP estimates that the average work week for a home health aide is 30 hours per week. This figure is based on Genworth's 2016 Cost of Care Survey showing a national median hourly rate of $20.

7. N4a and MetLife Foundation, *The Maturing of America: Communities Moving Forward for an Aging Population* (Washington, DC: N4a and MetLife Foundation, June 2011).

8. N4a and MetLife Foundation, *The Maturing of America.*

9. N4a and MetLife Foundation, *The Maturing of America.*

10. The AARP Network of Age-Friendly Communities website, accessed December 6, 2016, http://www.aarp.org/livable-communities/network-age-friendly-communities/.

11. "The Member List," The AARP Network of Age-Friendly Communities, accessed December 6, 2016, http://www.aarp.org/livable-communities/network-age-friendly-communities/info-2014/member-list.html.

12. "Getting Started," The AARP Network of Age-Friendly Communities, accessed December 6, 2016, http://www.aarp.org/livable-communities/network-age-friendly-communities/info-2014/getting-started. html.

13. The AARP Network of Age-Friendly Communities website.

14. "Community AGEnda: Q and A," Grantmakers in Aging, last modified October 2014, accessed January 9, 2017, http://www.giaging.org/documents/141015_Community AGEnda_QA_FINAL.pdf.

15. Barbara Lipman, Jeffrey Lubell, and Emily Salomon, *Housing an Aging Population: Are We Prepared?* (Washington, DC: Center for Housing Policy, 2012), http://www.nhc.org/2012-housing-an-aging-population.

16. These are the latest data available from the New York State Office for the Aging. "Naturally Occurring Retirement Community Supportive Service Program (NORC-SSP) and Neighborhood NORC (NNORC)," New York State Office for the Aging, accessed July 14, 2016, http://www.aging.ny.gov/NYSOFA/Programs/CommunityBased/NORC-NNORC.cfm.

17. Viveiros and Brennan, *Aging in Every Place.*

18. Michael D. Ericksen, Nadia Greenhalgh-Stanley, and Gary V. Engelhardt, "Home Safety, Accessibility, and Elderly Health: Evidence from Falls," *Journal of Urban Economics* vol. 87, pp. 14–24 (May 2015), http://papers.ssrn.com/sol3/ papers.cfm?abstract_id=2344916.

19. Aging in Place Initiative, *A Blueprint for Action: Developing a Livable Community for All Ages* (Washington, DC: National Association of Area Agencies on Aging and Partners for Livable Communities, May 2007).

20. "Fair Housing—It's Your Right," U.S. Department of Housing and Urban Development, accessed October 14, 2016, http://portal.hud.gov/hudportal/HUD?src=/program_offices/fair_housing_equal_opp/FHLaws/yourrights.

21. "Home Modification Loan Program (HMLP)," Massachusetts Rehabilitation Commission, accessed July 14, 2016, http://www.mass.gov/eohhs/docs/mrc/hmlp-fact-sheet-2014.pdf.

22. Joint Center for Housing Studies, *Housing America's Older Adults: Meeting the Needs of an Aging Population* (Cambridge, MA: Harvard University, 2014), Appendix Table A-6, Characteristics of Stock Occupied by Older Adults: 2011.

23. Natalie Burg, "Affordable Housing: What Ann Arbor Can Learn from Santa Cruz, CA," *Concentrate*, http://www.secondwavemedia.com/concentrate/features/santacruzADUs0230.aspx.

24. Joint Center for Housing Studies, *Housing America's Older Adults*, Appendix Table A-10, Housing Cost Burdened.

25. Joint Center for Housing Studies. *Housing America's Older Adults*, Appendix Table A-6.

26. Joint Center for Housing Studies, *Housing America's Older Adults.*

27. National Low Income Housing Coalition, "Project-Based Rental Assistance," in *2014 Advocates' Guide to Housing and Community Development Policy* (Washington, DC: National Low Income Housing Coalition, 2014).

28. David Baer, *State Programs and Practices for Reducing Residential Property Taxes* (Washington, DC: AARP Public Policy Institute, May 2003).

29. These are the latest data available from the Lincoln Institute of Land Policy. "Significant Features of the Property Tax." Lincoln Institute of Land Policy and George Washington Institute of Public Policy. (Residential Property Tax Relief Programs, accessed October 14, 2016, http://datatoolkits.lincolninst.edu/subcenters/significant-features-property-tax/Report_Residential_ Property_Tax_Relief_Programs.aspx).

30. Karen Lyons, Sarah Farkas, and Nicholas Johnson, *The Property Tax Circuit Breaker: An Introduction and Survey of Current Programs* (Washington, DC: Center on Budget and Policy Priorities, March 2007).

31. Department of Assessments and Taxation, *The Seventieth Annual Report of the State Department of Assessments and Taxation for Fiscal Year 2014*, http://dat.maryland.gov/Pages/Statistics-Reports.aspx.

32. *Ibid.*

33. Center for Budget and Policy Priorities, *Policy Basics: Introduction to Medicaid, What Is Medicaid?* (Washington, DC: June 2015), http://www.cbpp.org/sites/default/files/atoms/files/policybasics-medicaid_0.pdf.

53. The Need for Safe and Healthy Homes in Order to Age in Place*

RACHEL L. FONTENOT *and* WILLIE L. BRITT

This chapter focuses on the impact that home repair and safety modifications completed by Rebuilding Together San Francisco, a non-profit organization, has on making it possible for the elderly homeowners they serve to age safely in their homes. Various perspectives were sought to measure this impact. Also, homeowners who requested service but did not receive home repair assistance were surveyed to determine if not receiving services adversely affected their ability to remain safe and healthy in their homes. Next, homeowners who did receive home repair and safety modifications were surveyed to explore the impact the services they received had on their ability to remain safe in their homes since repairs were made. Finally, key stakeholders were interviewed to obtain insights on what factors do and do not make the services provided by Rebuilding Together San Francisco vital to allowing seniors to age in place.

The number of seniors within the City of San Francisco is growing and challenging the existing public service system to meet their housing and health care needs at a time when financial resources are limited. As people age, there are frequent changes and modifications required and made in their living environment to help eliminate risks of falls and potential health hazards. Rebuilding Together San Francisco is a community-based organization that leverages volunteer labor with corporate donations to provide repairs and install safety modifications, free of charge, to low income seniors in the City of San Francisco.

Research Methodology

This study was designed to determine if the housing repair and modification services offered by Rebuilding Together San Francisco are making the homes of low income elderly safer and healthier. As of the date of the research in 2014, there had been no research targeting the scope of services provided by this type of service organization and the impact they have on older individuals in a metropolitan city such as San Francisco. The research question studied was: Is Rebuilding Together San Francisco making the homes they serve safer and healthier? The researcher's hypothesis was: Rebuilding Together San Francisco is making the homes they serve safer and healthier. The

*Published with permission of the authors.

independent variable in this research was Rebuilding Together San Francisco's services and the dependent variable was the impact result of making the homes of seniors safer and healthier. Although there is only one organization called Rebuilding Together San Francisco, the scope of their service can vary according to funding and volunteer labor. This organization also categorizes potential clients based on the nature of their need. If callers report the need for safety equipment, they are put on a list for volunteers to install home safety equipment. If they report needing larger scopes of work, such as painting, step repairs and roofing, they are added to a list that is matched with larger volunteer groups and sponsors. For the purposes of this research, all individuals who had requested services were merged into one list and sorted randomly.

The dependent variable, making homes safer and healthier, was expected to be a subjective evaluation made by the individuals being served and key informants.

Specific standards have been developed by the National Center for Healthy Housing that have been determined to represent a safe and healthy home. However, clients who have received services from Rebuilding Together San Francisco have not received training on this material.

Terms and Definitions

For the purposes of this research, the following operational definitions were used:

1. Rebuilding Together San Francisco is non-profit organization located in San Francisco California that leverages volunteers to provide home repairs.

2. home is a dwelling, either single or multi-family, whose legal owner is the individual being served.

3. Seniors will refer to individuals, over the age of 60 who received services from Rebuilding Together San Francisco during the 2014 calendar year.

4. The terms safer and healthier will refer to the standards identified by the National Center for Healthy Housing targeting twenty-two risk factors associated unsafe and unhealthy homes as described in the research.

Data Collection Process Overview

Primary data was collected by conducting telephone interviews with two groups of seniors as well as key Informants. Group One was comprised of seniors who had received services from Rebuilding Together San Francisco. Group Two had requested services but had not received services as of the time of the interview. Key Informants consisted of professionals in the fields of aging and Rebuilding Together San Francisco administration. The purpose of the interview was to determine what, if any, impact Rebuilding Together San Francisco had by providing or not providing services. A list of 168 names and phone numbers was provided to the researcher by Rebuilding Together San Francisco and identified as individuals who had received services from the organization during the 2014 calendar year. A similarly compiled list of 50 individuals who had requested services but had not received services to date was also provided. These lists did not include any service or need related information. Group 1, those who had received services from Rebuilding

Together San Francisco were asked to respond to four questions which were designed to obtain information about the impact, if any, the services provided to them had made on the health and safety of their home. Group 2, who had requested but not received services were asked three questions to determine if they were able to coordinate home repair needs without the assistance of Rebuilding Together San Francisco.

Four key informants were surveyed to obtain their perspective on the needs of aging individuals in San Francisco and the impact Rebuilding Together San Francisco has made toward helping this population age in place. The executive director of the San Francisco Department of Aging and Adult Services, represents the City agency responsible for advocating, coordinating and funding services for older adults and individuals with disabilities. The director of Aging Services for Catholic Charities in San Francisco leads a large community-based effort to provide support to aging individuals in order to allow them to age in their homes. The executive director of Rebuilding Together San Francisco had extensive experience in coordinating home modification and repair services to low income seniors in San Francisco. The president of Rebuilding Together San Francisco's Board of Directors had experience as a rebuilding project leader for teams that conduct repair services as well as the administrative vision for Rebuilding Together San Francisco.

Controlling for Internal and External Validity

Potential factors affecting the internal validity of this study included unexpected health conditions of the individuals being interviewed. Many conditions cannot be eliminated or prevented through the implementation of health and safety modifications and may prevent an individual from remaining in their home despite the availability of a safe environment. Additionally, personal finances may prohibit an individual from being able to pay required mortgages, taxes or utilities in order to remain in their home. In order to reduce the impact of these internal variables, the individuals included in the two interview groups had been screened for financial eligibility and determined to be in no immediate risk of eviction by Rebuilding Together San Francisco prior to providing the list to this researcher.

This research was externally valid to other national Rebuilding Together Affiliates of similar size to Rebuilding Together San Francisco. There were no other nonprofit community-based organizations that offer free home repair and safety modification services to low income homeowners in the San Francisco area. However, this research would be pertinent to medical service organizations that offer health care to low income seniors, families as well as the general public. The issue of safe and healthy housing has the potential to impact everyone because the home environment can impact all aspects of personal health.

Key Findings from Survey Data

As the survey data indicated, service recipients did not associate the services they received from Rebuilding Together San Francisco with making their homes safer and healthier. The majority of respondents associated the terms safe and healthy with their personal safety in their neighborhoods and their personal health conditions. These respondents recognized the changes that had been made to their homes but did not recognize the homes as being safe and healthy.

Survey data clearly showed that individuals who had not received services from Rebuilding Together San Francisco but had requested assistance, had not been successful in finding alternative methods to having the needed repairs made. Furthermore, data reflected falling, tripping and safety as a primary concern for all individuals who had and those who were still waiting for services. The research data reflected unmet needs among some service recipients. The researcher concluded that the repairs remaining as needed were costly and require a greater level of skills than smaller repairs. Roofing problems, windows, furnace replacement and other structural problems are very expensive to perform. Key stakeholders were selected based on their familiarity and experience in the field of aging services in San Francisco and their knowledge of services provided by Rebuilding Together San Francisco. Two questions were asked to obtain qualitative and quantitative information:

1. What do you see as the biggest barrier to seniors being able to age safely in their homes in San Francisco?
2. What impact do the services provided by Rebuilding Together San Francisco have on making homes of seniors safer and healthier?

Key Findings from Interview Data

Key informants unanimously identified lack of funds as the primary barrier to seniors being able to age safely in their homes. Because the homes in San Francisco are predominantly multi-floor, modifications will more than likely be required to assist aging homeowners with going up and down stairs, using the bathroom and safely maneuvering narrow hallways. Lack of knowledge of available resources was also reported as a barrier. Key informants clearly supported the research hypothesis that Rebuilding Together San Francisco is making the homes they serve safer and healthier.

Significant Findings from All Data

Research data clearly highlighted the areas in which Rebuilding Together San Francisco is successfully helping the low-income seniors they serve. Safety modifications and minor repairs were reported as having a significant impact on the service recipients. However, data also pointed out that this organization does not currently have the capacity to address the more expensive and structural repairs that are needed by a large number of seniors. Additionally, key informants clearly expressed their belief that Rebuilding Together San Francisco was making the homes of the seniors they serve safer and healthier. However, the majority of service recipients did not agree. It is worth pointing out that the difference in responses is reflective of the service recipients' lack of clinical understanding of a safe and healthy home.

Conclusions and Recommendations

1. Based on the majority of responses obtained from Group 1, aging individuals would benefit by receiving education on health and safety risk factors in their homes.

Data revealed that most respondents considered a state of health and safety to be applicable to their person and not their homes. Materials and training could help educate older residents of potential dangers and risks in their homes. However, it is also interesting to note that several respondents claimed that they did not know why they were referred or what the nature of their needs was. A possible explanation for this response could be that these individuals had a representative who requested assistance on their behalf, leaving the respondent unaware of the nature of the risks in the home.

2. Due to lack of funding, Rebuilding Together San Francisco was unable to perform repairs that are expensive and structurally complicated. The needs remaining for service recipients represented in Group 1 consists of stairs, windows, furnaces and foundations. Additional public funding for home repairs and modifications would allow a large portion of low-income seniors to be served and allow Rebuilding Together San Francisco to make a greater impact.

3. The scope of repairs Rebuilding Together San Francisco was able to complete is limited by their funding and skills capacity. As survey data indicated, some needed repairs were not addressed due to funding limitations and the skills needed to install the modifications. Additional funding would allow Rebuilding Together San Francisco to purchase the supplies and skill required to make such repairs.

4. Rebuilding Together San Francisco did not have the name recognition necessary to obtain additional funding from private corporations and donors. Additionally, low income seniors may not have been aware of the assistance available from Rebuilding Together.

Recommendations

1. By December 2015, Rebuilding Together San Francisco should develop educational materials addressing safe and healthy housing. Such materials should provide to seniors and families when being assessed and oriented for service. This material may also be shared with other direct service providers who serve the aging population in an effort to reach as many seniors as possible.

2. By August 1, 2015, Rebuilding Together San Francisco should contact the City of San Francisco Mayor's Office on Housing and Community Development to request additional funds. An initial funding request of $300,000, leveraged with volunteer labor and discounted materials would make it possible for Rebuilding Together San Francisco to address approximately 50 percent of the unmet need identified in this research.

3. By April 1, 2015, Rebuilding Together San Francisco should expand their reach into multiple funding options and investigate additional funding from health care institutions, medical insurance providers and long-term care providers.

4. By September 1, 2015, Rebuilding Together San Francisco should develop a marketing plan to guide the organization to new level of exposure and access to funding options.

These recommendations were developed to improve Rebuilding Together San Francisco's capacity to provide the help most needed by low income seniors in order for them to safely age in place.

Update 2019

Since completing the research in 2014, Rebuilding Together San Francisco has expanded their educational outreach to low income homeowners in San Francisco to educate them about potential health hazards in the home. They have also released a very successful initiative called SHE BUILDS over the past 4 years that has significantly increased the volunteer skill capacity and funding to make much needed repairs. Women in the construction industry have demonstrated a commitment to working together to expand the number of seniors helped. In conjunction with National Rebuilding Day, the last Saturday in April, teams of female carpenters, plumbers, engineers, attorney's, and general labor have joined together to provide a much-needed boost to Rebuilding Together San Francisco's impact.

Continuing Thought for the Future

"Improving the material integrity of one's home instills personal dignity, allowing safe and independent living as well as renewed pride in the home and one's history."

REFERENCE

Fontenot, Rachel L. The Need for Safe and Healthy Homes in Order to Aging in Place: Evaluating Rebuilding Together San Francisco's Impact, Golden Gate University, San Francisco, California, 2014.

54. Accessibility Solutions for Colton Hall*

CLAIRE MOELLER RYGG *and* WILLIE L. BRITT

The adequacy of handicap access to public historical sites is often overlooked and not considered significant unless you have a family member or friend who is adversely impacted. This may limit the opportunity to simply visit, never mind enjoying, which is often taken for granted by those who are not physically impaired (mobility, vision or hearing).

The City of Monterey is not only a tourist destination for those who want to explore the beauty of Monterey Bay and surrounding areas, but it also offers a rich history and cultural heritage, spanning from early colonial California to the sardine capital of the world and now an important tourist destination. Approximately four million tourists come to Monterey each year and many visit the Monterey Old Town Historic District, "an area that generally includes within its boundaries a significant concentration of properties linked by architectural style or a past event." This is prevalent throughout many cities and towns in the United States. In Monterey, several 19th century historic adobes and buildings are under the stewardship of the Monterey State Historic Park Association, and the City of Monterey, including Colton Hall. Colton Hall is the original site of California's 1849 Constitutional Convention ("the birthplace of California"). Colton Hall is owned and stewarded by the City of Monterey.

According to Melvyn Green, principal engineer of Melvyn Green & Associates, Inc., who wrote the "Historic Structure Report for Colton Hall" (Green, 1991), Colton Hall is "an interesting and unusual mixture of the prevalent California style and the Greek Revival buildings...[and] eminently worthy of preservation at any cost." The upper floor of the two-story building is a history museum that was established in 1948. City offices occupy the first floor. "One of the more remarkable facts about Colton Hall is that it has been in continuous use as a public building since its construction" (Conway, 2003).

Three part-time Museum Guides welcome over 14,000 annual visitors and interpret the history of the hall and of its multi-use significance as the site of the first California constitutional convention, a town hall and an elementary school, courthouse, and other various municipal, county, state and federal agencies. In 2012 on some occasions, the guides would meet with individuals in front of Colton Hall who could not access the second-story museum to interpret the history and the site. The hall is also a gathering

---

*Published with permission of the authors.

place for special events such as proclamations by the mayor, an annual reenactment of the 1849 Constitutional Convention, the venue for annual winter evening music concerts, art exhibits, hosting visiting dignitaries, for recognizing members of the community or professional organizations, and visiting educational and cultural groups.

In 1993, the City of Monterey's engineers estimated the cost of a mechanical lift for the rear second-story entrance of Colton Hall would be $75,000, excluding a building electrical upgrade and would have to be approved by the City Council as a Capital improvement Project budget or funded from an alternative source. In 2005, museum staff presented the subject of accessibility to Colton Hall and recommended the legislative body for policy on Colton Hall, the Colton Hall Museum and Cultural Arts Commission to consider "alternative approaches to making Colton Hall exhibits and services accessible to people with disabilities, rather than recommending construction of a lift to the second floor" (Conway, 2005). The commission directed museum staff to gather information on web-based technology or close circuit TV as alternatives to improve visitor access to Colton Hall. From that direction, the City explored the use of audio tours by cell phone and added flash tours (graphical representation or virtual tour of a site via internet browser) of some of the City's historic sites to its website www.monterey.org. In October 2011, the City began its development of a cell phone tour with two-minute descriptive audio-narrative for approximately twenty historic sites, and in January 2012, the cell tours became available to the public.

What happened between January 2012 and December 2017? The City decided that it needed to bid work for compliance with ADA accessibility requirements and an access compliance survey was performed in 2013 for the entire City, including Colton Hall. A proposal for an ADA accessibility study with recommendations was granted, the study completed, and the ADA accessibility improvements for Colton Hall was advertised on December 6, 2017. The Project Description was: "In general, the work consists of, but is not limited to, improvements to Colton Hall and City Hall buildings to comply with ADA accessibility requirements, including the reconstruction of parking stalls, installation of an elevator at Colton Hall and a lift at City Hall, construction of an access ramp to access the Planning Office (Colton Hall), construction of an ADA-compliant bathroom (Colton Hall), and construction of an ADA-compliant path around both buildings."

In October 2018, for the first time in its 169-year history, Colton Hall is accessible to visitors with special needs. The City of Monterey has completed a $353,000 improvement project, which includes a reconstruction of the back stairs and deck, a new Limited Use/ Limited Access (LULA) lift to provide Americans with Disabilities Act (ADA) access to the second floor. Additionally, a new ADA compliant restroom that can accommodate a wheelchair, an access ramp in the rear courtyard, and an adjacent ADA parking area was added.

With the passage of the Americans with Disabilities Act in 1990, many persons with disabilities have gained their civil rights and enjoy a life of independence. The ADA is a civil rights law that prohibits discrimination against individuals with disabilities in all areas of public life, including jobs, schools, transportation, and all public and private places that are open to the general public.

However, there were/are obstacles that made/make accessibility to historic buildings, such as Colton Hall, difficult for this minority group, because of the goal to preserve the building's historic integrity. A review of literary sources revealed how public venues accommodate people with disabilities, how individuals perceive of the effectiveness of the ADA, and how handheld technology may be used to provide accessibility to historic building.

In reviewing the intent and provisions of the ADA, some key observations have been made that appear relevant for the issues of accessibility for historic buildings while preserving their structural integrity:

Griff Hogan in *Inclusive Corporation: A Disability Handbook for Business Professions* (2003) referenced that O'Quinn cautioned that: "legislation enacted with the least partisan dispute often turns out to be the worst law because its provisions were never really tested in any serious public debate.... Congress drafted the ADA broadly, using imprecise and undefined terms, and consequently left the task fleshing out the meaning of its provision to the federal judiciary.... Contrary to the claims of its proponents, the ADA imposes significant costs on American business firms and government entities" (pp. 27–28).

For a greater understanding of the complexities involved with public accommodation, the authors listed below provide relevant insights:

Kozue Handa, Hitoshi Dairoku and Yoshiko Toriyanna sought adult members of the visually impaired community and conducted a study entitled "The Investigation of Priority Needs in Terms of Museum Service Accessibility for Visually Impaired" (2010), analyzing facilities for wayfinding, exhibitions, information in Braille, audio or large print, and how museum staff would assist those who required those services.

Thomas Jester and Sharon Park listed recommendations in their preservation brief *Making Historic Properties Accessible* (www.nps.gov, 1995) without destroying the historic integrity of the building.

Ellen Giusti in her article "Improving Visitor Access" (2008) briefly described the creation and advancement of audio tour technology, and that today's consumer's cell or smartphone technology has rapidly advanced to become the wayfinding agents with "audience-specific narration" which provides independence for the museum visitor. C. Reich and A. Lindgren-Streicher state (as cited in Giusti, 2008) that access is more than just physical: "While the publication of [disability regulation] ... have led to significant changes in the industry, they predominantly focused on providing physical access to museums and did not address providing intellectual access to learning. Understanding physical difference among individuals and the resulting space and architectural requirements are important first steps. However, this information is not sufficient for providing true access to learning for all. Universal design for learning goes beyond physical accessibility. It involves creating multisensory, multimodal learning experiences from which all visitors can learn by touching, seeing, listening, smelling and sometimes even tasting."

In 2011, research was done relative to Colton Hall's accessibility. Members from the sensory and physically impaired communities participated in a brief survey, and disability service coordinators, representatives from municipal government, and ADA professionals were interviewed for their insights on priority needs for accessing a historic museum building in order to receive its history interpretive services and cultural arts programs. The results of this research is summarized herein to provide further information to other public and private entities that are responsible for the stewardship of historic buildings. This may be of some significance to enhance the overall view for accessibility and may inspire more innovative solutions for access for persons with disabilities.

Policy Recommendations and Future Research

In 2012, Claire Moeller Rygg provided policy recommendations, some she indicated may be implemented within a few months to two years (Phase I), and some may span over a few years (Phase II):

Phase I

- Install larger font exhibit labels in Colton Hall for the visually impaired. The museum staff may recommend to the Colton Hall Museum and Cultural Art Commission that the installation of larger font exhibit labels may be beneficial to the visually impaired.
- Build collaborative partnerships between the City of Monterey and local sensory impaired service centers in an effort to develop an outreach program to present informal lectures on early California history, for example, an annual event consisting of one, half-hour presentation during a luncheon at the Blind and Visually Impaired Center.
- Develop a training program for museum docents to guide blind and visually impaired individuals upon their request and provide history interpretive services on Colton Hall and early California history.
- Install Quick Response (QR) Codes on the City's Explore Monterey cell phone tours so the deaf may access a video of an American Sign Language interpreter signing historical information about Colton Hall and each of the other twenty-one historic sites listed on the tour.
- Develop a policy on access to the Colton Hall Museum. This policy may explain to interested individuals some of the standards of the American with Disabilities Act and the National Preservation Act for providing access to public services in a historically significant building.
- Review feasibility of a vertical lift system for Colton Hall. Once the final Access Compliance Survey has been completed, further action may be taken by the municipal leadership upon the counsel of the ADA consultant, the architect preservation professional staff who assess the historic integrity of Colton Hall and submits its findings in a historic structures report to the City's Museum and Cultural Arts Division and Planning and Historic Preservation staff.

Phase II

- Develop plan for future phase funding via grants for access solutions for Colton Hall. This may be dependent upon the results of the feasibility study as suggested in Phase I.
- Revisit Phase I policy recommendations after one year.

Future Research

- Conduct a follow-up survey with a larger population of people with disabilities and inquire about their level of satisfaction of the types of effectiveness of accessible solutions at historic buildings and museums in Monterey County.

- Conduct a survey of the stewards of historic buildings and museums to find out if accessibility for persons with disabilities exist and if they are implemented.
- Collaborate with other public and private entities to develop and implement a display of cultural heritage outreach program and accessibility service listings via the Internet and/ or a cell phone application.

2019 Update

Based on the 2012 proposed recommendations and areas for future research, a follow-up was completed at the beginning of 2019. Those results are listed below:

Construction for a rear stairway including a Limited Use/Limited Access (LULA) lift, an ADA accessible restroom and parking spaces was completed at historic Colton Hall in the fall of 2018. The funding for the project was obtained by the City's capital improvement and Neighborhood Improvement Programs, and foundation grants.

The Museums and Cultural Arts Commission reviewed their strategic plan for 2017/2019, and a subcommittee for the Colton Hall Museum and Old Monterey Jail was formed in 2017 with three Commission members who will assist museum staff to identify interpretive plan elements including technology (MCAC Minutes; Strategic Plan Goals for FY 17/19, August 28, 2017). The subcommittee met on December 18, 2018, to review the staff's work plan for short-term interpretive plan recommendations, electronic media display, and discussed exterior signage identifying Colton Hall. The subcommittee will meet again sometime in the spring of 2019.

Some of the recommendations listed in Phases I and II of this article may be reviewed by staff and brought forth for consideration in the future to the Colton Hall Museum and Old Monterey Jail subcommittee and it will make recommendations to the Museums and Cultural Arts Commission for action that can be taken to the City Council. Staff may want to prioritize the recommendations in Phase I and develop a policy for access to Colton Hall with additional explanations about the ADA and the National Preservation Act. In addition, a phase funding plan needs to be developed for interpretation for those with sensory challenges or who are differently abled.

The Commission also has purview over other historic sites: the Presidio of Monterey Museum located at the Lower Presidio Historic Park, the three historic Worker Shacks and the Pacific Biological Laboratories (also known as Ed Ricketts's Lab) both located at Cannery Row. The City was awarded a foundation grant to develop an ADA accessibility study for the Pacific Biological Laboratories.

All of these historic sites require responsible stewardship, and stewardship requires not only funding but the vision and support of local citizens and City officials who are determined to keep these historic sites available for future generations to enjoy.

REFERENCES

Colton Hall & City Hall Accessibility Upgrades Project. https://www.ebidboard.com/public/projects/showproject.asp?mbrguid=%7B1E39C53B-96B0-4BA8-A87B-ABAB42633190%7D&projectguid=%7B9C453754-F401-4D75-AF1B-322ED48F0457%7D, January 16, 2018.

Rygg, Claire. "Accessibility Solutions for Colon Hall," Golden Gate University, February 27, 2012.

55. Engaging Nonprofit Sector Institutions for Housing Seniors*

Joshua Odetunde

Effective engagement of nonprofit sector institutions is indispensable to ensure social justice in community development and urban planning for seniors. Commonly, it is assumed economic development land use planning issues are parallel to institutionalized social issues in the processes of public policy formulation and implementation. Community participation does not always correct this misconception because "efforts to achieve public participation are often less sophisticated" as Tommy Engram pointed out in a November 2016 *PA Times* issue. Sometimes, recognizing related issues requires professional knowledge. A case in point is real estate management issues intertwined with public policy issues in community development and urban planning. Often, they are kept separate to protect individual rights and privacy. Sometimes, this results in absurdity. For example, although it is public policy to ensure that every American family has a decent home, homelessness remains a concurrent problem with vacant and abandoned residential properties in many cities in the United States. Nonprofit sector institutions with professional capacities are needed to link economic efforts of institutions in both private and public sectors.

At present, nonprofit sector institutions commonly engage as charitable social service agencies providing housing assistance subsidies where relevant to their mission goals. This approach has not effectively impacted the local housing markets because currently the public perceives housing needs as private social issues such as basic need for shelter. Community development and urban planning for seniors should link their housing needs with their private social needs. Housing needs are not necessarily the same as social needs because housing units are not just shelters for living. Housing units are investments in landed properties. They are capital assets which can generate incomes for seniors who are homeowners. However, their housing needs as seniors have to be linked with real estate management of their capital assets. This will involve reconciling some conflicting public policy issues because of the general tendency to separate social and economic needs.

Social change is needed in the current public perception of housing as consumption goods. Residential landed properties are investment goods. Public policy in housing

*Originally published as Joshua Odetunde, "Engaging Nonprofit Sector Institutions for Housing Seniors," *PA Times*, https://patimes.org/engaging-nonprofit-sector-institutions-housing-seniors/ (February 3, 2017). Reprinted with permission of the publisher.

finance could also promote the social change. At present, financial institutions such as mortgage companies and credit card companies use various strategies to indirectly force homeowners to refinance instead of preserving their equities. Many homeowners, including seniors, may not have enough equities to make necessary changes in their housing needs. Worse still, most foreclosure processes do not include adequate protection of equitable landed property interests of homeowners. Hence, real estate dealers prey on many low income homeowners including seniors in their local housing markets. Therefore, public policy news to complement nonprofit sector institutions in various local housing markets to ensure social change.

Furthermore, while focusing on their charitable missions, nonprofit sector institutions tend to underestimate the economic force of the sector in community development programs. As a result, either some critical economic goods and services are undervalued, or those critical goods and services cannot be attracted for implementing development programs. Where those critical elements are appropriately valued and involved, nonprofit sector institutions may have to compete with for-profit private establishments to achieve their mission goals. Rather than take on competition in terms of financial outcomes however, the mission goals of the nonprofit sector institutions should clearly identify the unique social justice outcome of programs. One of such social justice outcomes is to ensure seniors are not perceived as economic liabilities because their social and economic needs are severed. Well-blended nonprofit charitable social services could constitute significant economic force in community development.

For promoting social change, public policy administrators particularly need to engage with nonprofit sector institutions in community real estate management for mutual benefits in local housing markets across the United States. The public policy issue of housing affordability is being confused with housing needs as landed properties in local housing markets. Rather than encouraging effective real estate management of existing housing stock as investments, public policy administrators are seeking for solutions in developments and designs to meet housing needs. The current public policy approach has resulted in ambivalent dichotomy in local housing markets comprising of market rate and subsidized housing units. Therefore, many low-income households including seniors are either homeless or occupying inadequate housing while some residential properties are vacant or abandoned. Also, foreclosures and tenant evictions remain common features of local housing markets. According to the 2014 study on housing America's older adult by the Joint Center for Housing Studies of Harvard University, it is projected one out of five people will be 65 years or older by 2030. A decent home is the linchpin of well-being. The need for social change is urgent. Engagement of nonprofit sector institutions in community real estate management is needed to complement public policy in local housing markets for social change.

An example is the Community Housing Market Support Network (CHMSN) Inc. a 501 (c) 3 Christian-faith-based nonprofit organization under the Internal Revenue Service code. The organization is based on the concept that low-income families and the poor will always be an integral part of any country's economy while they depend on charitable assistance and generosity to one another in their communities (Deuteronomy 15: 4 & 11). Therefore, CHMSN Inc. provides nonprofit real estate services and management for low-income households and the poor as leverage in line with the Christian principles of associating with those in low positions (Romans 12: 16). Since houses are capital resource assets, every family directly or indirectly receives some public assistance or leverage through financial engineering of the housing industry. The financial engineering makes helping families to meet their housing needs go beyond the traditionally charitable assistance. The housing market has evolved into the communal strategy of leveraging one another through home mortgage loans. Therefore, community-based nonprofit organizations are needed to complement public policy in the housing market and ensure social justice.

Such nonprofit organizations are needed because public policymakers have translated the invaluable mutual benefits of the communal strategy into monetary values for property tax, sales tax, user fees, and utility surcharges making complementary public policy imperative in local housing marketplaces. Otherwise, the housing finance system cannot evolve into equitable access for every family to have a decent home as reasonably envisaged in the goal of the United States' Housing Act of 1949. The mainstream thinking about the free market economy remains dominated by individualism, personal achievements, and competition with unsettled gaps in knowledge and practice in local housing marketplaces. While policymakers now tend to rely less on the traditional progressive income tax principles for economic efficiency to promote capitalism, renting homes to meet their housing needs has become the necessity for low-income households.

Therefore, our networking and innovative real estate management strategies in Louisville metro will involve:

- helping individuals and families to find affordable housing and to become homeowners
- helping families to become a network of investors collaborating to protect their home equities
- helping low-income households to prevent foreclosures
- providing homeownership counseling to help low-income households build equity in their homes
- helping to rehabilitate the homeless and providing a range of temporary shelter for households
- providing real estate management and services for single-family homes, small-scale investors, and landlords

56. Township Taps Former Mayor for Age-Friendly Initiative*

International City/County Management Association

As the U.S. population ages, most communities will wrestle with a variety of issues related to elderly residents. Top of mind would be emergency services, transportation, engagement and activities, and appropriate housing.

Teaneck, New Jersey (pop. 40,000), is getting ahead of the curve with a program called Age-Friendly Teaneck. The planning phase of the program began in January 2016 and the three-year implementation began in October 2016.

"My many years in Teaneck have made me realize what a priority it should be to keep our residents here, safe and engaged," said Township Manager William Broughton.

Age-Friendly-Teaneck

So far, the group has launched a website, www.agefriendlyteaneck.org and Twitter channel @AFTeaneck, which already is full of resources for the town's elderly population. The group has formed task forces and developed materials and ancillary programs in support of its initiative to make Teaneck an age-friendly and livable community. Already, the initiative has 16 steering committee members, 60 residents serving on five task forces, and partnerships are emerging quickly.

None of this would have been accomplished without the involvement of the former mayor, Jacqueline Kates. "Mrs. Kates and her drive have really helped the Age Friendly Initiative come to fruition," said Broughton.

"Most people would like to age in place, near the people and activities that have been part of their lives. But most cities, towns, and villages are not organized to help residents stay connected and engaged, may not have safe and affordable housing options, do not provide adequate access to transportation and mobility, enable economic opportunity, or allow seniors to be financially secure as they age," said Kates, who is project coordinator for Age-Friendly Teaneck said. "Communities are often unprepared for the increasing

*International City/County Management Association, "Township Taps Former Mayor for Age-Friendly Initiative," *PM Magazine*, https://icma.org/articles/article/success-story-township-taps-former-mayor-age-friendly-initiative (April 24, 2017). Originally published in the April 2017 issue of *Public Management* (*PM*) magazine and copyrighted by ICMA, the International City/County Management Association (icma.org); reprinted with permission.

number of older people, but we want to make sure that Teaneck is a community where we can remain and enjoy living, whatever age we are."

Starts with a Survey

The initiative began with a survey in which older adults identified these top concerns:

- Staying in their homes despite reduced incomes, higher taxes, and accessibility issues.
- Maintaining their homes when funds, information, and resources are scarce.
- Transportation when driving is no longer an option.
- Access to the adequate community, medical, and healthcare resources.
- Continued access to the Richard Rodda Community Center for activities and social interaction even if they are living alone.
- Managing finances and access to related resources and economic assets

"Our task forces are addressing the issues of concern that were identified during the planning phase, through the survey, as well as interviews and focus groups," Kates said. Task forces include:

- Transportation and Pedestrian Safety Task Force
- Health and Social Engagement Task Force
- Community Resources and Communications Task Force
- Housing Options Task Force
- Business and Banking Task Force.
- Street Safety

The first successful advocacy effort was led by Broughton, who responded to the concerns of the Age-Friendly group by interceding with Bergen County to increase crossing time at an intersection.

"That doesn't sound like a lot, but it really does make a difference for anyone crossing that intersection who can now walk at a slower and safer pace, without feeling the need to run and possibly fall in the street," Kates said. "People are very happy about that. And this safety issue demonstrates that age-friendly improvements can benefit everyone in the community."

Continuing this effort, and in response to an unfortunate rash of pedestrian fatalities, Broughton's office has started working with an expert in Complete Streets at Rutgers University to incorporate ideas into the town's master plan for roads and intersections.

The Transportation and Pedestrian Safety Task Force also is trying to find more ways to expand the township's Senior Transportation Services to help those who don't drive and need to get to doctors' appointments, the supermarket, or the beauty salon. Options include the Independent Transportation Network of volunteer drivers and the Go Go Grandparent program that use Uber and Lyft.

The Community Resources and Communications Task Force is in the process of developing a directory of essential Teaneck resource phone numbers for first responders to leave behind when they respond to emergency calls. "We have learned from the first responders that people call 911 even when there isn't a true emergency because they know they'll get a response, and they don't know where else to turn for help," Kates said.

First responders will distribute the directory that people can put on their refrigerators or near their telephones so they can call the proper number for a problem that is important but does not require police, fire truck or ambulance. The cooperative project is being underwritten by Five Star Senior Premier Living, one of the program's community partners.

On the flip side, Age Friendly Teaneck is promoting the Fire Department's Good Morning Check-In program for those who live alone. Residents who register with the Fire Department will receive a daily call to make sure they are okay, and if there's no response, a hose and ladder fire truck will be there to help.

The Health and Social Engagement Task Force and the Township and the Holy Name Medical Center are cosponsoring a series of four events, Conversation of Your Life, to raise awareness of the importance of anyone over 18 having an Advance Medical Directive.

Housing Concerns Abound

"Housing is one of the biggest concerns of older adults who want to stay in Teaneck," said Kates. "I hear about that issue more often than any other. If there had been housing options in Teaneck for us to downsize, my husband and I would never have considered moving," added Kates, who had lived in Teaneck since she was in elementary school.

For those on limited incomes, the options are few. The Brookdale subsidized independent housing for older adults opened in April 2016 and has a 10-year waiting list. And while the township council is supportive of residential housing projects, with several new developments approved, Kates does not think any are specifically targeted for older people, with the required amenities that would make it more comfortable to live there.

Thus, the Housing Task Force is exploring options for seniors on a college campus, with residents benefiting from the educational and cultural stimulation of college life, since they would be required to take a number of credits as a condition of becoming a resident. The task force also is looking into publicizing information on home-sharing options that can formalize these situations and protect the elderly with follow-up visits and other parameters set forth in agreements.

For those having difficulty maintaining their homes, the task force is publicizing agencies that can give free volunteer repair and maintenance help to older adults, such as The Chore Service of Bergen Volunteer Center and Rebuilding Together North Jersey. These groups perform minor repairs, install grab bars, and other equipment needed by the elderly.

The task forces also are working with business and banks to ensure that the economic assets of older adult consumers are being maximized and special needs are being met, by improving lighting, using larger fonts on materials and advertising and providing access to public restrooms. Training bank and business staff to recognize signs of financial and physical elder abuse also are on the agenda.

The Teaneck program is funded by the Henry and Marilyn Taub Foundation. The planning phase grant was $35,000 and the implementation grant is for up to $75,000 per year for three years. Resources for local governments in the Aging topic area on the ICMA website.

57. Advancing Independence, Integration and Inclusion Throughout Life*

ADMINISTRATION FOR COMMUNITY LIVING

The Administration for Community Living (ACL) was created around the fundamental principle that older adults and people of all ages with disabilities should be able to live where they choose, with the people they choose, and with the ability to participate fully in their communities.

By funding services and supports provided by networks of community-based organizations, and with investments in research, education, and innovation, ACL helps make this principle a reality for millions of Americans.

Mission and Strategic Plan

All Americans—including people with disabilities and older adults—should be able to live at home with the supports they need, participating in communities that value their contributions. To help meet these needs, the U.S. Department of Health and Human Services (HHS) created the Administration for Community Living in 2012.

ACL brings together the efforts and achievements of the Administration on Aging (AoA), the Administration on Intellectual and Developmental Disabilities (AIDD), and the HHS Office on Disability to serve as the Federal agency responsible for increasing access to community supports, while focusing attention and resources on the unique needs of older Americans and people with disabilities across the lifespan.

Mission

Maximize the independence, well-being, and health of older adults, people with disabilities across the lifespan, and their families and caregivers.

---

*Public document originally published as Administration for Community Living, "Advancing Independence, Integration and Inclusion Throughout Life," https://acl.gov/about-community-living.

Vision

- For all people, regardless of age and disability, to live with dignity, make their own choices, and participate fully in society. Therefore, we will:
- For the people we serve: Promote strategies that enable people to live in their communities.
- For our networks: Provide leadership and support.
- For our partners: Be a source of collaboration, innovation, and solutions.
- For our employees: Support their contributions, professional growth, and work-life balance.
- For the public Be effective stewards of public resources and a source for information.

All people, regardless of age or disability, should be able to live independently and participate fully in their communities. Every person should have the right to make choices and to control the decisions in and about their lives. This right to self-determination includes decisions about their homes and work, as well as all the other daily choices most adults make without a second thought.

Why Community Living?

In survey after survey, when older adults and people with disabilities are asked where they would prefer to live, they say they want to live in their communities, not in institutions.

Many people have deep ties to their communities that go back decades, if not generations. Remaining in the community allows people to preserve a critical connection to meaningful memories, people, places, and things. These connections with the familiar can be particularly important for older adults.

Living in the community can also offer a level of social connection that is hard to find in a nursing home or other institutional setting. It offers the opportunity to interact with family members, friends, and neighbors. Being integrated in the community means having the opportunity to live with, and work alongside, people of all different abilities.

Community living offers many benefits for individuals and their families, but it also offers many benefits to the communities themselves. Communities miss out on valuable voices and perspectives when people with disabilities and older adults are left out. They are deprived of co-workers, volunteers, mentors, and friends who offer new ways of thinking about, and navigating, the world as well as wisdom collected over many decades. Older adults also often serve the critical roles of family historians and keepers of a community's memories.

Not only is community living rewarding for individuals and communities, but also happens to be less expensive than other options for most people. Skilled nursing facilities can cost an average of $75,000 a year and public residential facilities for people with disabilities average $225,000 a year. In most cases, these costs are not covered by Medicare or private health insurance.

Finally, a series of laws, court decisions, and administrative rules have established community living as a legal right. Most notably, in 1999, the U.S. Supreme Court ruled in Olmstead v. L.C. that people with disabilities must receive services in the most integrated settings possible. This landmark decision has been a critical tool in protecting the rights of people with disabilities and older adults alike.

Supporting People in the Community

Many older adults and people with disabilities need help with the daily tasks of life. For some people this is physical help such as help with dressing and eating. For others, it is help with making decisions and planning. Still others require a blend of supports. Each person is unique, and the help they may need is unique as well.

At ACL, we believe that the preferences and needs of older adults and people with disabilities who need assistance belong at the center of the system of services and supports that enable them to live the lives they want to live. We further believe that those needs and preferences should be defined by the individual receiving services and supports.

At the same time, ACL recognizes that some people with disabilities and some older adults experience challenges in understanding and communicating their preferences and needs, and family members and caregivers often play a critical role in ensuring that those preferences are honored and needs are met.

We also recognize that the preferences of the individual are not the only factor in determining how to best support that person. The availability of services and supports in a variety of settings, the resources and availability of family caregivers, and other factors also must be considered.

Making Community Living Work for You and Your Family

The realization that you or someone you love will need additional services or supports to stay in the community can feel overwhelming, especially after an unexpected event such as a fall or an accident. Many people do not know what services are available, to whom to turn for help, or where to start.

In many states, Aging and Disability Resource Centers can act as a gateway to a broad range of services and supports for older adults and people with disabilities.

For people with disabilities of all ages, Centers for Independent Living are a great first stop. These community-based centers are run by and for people with disabilities and offer a broad range of services to empower and enable people to stay in the community.

People with disabilities of all ages may also benefit from assistive technology (AT) devices and services. AT includes everything from "low tech" helping tools like utensils with big handles to high tech solutions like talking computers. Every state and territory has an Assistive Technology Act program that can help people find, try, and obtain AT.

For older adults, ACL's Eldercare Locator is a great place to start. Visit www.eldercare.gov or call (800)–677–1116 to be connected with your local Area Agency on Aging or Aging and Disability Resource Center. Those organizations can help you understand what services are available in your community and help you sign up.

• *F. Women and Domestic Violence* •

58. Safe Parking Program for Homeless Women in Pacific Grove, California*

Deidre L. McLay *and* Mickey P. McGee

This chapter is rooted in a research case study completed to determine the effectiveness of the One Starfish Safe Parking Program in Pacific Grove, California, a non-profit organization serving adult women who live in vehicles. This study incorporated the perspectives from the program participants, program staff, parking lot provider, city police and government officials, and program outcomes related to housing and employment of the program participants. Effectiveness was evaluated on four factors: housing and employment changes for the participants; perceptions of program value by the participants; acceptance and support of the program from the Pacific Grove police and City of Pacific Grove government; and perceptions of the program by the One Starfish staff and the organization providing the parking lot, First United Methodist Church of Pacific Grove.

The goal of the research study was to determine whether the One Starfish Safe Parking Program was effective. Research focused on:

1. What changes in participants' lives occurred in terms of housing status and job status?
2. What were the demographics of the participants in the program?
3. How was the program perceived by the participants?
4. What aspects of the program did the participants find most important?
5. How has the Pacific Grove police interaction with people sleeping overnight illegally in vehicles changed since the program has been in place?
6. How have complaints from the community about homeless people living in vehicles changed since the program has been in place?
7. Is the program operating at a capacity that meets the needs of the homeless people living in vehicles in Pacific Grove?

Several research hypotheses were examined to determine whether the One Starfish Program would results in participants moving into conventional housing; would maintain an existing job which was held at time of entering program; and would result in 40 percent of participants increasing their income while participating in the program.

---

*Published with permission of the authors.

Women who live in their vehicles confront the added concern of personal safety and often seek to park away from areas where homeless men are present due to fear of violence. Many existing homeless shelters and services programs are available only to men or to women with dependent children so unaccompanied women are underserved. Thus, vehicle living can be an attractive option for women as something better than living outdoors when shelters or conventional housing are not available.

The subset of homeless people who are vehicle dwellers is growing. Lack of affordable housing leaves many employed people unable to afford rent in high cost areas and they end up living in their cars. Communities who object to their presence are taking steps to prohibit overnight parking and sleeping in vehicles. West Coast communities have more visible histories of dealing with homeless people living in vehicles and they also restrict parking and sleeping in vehicles. However, several communities have implemented safe parking programs to allow vehicle dwellers enrolled in organized programs to park and sleep overnight in designated parking lots.

The One Starfish Safe Parking Program was created to manage the program as safe parking lots were identified and approved in various communities. Lots first started in Carmel Valley, Monterey County. The initial attempt to get a program approved in the City of Monterey, California, was stymied by lack of government approval and opposition from neighbors. However, the necessary elements of local government support, a program manager, and a parking lot provider came together more quickly in the City of Pacific Grove and a One Starfish Safe Parking Program was started there. The City of Pacific Grove does prohibit sleeping overnight in vehicles in the city code Section 18.36.040, but in January 2015, the city passed Ordinance Number 15–001 to temporarily enact a safe sleeping pilot program. In 2016, it was codified into the city code Section 18.36.050.

In June of 2015, the First United Methodist Church of Pacific Grove (FUMC of PG) volunteered to allow up to five woman-occupied vehicles to use the church parking lot for the safe sleeping pilot program, under the provisions of Ordinance Number 15–001. Women with children were also allowed. The church only provides the parking lot and the One Starfish Safe Parking Program enrolls the participants and executes the program. As of June 2018, no other community organization in Pacific Grove has made parking spots available for the program as allowed under the City of Pacific Grove Ordinance. However, the One Starfish organization now has several other parking locations in service in the surrounding areas of the Monterey Peninsula, including lots in Carmel Valley, Carmel, Marina, and Monterey,

Homeless women in Pacific Grove who live in vehicles need a safe and legal place to park overnight. The women could benefit from assistance to determine how to move into conventional housing, keep or obtain employment, and access other social services. The One Starfish Safe Parking Program in Pacific Grove was created in 2015 to address this problem and has been in operation for three years.

A qualitative assessment of overall program effectiveness was determined from the four areas of emphasis: housing and employment outcomes for program participants; participants' perception of program value; local police and government support for the program; and non-profit program manager and parking lot provider support for the program.

There were two groups of people that provided data for this study. The first group consisted of key informants from the organizations involved in the creation and operations of the safe parking program: local government, local police, non-profit program staff, and the parking lot provider. Key informant interviews were conducted with representatives of the Pacific Grove Police Department, the Pacific Grove local government, the First United Methodist Church of Pacific Grove, and the One Starfish Program staff. Interviews were conducted with the First United Methodist Church of Pacific Grove and included the pastor, the office administrator, and the husband and wife lay leader team. Interviews were conducted with the City of Pacific Grove police and government personnel to include the chief of police, the police commander, and the police administrative manager.

The second group consisted of the vehicle-dwelling women participating in the program in Pacific Grove. Data was collected using a paper survey with twelve questions and a request for participation in follow-up interviews. The survey included an introduction describing the purpose of the research and a request for response and several questions used a Likert-type scale response for perceptions of program value such as safety, stability, and restfulness. The survey was anonymous in that it did not ask for any personally identifying information. Survey responders who agreed to follow-up interviews were interviewed in-person using a semi-structured interview, recorded, with permission, to a digital audio file. The surveys were distributed and collected by the One Starfish Safe Parking Program case manager during meetings regularly scheduled in her office for ongoing program management updates. An envelope was included with each survey and responders were told to place the survey in the envelope for privacy of answers before returning it to the case manager. Attempts to find and contact women who had previously participated in the program at the Pacific Grove lot were unsuccessful. However, four of the five women currently in the Pacific Grove lot responded to the written survey and three of them agreed to an in-person interview.

Secondary data was collected from a record review of data maintained by the One Starfish Program staff. The data was in a less structured form than anticipated, with much of it being gathered by e-mail reports from the case manager to the program founder and program director. Ultimately, the best source of data about the women in the Pacific Grove lot came from the hand-written notes of the case manager. She provided ages, disability status, intake dates, exit dates, and exit status for the women in the program during her tenure in response to a request from the author.

Conclusions

This case study examined the One Starfish Safe Parking Program in Pacific Grove from multiple perspectives to answer the question whether the program was effective. The answer revealed in this study is that it is effective in some ways yet ineffective in other ways.

The One Starfish Safe Parking Program in Pacific Grove is effective in these ways:

1. Pacific Grove police and government concerns about where vehicle dwellers could park legally after laws changed are resolved

2. The First United Methodist Church of Pacific Grove and the One Starfish Program staff are able to help serve the homeless, thus fulfilling a desire to help the needy

3. The homeless women participants feel safer and have better quality sleep and more predictable nights.

The One Starfish Safe Parking Program in Pacific Grove is not effective in these ways:

1. The goal of transitioning 40% of the participants to housing is not achieved
2. The goal of increasing the income of 40% of the participants is not achieved.

What Was Learned

This study has not discovered new insights about the plight of homeless women living in their vehicles. Rather, it has confirmed that the circumstances and attitudes described in the existing literature about homelessness are present in Pacific Grove. Older women who are homeless primarily because of being too poor to afford housing constitute a growing segment of the homeless population. Many of them live in vehicles as a step in between being conventionally housed and sleeping in the forest or on the street. The autonomy and privacy that a vehicle provides is valued, but the laws against parking and sleeping overnight make it difficult to avoid disruption and ticketing without authorized safe parking locations. The women take actions to avoid being stereotyped with the negative image of homeless people as dirty, criminal, addicted, and mentally ill.

The One Starfish Safe Parking Program provides its participants with a greater sense of safety, more restful sleep, and a more predictable day than when not in the program. In Pacific Grove, the program is perceived as effective by the local government, police, the church providing the parking lot, and the One Starfish staff. However, the program is not very effective in transitioning the homeless women to conventional housing, primarily due to lack of available market-rate housing resources that are in their price range and lack of supply of and eligibility for subsidized or special program housing.

This case study showcases an example of cooperation between government and non-governmental organizations to try to solve a problem. The combination of efforts between non-profit homeless service providers and religious institutions, with the approval of local government, to address a problem of public concern that government is not able to resolve also follows the pattern observed in other communities. And, the lack of subsidized housing or other dedicated housing resources for people who don't fit into special categories such as veterans, youth, substance abusers, those with mental health concerns, women with dependent children, or women fleeing domestic violence, is a significant barrier to getting the homeless vehicle dwellers out of their cars and into apartments or houses.

Final Thoughts

Absent a sufficient inventory of affordable or subsidized housing, safe parking programs essentially become homeless shelter-like accommodations for vehicles. Instead of lining up nightly for a bed in shelter, vehicle dwellers sign up monthly for a reserved spot in an authorized location. Like most traditional shelter programs, they serve a client base that follows certain rules and they are space limited. Also, like shelters, some people will choose not to seek the service because they don't want to conform to any rules at all. Unlike a traditional shelter, a safe parking program essentially disappears each morning as the vehicles disperse. This aspect can make safe parking programs more acceptable in some neighborhoods because there is not a visible reminder of the homeless population during the day as there is with a permanent homeless shelter building. But just like a shelter, a safe parking program does not house the homeless permanently. It is only a stop gap measure.

Safe parking programs for homeless people living in vehicles is like treating a chronic disease. It does not often solve the "disease" of homelessness, but it mitigates some of the harmful effects. Even if transition to housing is unlikely or long-delayed, providing safe parking as a treatment is worthwhile, even as efforts towards prevention and an ultimate "cure" to homelessness are pursued.

> A woman was walking on the beach one day and noticed a girl who was reaching down, picking up a starfish, and throwing it in the ocean. As she approached, she called out, "Hello! What are you doing?" The girl looked up and said, "I'm throwing starfish in the ocean." "Why are you throwing starfish into the ocean?" asked the woman. "The tide stranded them. If I don't throw them in the water before the sun comes up, they'll die," came the answer. "Surely you realize that there are miles of beach, and thousands of starfish. You'll never throw them all back, there are too many. You can't possibly make a difference." The girl listened politely, then picked up another starfish. As she threw it back into the sea, she said, "It made a difference for that one" [*The Star Thrower*, by Loren Eiseley].

References

Applied Survey Research. (2017). *2017 Monterey County Homeless Point-in-Time Census and Survey*. Watsonville, CA: Applied Survey Research. Retrieved April 16, 2018, from http://www.chspmontereycounty.org.

Baker, M. M. W., Sugar, N. F., & Eckert, L.O. (2009). Sexual Assault of Older Women: Risk and Vulnerability by Living Arrangement. *Sexuality Research & Social Policy: Journal of NRSC, 6*(4), 79–87. Retrieved from http://nsrc.sfsu.edu.

Biscotto, P. R., Jesus, M. C., Silva, M. H., Oliveira, D. M., & Merighi, M.A. (2016). Understanding the life experience of homeless women. *Rev Esc Enferm USP, 50*(5), 749–755. doi:10.1590/S0080–623420160000600006.

Casey, R., Goudie, R., & Reeve, K. (2008). Homeless Women in Public Spaces: Strategies of Resistance. *Housing Studies, 23*(6), 899–916. doi:10.1080/02673030802416627.

Gonyea, J. G., & Melekis, K. (2017). Older homeless women's identity negotiation: agency, resistance, and the construction of a valued self. *The Sociological Review, 65*(1), 67–82. doi:10.1111/1467–954X.12369.

Hecht, L., & Coyle, B. (2001, September). Elderly Homeless: A comparison of older and younger adult emergency shelter seekers in Bakersfield, California. *The American Behavioral Scientist, 45*(1), 66–79.

Hudson, A. L., Wright, K., Bhattacharya, D., Sinha, K., Nyamathi, A., & Marfisee, M. (2010). Correlates of Adult Assault among Homeless Women. *Journal of Health Care for the Poor and Underserved, 21*, 1250–1262.

Kisor, A. J., & Kendal-Wilson, L. (2002). Older Homeless Women: Reframing the Stereotype of the Bag Lady. *AFFILIA, 17*(3), 354–370.

McNamara, R. H., Crawford, C., & Burns, R. (2013). Policing the homeless: policy, practice, and perceptions. *Policing: An International Journal of Police Strategies & Management, 36*(2), 357–374. doi:10.1108/13639511311329741.

Meinbresse, M., Brinkley-Rubinstein, L., Grassette, A., Benson, J., Hall, C., Hamilton, R., ... Jenkins, D. (2014). Exploring the Experiences of Violence Among Individuals Who Are Homeless Using a Consumer-Led Approach. *Violence and Victims, 29*(1), 122–136. doi:10.1891/0886–6708.VV-D-12–00069.

Molinari, V. A., Brown, L. M., Frahm, K. A., Schinka, J. A., & Casey, R. (2013). Perceptions of Homelessness in Older Homeless Veterans, VA Homeless Program Staff Liaisons, and Housing Intervention Providers. *Journal of Health Care for the Poor and Underserved, 24*, 487–498.

Moxley, D. P., Washington, O. G., & McElhaney, J. (2012). "I don't have a home": Helping Homeless People Through Faith, Spirituality, and Compassionate Service. *J Relig Health, 51*, 431–449. doi:10.1007/s10943–010–9363–6.

Murray, S. (2011, September). Violence Against Homeless Women: Safety and Social Policy. *Australian Social Work, 64*(3), 346–360. doi:10.1080/0312407X.2011.552983.

National Law Center on Homelessness and Poverty. (2016). *Housing Not Handcuffs: Ending the Criminalization of Homelessness in U.S. Cities*. Washington, DC: National Law Center on Homelessness and Poverty. Retrieved April 16, 2018, from http://www.nlchp.org.

One Starfish Safe Parking and Supportive Services. (2017). *Partnering with One Starfish Guests to Find Housing, Fund for Homeless Women 2017 Grant Application*. Monterey CA: One Starfish Safe Parking and Supportive Services.

Robinson, T. (2017). No Right to Rest: Police Enforcement Patterns and Quality of Life Consequences of the Criminalization of Homelessness. *Urban Affairs Review*, 1–33. doi:10.1177/1078087417690833.

Salem, B. E., Kwon, J., & Ames, M. (2017). On the Frontlines: Perspectives of Providers Working with Homeless Women. *Western Journal of Nursing Research*, 1–23. doi:10.1177/0193945916689081.

Shinn, M., Gottlieb, J., Wett, J. L., Bahl, A., Cohen, A., & Ellis, D.B. (2007). Predictors of Homelessness among Older Adults in New York City: Disability, Economic, Human and Social Capital and Stressful Events. *Journal of Health Psychology, 12*(5), 696–708. doi:10.1177/1359105307080581.

Wakin, M. (2005, April). Not Sheltered, Not Homeless. *American Behavioral Scientist, 48*(8), 1013–1031. doi:10.1177/0002764204274197.

Wakin, M. (2014). *Otherwise Homeless: Vehicle Living and the Culture of Homelessness*. Boulder, Colorado: FirstForumPress.

Wasserman, J. A., & Clair, J.M. (2011). Housing Patterns of Homeless People: The Ecology of the Street in the Era of Urban Renewal. *Journal of Contemporary Ethnography, 40*(1), 71–101. doi:10.1177/0891241610388417.

Watson, J. (2016). Gender-based violence and young homeless women: femininity, embodiment and vicarious physical capital. *The Sociological Review, 64*, 256–273. doi:10.1111/1467-954X.12365.

Wehman-Brown, G. (2016). Home Is Where You Park It: Place-Making Practices of Car Dwelling in the United States. *Space and Culture, 19*(3), 251–259. doi:10.1177/1206331215596489.

59. Veteran, Minority, Woman and Homeless*

GINGER MILLER

My upbringing was simple. I grew up in Hempstead, New York, with my two brothers and one sister. Our parents were immigrants from Honduras, so my culture was different from most of my friend's and that always made me feel a little different, making me feel a little awkward. My mother and father were both proud Hondurans and they both spoke Spanish, but my mother didn't want to teach us Spanish for the fear of us getting confused in school. Things were a lot different during '70s for bilingual students, and she didn't want us to be singled out by teachers, or laughed at by the other kids.

I watched my parents do the best with what they had which was not a lot and no matter the situation they found themselves in they always appreciated the smaller things in life. If we had breakfast for dinner it was not frowned upon because it was food and at least we had something to eat and a roof over our heads. I remember my mother getting used clothes from one of our neighbors who would get clothes from a wealthy client and while most people would frown upon used clothes, I was simply grateful. It was times like this that instilled lifelong lessons in my heart that would carry me through some of the worst times in my life.

When it came time for me to go to college, I would have been the first one in my immediate family to attend and I was excited. Initially I had dreams of attended the Katharine Gibbs Secretarial School on Long Island, New York, and then I decided that I wanted to be a flashy accountant on Wall Street but all of that was just a dream. Unfortunately for me, my parents did not have money for me to go to college, and that's when I made the decision to go into the Navy to get the GI Bill so that I could have the money to pay for college.

That was an exciting time for me. Here I was, a young girl about to see the world, and embark on an entirely different life. I was both excited, but afraid at the same time. I mean, I was about to leave the only world I had ever known. It wasn't filled with lots of money, status, or luxury, but it was mine. It's where I felt safe. It's what I called home and it belonged to me.

But because I was always a dreamer, I knew that I had to go. I had to go because of the experiences that I would have. I also had to do it for my mom and dad who sacrificed so much for me and my siblings to have a better life. I knew that even though I was a little scared, I had what it took deep down inside of me to do the job.

*Published with permission of the author.

In life you never know what's going to happen you set out to do one thing and everything else happens besides that one thing. I had no idea what would be waiting on me, but I knew that I always wanted to see the world and enjoy my life, never get married and probably never have kids. But when I got to my first duty station in Annapolis, Maryland, all that wishful thinking with right out of the window. I met and fell in love with a young lance corporal. We got married after dating for six months of courtship, and shortly after getting married we were shipped off to Camp Lejeune, North Carolina.

While at Camp Lejeune, I was station with the Navy Boat Crew and my husband was stationed with a Marine Corps Expeditionary Unit that deployed often. My husband's unit served in Operation Sharp Edge and Operation Desert Storm.

When he came back off his last deployment he was different. He was quieter, drank more than usual and he was somewhat explosive. I didn't think much of it and I just thought it was a little stress. Boy was I wrong.

After serving five years in the Marine Corps, my husband got out and I planned to stay in the Navy for twenty years. That plan derailed when I got a medical discharge out of the Navy in 1992 due to injuries from the car accident and two boat accidents I had while on duty. All the accidents left me with physical pain and a decrease in my physical abilities. I had a broken back and suffered from severe migraines. I was hurt that my dream of serving in the military had now taken a cruel turn. It seemed like every step forward, there were three steps backwards. I was pregnant with our first son, and I had no idea what we were going to do next, but I knew we had to think fast.

When you're living the military life, it's different from the civilian life. While being enlisted in the military the government makes sure all your needs, housing, shelter and healthcare are taken care of. I was being faced with having to leave this security blanket behind, and now having to take care of these things with a baby on the way. My only skill set was driving boats. How were we going to do this?

We decided to put our furniture in storage and went to stay with my family in New York for one year until we could move to Pennsylvania where my husband had secured a job at a correctional facility that was being built.

Everything was planned out nicely. So we thought. It may not have been a big deal to most, but that job in Pennsylvania that we were depending on didn't happen. They canceled his assignment due to lack of funding and my husband's PTSD kicked into high gear, because we had a lot riding on that job.

My husband's mood swings came more and more and would elevate beyond my understanding. It was always like sitting on a firecracker and never knowing when it would explode. I did everything I could to try to keep him calm. I would reassure him that we would be ok. Even when I wasn't sure, I knew that I couldn't make things worse by being upset with him for yelling at me. I knew what he was dealing with was real. Maybe because I was in the military as well, I have seen the effects of others with this diagnosis. If you are not faced with this, you can't fully understand what people are going through. It's like suffering inside of your very own skin, and you can't get out.

When I tried to get him help from the local veteran and VSO support groups it would last long. My husband could not relate to the support group because most of the members were not his age and were mostly Vietnam veterans, so my husband stopped going and his PTSD just seemed to escalate.

I don't come from a military town or a military family so my family we were staying with in New York could not comprehend nor sympathize with what my husband was going through. The mood swings, anxiety, depression was just too much, and they told us that we had to find someplace else to stay.

Where do you go with a husband suffering from PTSD, being a young mother, and having a young toddler, no formal training and an associate's degree? I was afraid to ask for help and we ultimately became homeless. My world as I had known it and the one that I imagined were all gone in the blink of an eye! I served my country, got a medical discharge, never had time to prepare for the civilian world, and like a lot of veterans we went back home to stay with family and it didn't work out according to plan.

Every ounce of pride and patriotism had left my body! How could this be happening? I felt alone and too ashamed and even if I knew where to reach out to for help, there was no way I could bring the words "I'm a homeless veteran" up out of the pit of my stomach through my mouth. Unfortunately, in the early '90s there were not any major efforts under way to support younger veterans, homeless veterans or women veterans and if it was the outreach to our population was almost nonexistent.

I packed my family up along with my pride and jumped into a world that no person who has served their country should ever have to experience, a world of uncertainty, darkness, desperation and despair. I felt, isolated, scared, depressed, anxious, alone, confused and desperate but I thank God that my will to survive was strong enough to override all those emotions!

There were times when we had to sleep in our car or make a choice to eat little and stay in a hotel. I thought to myself, You are still the same Ginger Miller with drive, hopes and ambitions with a few major setbacks and rather succumbing to my situation, I decided to take matters into my own hands.

It was exhausting hiding that secret from everyone. There were so many times I just wanted to scream out to my friends and my family and tell them that I needed help. So many times, I wanted to share it with my counselor, but I was too afraid of how she and everyone else would look at me. I was embarrassed, and I felt like a failure as if I had let everyone down. They all believed that I was living the American Dream but, I was living the American Nightmare.

I worked three jobs and went to school full time to pull us out of our homeless state. As an unskilled worker, I had to take whatever jobs would bring in money to support my family and I worked during peak hours as a bank teller, as a nighttime cashier at a gas station and a work study job at the University I attended.

It wasn't easy at all. I remember going from house to house, hotels, our car, and when I think about it sometimes it just leaves me speechless. When you're living in that type of fear, you are on heightened alert all the time. But I had to just keep going anyway so that we could eventually do better and get our own place. I often look back and think to myself, how did we ever make out of hell alive and intact as a family?

I was in a confused state where I felt, My God, I just must survive, and then I looked at our son every night, and would think, okay, he doesn't deserve this, this is not why you brought him into this world. And then I would look at my husband and think, okay he really can't help because he's off the charts right now. I remember thinking to myself, okay Ginger Miller, either you take control of the ship, or you're going to go down with it.

As a woman veteran who was previously homeless, I consider myself to be one of the lucky ones because I made an incredible comeback and I am grateful to God!

I was homeless in the early '90s and here we are well into the twenty-first century and women veterans are the fastest growing segment of the homeless population and this should not be! Homelessness should never be an option and can be prevented with proper outreach, training, education and resources. Anyone who served their country should never ever become homeless and it is because of my experience with homelessness that I have dedicated my life's work to serving and supporting women veterans.

60. Homeless Women Veterans*

Alexandra Logsdon *and* Kayla M. Williams

When asked where she is from, Tracey Staff answers, "everywhere, and nowhere." Following in her mother's footsteps, who served 15 years in the Army, Tracey enlisted in the U.S. Air Force before graduating high school. She served for six years but struggled to find a place for her and her son to call home after being discharged in 2002. She bounced from city to city, spending no more than a couple of years in each location. Finally, she landed in Houston and knew she wanted to stay, however, she found it difficult to secure a job that offered the right combination of income and schedule for her lifestyle. Without steady employment, Tracey and her son found themselves living in low-rate motels and couch-surfing at friends' houses.

A woman's face may not be the image that springs to mind when someone mentions homeless Veterans, but Tracey's story is similar to those of other female veterans who bravely served our country. For instance, Krystal Ridley grew up in New York City before joining the Army. After being discharged with a service-connected disability, Krystal and her four young children found themselves couch-surfing at the houses of various family members.

Though it is often unrecognized in national discussions, these women are part of a proud legacy of military service: American women have fought in every conflict since the Revolutionary War, but their military participation was originally informal and later limited by law: not only were they barred from certain jobs and units, but women's enlistment was capped at 2 percent of the military until 1967. Their representation in the military increased to roughly 15 percent by the early 1990s, where it remains today. Accordingly, women made up a small fraction of the population of veterans through much of U.S. history. Women now make up about 9.5 percent of veterans, which will climb to 10.5 percent by 2020 and nearly 16 percent by 2040, making them one of the fastest growing subgroups of veterans (Aponte, 2017).

Compared to male veterans, women are younger (with a median age of 50, compared to a median age of 65 for male veterans), more ethnically diverse, less likely to be married, and more highly educated; compared to women who have never served, women veterans have higher median household incomes, and are less likely to live in poverty or have no health insurance. ("Profile of Women Veterans," 2016). Differences between men and women veterans—and between women who have and have not served in the military—are also reflected in the homeless population.

---

*Published with permission of the authors.

Homeless Women Veterans

Historical Data. Women veterans are estimated to make up a relatively small, but growing, proportion of the homeless Veteran population. (Perl, 2015). The U.S. Department of Housing and Urban Development (HUD) began identifying veterans in its annual Point-in-Time count in 2009. Point-in-Time (PIT) Counts are unduplicated one-night estimates of both sheltered and unsheltered homeless populations. The 1-night counts are conducted by Continuums of Care nationwide and occur during the last week in January of each year. Continuums of Care (CoC) are local planning bodies responsible for coordinating the full range of homelessness services in a geographic area, which may cover a city, county, metropolitan area, or an entire state. For PIT Count purposes, a veteran refers to any person who served on active duty in the armed forces of the United States. This includes Reserves and National Guard members who were called up to active duty (Henry, 2017).

In 2010, female veterans comprised eight percent (8 percent) or 5,926 of the 74,087 total homeless veterans. Between 2010 and 2017, the number of homeless female veterans has decreased by a total of forty percent (40 percent), though the numbers fluctuated year-to-year during this period.(Abt Associates, Inc., 2010).

Data Trends. In 2017, there were a total of 215,709 women identified as homeless in the U.S. Department of Housing and Urban Development (HUD) Point-in-Time Count. Of these women, 3,571 were veterans. Of the homeless female veterans, 2,071 were sheltered and 1,500 were unsheltered. Female veterans represent 8.9 percent of the 40,056 total veterans identified in the 2017 Point-in-Time Count. Since 2016, the number of homeless veterans who were women increased by seven percent (7 percent) or 243 additional female veterans (Henry, 2017).

Risk and Protective Factors. Research indicates that characteristics associated with homelessness among women veterans include "sexual assault during military service, being unemployed, being disabled, having worse overall health," and certain mental health conditions; protective factors were having graduated college or being married (Washington, 2010). Women veterans are more likely to have experienced many of those risk factors than civilian women and/or male veterans. Before, during, and after their military service, women veterans may be more likely to have faced certain challenges than men. Adverse Childhood Experiences (ACEs) are known to have an impact on lifelong outcomes; women with military backgrounds are more likely to have experienced the Adverse Childhood Experiences of physical abuse, household alcohol abuse, exposure to domestic violence, and emotional abuse than nonmilitary women (Blosnich, 2014).

While serving, women are more likely than men to experience military sexual harassment and assault, collectively referred to as Military Sexual Trauma (MST); in addition, women veterans who were sexually assaulted are significantly more likely to develop post-traumatic stress disorder (PTSD) and substance abuse disorders. (Hamilton, 2015; Hyun, 2009). Intimate partner violence (including psychological, physical, or sexual violence from a current or former intimate partner; IPV) is also a major contributor to housing instability among women in general, and women veterans in particular. (Hamilton, 2011). Overall, women are also more likely to experience wage disparities, domestic violence, and gender discrimination. Women veterans are, however, more likely to have graduated college than either civilian women or male veterans.

Unmet Needs. Since its launch in 1994, the Department of Veterans Affairs has administered Project CHALENG (Community Homelessness Assessment, Local Education, and Networking Groups) each year to bring together homeless providers, advocates, veterans, and other concerned citizens to identify the needs of homeless veterans. Project CHALENG has two components: A CHALENG survey, in which participants rate the needs of homeless veterans in their local communities, and CHALENG meetings, which encourage partnership development between VA and community service providers ("Community Homelessness Assessment, Local Education and Networking Groups," 2017).

In 2016, 5,280 individuals completed a CHALENG Participant survey. This included 3,191 homeless veterans and 2,089 non-homeless veterans (VA staff, state and public officials, community leaders, volunteers). Twelve percent (12 percent) of the homeless veteran survey participants were women. Over 50 percent of the female veterans surveyed were between the ages of 45–60, and 84 percent were of non–Hispanic/non–Latino decent. At the time of the survey, 32 percent of the women surveyed were living in permanent subsidized housing, such as HUD-VASH and 25 percent were literally homeless.

The top ten highest unmet needs of female veterans surveyed were as follows (in order descending from highest unmet need): registered sex offender housing, child care, family reconciliation assistance, dental care, credit counseling, financial guardianship, legal assistance for child support issues, legal assistance to prevent eviction and foreclosure, legal assistance to help restore a driver's license, and discharge upgrade. The top ten highest met needs of female veterans surveyed were as follows (in order descending from highest met need): medical services, tb testing and treatment, case management, HIV/AIDS testing and treatment, food, services for emotional or psychiatric problems, hepatitis C testing and treatment, clothing, substance abuse treatment, and medication management.

VA Progress

VA Homeless Programs. The VA takes a three-pronged approach to ending veteran homelessness: conducting coordinated outreach to proactively seek out veterans in need of assistance; connecting homeless and at-risk veterans with housing solutions, health care, community employment services, and other required supports; and collaborating with federal, state, and local agencies, housing providers, faith-based and community nonprofits, and others to expand employment and affordable housing options for veterans exiting homelessness. The VA provides key health care, housing assistance, mental health, and employment/job training resources for homeless and at-risk veterans ("Homeless Veterans," 2018). Through coordinated efforts, a growing list of 57 communities, including the states of Connecticut, Delaware, and Virginia, have effectively ended veteran homelessness as of the end of 2017, while also building and sustaining systems that can effectively and efficiently address veterans' housing crises in the future ("Ending Veteran Homelessness," 2017).

VA Services for Women Veterans. HA now provides health care to over 500,000 women veterans at 151 medical centers and 985 outpatient clinics nationwide ("Women Veterans Health Care," 2018). VHA out-performs all other sectors of care in providing gender-specific care for women veterans, including cervical cancer and breast cancer screening rates. All VA Medical Centers (VAMCs) have at least one Dedicated Women's Health Provider (DWHP) since VA has trained over 3,000 providers in women's health and continues to train hundreds more annually. VA provides prenatal and pre-conception care, maternity care services, and seven days of newborn care for women veterans, all managed by dedicated Maternity Care Coordinators. To continually improve our ability to provide high-quality evidence-based, culturally competent mental health care to women, VA held a National Women's Mental health Mini-Residency at which approximately 200 participants from across the country were trained on gender-specific aspects of psychotherapies and psychiatric medications, trauma, integrating peer counselors, and more (Williams, 2016). VA provides all care related to military sexual trauma (MST) free of charge; all veterans are screened and each VAMC has an MST Coordinator. VBA benefits can be a vital part of veterans' economic stability, and outreach efforts to women veterans have worked: women veterans now access disability compensation at rates equal to men, and utilize other benefits at equal or higher rates. Over 26,000 women have accessed their Post 9/11 GI Bill education benefits so far, and women veterans graduate at higher rates than all other groups. In FY15, nearly 66,000 women veterans (10 percent of veterans served) were guaranteed home loans totaling $16 billion.

Partnerships. Though their paths to permanent housing may have diverged, both Tracey and Krystal relied on vital resources from the Department of Veterans Affairs and other community and government partners to secure stability for their families. Tracey's path to success started with a referral to a VA community partner that helps veterans transition from service to civilian life. VA facilities nationwide rely on critical community and inter-governmental partnerships to fill in the gaps and provide wraparound services where VA programs and resources fall short. Tracey became an active participant in her local Supportive Services for Veteran Families (SSVF) program. The SSVF program awards grants to private nonprofit organizations and consumer cooperatives who provide a range supportive services to very low-income veterans and their families residing in or transitioning to permanent housing to promote housing stability (Williams, 2016). SSVF offered Tracey employment services, referrals to housing, case management, and temporary financial assistance while she applied for VA benefits. Tracey gained a renewed sense of confidence and determination. Through SSVF, she found meaningful employment with a community partner to not only provide for her family, but to also support local veterans like herself. Most importantly, Tracey was able to secure permanent housing for her and her son.

Along with SSVF, VA maintains other important partnerships including programs such as HUD-VASH Program (U.S. Dept. of Housing & Urban Development—VA Supportive Housing), Grant and Per Diem (GPD) Program, Health Care for Homeless Veterans, Homeless Veteran Community Employment Services, Veteran Justice Outreach, and many more. The most heavily utilized of these programs is HUD-VASH. HUD-VASH is a partnership between the U.S. Department of Housing and Urban Development and VA Supportive Housing Program to provide permanent, supportive housing and treatment services for homeless Veterans.

Krystal consulted with her local VA medical center in New York City to determine a path to permanent housing. Due to unavailability of childcare, Krystal brought her kids along to her meeting with her case manager. Understanding the great need of putting this family in housing immediately, Krystal's case manager contacted the HUD-VASH Coordinator at the facility. Coincidentally, a HUD-VASH voucher had just come available for

Krystal and her kids. The case manager performed a warm hand-off to the HUD-VASH team who were able to secure a residence for the family within a few days of Krystal's initial meeting at the VA Medical Center. As of Sept. 30, 2015, HUD had allocated more than 78,000 vouchers to help house veterans across the country. The HUD-VASH Program is for the most vulnerable veterans, and provides special services for women veterans, those recently returning from combat zones, and veterans with disabilities.

REFERENCES

Abt Associates, Inc. (2010). Veteran Homelessness: A Supplemental Report to the 2010 Annual Homeless Assessment Report to Congress. Retrieved January 11, 2018, from https://www.va.gov/HOMELESS/docs/Center/AHAR_Veterans_Report_2010.pdf.

Aponte, M., Balfour, F., Garin, T., Glasgow, D., Lee, T., Thomas, E., & Williams, K., Women Veterans Report: The Past, Present, and Future of Women Veterans. National Center for Veterans Analysis and Statistics, Department of Veterans Affairs, Washington, DC. (2017, February). Retrieved from https://www.va.gov/vetdata/docs/SpecialReports/Women_Veterans_2015_Final.pdf.

Blosnich, J., Dichter, M., Cerulli, C., Batten, S., & Bossarte, R. (2014). Disparities in Adverse Childhood Experiences Among Individuals with a History of Military Service. *JAMA Psychiatry*. doi: 10.1001/jamapsychiatry.2014.724.

Community Homelessness Assessment, Local Education and Networking Groups. (2017, June). Retrieved January 11, 2018, from https://www.va.gov/HOMELESS/docs/CHALENG-2016-factsheet-508-2017-07-29.pdf.

Ending Veteran Homelessness. (2017, August 4). Retrieved January 11, 2018, from https://www.usich.gov/goals/veterans.

Hamilton A.V., Poza I., Washington D.L. (2011). Homelessness and Trauma Go Hand-in-Hand: Pathways to Homelessness Among Women Veterans. *Women's Health Issues, 21*(4):S203-S209.

Hamilton, A. (2015, November 3). Military Sexual Trauma: Prevalent and Under Treated. Retrieved January 11, 2018, from http://www.apa.org/news/press/releases/2015/11/military-sexual-trauma.aspx.

Henry, M., Watt, R., Rosenthal, L., & Shivji, A. (2017, December) The 2017 Annual Homeless Assessment Report (AHAR) to Congress. Retrieved January 11, 2018, from https://www.hudexchange.info/resources/documents/2017-AHAR-Part-1.pdf.

Homeless Veterans. (n.d.). Retrieved January 11, 2018, from https://www.va.gov/homeless/.

Hyun, J.K., Pavao, J., Kimerling, R. (2009). Military Sexual Trauma. *PTSD Research Quarterly, 20* (2). Retrieved January 11, 2018, from http://www.ncdsv.org/images/NCPTSD_MilitarySexualTrauma_Spring2009.pdf.

Perl, L. (2015, November 6). Veterans and Homelessness. Retrieved January 11, 2018, from https://fas.org/sgp/crs/misc/RL34024.pdf.

Profile of Women Veterans: 2015. (2016, December). Retrieved January 11, 2018, from https://www.va.gov/vetdata/docs/SpecialReports/Women_Veterans_Profile_12_22_2016.pdf

VA Programs to End Homelessness Among Women Veterans. (n.d.). Retrieved January 11, 2018, from https://www.va.gov/homeless/for_women_veterans.asp.

Washington, D.L., Yano, E.M., McGuire, J., Hine, V., Gelberg, L. (2010, February). Risk Factors for Homelessness among Women Veterans. *Journal of Health Care for the Poor and Underserved, 21* (1): 82–91. doi: 10.1353/hpu.0.0237.

Williams, K. (2016, July 15). VHA Mini-Residency Program Focuses on Providing Mental Health Services for Women Veterans. Retrieved January 11, 2018, from https://www.blogs.va.gov/VAntage/29140/.

Women Veterans Health Care. (n.d.). Retrieved January 11, 2018, from https://www.womenshealth.va.gov/WOMENSHEALTH/womenshealthservices/healthcare_about.asp.

61. Finding Shelter[*]

Addressing Housing Challenges for Survivors of Domestic Violence

REBECCA DeSANTIS

October is Domestic Violence Awareness Month, and it is important to reflect on an issue that communities can face when combatting domestic violence: housing for survivors. According to the National Network to End Domestic Violence, domestic violence is the leading cause of homelessness for women and children. More shockingly, according to a study by the Centers for Disease Control Prevention, more than half (51.5 percent) of domestic violence victims who identified a need for housing services did not receive them. This is a challenge that local governments are working to address, knowing that a lack of shelter or temporary housing can increase survivors' vulnerability.

Following, we highlight some of the important steps that local governments around the country and abroad have taken to address housing challenges for survivors of domestic violence.

Orange County, Florida

Central Florida agencies working with victims of domestic violence reported that this past summer was particularly difficult in terms of housing challenges. Harbor House of Orange County, which is the largest shelter in the region, found itself at full capacity for most of the summer months and turning to alternative solutions for families in need. Although the region has many shelters for survivors, with the continued need for more beds, Orange County, Osceola County, and Seminole County shelters are partnering to apply for a nearly $800,000 federal grant for "rapid rehousing." This would mean that survivors seeking refuge would bypass shelters and go immediately into their own apartments, providing a needed level of security and stability in a time of transition.

---

*Rebecca DeSantis, "Finding Shelter: Addressing Housing Challenges for Survivors of Domestic Violence," *PM Magazine*, https://icma.org/blog-posts/finding-shelter-addressing-housing-challenges-survivors-domestic-violence (Oct. 29, 2018). Originally published in the October 2018 issue of *Public Management (PM)* magazine and copyrighted by ICMA, the International City/County Management Association (icma.org); reprinted with permission.

Lake County, Illinois

A Safe Place, the Lake County agency that provides services addressing domestic violence, prides itself on its ability to meet clients where they are, whether it be the first call or treatment years later. The agency works hard to combat domestic violence through a whole-community response, which includes an emergency shelter and temporary housing facilities. In 2017, according to its website, 45,212 nights of safe housing in transitional and permanent housing facilities and 7,501 nights of emergency shelter in a 35-bed shelter were provided. Lake County is working hard to reduce the stigma of domestic violence by speaking to the community and providing needed resources to families at risk.

Washington, D.C.

The District Alliance for Safe Housing (DASH) is Washington, D.C.'s largest safe housing provider, and it is seeing an unfortunate increase in the number of domestic violence cases based on a dramatic increase in the number of district residents it serves through housing solutions, financial assistance, and safety planning. According to its website, DASH envisions "a culture where safe housing is a human right shared by everyone." With this mindset, it works to help survivors avoid homelessness by providing a wide range of housing solutions from emergency shelter and temporary housing to finding them apartments where they can sign a lease. DASH receives most clients through referrals, but they also host a weekly clinic in the community to reach more families in need.

Abilene, Texas

The Noah Project of Abilene shelters and cares for victims of family violence in its center, which can accommodate 96 residents. With an increase in care needed for the community, North Project announced the creation of a new wing to its facility. The city of Abilene has taken domestic violence concerns seriously and has been working with the Noah Project and other local organizations to target this issue. According to Stan Standridge, chief of police for the Abilene Police Department, "Our goals were many: reduce violence; end domestic violence homicide; shift emphasis from victims to suspects; prosecute offenses even when victims refused to follow through; adopt bond conditions as normative protocols for bond; streamline emergency protective orders; and increase awareness."

Alta Verapaz, Guatemala, and Stockton, California

As part of the CityLinks partnership managed by ICMA and funded by USAID, the department of Alta Verapaz, Guatemala, and the city of Stockton, California, were partnered to connect officials in identifying and implementing solutions to local crime and violence. One of the priorities of this partnership was to help Alta Verapaz, which is located in a region of high rates of domestic violence, create strategies to shelter women and children who are victims of domestic violence. As part of this exchange, Dr. Joelle Gomez, director of the Women's Center Youth & Family Services in Stockton shared the center's experience providing shelters for homeless and runaway survivors of domestic violence, sexual assault, and human trafficking, among its other services. These types of partnerships help share best practices around providing housing for survivors of domestic violence.

There are communities worldwide finding innovative strategies to providing housing for survivors of domestic violence.

• *G. Youth* •

62. Helping Homeless Youth*

Jon Ruiz

Eugene, Oregon (pop. 160,000), is renowned for its exceptional quality of life, featuring such attributes as University of Oregon football, TrackTown USA, social activism, a high-tech community, wood products, world-class arts, an outdoor lifestyle, and craft beer. Those who intend to visit for a few months or years often stay for decades.

However, like many communities, Eugene is challenged by the plight of homelessness, and is continually seeking compassionate, caring, and equitable ways to support and improve the lives of all community members. WalletHub's 2018 article "States with the Most Underprivileged Children" reports that Oregon is one of three states with the highest rate of homeless youth in the country. In Eugene, over 1,500 K-12 students are homeless, and over 350 of them are unaccompanied by a parent or guardian. They often struggle to stay in school while grappling daily with where to sleep, and how to eat, wash clothes, and get to school the next day. These students often end up couch surfing at friends' homes or staying in hotels, trailer parks, or cars.

Tragically, about one-third of these youth drop out of school within a year. Many report that within the first couple of nights away from the relatively structured setting of school, they ended up on the street where they were approached by drug dealers or sex traffickers and felt their lives were in danger. They are particularly vulnerable to physical and emotional trauma, mental health problems, self-harm, substance abuse, poor education, and a decline in overall health. They are scared, confused, and desperate. As the days pass, they say their circumstances force them to engage in the dangerous street culture to survive.

Community Unites to Support 15th Night

In September 2015, a broad array of public, private, and nonprofit organizations came together to spark 15th Night, a youth-informed community movement to end youth homelessness by helping unaccompanied students stay engaged in school, safely housed, and off the street.[1] According to Looking Glass Community Services, a nationally accredited local nonprofit agency committed to supporting at-risk youth, a youth who spends

*Jon Ruiz, "Helping Homeless Youth," *PM Magazine*, https://icma.org/articles/pm-magazine/helping-homeless-youth (June 4, 2019). Originally published in the June 2019 issue of *Public Management* (*PM*) magazine and copyrighted by ICMA, the International City/County Management Association (icma.org); reprinted with permission.

more than 14 consecutive nights on the street is 80 to 85 percent more likely to become chronically homeless. We not only want to avoid that 15th night, we want to avert even one night on the street.

In addition to the trauma experienced by homeless youth, there is a financial cost to the community as well. Citing previous findings from other studies, the Oregon Department of Human Services' Homeless Youth Advisory Committee reached these conclusions in 2016[2]:

- The average annual cost per homeless youth placed in the criminal justice system is $53,665 versus $5,887 for moving a homeless youth off the streets. Moreover, runaways are 2.5 times more likely to be arrested as adults.
- Former runaways are 50 percent more likely than their counterparts to not have a high school degree or GED as adults. High school dropouts that are unemployed are estimated to impose a future lifetime taxpayer burden of $170,740 and a social burden of $525,030.
- More than 30 percent of formerly homeless youths report an alcohol problem, 40 percent report drug problems, and 50 percent report mental health problems over their lifetimes.

The Collective Impact Model

The 15th Night Movement is a broad community partnership committed to preventing youth from going on the street, but also intervening quickly if they do. 15th Night has intentionally chosen not to become its own nonprofit organization. We instead chose the Collective Impact model to leverage and align existing community resources in innovative ways. We intend to inspire a cultural shift, one in which our community not only finds it unacceptable for our kids to be living on the streets, but also commits to the next steps of making it stop.

John Kania and Mark Kramer of Stanford University first introduced the Collective Impact framework in 2011. They defined Collective Impact initiatives as "long-term commitments by a group of community leaders who have decided to abandon their individual agendas in favor of a collective approach."[3]

The social sector is filled with examples of partnerships, networks, and other types of joint efforts. But Collective Impact initiatives are distinctly different. Unlike most collaborations, Collective Impact initiatives involve a centralized infrastructure, a dedicated staff, and a structured process that leads to a common agenda, shared measurement, continuous communication, and mutually reinforcing activities among all participants.

Five Key Principles

Within the Collective Impact framework, 15th Night focuses on five principles: innovation, invitation, youth centered, sustainability, and replication.

Innovation. Timely intervention is often critical to keeping students in school and off the streets. In February 2016, 15th Night partnered with the Technology Association of Oregon (TAO) to develop an alert system known as the Rapid Access Network (RAN).

This web-based program connects service needs with service providers in real time. A diverse group of over 30 organizations are connected to RAN, ready to respond within one hour if possible, providing 65 different resources to help support homeless students. Since its inception, 336 students have connected to RAN providers for everything from such basic necessities as food, clothing, and shelter to services such as counseling, mentoring, and health care. RAN also provides some of the data needed to help us better understand youth needs, identify resource gaps, and address barriers in our effort to help end youth homelessness.

Invitation. 15th Night has cast a wide net, inviting many to join the movement. As part of the 15th Night Catalyst Team, schools, public safety providers, businesses, service providers, faith organizations, government agencies, and the public are all at the table. Their collective wisdom and teamwork guide the planning and ensure alignment while removing barriers and finding creative solutions for sustaining the 15th Night movement.

One group is a cohort of over 50 volunteers who respond when the 15th Night network is unable to meet a specific need of a student, often in less than 30 minutes of the request. 15th Night efforts have also resulted in systemic change. For example, without a state identification card, navigating myriad support systems can be challenging and the process for receiving a card can be difficult. The Junior League of Eugene figured out how to provide funding and easier access for homeless students to obtain identification cards.

Similarly, students applying for SNAP benefits face many barriers and have often given up trying to access this resource because of confusion, limited access, and other obstacles. In response, the Oregon Department of Human Services trained staff members in each branch to specifically help unaccompanied youth, respond to RAN requests for help with SNAP applications, and coordinate appointments.

Youth Centered. From its inception, 15 Night has reversed the power dynamic and empowered youth to be involved at all levels. "Nothing about us without us" is the underlying motto of the Youth Action Council (YAC), which is using its voice to impact change in our community. YAC members have a variety of life experiences. Some are very familiar with living on the street while others, who have never experienced homelessness, care deeply about the issue. To mitigate potential barriers to youth participation, we have ensured meeting times are after school and have provided transportation, meals, and $20 stipends per meeting. YAC facilitators help build relationships, provide training, ensure a safe and supportive environment, and assist with project management for activities such as summer outreach, Back to School BBQ, clothing drives, and the Youth Point in Time (PIT) Count, a comprehensive unsheltered count of youth experiencing homelessness conducted by the Human Services Division of Lane County, Oregon. The youth lead the planning, the projects, and the meetings.

Sustainability. Two years ago, 15th Night developed and initiated the School Mobilization Model (SMM) as a strategy to sustain the 15th Night movement. The SMM was piloted in school year 2017/2018 at South Eugene High School, one of Eugene's five public high schools.

The intents of the SMM are to directly connect youth in need with someone who can meet the need, broaden the base of support, and systematically identify and address the issues within and unique to a school catchment area, which includes the elementary and middle schools that feed a high school. To accomplish this, the SMM creates a community of students, school staff and teachers, parents, neighbors, alumni, faith organizations, and others nearby the school to meet students' basic needs. This consortium breaks down barriers that prohibit or discourage unaccompanied youth and/or students at risk of homelessness from accessing services (e.g., food, clothing, and mental health) that enable students to stay in school and off the street. The SMM integrates community awareness and engagement, RAN technology, and the same Collective Impact model framework used by 15th Night.

Replication. In partnership with United Way of Lane County, 15th Night is replicating the successful experience at South Eugene High School in nine additional high schools in Eugene and the greater metro area. As part of the pilot program, RAN 2.0 was developed, allowing school-specific networks to connect to the larger community network.

Researchers at the Eugene-based Oregon Social Learning Institute are collecting 15th Night data to develop a predictive model to identify risk factors for student homelessness and assess the effectiveness of the SMM. As the SMM expands to other schools, practices that produce the best outcomes will be developed into a tool kit, which, along with the RAN, will be made available to schools and communities in Oregon and throughout the country.

The costs of youth homelessness far exceed the community resources needed to address the challenge. In Eugene, we are pursuing a cultural movement and raising the expectation we have for our community. We are igniting the possibility that none of our youth will ever experience a 15th Night.

NOTES

1. www.15thnight.org.
2. Oregon Department of Human Services, Homeless Youth Advisory Committee, "Oregon's Runaway and Homeless Youth: An Overview and Strategic Framework," 2016.
3. John Kania and Mark Kramer, "Collective Impact," *Stanford Social Innovation Review*, 9(1) 36–41, Winter 2011.

63. Navigating Student Housing Challenges[*]

RYAN JENSEN *and* KATELYN HANSEN

Empty cups in the yard, old couches curbside, and loud music into the middle of the night. If these scenes are familiar, you may find yourself within a campus town neighborhood surrounding any number of colleges across the country.

While the complaints may sound clichéd, the housing conflicts created by large student populations infiltrating traditional single-family neighborhoods are no laughing matter. They affect local housing markets, leading to challenges related to differences in lifestyle and behavior, and in many cases, significantly impacting the supply of owner-occupied housing, diminishing neighborhood character, and straining local resources.

These challenges can be addressed. A study of town-gown communities nationwide, reveals a variety of case studies wherein a school and its surrounding neighborhood(s) have worked together to develop strategies that lessen these housing challenges.

The study was part of the 2017 Strategic Housing Plan for the University of Iowa and surrounding communities. The intent of the study was to analyze town-gown best practices and address university and local housing issues at other flagship and land grant institution communities across the country. The intent was also to devise cohesive housing strategies applicable to the university and its surrounding areas.

Even beyond town-gown communities, many of these strategies are applicable to housing issues experienced in communities of all types and sizes across the country.

While the potential approaches are vast, they generally fall into one of the three categories outlined here.

1. Mitigating Challenges—Reactive Approach

Many communities have attempted to deal with student-renter conflicts after problems have arisen through reactive strategies. These approaches typically include educating student renters on how to be better neighbors.

---

[*]Ryan Jensen and Katelyn Hansen, "Navigating Student Housing Challenges," *PM Magazine*, https://icma.org/articles/pm-magazine/navigating-student-housing-challenges (November 30, 2018). Originally published in the November 2018 issue of *Public Management* (*PM*) magazine and copyrighted by ICMA, the International City/County Management Association (icma.org); reprinted with permission.

Urbana, Illinois, has enacted an educational outreach program for student renters in which the city distributes welcome packets to inform students of such residential neighborhood regulations as trash pickup and parking.

Other communities have taken a more common regulatory approach by enacting noise ordinances, parking limitations, and occupancy limits per dwelling unit, among other strategies.

While these policies can be effective in campus towns, they are not unique to student renters and could be applied to any renters or transient population.

For communities trying to reverse the trend of owner-occupancy to student-rental conversions, rehab programs provide an incentive for this type of housing. The Univer-City Program in Iowa City, Iowa, for example, will fund up to $50,000 in renovations to single-family homes close to downtown and the University of Iowa in exchange for a 20-year owner-occupancy deed restriction.

The program focuses on areas in the center of the housing conflict—single-family character but located close to downtown and the university, making them heavily demanded by renters. To date, more than 60 properties have been renovated and sold as owner-occupied through this program.

2. Guiding Development—Proactive Approach

Some communities partner with their neighboring higher education institution(s) to get ahead of any housing challenges through a proactive approach. These strategies generally try to spur or influence the type, location, and character of development to limit negative interactions.

One proven strategy includes encouraging development in other areas better suited to accommodate students; this approach could work for any specific population subgroup that may require specialty housing, including senior housing near health-care facilities, workforce housing adjacent to specific centers of employment, or housing targeted at post-grad young professionals in central business districts.

One such example includes the creation of a development district encouraging high-density, student-oriented rental housing near a campus edge. A primary objective of creating these districts is to allow for high-density, attractive development within close walking distance to campus, which in turn relieves the pressures from student renters encroaching into single-family, owner-occupied neighborhoods.

Lawrence, Kansas, has used this approach by creating the Oread Neighborhood Plan adjacent to the University of Kansas, which upzoned portions of a historically single-family residential area that had transitioned to primarily student house rentals. The overlay zoning district allows for high-density housing and mixed-use development targeting students.

The types of purpose-built housing options encouraged in this area help keep off-campus student renters proximate to campus resources, limiting the encroachment into other areas of the community while keeping students more engaged in the on-campus environment.

Purpose-built student housing properties are defined as facilities catering specifically to student renters by offering individual bed leases, academic lease terms, roommate matching, and all-inclusive utilities. Industry research has shown that town-gown communities with less than 30 percent of student renters in purpose-built housing are at risk of greater housing conflicts with more pressures on the general housing stock, including single-family neighborhoods.

Other communities have actively worked to spur development through investment in infrastructure. West Lafayette, Indiana, home of Purdue University, used a public-private partnership (P3) to fund infrastructure improvements that encouraged the redevelopment of land west of campus.

The $120 million project, which included roadway improvements and streetscape enhancements among other components, is funded through a tax increment financing district, along with the Purdue Research Foundation. The State Street Corridor Project has a long-term goal of attracting a mix of uses supporting a live-work-play technology hub that will include 2,000 to 3,000 beds of new student housing.

The initiative's goal is threefold: provide a better campus gateway and jump-start development of the Discovery Park District; support the needs of a growing institution; and ease development pressures in other areas of this relatively small community.

3. Controlling Supply—University Approach

Often the most direct solution to take pressure off the general housing market is for universities to provide more housing options to students. While this may sound straightforward, it is often not desired by the institution due to such reasons as limited debt capacity, land availability, and other competing priorities, to name a few.

Institutions, however, have found creative ways to partner with the private sector to deliver the needed student beds while limiting their risk and responsibility. One example is the private-certified housing program at the University of Illinois.

This program provides more than 3,000 beds of student housing that are privately owned on non-university land but fulfill the institution's first-year, live-on campus requirement. For them to remain certified, the facilities must adhere to strict residence life programming requirements and pass annual facility inspections from the city.

There are also examples of institutions partnering with the private sector to develop new housing facilities on university land. These P3s can be structured through long-term ground lease agreements where the private sector designs, builds, finances, and, in some cases, operates and maintains the facility.

University of Massachusetts Boston is just one of many examples of this type of arrangement. It is opening a 1,077-bed residence hall in 2019 as its first on-campus housing option.

Part of the reason for this development is a response to Boston's initiative, as outlined in "Housing a Changing City: Boston 2030" to create 16,000 new on-campus student housing options across the city's universities to help combat escalating rent and unsafe living conditions in the private rental market.

The goals of this project are to provide safe, affordable, and convenient living options for students while also taking pressure off of an overheated housing market.

University and college employees also must navigate local housing issues and proximity challenges. Institutions can foster live/work environments for their faculty and staff by providing financial assistance programs (i.e., primary mortgage assistance), referral programs, or rental or for-sale housing developments.

An example: University of California, Irvine created its own Irvine Campus Housing Authority, which developed the University Hills community, providing rental and for-sale housing options to university employees. Another example is Bucknell University, which offers a mortgage guarantee program for employees relocating to the Lewisburg area.

Such strategies are crucial in campus and town environments surrounded by expensive housing markets or markets needing to bolster homeownership.

No matter the situation, whether a rural community with a large land-grant institution or an urban center with a small liberal arts campus, it is vital for stakeholders to work together on a comprehensive housing strategy. Even communities without a higher education institution face challenges related to a housing supply that provides for a diverse mix of residents whether young professionals, workforce, seniors, homeless populations, or others.

64. The Hidden Homelessness Among America's High School Students*

Stacey Havlik

One in 30.

That's what a new first-of-its-kind study found was the number of students ages 13 to 17 who have experienced homelessness in the past year. The figure represents about 700,000 young people nationwide.

When a student is homeless in high school, it can cause high levels of stress and anxiety. While other students are able to focus on getting good grades and planning for college, students who are homeless often worry about basic necessities, such as food, clothing and shelter.

In order to turn things around and help homeless students succeed and have a decent shot at college, school counselors should be seen as our first line of support. I say that based on years of experience as a researcher who has focused on the critical role that school counselors play in helping low-income and first-generation college students make it to college.

Unfortunately, what I have found through my research is that school counselors often feel helpless despite their desire to help students who are experiencing homelessness. They also feel underprepared to support the needs of such students. With increased preparation and knowledge on homelessness, school counselors would be in a much better position to help homeless students succeed.

School counselors may meet homeless students' basic needs by collecting school supplies, clothing or food items for students in need. This can be done by coordinating community or school donation programs, collecting monetary donations from the community, or applying for grants through the Department of Education. They may also identify resources in the community and collaborate with stakeholders, such as social workers and teachers to form a supportive system. But my research has found that school counselors often lack knowledge about students who are homeless and have limited training to support their needs. This in turn puts the educational future of students experiencing homelessness in jeopardy.

*Originally published as Stacey Havlik, "The Hidden Homelessness Among America's High School Students," *The Conversation*, https://theconversation.com/the-hidden-homelessness-among-americas-high-school-students-88925 (January 4, 2018). Reprinted with permission of the publisher.

One of the reasons homeless students can be difficult to identify is because homelessness is often thought of as individuals living on the street or in a shelter. The reality is that homelessness can also take many other forms. In fact, the federal definition of homelessness includes those who lack a "fixed, regular, and adequate nighttime residence." This includes individuals and families who are living with others due to a loss of housing, often referred to as "doubling up." Those living in shelters or locations such as motels, hotels, trailer parks or campgrounds because they lack other consistent housing options may also be considered homeless. Individuals who are under 18 and living without a parent or guardian and lack consistent housing are considered "unaccompanied homeless youth." Through having a clear understanding of the various definitions, school counselors can identify students experiencing homelessness quickly and educate others so that if there is a housing loss, students can be provided with the supports they need.

Counselor Contact Is Critical

Research indicates that students from low-income backgrounds are more likely to go to college after they graduate when they have a series of contacts with their school counselors, as opposed to seeing their counselor only once. Unfortunately, my work suggests that school counselors are often forced to focus on meeting homeless students' basic needs. This leads counselors to offer homeless students the kind of general college support that they would give all students.

Consequently, many counselors may neglect the highly specialized college planning needs of students who are homeless. Further, one report suggests that although school counselors are in a position to positively impact students' career and college readiness, they need more extensive graduate and in-service training on college and career counseling.

Generally speaking, students who are homeless face emotional distress in the form of anxiety or low self-esteem and lower academic achievement. School can be a place of consistency that can support their postsecondary planning, but only if schools are mindful of the unique needs of high school students experiencing homelessness. Schools must provide individualized support that focuses on enhancing students' expectations of college attendance and their belief in their ability to attend.

When they are identified, students experiencing homelessness can be supported through the McKinney-Vento Homeless Assistance Act. The federal law includes provisions meant to remove barriers, such as by providing transportation for students who move out of a district because they became homeless. It also allows for quick enrollment for students experiencing homelessness regardless of the required paperwork, and funding for programming such as academic support or afterschool programs. It also allows for a local liaison to ensure students are identified and receiving supports they need. Further, when McKinney-Vento was revised under the Every Student Succeeds Act, it specifically stated that school counselors and local liaisons must provide "individualized" college support for students who are homeless. But ultimately, the federal law by itself won't do anything to help students experiencing homelessness. It's all about how well the law is executed at the school level.

Information Is Crucial

Schools should also include information about McKinney-Vento and college planning that would be directly beneficial to homeless youth on their websites. Unfortunately, few schools are doing so.

Schools can also develop systems of support in the community to support homeless students' basic needs. This will allow them more time to focus on other things, such as college planning.

When advising about college, counselors must determine things such as whether students need campus housing during breaks, if the school has affordable meal plans and if the university has support systems in place for additional counseling, advising, mentoring or tutoring. Directing students to apply to universities that are a good fit will help them to be more successful.

With intentional planning, schools can be a resource for students experiencing homelessness that helps them to stay on track, graduate and go on to college. But if we continue to neglect the specific needs of homeless students, we run the risk of consigning them to lives of uncertainty and placing their college dreams further out of reach.

PART IV

The Future

65. Shelter Design Can Help People Recover from Homelessness*

JILL PABLE

Some 544,000 people in the United States have no shelter every night, according to the U.S. Department of Housing and Urban Development. Homeless families make up over one-third of this total.

Beyond exposing them to weather, crime and unsanitary conditions, homelessness can also damage people's self-esteem, making them feel helpless or hopeless. Being homeless is a traumatic experience, in part because of the stigma associated with this situation.

Recovering from homelessness may therefore involve not just finding a job and permanent home but also rebuilding one's self-esteem.

My research on the built environment suggests that the interior design of homeless shelters can either support or hinder people's ability to assert control over their future.

How Design Affects People

Research has long demonstrated that physical spaces affect human moods and behaviors.

Office environments with many common spaces foster collaboration, for example, while stock investors who work on higher floors take more risks.

Homeless shelters, too, can influence how residents see the world and themselves. A shelter with sterile corridor and glaring lights may silently send the message that, "People don't think you deserve a nice place to live."

Homeless housing designed with warm colors, thoughtful lighting and useful signage, on the other hand, can send the opposite message: "Someone cares."

In my experience, most homeless shelters are designed simply to house as many people as possible. Others are so dilapidated, violent or dirty that people actually prefer to sleep outside.

---

*Originally published as Jill Pable, "Shelter Design Can Help People Recover from Homelessness," *The Conversation*, https://theconversation.com/shelter-design-can-help-people-recover-from-homelessness-98374 (July 5, 2018). Reprinted with permission of the publisher.

What Unhoused Families Need

I undertook a three-month field experiment at a shelter in Florida to understand how bedroom design could support or hinder two families trying to transition from homelessness into permanent housing.

Each family consisted of a single mother with two children. One family had two girls, ages 3 and 4. The other had two boys, ages 3 and 18.

Both parents had generally positive relationships with their children, had completed high school through the 10th grade and were living in the shelter because they had lost their jobs.

Initially, both families stayed in identical 9-by-12 bedrooms. Each had two metal bunk beds, one dresser, pale green walls, a single light fixture and a bathroom shared with a family of four. With so little storage, the families piled their belongings on the unused fourth bunk.

The bedroom door had no lock, so that staff could check in on residents as needed. This is common in shelters.

Housing That Looks Like Jail

After two months, one family moved into a room that our team had upgraded with 18 new features intended to empower residents by offering them control over their environment.

These included drawer-and-bin storage for their possessions, lap desks, privacy curtains around the beds, bulletin boards and shelving. We also painted the walls a light blue.

I interviewed the mothers in the beginning and the end of their experience.

The mother who would later move into an upgraded room felt "aggravated and frustrated" in the first space. The mother who stayed in that room for all three months described it as "crowded," "claustrophobic" and "grim." She even said the metal beds and hard, cold floors reminded her of jail.

Both families piled their belongings on the unused fourth bunk for lack of other storage.

"The more time you spend in it, the more you feel like the walls are closing in," she told me after four weeks, explaining that she often stayed out late to avoid coming home to this cramped situation.

So did her older son, who sometimes spent all night in the shelter's computer lab. His mother worried about her son's "vampire" hours.

This family seemed agitated throughout the three-month study. They sought relief from their housing situation—and from each other—elsewhere.

The Family's Experience in the Altered Room

Things looked different for the other family.

The good lighting and wall cushions encouraged them to read together. They had guests more often. A case worker told me that the family would sometimes spend the entire day together in their shelter bedroom—something they'd never done in their previous space.

Though the two rooms were the same size, a divided Dutch door and bed curtains allowed the residents in the altered room to create personal spaces for listening to music or reading.

They organized and put away their possessions in the storage provided, reducing clutter.

The children liked drawing on the marker boards, so the mother allowed them to use it as a reward for good behavior, exerting parental authority in a positive way.

Signs of Ownership

Tellingly, the families also expressed themselves differently in the two rooms.

In the upgraded room with shelving, the family displayed photographs, art and beloved stuffed animals. The kids played dress up in front of the mirror. These are both territorial acts that define and confirm identities.

The family in the unaltered bedroom displayed little art, in part because the mother felt it was an imposition to ask shelter staff for tape to affix items to the wall.

When her 3-year-old boy tried to play cars on the floor, his mom told him it was too dirty. Bored, he would peel paint off the wall near his bed.

She reprimanded him for this behavior, causing arguments. The children also argued frequently with each other.

A Place to Call Home

At the study's end, I asked the mother living in the upgraded space how she would have felt if her family had stayed in the unaltered bedroom. Her answer reflected the role housing plays in keeping a family happy and healthy.

"I don't know if I would say I would be depressed, but I would have had a different feeling," she responded. "Sometimes you just want peace and quiet"—which the bed curtains and Dutch door now offered her.

She also thought her kids might have eventually "cracked," she said, because they couldn't act as they would in "a regular home."

"My older girl will pull the curtains and read books to her sister" now, the mother said. "She feels like she has something that belongs to her."

The new bedroom, which could be adjusted to fit the family's needs, empowered them to take ownership of it. I believe such actions may help combat underlying feelings of helplessness.

This small, only partially controlled study is not the final word in shelter design.

But it certainly suggests that shelter architecture can help families experiencing homelessness by giving them a calm, positive and supportive home base for planning their future.

66. Improving Resident Services[*]

Using Blockchain Technology to Benefit the Community

Rebecca DeSantis

The city of Austin, Texas, was in a tough position when an annual census for 2018 found a 5 percent rise in homelessness in Austin and Travis County compared with 2017. While planning and developing strategies to reduce the number of residents experiencing homelessness, the city also wanted to find an innovative solution to a serious issue that makes access to healthcare and government services especially challenging for those experiencing homelessness: storing essential documents.

For someone living on the streets or moving between shelters, identification documents like Social Security cards or insurance cards can be lost, stolen, or ruined by rain. According to the Ash Center for Democratic Governance and Innovation at the Harvard Kennedy School, "For homeless individuals, a secure place to store identification is not always an option." In addition to not having a storage location for important documents, having to reapply for replacements multiple times can be a damaging cycle.

Inspired by the World Food Programme "Building Blocks" in Jordan, which keeps family accounts on a "permissioned," or private, variant of the Ethereum blockchain, Austin developed the MyPass Initiative. This program is a partnership between the city, Austin-Travis County Emergency Medical Services, and Dell Medical School at the University of Texas, and it is being tested by a sample of homeless residents. According to the cities MyPass website, blockchain technology digitally scatters the user's records, and the user would sign in with a password or another login tool, using a computer or mobile phone when accessing such services as at a clinic.

Blockchain technology can be used by local governments to improve services and empower communities. ICMA and the Government Finance Officers Association (GFOA) released a whitepaper "Blockchain Technology: Local Government Applications and Challenges" that illustrates the benefits and challenges of blockchain technology by exploring case studies, like that of Austin, as well as the application and implementation of blockchain in other levels of government internationally.

---

[*]Rebecca DeSantis, "Improving Resident Services: Using Blockchain Technology to Benefit the Community," *PM Magazine*, https://icma.org/blog-posts/improving-resident-services-using-blockchain-technology-benefit-community (November 19, 2018). Originally published in the November 2019 issue of *Public Management* (*PM*) magazine and copyrighted by ICMA, the International City/County Management Association (icma.org); reprinted with permission.

Based on Austin's experience with testing blockchain technology through the MyPass program, and other cities and counties who have implemented blockchain, here are a few suggestions of ways local governments can use blockchain technology to improve resident services and benefit the community.

Minimize Risk of Loss of Vital Records. In addition to the homeless population struggling with identification record security, government agencies also deal with challenges around securing vital records. In the past, agencies have dealt with records lost in fires and database failures, and if the office does not have sufficient backups, recreating those records can be a serious challenge for the agency. The distributed nature of a blockchain means that the records are not kept in one location, but across the ledger in multiple locations. If vital government records are maintained on an immutable distributed ledger accessible from many locations, then their risk of loss is greatly reduced.

Putting Power in the Hands of the Community. One of the potential benefits to a public blockchain in local government is that it enables people to deal directly with each other in transactions validated by the public. On a public blockchain, anyone can join the network and validate transactions. Such a system makes it difficult for any one person or agency to tamper with or forge transactions, giving the power of exchange and validation to the community.

Increase Ease of Access to Health Services. For an individual experiencing homelessness or another life situation where they may not have access to their identification or health documents, seeing a doctor or other healthcare provider may be arduous. In a community like Austin, which is testing blockchain technology for recordkeeping, those individuals who are part of the program can access services at a participating health clinic or doctor's office because their documents live on the blockchain and can be accessed by cell phone, computer, and text message and shared among healthcare staff. Allowing homeless individuals to access health services may not only allow them to get the treatment they need, but it may also help them access coordinated programs with health and social services with the aim of breaking the cycle of homelessness.

Want to learn more about the potential applications of blockchain technology for local government use? Download the whitepaper "Blockchain Technology: Local Government Applications and Challenges" at https://icma.org/sites/default/files/2018-Nov%20Blockchain%20White%20Paper.pdf.

67. Libraries on the Front Lines of the Homelessness Crisis in the United States*

Richard Gunderman *and* David C. Stevens

Libraries are increasingly a sanctuary for people who are homeless or mentally ill. We wondered how libraries function on the front lines of social service provision.

Prevalence of Homelessness in the United States

On any given night in 2014, over half a million people in the United States found themselves without a home. While the majority of these people (69 percent) secured shelter for the night, many shelters do not provide daytime accommodations for their patrons. This leaves many in search of daytime activity and protection from the elements.

Unfortunately, many homeless are also living with debilitating mental illnesses. The intimate relationship between homelessness and mental illness is well-established. Almost all psychiatric conditions are overrepresented in homeless populations.

The transition from inpatient to outpatient psychiatric treatment that began in the 1960s, including the closure of state-run psychiatric hospitals, may contribute to the prevalence of mental illness among the homeless. Today, adjusting for changes in population size, U.S. state mental hospitals house only about 10 percent the number of patients they once did.

So it is no surprise that libraries are coping with a large number of patrons who are homeless or have mental illnesses. Public libraries are, after all, designed to be welcoming spaces for all.

This can leave libraries struggling with how to serve a population with very diverse needs.

A Major Metropolitan Library

This is an issue we know that librarians at a metropolitan public library we visited are grappling with. We became aware of this issue in speaking informally with librarians

---

*Originally published as Richard Gunderman and David C. Stevens, "Libraries on the Front Lines of the Homelessness Crisis in the United States," *The Conversation*, https://theconversation.com/libraries-on-the-front-lines-of-the-homelessness-crisis-in-the-united-states-44453 (August 18, 2015). Reprinted with permission of the publisher.

267

who work there. To our surprise, we learned that the library serves a large number of homeless and mentally ill patrons.

The librarians told us about some of these patrons. There is Big Bob, a large man in his 40s who frequently regales the librarians with accounts of his exploits as a member of special ops forces in the military. There is John, a reclusive man always attired in combat fatigues and heavy-duty army boots who turned out, in the bitterest cold of winter, to be suffering from severe frostbite.

And there is Jane, a young woman who, when it emerged that she was temporarily living in her car, turned the tables on the librarians by saying, "Shh," so no one else would learn of her plight.

Some of these library patrons are homeless. Others have been diagnosed with a mental illness, such as bipolar disorder, schizophrenia, depression, or substance dependence. Tragically, many are experiencing both.

They come to the library for all sorts of reasons: to seek warmth and shelter, to use the restroom, to access the internet, to meet friends, and yes, even to read books and newspapers. One librarian estimates that about half of the library's regular patrons are either mentally ill or homeless.

The library's long-term employees report that the mentally ill were not always such a prominent component of its clientele. Their presence increased dramatically 20 years ago, with the closure of a local mental hospital.

How Librarians Can Help Patrons Who Are Mentally Ill or Experiencing Homelessness

Helping homeless and mentally ill clients is a challenge that libraries all over the country are grappling with, but library science curricula don't seem to have caught up.

According to one newly minted librarian who received her master's degree in library science a few years ago, contemporary library education typically includes no coursework in mental illness. It focuses on the techniques and technology of library services, especially meeting the needs of patrons for access to information.

Learning strategies to assist mentally ill and homeless patrons might not be on library curricula, but the American Library Association has long had policies in place emphasizing equal access to library services for the poor, and in 1996 formed the Hunger, Homelessness, and Poverty Task Force.

Across the country, libraries have developed helpful strategies for serving homeless and mentally ill patrons. One, at least for large libraries with sufficient numbers of personnel, is to designate a member of the staff as a specialist in these matters, who serves as a resource person for other employees.

At the metropolitan library we visited, one of the more civically oriented librarians acts as a liaison between various local mental health agencies and homeless shelters. She has cultivated a relationship with a mental health crisis clinician at the county hospital, who has organized workshops to educate the library staff about mental health and substance abuse.

This librarian's work with homeless and mentally ill library patrons is currently supported by the library's budget, but much of her progress was driven by her personal commitment. As she looks toward retirement, she worries that these services will fade when she leaves.

However, there are signs that libraries are embracing their role as a safety net. Libraries in San Francisco, Washington DC and Philadelphia are hiring social workers to assist with the needs of homeless and mentally ill patrons. Others in Queens, New York and Denver, Colorado have outreach programs that bring training services to homeless shelters and educate residents about library services. The Denver program even provides the bus fare to visit the library.

The librarians we talked to take their role as surrogate mental health workers in stride, and many regard their mentally ill patrons with a sense of mission.

Said one librarian who has worked at the downtown library for more than 30 years: "The library often serves as a destination for people who have no place to go. They can always come here, to be warm, safe, and entertained. At first, I didn't know how important the library is to them, but one day before a holiday, a patron came up to me and said, 'You guys will really be missed tomorrow.' Some may resent the presence of the mentally ill in the library, but as far as I am concerned, everyone deserves a chance to use it."

68. Homeless and the Courts*

RUTH ASTLE SAMAS

"The law, in its majestic equality, forbids rich and poor alike to sleep under bridges, to beg in the streets, and to steal their bread."
—Anatole France, *The Red Lily*

In 2018, the United States Court of Appeals, Ninth Circuit, decided the case of *Martin v. City of Boise* 902 F. 3rd 1031. This case holds that it is a violation of the Eighth Amendment to the United States Constitution to prosecute people criminally for sleeping out-side on public property when those people have no home or other shelter to go to. It also holds that cities cannot force homeless to use religious-based shelters (https://scholar.google.com/scholar_case?case=17340329580133284185&hl=en&as_sdt=6&as_vis=1&oi=scholarr).

This case is significant. It reflects the conclusion that criminalizing homelessness is not effective public policy. The city of Santa Cruz, California, has been dealing with a growing number of homeless living on the beach. There is a move to enact a curfew. However, it is not clear if that would violate the *Martin* decision. Los Angeles and Sacramento have also questioned the wisdom of the *Martin* decision. The Ninth Circuit denied a request to hear this matter *En Banc* and On August 22, 2019, the City of Boise filed a petition for a writ of certiorari in the Supreme Court of the United States requesting the Supreme Court to hear the case.

Some homeless find themselves charged with petty criminal offenses. Many counties in California have set up Community Homeless courts to deal with quality of life crimes. Special court sessions are held in local shelters or other community sites. These courts are designed to resolve outstanding misdemeanor warrants for such charges as disorderly conduct and public drunkenness. San Diego county holds monthly sessions at Saint Vincent di Paul and Veteran's Village. Los Angeles county holds sessions at the Salvation Army (https://www.ncsc.org/Topics/Alternative-Dockets/Problem-Solving-Courts/Homeless-Courts/State-Links.aspx#California).

The Administrative Office of the Court's Collaborative Justice Unit held the first in a series of conference calls with California Homeless Courts. The participating courts provided summaries of program development and case processing strategies that were effective in their courts. Alameda County: The Alameda Homeless Court has informally participated in the past two bi-annual (every two years) Veterans Stand Down events.

---

*Published with permission of the author.

The court began exploring the question of homelessness and quality of life infractions and misdemeanors that clutter the court's calendars and learned that the County of Alameda was conducting the first ever census of homeless persons in March 2003. They made contact with those conducting the study and invited them to attend the court's community focused court planning committee meetings to update the committee on the study's progress.

Based on the Veterans Stand Down experience and information from the study, they decided to explore creating a homeless court. Alameda anticipates having their first homeless court session as early as March 2004 likely to be held in a shelter in Oakland. The pace and scope of the project depend upon a number of factors, mostly revolving around the availability of voluntary resources.

Los Angeles: Similar to Kern County, Los Angeles conducted a site visit to the San Diego Homeless Court prior to opening their court. The Los Angeles Homeless Court operates out of the Ninth Circuit Court through the City Attorney's Office. They have handled a total of 500 cases since the court opened in November 2000. The court operates 23 sessions every month at different shelter locations. Los Angeles does not have the funds or staff to develop a follow-up program nor do they have the funding to track outcomes. The court would like to develop a system for statistical reporting for clients who re-offend.

Orange County: Orange County conducted site visits to Los Angeles, San Diego and Ventura: prior to opening their homeless court in October 2003. They developed a needs assessment by surveying county shelters. The court accepts misdemeanors and other infractions during their monthly sessions.

San Diego: The San Diego Homeless Court started in 1989 and is conducted on a monthly basis.

California Homeless Courts

Alameda County. Alameda County Superior Court's website provides general details on its Homeless and Caring Court. The website also provides a phone number leading to more resources on the matter.

Bakersfield. The Greater Bakersfield Legal Assistance, Inc. provides basic information on the Community Homeless Law Center Project and how its legal services can assist homeless clients.

Fresno County. The Fresno County Superior Court website provides basic information on its Homeless Court proceedings and requirements to participate in the specialty court.

Kern County. The Kern County Mental Health Department has developed a specialized division, the Kern Linkage Program, which serves homeless adults who have chronic and persistent mental illness. The KCMH Kern Linkage Program website provides details on its case management program, including participation requirements and procedure steps. It is important to note that Bakersfield is a city located in Kern County.

Los Angeles. Public Counsel, the largest pro bono law firm in California and the nation, provides brief information on the Homeless Court Program of Los Angeles, including what the court addresses regarding charges. Though Public Counsel no longer handles the Homeless Court Program, it directs attention to the Los Angeles City Attorney's Office, which does handle the Homeless Court Program. Appropriate contact information is posted for additional inquiry (LA City Attorney's Office).

Orange County. The Orange County Superior Court's website briefly describes the Homeless Outreach Court and its goals.

Sacramento. The Sacramento Superior Court's website provides detailed information on its homeless court program, Loaves and Fishes Court. The featured information includes requirements for court access and offenses addressed. The Sacramento County District Attorney's Office also addresses the Loaves and Fishes Court, providing contact information for further inquiry.

San Diego. The San Diego Homeless Court started in 1989 and is conducted on a monthly basis. On average the court sees 35 to 40 clients per month on a full range of misdemeanors. including DUI, sleeping in public and traffic related infractions. San Diego is starting to negotiate with their district attorney, an addition to the city attorney with whom they normally collaborate. Increasingly local programs involved in the homeless court are reporting back to the court about the status of clients. Client tracking is usually conducted anecdotally although the city attorney does track who returns to the court and why. Clients are expected to complete community service, which is anything considered positive, i.e., life skills training, 12-step programs or anger management.

San Diego has just completed a second video through the American Bar Association.

Santa Clara. The Santa Clara Outreach Court opened in January 2003. The court is called an outreach rather than a homeless court to dispel the demeaning quality of homelessness. They hold sessions during the first Saturday of the month at the city's largest homeless shelter. Sessions are held with the judge, public defender and district attorney with an average of 30 to 40 participants. The Outreach Court includes 12 participating shelters which include 20 different referral agencies. Lunch is also served which boosts client attendance. The court has processed 400 cases since January 2003. The court is primarily interested in clearing outstanding warrants and saving money for the court. Secondarily, the court recognizes that the program improves the quality of life for the client.

Ventura. The Ventura Court opened three years ago and is conducted through various agencies that serve the homeless. The court averages 50 cases per session every other month. The cases are calendared only if the client has started community service. Ventura does track their cases through the assistance of a work-study student. The student tracks each case with the guidance of the social worker through the originating referral agency. Like other California homeless courts, Ventura operates their court with a minimal of funding.

Alameda County is a good example: www.Alameda.courts.ca.gov/Pages.aspx/Court-Community-Outreach-Programs#7 .

Homeless and Caring Court

The Homeless and Caring Court seeks to address some of the legal barriers confronting homeless individuals. The Court holds bimonthly court sessions in homeless shelters and community sites in Alameda County. Typically, participants have been cited for various minor nonviolent offenses. These matters often escalate when homeless defendants fail to appear in court and arrest warrants are issued, creating new or additional sanctions and preventing these defendants from obtaining housing and other social welfare assistance. The individuals who participate must demonstrate their readiness to come to court in a variety of ways depending upon their particular circumstances, including seeking employment, education, pursuing sobriety, and general stability in their lives. The defendants are identified as good candidates for the Homeless Court through a consortium of local service providers.

San Diego also has a program to help the homeless, as well. "The San Diego Homeless Court Program (HCP) is a special Superior Court session for homeless defendants— convened in a homeless shelter— to resolve outstanding misdemeanor offenses and warrants. To counteract the effect of criminal cases pushing homeless defendants further outside society, the HCP combines a progressive plea bargain system, alternative sentencing structure, assurance of 'no custody,' and proof of program activities to address a full range of misdemeanor cases. Each month, a local homeless service agency hosts a special Superior Court session. The HCP builds on partnerships between the court, prosecutor, public defender, and local service agencies to help resolve the problems that homelessness represents with practical and effective solutions. We believe that when homeless participants work with agency representatives to identify and overcome the causes of their homelessness, they are in a stronger position to successfully comply with court orders" (https://www.homelesscourtprogram.org/).

Conclusion

Criminalization of Homelessness is not the answer. Housing the homeless in jails is not good public policy. Charging the homeless with petty crimes does nothing to abate the problem. It is an added expense to cities and counties to pursue criminal charges with no real consequences.

69. A Case for Transition Shelters*

Gabby V. Moraleda

Historical data suggests that a mere 15 percent of the people affected by disasters are reached by all forms of combined assistance and are able to recover. The remaining 85 percent are left on their own to rebuild their homes and lives. Surely, difficult for those who do not have the means to lift themselves out from becoming homeless because of natural and climate change hazards.

Understandably, humanitarian shelter gets first priority.

Foreign/International aid and diaspora donations are primarily designated for food, medicines and short-term shelter. In the absence or shortage of covered spaces (ex.: basketball courts), tents (or tent-like shelters) have become the most convenient and visible structures in evacuation areas. Tents are portable, relatively easy to setup and reasonably priced—becoming the quickest way to provide a roof over one's head. Not durable, limited functionality but given the situation, the most practical.

These tents, by their very nature and given their technical specifications, are meant for a few weeks of stay only. Temporary in nature—for emergency. Beyond that, their value and utility diminishes substantially. Its continued use exposes the people living in them—the elderly, infants, handicapped and nursing mothers to more harm than good. In the normal course of recovery, it is envisioned that if homes are livable after a disaster, then the people are ushered back into their permanent homes. If homes are severely damaged, they are moved to transition shelters, fitted for better living—up to a point in time when the homes are repaired.

Building back better permanent houses is a straightforward proposition. Financing is readily available from usual lending sources backed by government mortgage institutions. In the Philippines, access to these funds can be through the Social Security System (SSS) and the Government Service Insurance System (GSIS) housing loans in conjunction with PAGIBIG's Home Development Mutual Fund. Most of these lenders have structured lending protocols skewed in favor of low-risk borrowers, basically their contributing members. If you can demonstrate the capacity to pay (i.e., have a regular job), these lenders will lend you. After the appropriate building permits have been properly secured, repair/rebuilding can take several months.

In other words, the upper and middle-income groups have a clear pathway to recovery.

The case for low-income, high-risk families (marginal farm workers and fishermen)

---

*Published with permission of the author.

is different. Quite the opposite. They have no one to run to. No parameters to work with and no access to lenders.

They are left on their own to source funds, if they can, from friends, family members—local and overseas. The obvious consequence is that if they are unable to secure funds, they linger in a "state of limbo," the default option, and stay in humanitarian shelters for an "extended" period of time. This can be "forever." When this happens, migration becomes the one avenue left—as in the case of Typhoon Haiyan and the Marawi siege.

Inequity, even in disasters.

As such, it is clear, transition shelter presents itself as the vital link—from humanitarian shelter to permanent housing—the only option open, not for those who can afford but for the poor and underprivileged. Unless these better built shelters are made available, the people will remain in deplorable emergency-living conditions.

Without a doubt, there are fundamental fiscal policy and operational considerations—especially when destruction is widespread and extensive as in Tacloban. For one, the magnitude alone can be overwhelming, overpowering and consuming—and when help is nowhere in sight. Private donations generally taper off after a week of giving. Whose primary responsibility is it then to rebuild—government, the diaspora, the international community or themselves? No one seems to have a definite answer—or even paying attention.

And, since time is of the essence, "speed of delivery" is a second major factor. Time does not stand still. When bureaucracy seeps in, gridlock happens and everything is pushed back—or out. As a result, a great majority are left unattended, alone to fend for themselves for months, if not years. Indeed, a sad plight repeatedly heard off and ignored.

The starting (humanitarian) and end (permanent) points of the shelter recovery process are, in a way, "covered." It is in place and defined. The middle (transition) phase, the most critical, is not. It is no wonder the responses of the "community" in past major disasters have been consistently lacking and inadequate.

The pursuit of aggressive transition shelter solutions and settlements becomes compelling. For without it, the defenseless will always be left out in the dark, remain homeless, hopeless and will stay in makeshift shelters—vulnerable, if not perish, when the next disaster strikes.

The Assumptions

As we chart out our best options, it is wise to review four simple assumptions that have guided our approaches and proposed solutions. These are;

First, we must be cognizant of the fact that in these changing times, in the context and reality of climate change—*nature always wins*. Given its strength, it takes anything along its path. There is no way around this. For disaster volunteer groups—be forewarned, it is a myth to believe otherwise.

Second, in the face of any impending disaster (super typhoons) and the context of crudely built homes, on "no build or hazard zones" and are unable to withstand nature—the first line of "defense" is—*to run to safer/higher ground*, to places of (temporary) refuge. Evacuation to safe areas and structures is the first order of business. This is the most logical thing to do, no ifs and buts.

Third, given the repetitiveness and increasing strength of typhoons, and to the extent we can, we must realize—*man can only mitigate* or minimize the risks, through better building technologies, common sense engineering solutions in flood control/water management including the adoption of environmentally-based solutions such as erosion prevention, among others. These interventions are technologically sound, readily available from experienced engineers and can be put in place, way before a disaster strikes. No rocket science needed.

And fourth, "prevention" pays off—or costs related to "upgrading" or retrofitting poorly built homes with inferior materials to conform with acceptable standards are worth the expense. A dollar spent in prevention equates to four dollars in rebuilding—a $1: $4 ratio, validating the classic principle that "an ounce of prevention is worth a pound of cure."

If you look at it closely, literally, figuratively and profoundly, the task at hand is really to find or build places of refuge—safe, secure shelters that can withstand the storms that are sure to come.

The sad experiences of the past must not be repeated. Unfortunately, it is. The prolonged misery we continually witness in each disaster is a raison d'etre to put on each of our shoulders the burden and tremendous challenge to respond—collectively.

A Work in Progress: Portable Container Vans, Bamboo Homes and Available Spaces

Haiyan is a game changer. It is a first and certainly not the last. Our interest paper "After Haiyan: Where?" highlighted the following points;

1. That, there is an urgency to start discussions on how we can, at least, start a rebuilding and renewal program that shall prepare the nation.

2. In the short run, there is a need to move the evacuees from emergency centers to habitable "transition homes and communities" before the next rainy season. Retrofitted container vans are a possibility because they are portable and reusable.

3. We foresee the need to "challenge" the boundaries of engineering and architectural science and explore its boundaries to "Build Better Than Before" solutions.

As detailed out (parts of our paper are quoted below), container vans as transition shelters have become a desired solution. Strength, portability and reuse are its strengths. With compact, configurable, and Lego-like properties, the vans can withstand the fiercest of storms.

It is envisioned that 40 × 8 foot containers be used having a total area of 320 square feet (or, 30 square meters) for these living quarters to make a decent livable space for a household of five (5) persons. Container dimensions are 10 feet high and vary from 10, 20, 30 and 40 feet long so they can be modularly combined. They are structurally sound, being able to load up to 20 tons of cargo and stacked up 9-high. These can be locked with a mechanism side-by-side and on top of each other such as can be observed on container ships.

Containers are cost effective. They need to undergo sandblasting, painting, cutting window openings, and conversion of steel gates to maintenance free pvc doors. Interior features of the containers are R-15 fiberglass insulation on the ceiling and sides conforming to container corrugation, finish-painted ceiling and side walls of riveted ½-inch marine plywood, 2 white pvc windows of 2 ft × 4 ft, and 12 CFL overhead lights/switches, wiring for 12 outlets. In addition, foldable bunk beds, and tables and space separators will be installed. The specific layout of these temporary container shelters within or around the city shall be such as to minimize obstructions and interference to rapid reconstruction of the Tacloban commercial districts. The locations and configurations of these shelters will be environmentally sound and conform to space planning standards. Access roads need to be included in the site preparation as well as electrical connections to each container shelter with power to be provided by the local utility.

These refurbished container vans will <u>not</u> be fitted with toilets and bathrooms. Instead, a communal system will be provided in a central location to centralize water supply and delivery and a septic tank for disposal of biohazard wastes. Fresh water shall be drawn from deep wells, where available and pumped into a 10,000-gallon elevated water tank. From the tank, water delivery will be piped into dedicated lines for drinking water and another line for washing, bathing and laundry needs. Large garbage bins will also be provided for solid wastes destined for landfill and composting. Moreover, inhabitants will be taught to segregate biodegradable, recyclable and true wastes.

Assuming that land, containers and most importantly, funds, are available, these temporary village shelters can be completed in six (6) months on a compressed schedule to create a quick and welcome response to this disaster and well ahead of the next devastation storm that can be expected in approximately eight (8) months. As these container vans are planned to transition beneficiaries to permanent homes, it is imperative that a long-term viable housing project be simultaneously put in place.

A second option is to use bamboo.

The plant, actually a grass, is pretty abundant in the countryside and easy to cultivate. It can be farmed and commercially grown. Bamboo is used for food, charcoal, furniture and construction—as scaffolding. Its roots hold the soil, prevents erosion and is a climate change agent. For some time now, bamboo has been on the radar screen as a possible construction material. To this day, there are pro and con discussions on its technical properties as a substitute for steel. In the last few years, a non-governmental organization (NGO) has adopted treated bamboo for home construction. It is pioneering its use for shear walling and roofing frames or the cement-bamboo framing technology. They claim model homes built out of bamboo can withstand above normal wind loads and conforms with the National Structural Code of the Philippines.

A second NGO supplies the treated bamboo. The company is making a strong pitch in the housing and construction industry for its regular usage. They are confident with their findings on the properties, structural strength and usefulness of bamboo—to a point they have invested in a treatment plant in Negros. With the 2 NGO's, the supply chain is taking shape.

The third option is to utilize available spaces in schools, churches—even shopping malls as transition shelters. It is sensible because in most towns and cities, they are in existence. No need to build, just design and assign space.

These buildings are equipped with the necessary hygiene facilities and running water, essential for daily living. The engineering challenge is to evolve functional designs that will convert available spaces into a "mix use" and provide "zones" as living quarters for extended stay. For structures that have daily and heavy "consumer traffic" such as shopping malls, they may offer some resistance. Churches and schools, inherent places of refuge and learning may be more "flexible" in configuring their workspace to accommodate the modified living needs of these transients.

Finding Financing

By the sheer size of the problem, finding funds remain the biggest barrier to implementation. In spite of the global prosperity, we find the usual sources of financing—the international community of donors, are seemingly running out of funds. The reason for this is the high incidence and intensity of disasters worldwide as a result of climate change and conflict—i.e., more to serve with limited funds. Notwithstanding the geo-political realities, there is growing perception, the have's (industrialized nations) are gradually "distancing" themselves from the have not's (developing counties) in disaster response—unable to hear the plea, that universally held development tenets are no longer valid when viewed in context of recurring disasters.

In itself, an imminent "disaster"—on the horizon?

In this day and age of natural disasters and political turmoil, development implies disaster planning. Both are two sides of the same coin, with a caveat—disaster planning must drive development.

This situation undoubtedly has created a scare and put pressure on countries prone to disasters (those in the typhoon belt) to search for creative ways outside the norm to raise the necessary funds. Though still very raw and tentative, in discussions, there are three ideas that have been put forth.

The first is to tap the local government units (LGU) Internal Revenue Allotments (IRA). The IRA is the LGU's yearly share of the national revenue. This can go anywhere upwards from

120 million pesos for a first-class municipality. At least 5 percent of the IRA is mandated to fund disaster response and preparedness—or at least 6 million pesos is available each year. The LGUs can leverage these disaster funds and are allowed to borrow on it. So, assuming only half or 3 million pesos is allotted for preparedness—using this amount, the LGU can secure a substantial loan, say 15 million pesos, which could be smartly used for transition shelters. The loan can securely be paid off in five years—without compromising their financial status.

Another idea is to tap the increasing overseas dollar remittances to share in the burgeoning cost of disaster recovery. The idea behind is to engage the participation of the U.S. diasporas of the most vulnerable nations. The suggestion is to take a small piece of the remittance fees and/or tag on an additional amount for this purpose. Somewhat akin to asking donations when you pay at a Safeway counter.

The last one is to partake in the "rounding off" receipts—when the rates are mathematically expressed beyond 2-decimal places. This can be significant when you factor the huge amounts of annual remittances.

Overall, the plan is to lodge these cumulative funds into some sort of a rainy day fund—for disaster preparedness. The administrative and legal details have not been ironed out. They need to be. However, this should not stop us from pursuing these mutually independent courses of action—with focus, passion and a sense of mission.

Appendices

A. Glossary of Homelessness*

ALAN R. ROPER

Addictions Programs: Programs that consists of self-help residential or outpatient treatment facilities, harm reduction programs, individual or group counseling, abstinence-only housing and support from community programs.

Adequate Housing: Housing that is reported by residents as not requiring any major repairs. Housing that is inadequate may have excessive mold, inadequate heating or water supply, significant damage, etc.

Adults with a Serious Mental Illness (SMI): This subpopulation category of the PIT includes adults with a severe and persistent mental illness or emotional impairment that seriously limits a person's ability to live independently. Adults with SMI must also meet the qualifications identified in the term for "disability" (e.g., "is expected to be long-continuing or indefinite duration").

Adults with a Substance Use Disorder: This subpopulation category of the PIT includes adults with a substance abuse problem (alcohol abuse, drug abuse, or both). Adults with a substance use disorder must also meet the qualifications identified in the term for "disability" (e.g., "is expected to be long-continuing or indefinite duration").

Adults with HIV/AIDS: This subpopulation category of the Point in Time (PIT) includes adults who have been diagnosed with AIDS and/or have tested positive for HIV.

Affordable Housing: Any type of housing, including rental/home ownership, permanent/temporary, for-profit/non-profit, that costs less than 30 percent of a household's pre-tax income.

Asset-Based Approaches: Wide-range of projects and initiatives that promote savings and the acquisition of assets among people with low incomes.

At-Risk of Homelessness: People who are not experiencing homelessness, but whose current economic and/or housing situation is precarious or does not meet public health and safety standards. (Reference)

Best Practice: an intervention, method or technique that has consistently been proven effective through the most rigorous scientific research and has been replicated across several cases or examples.

Busking: A subsistence strategy that refers to providing entertainment for money. The activity is considered to be part of informal economy and is commonly associated with homelessness.

Case Management: A collaborative and client-centered approach to service provision for persons experiencing homelessness. In this approach, a case worker assesses the needs of the client (and potentially their families) and when appropriate, arranges, coordinates and advocates for delivery and access to a range of programs and services to address the individual's needs.

---

*Published with the permission of Alan R. Roper.

Child Poverty: Child poverty refers to the proportion of children 17 years and under living in households where disposable income is less than half of the median in a given country.

Chronic Disease: A long-lasting medical condition that cannot be prevented by vaccines, or in many instances, be cured.

Chronically Homeless:
1. An individual who:
   a. Is homeless and lives in a place not meant for human habitation, a safe haven, or in an emergency shelter; AND
   b. Has been homeless and living or residing in a place not meant for human habitation, a safe haven, or in an emergency shelter continuously for at least twelve months or on at least four separate occasions in the last
   c. Can be diagnosed with one or more of the following conditions: substance use disorder, serious mental illness, developmental disability (as defined in section 102 of the Developmental Disabilities Assistance Bill of Rights Act of 2000 [42 U.S.C. 15002]), post-traumatic stress disorder, cognitive impairments resulting from brain injury, or chronic physical illness or disability;
2. An individual who has been residing in an institutional care facility, including a jail, substance abuse or mental health treatment facility, hospital, or other similar facility, for fewer than 90 days and met all of the criteria in paragraph (1) of this definition, before entering that facility; or
3. A family with an adult head of household (or if there is no adult in the family, a minor head of household) who meets all of the criteria in paragraph (1) of this definition, including a family whose composition has fluctuated while the head of household has been homeless.

Chronically Homeless Family with Children: A family with children with an adult head of household (or if there is no adult in the family with children, a minor head of household) who meets all of the criteria for a chronically homeless individual, including a family with children whose composition has fluctuated while the head of household has been homeless.

Collaborative: Is the term used to describe loosely affiliated networks as well as more formal partnerships between people working across departments, organizations or sectors. Unlike integration, collaboration does not require formal infrastructure to merge work processes across organizational sites.

Co-location: Refers to the practice of housing services in a single location to improve service access and communication/collaboration between service providers.

Community Services: Any programs delivered through non-profit or faith-based community organizations to assist people experiencing homelessness.

Concurrent Disorders (Dual Diagnosis): Describes a condition in which a person has both a mental illness and a substance use problem.

Continuum of Care (CoC): A community plan to organize and deliver housing and services to meet the specific needs of people who are homeless as they move to stable housing and maximize self-sufficiency. It "includes action steps to end homelessness and prevent a return to homelessness." In Los Angeles County, there are four CoCs. The Los Angeles Homeless Services Authority serves all cities of the County with the exception of Long Beach, Pasadena, and Glendale, who each have their own CoC.

Coordinated Assessment: A standardized approach to assessing a person's current situation, the acuity of their needs and the services they currently receive and may require in the future. It takes into account the background factors that contribute to risk and resilience, changes in acuity, and the role of friends, family, caregivers, community and environmental factors.

Coordinated Entry System (CES): A regionally based system that connects new and existing programs into a "no-wrong-door network" by assessing the needs of individuals/ families/

youth experiencing homelessness and linking them with the most appropriate housing and services to end their homelessness. The goal of the CES is to streamline processes through which communities assess, house, and support housing retention for individuals/families who are homeless; to ensure all of our homeless neighbors are known and supported; to target and maximize limited housing resources; and comply with the federal mandate to adopt a standardized intake and coordinated assessment process for housing. The essential components of CES are: (1) a system that is low-barrier and easy to access; (2) a system that identifies and assesses people's needs; and (3) a system that prioritizes and matches housing resources based on those needs.

Coordinated Intake: A standardized approach to assessing a person's current situation, the acuity of their needs and the services they currently receive and may require in the future. It takes into account the background factors that contribute to risk and resilience, changes in acuity, and the role friends, family, caregivers, community and environmental factors.

Core Housing Need: When a household spends more than 30 percent of its pre-tax income on housing costs.

Crisis Housing: An emergency shelter in the homeless coordinated entry system. Crisis Housing means any facility, the primary purpose of which is to provide temporary shelter for the homeless or to provide a bridge to permanent housing.

Demonstration Projects: Large-scale studies focused on a theory or concept that has already gone through an initial testing process to sort out any logistical and/or core issues. The focus of the demonstration project is, as the name suggests, to demonstrate the value of the theory or concept by allowing as much relevant information as possible to be collected. This information is then evaluated by researchers and used to assess the effectiveness of the theory or concept.

Discharge Planning: Preparing someone to move from an institutional setting (child welfare system, criminal justice system, hospital etc.) into a non-institutional setting either independently or with certain supports in place.

Discrimination: Intentional or unintentional actions that negatively affect people, based on biases and prejudices.

Early Intervention Strategies: Strategies designed to work quickly to support individuals and families to either retain their housing, or to use rapid rehousing strategies.

Emergency Response: Providing emergency supports like shelter, food and day programs while someone is experiencing homelessness.

Emergency Sheltered: Staying in overnight emergency shelters designed for people who are experiencing homelessness.

Empowerment Evaluation: The application of evaluation techniques in facilitating self-determination.

Enforcement: Interventions that seek to strengthen community safety by responding to the crimes and community disorder issues associated with the importing, manufacturing, cultivating, distributing, possessing and using legal and illegal substances.

Episodically Homeless: Those who move in and out of homelessness

Eviction Prevention: Any strategy or program, usually geared at renters that is designed to keep individuals and families in their home and that helps them avoid homelessness.

Family and Natural Supports: Include family, friends and community. By providing young people with family and natural supports that align with "place-based" supports (ex. schools), we reduce the probability that a young person will leave their community in search of supports and become mired in homelessness.

Family Reconnection (and Reunification): Client-driven case-management approach that seeks to identify and nurture opportunities to strengthen relationships and resolve conflicts between young people who leave home and their caregivers.

Follow-Up Support Workers (FSW): An individual who helps an already housed client maintain their housing and connects the client with resources and services in the community.

Hard Skills: The learning of marketable skills, such as carpentry, computer repair or restaurant work, that increase the employability of people wanting to get jobs.

Harm Reduction: Policies, programs and practices aimed at reducing the risks and negative effects associated with substance use and addictive behaviors for the individual, the community and society as a whole.

HART (Homelessness Assets and Risk Tools): A tool used to measure risk of homelessness.

Hidden Homelessness: Persons who live temporarily with others without the guarantee of continued residency or immediate prospects for accessing permanent housing.

Homecare and Continuing Care: A wide range of inpatient and outpatient services that may be offered in the home, in the community or in a hospital or medical setting.

Homeless: An individual who lacks a fixed, regular, and adequate nighttime residence; AND is an individual who: has a primary nighttime residence that is a supervised publicly or privately-operated shelter designed to provide temporary living accommodations; an institution that provides a temporary residence for individuals intended to be institutionalized; or a public or private place not designed for, or ordinarily used as, a regular sleeping accommodation for human beings.

Homelessness: Describes the situation of an individual, family or community without stable, safe, permanent, appropriate housing, or the immediate prospect, means and ability of acquiring it. It is the result of systemic or societal barriers, a lack of affordable and appropriate housing, the individual/household's financial, mental, cognitive, behavioral or physical challenges, and/or racism and discrimination. Most people do not choose to be homeless, and the experience is generally negative, unpleasant, unhealthy, unsafe, stressful and distressing.

Housing Accommodation and Supports: The provision of housing and ongoing supports as a means of moving people out of homelessness.

Housing Choice Voucher (HCV): The federal government's major program providing rental subsidies to assist very low-income families, the elderly, and the disabled to afford decent, safe, and sanitary housing in the private market.

Housing Exclusion: The failure of society to ensure that adequate systems, funding and support are in place so that all people, even in crisis situations, have access to housing.

Housing First: An approach that offers permanent housing as quickly as possible for people experiencing homelessness, particularly for people with long histories of homelessness and co-occurring health challenges, while providing the supportive services people need to keep their housing and avoid returning to homelessness.

Housing First for Youth (HF4Y): A recovery-oriented approach to ending homelessness that adapts the approach to the needs of young people. It centers on quickly moving people experiencing homelessness into independent and permanent housing. It is followed by provision of additional supports and services as needed.

Housing Inventory Chart (HIC): Consists of three housing inventory charts for: emergency shelter, transitional housing and permanent supportive housing

Housing Navigator(s): Housing Navigator is the client's primary point of contact in CES, often a social worker, case manager, outreach worker, or volunteer. The primary function of the Housing Navigator is to: (1) assist clients in collecting necessary documents for housing applications,

(2) accompany clients to housing appointments, and (3) assist clients in navigating the entire housing search and placement process.

Housing Policy: The actions of government, including legislation and program delivery, which have a direct or indirect impact on housing supply and availability, housing standards and urban planning.

Housing Workers: Individuals employed, usually by community agencies/non-profits but sometimes working directly for a specific level of government, who are able to assist individuals in finding housing and supporting them with the related services that are part of that process.

ICM (Integrated Case Management) teams: A team approach taken to co-ordinate various services for a specific child and/or families through a cohesive and sensible plan. The team should include all service providers who have a role in implementing the plan, and whenever possible, the child or youth's family.

Indigenous Homelessness: A definition of homelessness that takes into account a country's legacy of marginalization and displacement of Indigenous Peoples, created through settler colonialism. It requires an understanding of the Indigenous philosophy "All My Relations" as Indigenous homelessness and the Indigenous concept of "home" goes beyond one's physical structure of habitation.

Individual and Relational Factors: The personal circumstances of a homeless person, and may include: traumatic events, personal crisis, mental health and addictions challenges, which can be both a cause and consequence of homelessness and physical health problems or disabilities. Relational problems can include family violence and abuse, addictions, mental health problems of other family members and extreme poverty.

Informal Economy: Economic activities that fall outside the formal labor market. Generally, refers to production, distribution and consumption of goods and services that are not accounted for in formal measurements of the economy.

LGBTQ2S: The acronym stands for lesbian, gay, bisexual, transgender, transsexual, queer, questioning, and Two-Spirit people.

Life Skills: The skills that are essential for living independently and includes skills such as managing money, shopping, cooking, etc.

Low-Barrier Shelter: A form of congregate housing where a minimum number of expectations are placed on people who wish to stay there. The aim is to have as few barriers and rules as possible to allow more people to access services.

Measuring Integration: Efforts in assessing the degree to which clients are receiving appropriately integrated services and/or used to improve coordination efforts.

NIMBY (Not in My Backyard): describes when residents of a neighborhood designate a new development (e.g., shelter, affordable housing, group home) or change in occupancy of an existing development as inappropriate or unwanted for their local area.

Outreach Programs: Services and programs involved in bringing services directly to where people are rather that requiring someone to go into an agency.

Panhandling: A subsistence strategy that refers to begging for money, food and other items. The activity is considered to be part of informal economy and is commonly associated with homelessness.

Parenting Youth: A youth who identifies as the parent or legal guardian of one or more children who are present with or sleeping in the same place as that youth parent, where there is no person over age 24 in the household.

Permanent Housing (PH): Community-based housing without a designated length of stay, which includes both Permanent Supportive Housing (PSH) and Rapid Rehousing (RRH).

Examples of permanent housing include, but are not limited to, a house or apartment with a month-to-month or annual lease term or home ownership.

Permanent Supportive Housing (PSH): Long-term, community-based housing that has supportive services for homeless persons with disabilities. This type of supportive housing enables the special needs of populations to live independently as possible in a permanent setting. Permanent housing can be provided in one structure or in several structures at one site or in multiple structures at scattered sites.

Point in Time (PIT): A snapshot of the homeless population taken on a given day. Since 2005, HUD requires all CoC applicants to complete this count every other year in the last week of January. This count includes a street count in addition to a count of all clients in emergency and transitional beds.

Poverty: There is a lack of international consensus on the definition of poverty. Low-Income designation as a tool in identifying individuals and families who are substantially worse off than the average.

Prevalence Counts: An alternative to the PI counts and are often used in some small and rural communities. They determine how many people were homeless over a set period in time.

Progressive Engagement: A best practice strategy of providing services and financial assistance that preserves the most intensive and expensive interventions for households with the most need in order to preserve resources and provide assistance to the widest number of people.

Provisionally accommodated: Those whose accommodation is temporary or lacks security of tenure.

Racism: A form of prejudice and discrimination directed towards someone based on one's race, which produces impenetrable systemic and societal barriers.

Rapid Rehousing (RRH): A support intervention that uses a combination of case management, Housing Navigation, and short to medium term financial assistance to assist mid-range acuity homeless households identify and stabilize in tenant-based, scattered site, permanent housing.

Regional Coordination: Oversight of wide partnerships across public and private entities that ensure homeless persons are fully supported and connected to housing and services within their respective communities. Regional and coordinated access to housing and services ensures that a homeless person does not have to go to multiple agencies to obtain housing and services assistance.

Rent Reasonableness: The total rent charged for a unit must be reasonable in relation to the rents being charged during the same time period for comparable units in the private unassisted market and must not be in excess of rents being charged by the owner during the same period for comparable non-luxury unassisted units.

Rental Supplement Program: Rent-geared-to-income housing with private landlords. Rent supplements are subsidies paid by government to private landlords who are part of this program.

Respite Accommodation: Services that provide young people with emergency supports as an alternative to the shelter system.

Scattered Site Housing: Housing that is provided at individual locations, usually in the private rental market, as opposed to an affordable housing building or project.

Self-care: The process of maintaining and promoting one's health, well-being and development to meet the everyday challenges and stressors.

Severe Housing Needs: when a household spends more than 50 percent of its pre-tax income on housing costs.

Severe Mental Illness: Defined as a serious and persistent mental or emotional disorder (e.g., schizophrenia, mood-disorders, schizoid-affective disorders) that interrupts people's abilities to carry out a range of daily life activities such as self-care, interpersonal relationships, maintaining housing, employment or stay in school.

Sexual Identity: How a person identifies to whom they are sexually and romantically attracted (e.g., lesbian, gay, bisexual, heterosexual, etc.)

Shelter Diversion: A strategy targeting homeless youth that refers to the provision of alternative temporary housing options, supports and interventions designed to reduces the young people reliance on emergency shelter system.

Shelter Inventories: Counts the number of beds available in a shelter system (which may or may not include Violence Against Women shelters) and determines what percentage of these beds are occupied on a given night.

Shelter Workers (Residential Counselor): Individuals working in a shelter who provide support to the residents to help maintain order in the shelter and to help the residents achieve success in transitioning to housing.

Squeegeeing: A subsistence strategy that refers to washing car windshields for money. The activity is considered to be part of informal economy and is commonly associated with homelessness.

Street Outreach: Incredibly important work that involves moving outside the walls of the agency to engage people experiencing homelessness who may be disconnected and alienated not only from mainstream services and supports, but from the services targeting homeless persons as well.

Substance Use: All types of drug and alcohol use.

Substance Use Prevention: Interventions that seek to delay the onset of substance use, or to avoid substance use problems before they occur.

Suitable Housing: Housing has enough bedrooms for the size and composition of the resident household, according to National Occupancy Standard (NOS) requirements.

Support Workers (SW): Are usually assigned individual clients to monitor and conduct case management with in order to place clients into housing.

System Integration: Formalized coordinated approach to planning, service delivery, and management. An integrated system is an intentional, coordinated, suite of services that is centrally funded and managed. Systems integration aims to align services to avoid duplication, improve information-sharing, increase efficiency (e.g., reduce wait-times), and provide a seamless care experience for individuals and families.

System of Care: Strengths-based, culturally relevant, participatory framework for working with children and families.

System Prevention: Working with mainstream institutions to stop the flow of individuals from mental health care, child protection and corrections into homelessness.

Systems Failures: Occur when other systems of care and support fail, requiring vulnerable people to turn to the homelessness sector, when other mainstream services could have prevented this need.

Transition: When a transgender individual begins to live life in the gender with which they identify, rather than the sex they were assigned at birth. For some, this includes changing one's first name and/or other legal documents (e.g., health card, driver's license, etc.), dressing differently, taking hormones and/or undergoing surgery. Each person's transition is different and deeply personal.

Transition Age Youth (TAY): An individual between the ages of 16 and 24.

Transitional Housing (TH): Transitional housing (TH) is designed to provide homeless individuals and families with the interim stability and support to successfully move to and maintain permanent housing. Transitional housing may be used to cover the costs of up to 24 months of housing with accompanying supportive services.

Transitional Housing Services: Supportive, yet temporary type of accommodation that is meant to bridge the gap from homelessness to permanent housing by offering structure, supervision, support, life skills, education, etc.

Transitionally Homeless: Short-term homelessness, usually less than a month.

Unaccompanied Youth: Unaccompanied youth are persons under age 18 who are not accompanied by a parent or guardian and are not a parent presenting with or sleeping in the same place as his/her child(ren). Unaccompanied youth are single youth, youth couples, and groups of youth presenting together as a household.

Unduplicated Count: The number of people who are homeless within a specified location and time period. An unduplicated count ensures that individuals are counted only once regardless of the number of times they entered or exited the homeless system or the number of programs in which they participated.

Unsheltered: Living on the streets or in places not intended for human habitation.

Veteran: This subpopulation category of the PIT includes adults who have served on active duty in the armed forces of the United States. This does not include inactive military reserves or the National Guard unless the person was called up to active duty.

Victim Service Provider: A private nonprofit organization whose primary mission is to provide services to victims of domestic violence, dating violence, sexual assault, or stalking. This term includes rape crisis centers, battered women's shelters, domestic violence transitional housing programs, and other programs.

Youth Assessment Prioritization (YAP) Tool: A strength-based assessment of youth who are experiencing, or are at-risk of experiencing, homelessness that strives to be as non-clinical and non-prescriptive as possible. YAP is an assessment that is undertaken when a vulnerable young person comes into contact with the service system. Read more about the YAP Tool.

Youth Homelessness: Young people between the ages of 13 and 24 who are living independently of parents and/or caregivers, and lack many of the social supports deemed necessary for the transition from childhood to adulthood.

Youth Who Leave Home: Youth who choose to leave home/parents/caretakers for various reasons. This is the term used instead of "runaway youth."

REFERENCES

The Canadian Observatory on Homelessness, (2019) Homeless Hub, retrieved from https://www.homelesshub.ca/.

Los Angeles Homeless Services Authority, (2019) retrieved from https://www.lahsa.org/.

Virginia Housing Alliance, (2018), Understanding Homeless Programs and Policies: A Glossary of Terms, retrieved from https://vahousingalliance.org/.

B. Right 2 Survive FAQ*

Denver Homeless Out Loud

Question: *What is the overall problem this legislation is trying to solve?*

Response: The prevalence of homelessness in the 21st century's economic and political system has not only led to violations of internationally recognized human rights; it also threatens the public health of entire communities. The Right to Survive Initiative seeks to protect the basic human rights of people to rest by outlawing municipal laws that criminalize homelessness and the survival acts of resting and sharing food in public. This will shift focus to addressing the true root causes of homelessness and its consequences on families, communities, and society.

Question: *Don't homeless people need services, so isn't it important that we have camping bans and other such laws to give police a tool to connect people with those services?*

Response: While it is true that many people who are homeless need services, including mental and physical health care, drug and alcohol rehabilitation assistance, shelter, and the like, these services do not address the basic need and right to be in public spaces. Efforts to connect homeless people with services through laws against being in public do not work. For those who need these services, such services are so severely limited that many people do not have the option to access them—and thus being told to "move along" out of public spaces into these services is often not possible. Furthermore, many people do not need any of these services, what they need is attainable housing. Trying to force them into these services is counterproductive and a violation of their rights and freedoms. Using camping bans—and other such laws criminalizing necessary life-sustaining acts—as a "tool" to connect people with services is wrong and unnecessary. If the goal is to help connect those needing mental health or other such services with those resources, this could be better done by hiring social workers to connect with people on the streets and by investing in providing the needed services so those needing them have an option to receive them.

Question: *Isn't housing the solution to homelessness? If we just focus on housing, we won't need to worry about homeless people being criminalized.*

Response: We agree that the solution to homelessness is permanent housing, and that our entire society must work together to ensure that truly attainable housing is

*Denver Homeless Out Loud, "Right 2 Survive FAQ," https://denverhomelessoutloud.files.wordpress.com/2018/04/right-2-survive-faq.pdf. Reprinted with permission of the publisher.

available to all who need it. But this solution is not being executed at a rate to meet the need, nor unfortunately does it seem to be "just around the corner." Meanwhile, people who lack housing and must therefore conduct their survival activities in public space are being treated as criminals for this activity.

Such criminalization is unconstitutional, immoral, counterproductive, and just plain wrong. Law protecting this human right is needed to protect people's right to survive in public space, even while we work to create the public will to provide affordable housing opportunities to all who need it. There is every reason why we must work to correct both wrongs—the criminalization of homelessness and the lack of affordable housing for all—at the same time.

Question: *The people who sleep outside do so by choice. If you make it legal, won't more and more people do it?*

Response: Most people who sleep outside would move indoors if "choices" that were appropriate for their needs, like housing, were available to them. Many people are afraid of sleeping outside and choose to sleep in shelters whenever possible. Others sleep outside rather than in a shelter because there are not nearly enough shelter spaces for all who need them, and shelter is not a permanent solution for homeless. Many people with mental health conditions are unable to tolerate shelters. There's a lack of shelter spaces for couples, LGBTQ individuals, families, young people, people with disabilities, and people with pets. Many are fearful of the bugs, violence, theft, and unsanitary conditions which they often associate with shelters. Many who have jobs cannot stay at shelters because shelters have strict check in times that conflict with their work schedules.

As Denver Homeless Out Loud's 2013 report on the effects of the Urban Camping Ban revealed, making outdoor "camping" illegal did not stop people from doing it. It just pushed them away from safer, more accessible, better lit areas into more hidden, less lit and therefore more dangerous areas—which also made it harder for outreach workers to engage with them.

The way to reduce the number of people who are sleeping and living outside is not to criminalize their efforts to exist in public space, but rather to make appropriate housing available. One reason we do not have adequate housing and services to meet the needs of homeless Coloradans is because of the high priority municipalities have placed on law enforcement activities against homeless people. If the money spent on the enforcement of anti-homeless laws (including policing, court processing, and incarceration) were instead spent on permanent affordable housing, we could create real housing options for people experiencing homelessness.

Question: *But aren't most homeless people dirty? Don't they make our downtown areas look gross and push visitors away?*

Response: The way to keep homeless people from looking dirty is not by criminalizing their existence, but by providing appropriate restrooms, showers, storage facilities, day centers, and especially housing! Homeless people do not *want* to be dirty.

Question: *If we allow people to rest in public won't they leave trash everywhere?*

Response: This bill does not give people the right to leave trash about. Laws against littering would still exist. This bill only allows people to rest in a non-obstructive manner—not break other laws like littering. Furthermore, in order to address trash in public spaces adequate trash containers and trash servicing is needed. This bill would enable city money to be redirected to these needs.

Question: *Don't we need laws to keep homeless people from hanging out and sleeping downtown and in neighborhoods in order to keep crime down?*

Response: There is no statistical evidence to support stereotypes about a relationship between homelessness and real crime, like assaults or burglary. The idea that homeless people are criminals is nothing but a myth that has been perpetuated to make others afraid of homeless people and willing to support draconian measures against them—such as passing bans on sleeping outside and spending millions of dollars on policing their activities and "moving them along"—money that should be spent on needed services and on combating REAL crime. The real problem is crime and violence experienced by homeless people—especially the many elders, youth, women, and disabled among the community—whose need to survive outside makes them so vulnerable to violence.

The National Coalition for the Homeless' 2013 report, "Vulnerable to Hate: A Survey of Hate Crimes and Violence Committed Against Homeless People," documented 1,437 acts of violence against homeless people committed by housed perpetrators between 1999 and 2013—including murders, rapes, beatings and mutilations. By criminalizing homelessness instead of dealing with its root causes, our local governments are forcing homeless people into more hidden, and therefore less secure, areas—where the risk of being attacked is increased. And criminalizing homelessness instead of providing appropriate solutions sends the public the message that "homeless lives don't matter"—they're fair game.

Question: *If we can't have park curfew laws, camping bans, and "no loitering" ordinances, won't homeless people take over the parks, causing other people to stay away?*

Response: Please remember that housed people have houses in which to sleep, rest and socialize. They also, to varying degrees, have a greater ability to go to coffee shops, restaurants, movies, plays and clubs to socialize and be entertained. Unhoused people, on the other hand, have shelters (if they can get in and tolerate the environment), a few overcrowded day centers in which they are segregated from everyone else, and public spaces, such as libraries, downtown areas, and parks. If homeless people tend to dominate certain parks, it is only because they have nowhere else to go and have a perfect right to be there. Anyone, housed or unhoused, who violates any law or legitimate rule that does not violate our human rights, is subject to being removed and/or prosecuted. There is no reason why other people should "stay away" from public spaces in which homeless people congregate. If public officials and the media didn't perpetuate the myth of homeless people as criminals, others would probably not be as scared to be near them, and people would come to know, understand and appreciate each other.

It is also important to remember that there are currently laws making sleeping with cover, sitting in certain areas, or the like illegal, and nonetheless thousands of homeless people currently are spending their days and nights in public spaces like parks. This activity is not a choice so that will not change with the passing of the Right to Survive. What will change with the passing of the Right to Survive is that homeless people will not be harassed by police, continually told to move along from one place to another, moved to more hidden far off less safe places, and left in the cold without needed protection from the elements.

Question: *But won't citing homeless people at least motivate them to move out of a certain neighborhood, or maybe move indoors?*

Response: No. As local police precincts race to respond to complaints about homeless people in their areas, most homeless people have nowhere else to go, so they are forced to remain in public space. As citations for "quality of life" activities add up, so do fines that are impossible to pay. When homeless people are arrested and even incarcerated just for being too poor to pay for these tickets, they acquire a criminal record that creates barriers to housing and employment. The criminalization of homelessness not only violates homeless people's human rights, but also perpetuates and deepens their poverty by creating legal barriers to exiting homelessness.

Question: *Why would I want people sleeping in their cars and trucks to park outside of my house?*

Response: What makes someone sleeping in their vehicle by your home—because they have nowhere else TO sleep—more threatening to you and the neighborhood than someone sleeping in their home next door? Get to know the people. You will likely find that there is nothing to be worried about, and even that they make the neighborhood safer by protecting your house from burglary and deterring other crime. Six to 10 percent of students at the Auraria colleges are homeless and many sleep in their cars for safety.

Question: *What do you mean by the right to share food? Don't we feed homeless people enough already?*

Response: It's not a matter of feeding them "enough." There are laws across the country criminalizing the act of simply sharing food with anybody in public. This Act will prevent laws like that from being passed in Colorado.

In many cases food-sharing programs are the only occasion in which some homeless individuals will have access to healthy, safe food. The 2013 Hunger and Homelessness Survey, conducted by the United States Conferences of Mayors, found that:

- 83% (19 of 25) of cities surveyed in 2013 reported an increase in the number of emergency food requests from the previous year.
- 91% reported an increase in persons requesting food assistance for the first time.
- 80% reported an increase in frequency of visits to food pantries and emergency kitchens each month.

The need for food assistance is growing in our communities and we must ensure that those who wish to share food with those in need can continue to do so in public space.

Question: *So, if this law passes homeless people can just start sleeping in my doorway?*

Response: No, they cannot block doorways. The bill states clearly that people can "rest in public spaces and protect oneself from the elements, in a non-obstructive manner." Current laws prohibiting obstruction of a passageway would still be in effect.

Question: *Will passage of this bill mean that city crews will no longer be able to clean up public areas?*

Response: No. Laws against littering and obstructing a right-of-way would still be in place, so cleanup crews could still do their job. It just means that cleanup crews will not be allowed to simply throw away possessions of value to people—like backpacks, sleeping bags, and blankets when those possessions are on public property and are not obstructing a right-of-way. This is in accordance with the constitutional 4th amendment right against unreasonable searches and seizures.

Question: *How will cities deal with people's bad behavior in public places if this bill passes?*

Response: The Right to Survive Initiative would not affect localities' ability to enforce laws against such things as assault, harassment, or blocking passageways. It would only end the practice of arresting or citing people for the simple acts of resting or sharing food in public—acts of survival.

About the Contributors

The **Administration for Community Living** is part of the U.S. Department of Health and Human Services and was created around the fundamental principle that older adults and people of all ages with disabilities should be able to live where they choose, with the people they choose, and with the ability to participate fully in their communities.

JoNel **Aleccia** is a senior correspondent focused on aging and end-of-life issues on the Kaiser Health News enterprise team.

Deborah **Bailey** is a visiting research scholar at Johns Hopkins University where she is conducting a study on social capital in the Sandtown-Winchester area of West Baltimore.

Charles **Barber** is a writer in residence at Wesleyan and a lecturer in psychiatry at Yale.

William **Bare** retired as a colonel with the Air Force and then became the executive director of a non-profit organization whose mission was to house and assist homeless veterans and their families.

Willie L. **Britt** is a distinguished adjunct professor of public administration at Golden Gate University, vice president of the Pilipino Senior Resource Center, and the business manager of Makati Chiropractic Center, USA.

The **California Department of Housing and Community Development** helps to provide stable, safe homes affordable to veterans, seniors, young families, farm workers, people with disabilities, and individuals and families experiencing homelessness.

Samantha **Carr** is a 2008 MPA alumni of Golden Gate University and executive director of Popular Nerd Consulting.

Carol **Caton** is a professor of sociomedical sciences (psychiatry and public health), Columbia University Medical Center.

The **Center for Public Policy** is at Virginia Commonwealth University's Wilder School of Government and Public Affairs.

Damon **Conklin** is a registered lobbyist and also is director of government affairs, California Builders, Sacramento.

Denver Homeless Out Loud works with and for people who experience homelessness to help protect and advocate for dignity, rights, and choices for people experiencing homelessness.

Rebecca **DeSantis** is program manager for career and equity advancement at the International City/County Management Association.

DaVina **Flemings** is chief, state government relations, Pacific Gas & Electric Company, Sacramento, California.

Rachel L. **Fontenot is** a graduate of Golden Gate University's EMPA program, has worked in the field of aging for more than 25 years and works for the State of California.

Susan **Fraiman** is a professor of English, University of Virginia.

Joaquin Jay **Gonzalez** III is Mayor George Christopher Professor of Public Administration at the Edward S. Ageno School of Business of Golden Gate University, former San Francisco Immigrant Rights Commissioner, and the president of the Pilipino Senior Resource Center of San Francisco, California.

Anna **Gorman** is senior correspondent with *Kaiser Health News* and writes about all things health: policy, reform and disparities.

Richard **Gunderman** is chancellor's professor of medicine, liberal arts, and philanthropy, Indiana University–Purdue University Indianapolis.

Shannon **Guzman** is a policy research senior analyst with the AARP Public Policy Institute.

Katelyn **Hansen** is an assistant project manager, Brailsford & Dunlavey.

Stacey **Havlik** is an assistant professor of education and counseling, Villanova University, and a 30-year executive manager with the City of Berkeley.

Jim **Hynes** is an adjunct professor of public administration and urban innovations at the Ageno School of Business, Golden Gate University.

Ana B. **Ibarra** is a web reporter at *Kaiser Health News*.

Roya **Ijadi-Maghsoodi** is an assistant professor of psychiatry and biobehavioral sciences/investigator at the VA Greater Los Angeles HSR&D Center for the Study of Healthcare Innovation, Implementation & Policy.

International City/County Management Association is the leading organization of local government professionals dedicated to creating and sustaining thriving communities throughout the world.

Ryan **Jensen** is a senior project manager, Brailsford & Dunlavey, Chicago, Illinois.

David **Kidd** is design director at *Governing*.

Patricia **Kime** is a contributor to *Kaiser Health News*.

Margot **Kushel** is a professor of medicine, University of California, San Francisco.

Alexandra **Logsdon** is a senior portfolio manager, Secretary's Center for Strategic Partnerships, U.S. Department of Veterans Affairs.

Mickey P. **McGee** is an associate professor of public administration and Director of the Doctor of Business Administration Program at the Edward S. Ageno School of Business of Golden Gate University. He co-developed GGU's Urban Innovations Program including the course, Inclusion, Diversion, Equity, and Accessibility.

Amanda L. **McGimpsey** is a community outreach specialist focused on creating partnerships to solve social issues.

Rachel D. **McGuffin** is a Chinese language instructor at the U.S. Defense Language Institute in Monterey, California.

Deidre L. **McLay** is a community volunteer in Pacific Grove, California.

Joseph W. **Mead** is an assistant professor at Cleveland State University.

Ginger **Miller** is a navy veteran and president and CEO of Women Veterans Interactive Inc.

Gabby V. **Moraleda** is executive director, Pilipino Senior Resource Center, San Francisco, California, and board member, University of the Philippines Alumni Association of San Francisco.

Cynthia **Nagendra** is director, the Alliance Center for Capacity Building, National Alliance to End Homelessness.

James P. **Nicholls** III is a department specialist with the Physician Information & Interoperability Services of Sutter Health, Sacramento, California.

Joshua O. **Odetunde** is a consulting director at Community Housing Market Support Network Inc., Louisville, KY.

Jill **Pable** is a professor of interior design and architecture, Florida State University.

Darby **Penney** is a long-time activist in the movement to protect the human rights of people with psychiatric disabilities.

Sukhdeep **Purewal** is an administrative analyst, County of Sutter, Yuba City, California.

Mattie **Quinn** is a staff writer with *Governing*.

Sara **Rankin** is a professor of lawyering skills, Seattle University.

Phillip **Reese** is a data reporting specialist and an assistant professor of journalism at California State University-Sacramento.

Alan R. **Roper** is a distinguished adjunct professor at Golden Gate University and instructional designer/curriculum developer for the University of California, office of the president.

Harriet Blair **Rowan** is a digital reporter for California Healthline.

Michael **Rowe** is a professor, Department of Psychiatry, Yale University.

Jon **Ruiz** is city manager of Eugene, Oregon.

Claire Moeller **Rygg** is with the Museums and Cultural Arts Division, Library and Museums Department, City of Monterey, California.

Emily **Salomon** was formerly with the National Housing Conference.

Ruth Astle **Samas** is a retired State of California law judge and a distinguished adjunct professor at Golden Gate University.

The **San Francisco Department of Homelessness and Supportive Housing** is a consolidated department that focuses on preventing and ending homelessness for people in San Francisco.

Kurt **Schake** is executive director of the Monterey County Veterans Transition Center in Marina, California.

Benedict **Serafica** is a navy veteran and is serving with the California Air National Guard and with the California Military Department as an executive NCO to the Command Senior Enlisted Leader.

Michael **Silliman** works as a program manager at the International City/County Management Association in Washington, D.C.

David C. **Stevens** is a resident, radiology, Indiana University–Purdue University Indianapolis.

The **Substance Abuse and Mental Health Services Administration** is the agency within the U.S. Department of Health and Human Services that leads public health efforts to advance the behavioral health of the nation.

Paul **Toro** is a professor of psychology, Wayne State University.

Town of Bedford is in the State of Massachusetts.

Nicole **Trupiano** is an administrative secretary for the Planning & Economic Development Department for the City of Santa Rosa.

The **U.S. Department of Housing and Urban Development** is a cabinet-level department of the federal government responsible for administering programs that provide housing and community development assistance.

The **U.S. Department of Labor** is a cabinet-level department of the federal government responsible for occupational safety, wage and hour standards, unemployment insurance benefits, reemployment services, and some economic statistics.

The **U.S. Department of Veterans Affairs** is a federal cabinet-level government agency that provides near-comprehensive healthcare services to eligible military veterans.

The **U.S. Interagency Council on Homelessness** is an independent federal agency within the executive branch that leads the implementation of the federal strategic plan to prevent and end homelessness.

Beth **Velasquez** is a member of the AARP team.

Janet **Viveiros** is a program and policy analyst at Nemours, Washington D.C.

Kayla M. **Williams** is a senior fellow and director of the Military, Veterans and Society Program at the Center for a New American Security.

The **White House** is official residence and the executive office of the president.

J.B. **Wogan** is a staff writer with *Governing*.

Johanna L. **Wong** is the quality and compliance data analyst for Samaritan House in San Mateo, California.

Jason J. **Yergler** is a Washington state-based professional with experience in the tech startup community of Seattle, Washington.

Index